Colonisation: A Comparative Study of India and Korea

Colonisation: A Comparative Study of India and Korea

Editors

Vyjayanti Raghavan

R. Mahalakshmi

ACADEMIC FOUNDATION
NEW DELHI

www.academicfoundation.org
www.academicfoundation.com

First published in 2015
by

ACADEMIC FOUNDATION
4772-73 / 23 Bharat Ram Road, (23 Ansari Road),
Darya Ganj, New Delhi - 110 002 (India).
Phones : 23245001 / 02 / 03 / 04.
Fax : +91-11-23245005.
E-mail : books@academicfoundation.com
www.academicfoundation.org
www.academicfoundation.com

in association with
Centre for Korean Studies, School of Language, Literature & Culture Studies, Jawaharlal Nehru University (JNU), New Delhi.

This work was supported by the Academy of Korean Studies Grant funded by the Korean Government (MEST) (AKS-2010-ANA-2101).

Disclaimer:
The findings/views/opinions expressed in this book are solely those of the authors and do not necessarily reflect the views of the publisher.

Cataloging in Publication Data--DK
Courtesy: D.K. Agencies (P) Ltd. <docinfo@dkagencies.com>

Colonisation: a comparative study of India and Korea / editors, Vyjayanti Raghavan, R. Mahalakshmi.
pages ; cm
Includes bibliographical references.
ISBN 9789332701823

1. India--Colonization. 2. Korea--Colonization. 3. India--Historiography. 4. Korea--Historiography. I. Raghavan, Vyjayanti, editor. II. Mahalakshmi, R., editor. III. Jawaharlal Nehru University. Centre for Korean Studies.issuing body.

DDC 325.30954 23

Typeset by Italics India, New Delhi.

Printed and bound by The Book Mint, New Delhi.
www.thebookmint.in

CONTENTS

PART III

Colonialism and its Impact

About the Editors/Contributors

Editors:

Vyjayanti Raghavan is Professor and Chairperson, Centre for Korean Studies at the School of Language, Literature & Culture Studies, Jawaharlal Nehru University (JNU), New Delhi. She has a Master's Degree in Korean History from Seoul National University and a PhD from the Department of Disarmament, School of International Studies, JNU. She has been teaching Korean language and culture at JNU since 2000. She has co-authored and edited many books and contributed a number of articles to journals and newspapers. Some of her recent publications are the co-authored *Sino-Indian and Sino-South Korean Relations* (2014), *Korean Wave in India: Present Status and Future Prospects* (2012), and *Comparative Security Dynamics in Northeast Asia and South Asia* (2010), among others. Prof Raghavan has been a visiting scholar at Yonsei University, Republic of Korea and a Senior Research Fellow at the Academy of Korean Studies.

R. Mahalakshmi is Associate Professor at the Centre for Historical Studies, Jawaharlal Nehru University (JNU), New Delhi. She specialises in the history of ancient and early medieval south India, and teaches several courses at the Master's and research levels in this field. Her research interests include: religion and society, art and architecture, gender studies and political economy. She was awarded the Professor Hiralal Gupta Research Award for the best book by a lady historian by the Indian History Congress in 2013, for her work *The Making of the Goddess: Korravai-Durga in the Tamil Traditions*. She has also authored *The Book of Lakshmi* (2009). She is currently working on brahmanical influence and iconography in early medieval Sri Lanka and Southeast Asia.

Contributors:

Aditya Mukherjee is Professor of Contemporary Indian History, Centre for Historical Studies, JNU, New Delhi. He is the Editor of the *Sage Series in Modern Indian History* (15 monographs already published). He was President of the Indian History Congress for Modern India, 2007-08. He has been Visiting Professor at Duke University, USA (1986), Japan Foundation Fellow (1999-2000), University of Tokyo and Visiting Fellow at the Institute of Advanced Study, Lancaster, UK (October 2007), Fellow Institute of Advanced Study at Nantes, France (2010) and Visiting Professor at La Sapienza, University of Rome, Italy (2013). His publications include: *India's Struggle for Independence* (1988, more than 50 reprint by 2014), and *India Since Independence* (2008), both translated into six languages. *Imperialism, Nationalism and the Making of the Indian Capitalist Class 1927-1947* (2002); and *RSS, School Texts and the Murder of Mahatma Gandhi: The Hindu Communal Project* (2008, co-author).

Alok Bajpai is an independent research scholar working on Mahatma Gandhi and Indian National Movement for over a decade. He has been a Fellow at Nehru Memorial Museum & Library, New Delhi. His research papers have been published in esteemed journals like *Proceedings of Indian History Congress*, *Mainstream Weekly*, and *Quarterly Review of Historical Studies*. He was awarded Prof P. S. Gupta Memorial Prize and J.C. Jha Prize in Indian History Congress in the year 2011.

Hulas Singh has done his MPhil and PhD from JNU, New Delhi. He specialises in intellectual history of 19th century Maharashtra. He is a senior public servant and has held several positions in Government of India.

Mridula Mukherjee is Professor of Modern Indian History at the Centre for Historical Studies, JNU, New Delhi. She has been the Director of the Nehru Memorial Museum & Library; President of the Indian History Congress (Modern India); Dean, School of Social Sciences, JNU and Editor of *Selected Works of Jawaharlal Nehru*. She is the Editor of the Sage Series in Modern Indian History (14 monographs already published). She specialises in agrarian history, peasant movements, the Indian national movement and Gandhi. She has been a Visiting Scholar at Duke University, USA and University of Tokyo, Japan; a Visiting Fellow at Nantes Institute of Advanced Study, France and at Institutes of Advanced Study at Lancaster, UK and Sao Paulo, Brazil; and Visiting Professor at La Sapienza, The University of Rome, Italy. She has co-authored two best-selling books called *India's Struggle for Independence* (1989, more than 50 reprints by 2014) and *India Since Independence* (2008), both of which have been translated into several languages. Her other publications are *Peasants in India's Non-violent Revolution, Practice and Theory* (2004); *Colonialising Agriculture: The Myth of Punjab Exceptionalism* (2006); and *RSS, School Textbooks and the Murder of Mahatma Gandhi: The Hindu Communal Project* (2008).

Neerja Singh is Associate Professor of History in Satyawati College (Eve.), University of Delhi, Delhi. She has published two books, namely *Nehru-Patel: Agreement within Differences* and *Gandhi-Patel: Differences within Consensus*. Her forthcoming book is called *Myth of the Indian Right: Patel, Prasad and Rajaji*. She has participated in various seminars and presented papers in India and abroad. She is also a UGC National Research Awardee.

Pankaj Mohan studied East Asian languages and history, initially at JNU, New Delhi, and subsequently at Peking University, Beijing, Seoul National University and the Australian National University, Canberra, from where he received his PhD degree. Prior to joining the University of Sydney in July 2002 as a tenured lecturer in Korean Studies/Asian Studies, he taught at the Australian National University for over six years and at the University of Copenhagen for three years. He has published numerous book chapters and papers on early Korean Buddhism in several journals, including *Korea Journal, Seoul Journal of Korean Studies, Review of Korean Studies, Korea Observer, Journal of Inner and East Asian Studies* and *Korean Culture*.

R. Venkataramanujam is an Assistant Professor in the Department of History, Madras Christian College (Autonomous), Chennai (since 2004). He did his MA (History) specialising in Modern India in the

Centre for Historical Studies, JNU, New Delhi. He then pursued his research, specialising in diplomatic studies, in the School of International Studies, JNU, from where he secured his MPhil and PhD. He has presented papers in international and national conferences, and has a few publications to his credit. His present areas of research interest are colonialism and nationalism, and temple art and administration.

Rakesh Batabyal is a Concurrent Faculty, Centre for Media Studies, School of Social Sciences and Associate Professor/Deputy Director, Academic Staff College, JNU, New Delhi. He has taught Contemporary History of Communication, Graduate School of Information Studies, Tokyo University. He has recently chaired sessions on field reports from the Resource Persons of the Balbandhu Scheme of the National Commission for the Protection of Child Rights, Discussant and Chaired session at the Review Meetings of the Balbandhu programme, NCPCR and the Seminar on BRICS and Regional Economic Powers in the Global Economy, Jawaharlal Nehru Institute of Advanced Studies. He has published *Communalism in Bengal: From Famine to Noakhali (1943-47)* (2005), *The Penguin Book of Modern Indian Speeches* (Edited, with an Introduction, 2007) and *JNU: The Making of a University* (2014).

Shin Yong-ha is a seminal thinker and foremost scholar of modern Korean history. He has studied at Seoul National University and Harvard University. He taught sociology and modern Korean history and served as Dean, College of Social Sciences at Seoul National University. He authored over 50 books on various aspects of Korean identity and the rise and development of Korea as a modern nation state. After retirement from Seoul National University, he was offered special chairs by several universities, including Hanyang University, Ehwa University and Ulsan University.

Shri Krishan completed his education from Delhi University and then JNU, New Delhi. He has published *Political Mobilization and Identity in Western India: 1934-1947* (2005). He has contributed several research papers and articles in a number of important journals. He has also worked as a course writer and editor for Indira Gandhi

National Open University, New Delhi. He was a Senior Fellow, Nehru Memorial Museum & Library, New Delhi (2009-2011). He is currently Chairperson, Department of History and Dean, Faculty of Social Sciences at Indira Gandhi University, Meerpur, Rewari, Haryana, India.

Sucheta Mahajan is Professor at the Centre for Historical Studies, JNU, New Delhi. She has been Gillespie Visiting Professor at the College of Wooster, Ohio, USA, a Fellow of the Indian Institute of Advanced Study, Fellow of the Rockefeller Foundation's Bellagio Center and a Visiting Professor at the Maison des Sciences de l' homme, Paris. Her significant books include *Independence and Partition: The Erosion of Colonial Power in India* (2000); *India's Struggle for Independence* (1988; with Bipan Chandra *et al.*); *RSS, School Texts and the Murder of Mahatma Gandhi: The Hindu Communal Project* (2008; with Aditya Mukherjee and Mridula Mukherjee) and *Education and Social Change: MVF and Child Labour* (2008). She has also edited many books such as *Rites of Passage, A Civil Servant Remembers: H.M. Patel* (2005); *Composite Culture in a Multi-Cultural Society* (co-edited with Bipan Chandra), and most recently, *Towards Freedom 1947: Documents on India's Freedom Struggle* (2013). Her fields of interest cover the short and long history of the 20th century, its politics, political economy and social change.

Vipan Chandra is Professor of History, Emeritus, at Wheaton College in Norton, Massachusetts, USA. He taught there for 35 years before retiring in 2012. He is a specialist in modern Korean and Japanese history and has contributed a research monograph (cited in the Note on Sources to chapter 14) and many articles in his field since 1974. He is also a former columnist for *The Korea Times* and *The Korea Herald*. Prof Chandra received his early advanced degrees from Meerut College, Meerut, a diploma in the Korean language from Yonsei University, Seoul, and his MA degree and PhD in History and East Asian languages from Harvard University.

Visalakshi Menon was Associate Professor at Jesus and Mary College, University of Delhi, New Delhi. She received her doctorate from JNU, New Delhi. Her publications include *Indian Women and*

Nationalism: The U.P. Story (2003); *From Movement to Government: The United Provinces, 1937-42* (2003); *Modern India* (co-authored with Narayani Gupta and Srimanjari, 2004); *The Dynamics of the Congress in UP, 1945-55* (forthcoming); and *Towards Freedom: Documents on India's Freedom Struggle, 1942* (forthcoming). Her research interests covered nationalism and colonialism with special reference to gender and north India.

Vladimir Tikhonov is Professor of Korean and East Asia Studies at Oslo University. He is the author of *Social Darwinism and Nationalism in Korea: The Beginnings (1880s–1910s)* (2010). He is currently researching on modern nationalist thought and modern Buddhism in Korea.

Acknowledgements

This study has been made possible by a grant received from the Academy of Korean Studies of the Republic of Korea. We would like to express our sincere gratitude to them for the support given for this area of inquiry which is completely new, both in the Korean as well as the Indian academic arena. Jawaharlal Nehru University (JNU), New Delhi, as the host institution of the project provided invaluable support in the form of infrastructure and facilitated the holding of workshops and conferences, and we gratefully acknowledge this.

We would like to thank Prof Vipan Chandra for his meticulous copy editing and incisive comments on the Korean papers in this volume. Also, a special thanks to Uddalok Bhattacharya for the same effort done for the Indian papers in the volume. Their efforts helped greatly in the final revision and in giving the book its final shape.

Our sincere thanks to Deepak Yadav who as a Research Assistant assisted us throughout the period of the project and also took on the burden of liaising with the paper contributors. Our special thanks to Dr Rakesh Batabyal for providing us with the venue of the Academic Staff College at JNU and other logistical support, at various stages of the project, that made this volume possible. Our gratitude is also due to Avanindra Kumar and Kunal Kumar who have assisted us with administrative and academic work as Project Assistants at various stages of the two-year project.

We would also like to acknowledge and thank the support of the library staff at the Academy of Korean Studies for providing space and material for the research. Thanks are also due to our colleagues at the Centre for Korean Studies and Centre for Historical Studies for their support and encouragement. Our contributors from different institutions in India, South Korea, China and USA were most supportive of our demands, particularly in the final stages of preparing the manuscript, and this volume is the outcome of their efforts as well. We tragically lost Dr Visalakshi Menon in June this year, who despite her long standing illness responded enthusiastically to our requests, including editorial queries until shortly before her demise. This book is dedicated to her.

We would also like to thank the editorial team at the Academic Foundation, New Delhi, for bringing out the volume in its present shape.

New Delhi Vyjayanti Raghavan and R. Mahalakshmi

VYJAYANTI RAGHAVAN AND R. MAHALAKSHMI

Introduction

Colonisation, or the process through which colonialism is manifested, is a very significant theme in world history. By the early 20th century, almost every country of the world was divided into two camps—that of the coloniser and of the colonised. However, very little effort has been made to understand the process from a larger perspective. The two-year project on "Colonisation: A Comparative Study of Korea and India" was proposed by Vyjayanti Raghavan and R. Mahalakshmi in December 2010 to enable us to take a step forward in our analysis of colonialism as a modern, primarily Western, phenomenon and its impact on different continents and countries. The Indian experience of colonisation began in the second half of the 18th century and continued for two centuries, whereas Korea was colonised in the early 20th century. The coloniser in the case of Korea, unlike in most parts of the world, was not a Western power, but an emerging Asian imperial power. The contexts were obviously different in these two regions, and the manner in which colonisation had an impact on these countries would also inevitably have been specific to the contexts. However, if we understand colonialism as a mode of production, specifically designed towards integration and enmeshing of the colony's economy and society to the metropolis coloniser in the context of the development of world capitalism,[1] we can realise the need for a comparative framework in understanding colonialism.

It has often been argued that British colonialism was benign, and that Japanese colonialism was far more brutal and intense in

1. Chandra, Bipan (1979). "Colonialism and Modernization", in *Nationalism and Colonialism in Modern India*. Hyderabad: Orient Longman. p.25.

comparison.[2] Japan's colonial conquest of Korea occurred rapidly when compared to the British colonial conquest of India. In the case of Japan, it had won two major wars—the Sino-Japanese War in 1894-95 and the Russo-Japanese War in 1905—and its conquest of Korea were an extension of its militaristic expansion in the region. The British colonial conquest of India, it is well known, occurred because of the mercantilist interests of the former, and was gradually extended over the entire sub-continent. Both the colonised countries, Korea and India, were at a disadvantage in all areas of military operations. Britain had superior artillery as a result of the industrial revolution, and Japan's Meiji Restoration had equipped their leaders with modern western guns and had also trained them in European infantry techniques. So even though there had been a number of uprisings and rebellions in Korea and India against the foreign powers before their colonisation, for instance the 1857 Revolt in India or the Tonghak rebellion of 1894 in Korea, the rebels did not stand any chance against the superior technology. It has been argued that the forms of protest in the latter years in both colonies followed the same pattern—through non-violent means or by boycotting British and Japanese products. Thus, passive forms of resistance were used as a weapon in both countries against colonial power, and in India in particular, non-violence was used as a moral force to counter British colonialism.

India was considered the 'Jewel in the Crown' by the British; similarly, Korea was the largest component for the Japanese imperial power. However, there are three counts on which we need to qualify this statement. First, Japan's annexation was late as Japan itself bloomed late as an imperialist power. It met with fierce Korean resistance from the start. Therefore, maintaining peace and public order became a priority for Japan. Hence, first the military police and after the 1 March Movement in 1919, the civilian police system acquired a central role in the colonial administration of Japan. Second, the occupation of Korea was unique in terms of the proximity of the

2. Kohli, Atul (2004). "The Colonial Origins of a Modern Political Economy: The Japanese Lineage of Korea's Cohesive-Capitalist State", in *State-Directed Development: Political Power and Industrialization in the Global Periphery.* Cambridge: Cambridge University Press. p.27.

colony to its colonial power. This not only made it easier for Japanese officials to settle in Korea and administer it, but also facilitated colonial migration into Japan. It is estimated that by 1942 the number of Koreans working and living in Japan was as high as 1.5 million and the Japanese population in Korea was almost 3.0 per cent of Korea's population.[3] On the other hand, the geographical distance made it equally difficult for Britain to station a large number of officials in India to administer it. They had to rely on the local population, and it is for this reason that the British introduced Western education in India, and not because of the mistaken belief in their benevolence. Even at the height of British Imperial presence, the number of Englishmen in India never exceeded 50,000, including their army. Third, the size and diversity of India meant that colonisation took effect in different ways and at different points of time in the sub-continent.

The defeat of Siraj-ud-Daula, the Nawab of Bengal, at the hands of British East India Company in the Battle of Plassey of 1757 was the first step towards colonisation of India. This was followed by the infamous "Plassey plunder"—the formal Company looting of the coffers of the state and the individual extortion that accompanied it. The Battle of Buxar in 1764 brought the British victory over Mughal emperor Shah Alam II, and in the Treaty of Allahabad of 1765, the British were granted the revenue-collecting rights in Bengal, Bihar and Orissa. The appointment of Warren Hastings in 1773 as the first Governor General for governing India under British East India Company marked the institutionalisation of colonial rule in India. A series of institutional mechanisms were put into place such as the Permanent Settlement (1793), the Subsidiary Alliance System (1798), the Mahalwari (1822) and Ryotwari (1820) System and the Bengal Tenancy Act (1822), which allowed the British to consolidate their political and economic interests in different parts of India. The Revolt of 1857 marked the first systematic attempt, although without a long-term vision, to challenge British rule and had repercussions throughout north, central and western India. After ruthlessly

3. Robinson, Michael E. (2007). *Korea's Twentieth-Century Odyssey: A Short History.* Honolulu: University of Hawai'i Press. p.36.

suppressing the revolt, British colonial rule entered a new phase with power passing on from the East India Company to the British Crown, through the Government of India Act 1858 (which was an Act of Parliament in Britain.)

Korea's Joseon dynasty had followed a policy of isolation in the 18th and 19th centuries, because of which it was referred to as the Hermit Kingdom by the Europeans. We know about an English merchant ship that was turned away in 1832 and a warship in 1845. There were several efforts by the French, Russians, Germans and Americans to enter the Korean peninsula, which were all repulsed by the Koreans.[4] This isolation was breached by the Japanese in the last quarter of the 19th century. Japan's hold over Korea began with the Unyo incident of 1875, wherein a small boat was sent to Korea's Kanghwa Island, ostensibly in search of drinkable water in the coastal waters of Korea. This invited opening of fire by the Korean forces but they were soon out-powered by the superior Japanese gun power. Japan returned the following year and forced Korea to sign the Treaty of Kanghwa. Japan forced on Korea all the unequal terms that they themselves had been subjected to by the Western powers. Japan liberated Korea from the Chinese hold, thereby ending the traditional tributary relationship, and also forcefully got Korea to open three of its ports to Japanese trade and give the Japanese extra-territoriality rights in Korea. This opened up Korea to other Western powers too and Korea signed a number of treaties. Politically, within Korea there was a power struggle between the pro-Chinese and pro-Japanese factions. This culminated in the Sino-Japanese War, fought on the Korean soil in 1894-95. Japan emerged as the victor. The Treaty of Shimonoseki signed with China gave it total access to Korea as China had to grant Korea full autonomy and independence. China also had to cede the Liaotung Peninsula, Formosa and Pescadores to Japan, besides having to pay a huge indemnity and open up its ports to Japan for commercial activities. However, Japan's wings were clipped later with the Triple intervention of France, Germany and Russia

4. Beck, Sanders (2008). *East Asia 1800-1949*. Goleta/California: World Press Communications. *www.san.beck.org/21-6-Korea.html*

and it had to cede the Liaotung peninsula back to China. This was the first step towards Japan gaining control over Korea. Following its victory over Russia after the Russo-Japanese War of 1904-05, Japan's annexation of Korea was unstoppable.

The 18th and early 19th centuries in India saw the French and the English competing to extend their control over the subcontinent from the enclaves where they had established themselves, and the latter won. It is said that it was the tribute extracted from India that played a critical role in sustaining the British war against the French.[5] In the case of Korea in the late 19th century, we see the Russians and the Japanese competing for control over the peninsula, in which the latter won through intrigue and by influencing a faction of the Korean leadership. Russia and Japan had been trying to develop their spheres of influence in East Asia, largely at the expense of China. What clinched Japan's hold in the region was the alliance it signed with Britain—the Anglo-Japanese Alliance of 1902. Assured that Britain would not interfere, Japan launched the war against Russia and emerged victorious, much to everyone's astonishment. This became the turning point at which Japan came to be recognised as a militarily powerful nation, and at the same time a colonial power to be wary of.

In India, the power of the colonial government in this second phase was constrained by the diversity of Indian society and the colonial knowledge production about India, its history and its traditions were undertaken with the liberal imperialist view of positively transforming the colony.[6] Japan, on the other hand, had a different historical relationship with Korea in the pre-modern and early modern period, and, in fact, the Koreans considered themselves culturally superior to the Japanese, and that Japan was at the receiving trail of culture and knowledge from China. Therefore, they were taken completely by surprise when Japan colonised them. The

5. Bagchi, Amiya Kumar (2010). *Colonialism and Indian Economy*. Delhi: OUP. p.xxvi.

6. For a discussion of the three stages of colonialism as enunciated by Bipan Chandra and a critique of the idea of British liberalism, see, Chandra, Bipan (1990). "Colonialism, Stages of Colonialism and the Colonial State", in H.V. Sreenivasa Murthy, B. Surendra Rao, Kesavan Veluthat and S.A. Bari (eds.), *Essays on Indian History and Culture: Felicitation Volume in Honour of Professor B. Sheik Ali*. Delhi: Mittal Publications. pp.141-62.

Japanese, which belonged to the same stock as the Koreans, even if they had set themselves on the path of modernisation after the Meiji Restoration, were not unfamiliar with the culture of Korea. In fact, the two not merely shared a long historical relationship; they also had a strong racial and cultural affinity. However, in its quest to modernise society and the system of governance of its colony, Japan tried to obliterate the Korean system of functioning and denigrate Korean culture. This greatly irked the Koreans and explains the vehemence of the anti-Japanese sentiment.

Since the reasons for colonising were basically the same in Japan and Britain, i.e., search for an overseas solution to the economic problems at home, the economic impact on the colonies shows a lot of similarities. It needs to be mentioned here that in the case of Korea the added reason for colonising was the fact that Korea was very logistically placed for Japan to access Manchuria as well as to launch its continental aggression. Besides, Japan curiously viewed Korea as "a dagger pointing at the heart of Japan", and wanted to ensure its own security by locking out Russia, Britain and others from the region. Scholars like Kang Ch'ang Il are of the view that the reason why Japan wanted to "Japanise" Korea was because of its desire to annex the Korean peninsula into the Japanese mainland as it did with Hokkaido and Okhinawa after the Meiji Restoration.[7]

The economic policies followed by the two imperial powers were either exploitative or self-serving, leading to lopsided development in the colonies. Both India and Korea were largely agrarian countries and it was the peasants who were greatly affected by revenue policies of the colonial governments. The Japanese colonial agrarian policy was to make Korea a granary for Japanese needs.[8] Therefore, Japan undertook a land survey as soon as it annexed Korea, between 1910 and 1918, and seized large tracts of land. By the end of the programme, the Japanese came to hold as much as 40 per cent of

7. Kang, Ch'ang-Il (1994). "*Ilche eui Joson jibae jeonch'aek*" (Japan's Policy of Occupying Joseon), *Yeoksa Wa Hyeonsil* (History and Reality). Vol.12. Korean History Research Committee. p.40.

8. Kang, Man-Gil (1994). *A History of Contemporary Korea*. UK: Global Oriental. p.98.

the land within Korea.[9] Having done that, they then launched a programme for increasing rice production and adopting advanced techniques of agriculture. The colonial authorities justified both these measures, i.e., the land survey and increasing the rice production, as being a policy of agricultural improvement. But, in fact, Japan undertook this as an outlet for its fast-growing population.[10] Moreover, "the rapid growth of Japanese monopoly capitalism during the years of the First World War brought destitution to the Japanese masses, particularly in rural areas. This resulted in a sharp drop in agricultural production... The urgency of the situation meant that the Japanese imperialists had to force increased production of food stuffs in Korea in order to secure a reliable source of foodstuff supplies."[11] Thus, rice production increased by 36 per cent between 1920 and 1928, and in the same time period, the amount of rice exported to Japan rose more than 400 per cent, i.e., the rate of increase in rice being exported to Japan was far greater than the rate of increase in production.[12] This brought down the per capita consumption of rice by Koreans by nearly 28 per cent during the 1920s.[13] This also resulted in increase in crop prices almost fourfold from 1910 to 1920.[14] Koreans had to switch to hulled millet from Manchuria, which was considered to be much inferior then the rice produced domestically. However, this programme of increasing rice production was stopped in 1934 because of various reasons. First, the imported rice was adversely affecting the Japanese rural economy during the depression. Secondly, the irrigation cooperatives that the Japanese had set up in Korea did not function the way it was envisaged because of lack of funds among the Koreans and lack of inclination among

9. Robinson *op. cit.* no. 3: 38.

10. Choe, Byung-T'aek (2010). *"Gangje Bunghap Jeonhoo Ilche eui 'nongeup kairyang' Bangch'im"* (The Japanese Colonial Authority's Policy of 'Agricultural Improvements' around the Time of Japan's Annexation of Korea), *Yeoksa Wa Hyeonsil* 78: 381-418.

11. Kang *op. cit.* no. 8: 103.

12. Ibid.: 104-05.

13. Ibid.: 105.

14. Gi-Wook, Shin (1996). *Peasant Protest & Social Change in Colonial Korea.* Seattle and London: University of Washington Press. p.44.

the Japanese. Thirdly, the Korean peasants had started protesting strongly against the rice exports, and finally and more importantly, by the 1930s, Japan's focus had shifted to its military aggression against Manchuria and China as a whole. It started paying more attention to developing the industrial sector, which consisted of largely war industries to meet Japan's requirements.

Japan's initial survey reported a lot of virgin soil and therefore they brought in an enormous amount of advanced agricultural technology for increasing rice production. But subsequently when they found that this was not the case, they tried to recover the cost of all this by imposing exorbitant duties and taxes on farmlands.[15] In Korea, the peasants had already become destitute because of over-taxation and exploitation by corrupt government officials under the Joseon dynasty. The Japanese laid open the door to their further exploitation by various means and to such an extent that many farmers who had earlier owned land and cultivated it became tenant farmers or in many instances even landless.[16] At times, it drove the peasants to such a state of penury that they either opted to leave the country or give up farming and take on other occupations.[17]

At the time of the Japanese annexation, rural society comprised landlords, owner-cultivators, semi-tenants, landless tenants and wage-workers. According to Gi-Wook Shin, tenancy tenure even during the latter period of the Joseon dynasty was unstable and insecure.[18] However, the 1910-1918 Land Survey, undertaken by the Japanese, recorded that over 77 per cent of households in Korea lived on their land either as tenants or semi-tenants. But by 1922, the landless tenancy rate increased to 41 per cent of the workforce and the figure rose to 60 per cent by the end of colonial rule.[19] Also,

15. Ibid.

16. Seok-Heung, Chang (2004). "Overseas Migration of Koreans in the Colonial Period and Historicality of Repatriation", *Korea Journal* 44(4) (Winter): 7.

17. Robinson *op. cit.* no. 3: 36.

18. Gi-Wook *op. cit.* no. 14: 22-38.

19. Janice, C.H. Km (2007). "The Varieties of Women's Wage Work in Colonial Korea", in *The Review of Korean Studies* 10(2): 122, June. For a detailed study of changes in the ratios of agrarian household types during the period 1916-1932, see, Kang *op. cit.* no. 8: : 103.

because tenant farming did not fetch enough income to meet the family needs, many started working for wages too. It is said that while 13 per cent of the tenants also worked for wages in 1913, this figure rose to 16 per cent by 1926 and by 1940 it was over 35 per cent.[20] Both the colonial powers claim that it was the land reforms undertaken by them that galvanised the agricultural economy of the colonised countries. But it cannot be denied that it was because both needed to finance their operations mostly from land that these reforms were undertaken and the pre-existing patterns of possession and ownership of land were interfered with.[21]

In the Indian context, British colonisation has to be located in its trading interests in Indian textiles and spices. This was because until the end of the 18th century, India was the major producer of raw cotton and exporter of textiles in the world.[22] The 18th century saw the volume of British trade in Indian textiles increasing and, in fact, financing the Atlantic slave trade: Indian textiles constituted 27 per cent of goods shipped to Africa in this period. This in turn was financed by the bullion 'rape' of Latin America.[23] But after the Battle of Plassey in 1757, Britain raised revenues from the conquered regions of India to pay for its (Britain's) exports, leading to the incredible drain of wealth from the country. Historian Irfan Habib describes this as the ultimate blissful dream of the merchant capitalist—"to be able to buy without having to pay, and yet to be able to sell at the full price."[24] It has been shown that in 1757-58, the East India Company brought bullion the equivalent of ₹31 lakh as payment for its exports; but from this time on, it did not bring in any capital at all.[25] However, this surplus appropriation did not end with the rise of "free trade" or industrial capitalism in England; it increased enormously throughout

20. Ibid.: 122.

21. See Bagchi *op. cit.* no. 5: 196.

22. Mukherjee, Aditya (2010). "Empire: How Colonial India Made Modern Britain", *Economic and Political Weekly* XLV(50): 75, 11 December.

23. Ibid.

24. Habib, Irfan (1995). "Colonialization of the Indian Economy", in *Essays in Indian History: Towards a Marxist Perception*. Delhi: Tulika. pp.299-300.

25. Mukherjee *op. cit.* no. 22: 76.

British colonial rule in India. Since agriculture was the backbone of the Indian economy, various revenue settlement policies attempted to grapple with the regional diversity in India. It has been estimated in official records of the East India Company that land revenue collection went up from ₹64.3 lakh in 1762-63 under the native rulers to ₹147.0 lakh in 1765-66 under the Company.[26] In the north Indian heartland around Agra, the land revenue demand went up from ₹2.1 crore in 1806-07 to ₹3.6 crore in 1829-30, and ₹5.6 crore in 1844-45.[27] This increase, accompanied by no substantial increase in prices but in fact a slight depression, meant that the land revenue increase was in real terms.[28] The same pattern can be seen in the Company territories in western and southern India, indicating the nature and magnitude of surplus appropriations in the form of land revenue by the British.

On the trade front, from beginning of the 19th century, the clamour for free trade led to the promulgation of the Charter Acts of 1813 and 1833. This was because of industrialisation in Britain, and the need to find markets for the finished products from British industries.[29] Not only were Indian exports hit, the domestic market was severely challenged as well. In 1815, the export of cotton goods from Britain to India was 0.8 million yards and by 1839, it had risen to 100 million yards,[30] leading to decline of the indigenous textile industry. Similarly, other crafts and industry were also hit, and together they led to massive unemployment and population decline in urban areas.[31] Given the un-productivity of Indian raw cotton because of it being short-stapled, cash crops like indigo were introduced, which however, could not compete with the West Indian competition. By the 1830s, opium was seen as the palliative for the ailing agrarian sector: poppy cultivation in India would pay for British exports of tea and silk from

26. Habib *op. cit.* no. 24: 300.

27. Ibid.: 310.

28. Ibid.: 311.

29. Ibid.: 319.

30. Ibid.

31. Ibid.: 322.

China.[32] The newly-worked out tribute in the form of opium from India in 1855 had an export value of £6.23 million, and the value of exports from China to England stood in the same year at £8.5 million. The Indian export value, along with England's own measly export value of about £1 million, provided the balance of trade for England.[33]

The third stage of British capitalism in the second half of the 19th century was one in which capital investment outside the metropole was pursued along with expansion of the market. The first major investment was in the railways in India, and although ostensibly there was a two-way flow of capital, "the principal and returns on this capital belonged to Britain, and not India," and in the long run, the railway network "served as the catalyst of complete colonialization."[34] The commercialisation of agriculture, mentioned earlier, resulted in the shrinking of food crop production, while conversely there was an increase in the export of food crops in this period. The repeated recurrence of famines in quick succession, the colonial policies that kept the food grain supply from reaching the local population, the decrease in real wages of the agricultural labourers, and the rise of a class of landlords and rich peasants from among the erstwhile *zamindars* of pre-modern Mughal society, all in all, characterised the colonial economy of India of the early 20th century.

The creation of an Indian army, the cost of which the Indian people had borne but which would be under the control of the British, occurred in the early years of British rule. The hierarchical division of the army into the miniscule British/Company army officers, on one hand, and sepoys, on the other, was put into place by middle of the 18th century. The Revolt of 1857 occurred initially because of disaffection among the sepoys of the Indian army because their religious sentiments were hurt by various practices followed in the army.[35] In the 20th century, the British Indian army was deployed all

32. Ibid.: 324-25.

33. Ibid.: 325.

34. Ibid.: 327-28.

35. Chandra, Bipan, Mridula Mukherjee, Aditya Mukherjee, Sucheta Mahajan and K.N. Panikkar (2000). *India's Struggle for Independence*. Penguin Books Ltd. pp.3-4.

over Asia and even beyond, not just to defend the interests of the British Indian Empire but also to extend the empire elsewhere.[36] In the Korean context, we can again see the raising of the colonial army, although the context was considerably different. The Korean people faced forced conscription and deployment to fight Japan's War in Manchuria and China. An added feature in the case of Japan was the enslavement of Korean women as sex slaves for the Japanese army. These women were called "comfort women" and at a point in time, there were as many as 200,000 in the Japanese army. The issue of the "comfort women" and the compensation paid to them after liberation is still a bone of contention between the governments of Korea and Japan. Be that as it may, it is estimated that the number of Koreans who migrated overseas, during the colonial period, on account of forced conscription and forced labour and enslavement was as high as 1.2 million.[37]

In the aftermath of the initial movements of protest in the two countries—the 1857 Revolt in India and the March 1 Movement of 1919 in Korea—changes in the policies of the two powers, Britain and Japan, followed a similar direction. Both the colonial powers set up modern state forms with more efficient instruments of rule, with more firepower, and better-organised police and newer legal concepts. From the 1930s, during the period of its military aggression in other parts of East Asia, Japan strove to convert the Korean cultural leaders into pro-Japanese elements and in the process used aggressive policies like eradicating the Korean language from the school curriculum, forcing people to take on Japanese names, etc. This came to be seen as Japanese colonial cultural policy in Korea, which was meant as a strategy to "divide and rule"—a familiar term in the Indian colonial context as well. Japan tried to foster the growth of pro-Japanese people in cultural, religious and economic circles.[38] It was a policy of dividing the leadership class of people within

36. Bagchi *op. cit.* no. 5: xxxi.

37. Seok-Heung, Chang (2004). "Overseas Migration of Koreans in the Colonial Period and Historicality of Repatriation", *Korea Journal* 44(4): 7, Winter.

38. Kang *op. cit.* no. 8: 149.

Korea on the basis of ideology and conception of what constituted a nation. As a result, the national movement could not have a fulcrum around which the people could rally to dislodge Japan. The 1 March Movement had taught the colonisers that they could neither abolish nor ignore local institutions without devastating consequences. Their solution was to strengthen alliances with the ruling class within the country and to use them to collect taxes and maintain political order, which they did effectively.

In the Indian context, having learnt their lessons from the Revolt of 1857, the British from the early 20th century followed a deliberate policy of divide and rule, which was meant to provide a safety net for the rulers against the growing appeal of nationalism, which had found a platform with founding of the Indian National Congress in 1885, and to find support among some sections of the Indian people to maintain their hegemony. In its long-term dimension, the British policies stimulated communal antagonism and politics, which would particularly serve as a counter to the legitimacy of mass-based nationalism of the Congress from the 1920s. In the short term, administrative policies that would contribute to the development of the long-term strategy were instituted.[39]

Another area in which the Japanese sought to dominate in order to totally subjugate Korea was in the field of education. They promulgated their first educational ordinance for their colony in 1911. However, the school system it introduced for Koreans was different from the ones for Japanese. The number of years of education or the curriculum followed at each of the levels—primary, secondary and high school—was either much less or inferior to the ones for the Japanese students. The curriculum also included learning the Japanese language and taking courses on ethics that taught them to be loyal to the Emperor and the state. The effort certainly was laudable in trying to educate the Koreans, but it seemed geared towards making them loyal subjects of the Japanese empire. Higher educational opportunities were available for very few

39. Chandra, Bipan (2008, 1984). *Communalism in Modern India.* Delhi: Har-Anand. p.277.

Koreans. Vocational training was encouraged to foster the growth of semi-skilled labour force to suit Japanese needs.[40]

The colonial domination included breaking down traditional forms of governance and introducing a modern system of administration, which had an unintended fall-out of increase in literacy rates and number of schools, industrialisation and the formation of various forms of collective identity including that of class and nationhood. But at the same time, it needs to be recognised that this does not mean that without the help of the colonial power all this would not have happened or that this was not already happening before the colonial takeover. In fact, tenets of modernisation were beginning to emerge within Korea even before their colonial domination. The Enlightenment group and the Tonghak rebels had risen and rebelled against the traditional and corrupt bureaucracy during the latter half of the 19th century, and had advocated modernisation even before the Japanese had taken over. Korea also possessed another feature that it had inherited from the Chinese form of governance, which could be regarded as a concept belonging to the modern state—the feature of a bureaucracy selected on the basis of merit through an examination process. It is said that the British had probably modelled their system of civil service examination on the old Chinese Mandarinate. A modern education system is also traced in Korea to the beginning of the 20th century but got stifled to serve Japanese colonial interests.[41]

A familiar argument in the Indian colonial context is about the benefits of British rule, and invariably the focus is on the education system introduced by the British. It has been argued that western colonial domination coincided with the rise of modern western knowledge, and in fact the latter served as an instrument of the former to entrench colonial power in obvious and subtle ways.[42] The new system resulted in not merely a shift in subjects of study, but also in the pedagogical basis of education.[43]

---

40. For details on Japan's educational policy, see Kang *op. cit.* no. 8: 150-54.

41. Ibid.: 154.

42. Seth, Sanjay (2007). *Subject Lessons: The Western Education of Colonial India.* USA: Duke University Press. p.1.

43. Ibid.: 4.

Given the circumstances under which Korean nationalism developed in the early stages, it was natural that it foundered and failed to achieve its objective for there were few foundations upon which it could be built. The Korean masses—mostly illiterate, poor and accustomed to a Confucian state of hierarchical authority—were unable to consolidate their actions. Korean activist leaders like An Ch'ang-ho, Park Yong-Man, Shin Ch'ae-ho and Syngman Rhee had either been imprisoned or chased out of the country. The provisional government set up by them in Shanghai or its branches in San Francisco or Hawaii were not successful in grooming any one leader to take hold of the reins. The leaders outside the country differed greatly in personal attributes and political ideas, all of which had a negative impact on the independence movement.[44] Political factionalism, in fact, was a legacy of the Japanese colonial policy of "divide and conquer",[45] a strategy they adopted to split the nationalist movement within Korea. Nevertheless, vigorous campaigns such as the Enlightenment Self-Strengthening Movement and Patriotic Enlightenment Movement resulted in dissemination of the idea of Korean nationalism and resurgence of Korean sovereign power.[46]

In the Indian context, the ideology of nationalism found an institutional base with founding of the Indian National Congress, and it provided a platform throughout its history for a variety of political thought. While the three phases of the Congress-led movement have been classified as the moderate, extremist and mass phases, it would be more appropriate to see these as different streams from within the broad nationalist frame taking centre stage, responding to particular periods of colonial rule. There were local, regional movements that addressed specific concerns related to colonial domination, as well as broader programmes addressing issues at a pan-Indian level. The

44. For details of the roles played by some of these leaders refer to Han-Kyo, Kim (2002). "The Korean Independence Movement in the United States", *International Journal of Korean Studies* VI(1): 1-27, Spring/Summer. International Council on Korean Studies.

45. Robinson, Michael E. (2007). *Korea's Twentieth-Century Odyssey: A Short History.* Honolulu: University of Hawai'I Press. p.103; Kang *op. cit.* no. 7: 40-42.

46. Shin Yong-Ha (n.d.). *Acceptance of Western Sociology in the Late 19th Century* and *Korean Social Thought.*

Communist Party added class struggle to the agenda of the liberation struggle, while certain community-based parties and organisations played tango with the British colonial authorities.

II

There is no dearth of studies on colonialism in Korea and India; however, it is rare to find any comparative history of the colonial experiences in the two countries. The inherent difficulties of comparing two completely different colonial powers and colonial subject countries, and the complexities of the subject matter itself make this comparison a challenging prospect. The editors were both daunted by the task before us, as well as provoked to undertake this study because of the sheer complexity and nuances that it would help us portray in the understanding of colonialism. Further, it is our view that since colonialism cannot be understood as an isolated phenomenon, the comparative framework allows us to open a window to the worldwide processes related to trade, socio-economic change and political transformations in the modern period.

The book is divided into several themes, which allow us to relate the colonisation experience in Korea and India. The first theme focuses on the pre-modern histories of Korea and India, with a view to understand the nature of the social formation before these regions were colonised. R. Mahalakshmi examines the nature of state formation from the early historical period to the late medieval period in India, focusing on transformations, diffusion, regionalisation and continuation of the state across diverse regions of the Indian sub-continent. Pankaj Mohan critically analyses the interpretations of the past in the colonial and nationalist historiography of Korea, and raises pertinent questions about how the past is used to mediate and even justify the present. The significance of this theme lies in its grappling with a question that was raised in colonial times and continues to be raised today—was colonialism the catalyst of positive change in static, pre-modern societies of Asia with despotic state structures?

The second theme, comprising eight essays, focuses on the colonisation process. Aditya Mukherjee draws our attention to debates in the colonial period and in recent times about the transformative power of colonialism—development is seen to have occurred under the aegis of the benevolent colonial power. He provides data to show that the economy was reeling under the impact of colonisation, so much so that from contributing 25 per cent to the world's GDP in 1800s, India's share was reduced to a dismal 4 per cent at the time of independence. He projects these figures against the development of the Indian economy after 1950, to show that the major industrialisation and modern economic restructuring occurred in this period, and even then given the century and a half of economic drain, India has barely been able to recover from the colonial exploitation of the British.

Other essays in this section focus on modes of colonial governance and institutional mechanisms that were put into place for this purpose. Shri Krishan's study of the military, legal and administrative structures provides the lead article here. Borrowing from Gramsci, we have tried to look not only at the coercive arms of the state but also the ideological apparatuses through which the state exerts its control. Visalakshi Menon's study of colonial education in India; Venkataramanujan's examination of the colonial state and its engagement with religious institutions and communities and Alok Bajpai's exploration of the institutionalisation of western science focus on the state's intervention in the social and cultural life of the colonised people in India.

The next section focuses on the issue of anti-colonialism, nationalist consciousness and the struggle for freedom, and the articles of Shin Young-Ha and Mridula Mukherjee provide us with the wide canvas against which we can see these issues. Shin Young-Ha gives us a fascinating view of Korean nationalism, rejecting the modernist roots and locating it within the primordialist identities of the pre-modern period. Mridula Mukherjee provides an overview of the anti-colonial movements in India, looking at various dimensions of the critique of colonialism that arose from these and the various sections that participated in these movements. Vyjayanti Raghavan's discussion of the Donghak rebellion brings to our attention an early anti-colonial movement, which despite its limitations, left a lasting legacy in the Korean nationalist psyche. Vladimir Tikhonov's study of representations of pre-colonial identities in the colonial period in Korea draws our attention to the contestation of identities—pre-modern, colonial and nationalist—that can be framed within the anti-colonialist discourse. While the discussion revolves around the representations of China and the Chinese, the author raises questions about the intense sentiments invoked on all sides, which ultimately corresponded with the debates on Korean identity. Neerja Singh and Hulas Singh draw our attention to the responses of Indian intellectuals in the 19th century, when British colonial power was well consolidated, towards key social issues and the need for reformation in Indian society. Thus, while accepting the post-Enlightenment ideals that emanated from Europe, these scholars see the repudiation of colonial arguments about the transformative power of colonisation, and emphasise the efforts of intellectuals to bring about reform without rejecting tradition in its entirety. Rakesh Batabyal focuses on Gandhi, widely considered the most influential figure of the national movement, and his critique of colonialism. While colonial apologists have tried to reduce his significance by referring to his caste-class background, or rejecting his politics as opportunistic, Batabyal stresses the deep insights of Gandhi about Indian society, colonial exploitation and the need to tread cautiously on the development path, which continue to have a contemporary relevance in India. Vipan Chandra also highlights the thoughts of two prominent Korean thinkers So Chaep'il and Yun Ch'iho, who were intellectual reformists of the late 19th century and brings new insights on the way they are perceived. The last paper in this section, also by Rakesh Batabyal, focuses on communalism as a specific ideology that emanates as a result of the colonial reactions to the nationalist movement, the divide and rule policy adopted by the British, and as rooted in modern politics and social transformations that occurred due to colonisation.

Our final chapter is in the nature of an epilogue by Sucheta Mahajan, who looks at imperialist strategies of retreat and the partition of India, which takes us back to the question of colonisation as bestowing benefits to the colony. The hasty pull-out of the British in the Indian context once it saw the setting sun over its erstwhile empire in no way reflected any benevolence or concern for the colony, and, in fact, brings home to us the spuriousness of such arguments.

There are many more topics of comparison that await basic research, and numerous issues waiting to be addressed. This book hopes to incite curiosity and further collaborative research in these areas.

R. MAHALAKSHMI

Colonialism: Issues and Perspectives

Introduction

Recent trends in scholarship on early modern history pose the colonial between a pre-colonial and a post-colonial phase, and in the process have de-contextualised the term and indeed drawn attention away from the phenomenon itself. Colonialism cannot be seen within a casual evolutionary framework, but as a phenomenon that occurred at different points of time in different parts of the world with the growth of capitalism in Europe. It constituted the occupation of regions by European powers, at first ostensibly for pursuing their trading interests, and over a period of time, the extension of European political control over these now designated colonies, for economic benefits to the home country. By seeing colonialism as a phase, the specific nature of the phenomenon was ignored and the umbilical cord connecting it to the development of world capitalism has been subsumed in studies on empire. The understanding that colonialism resulted in modernisation of the colonial economy and growth of capital formation, breaking asunder the pre-modern feudal social relations, have been recast in the 'development' debates from the 1960s, in the context of 'de-colonisation' and the emergence of colonies as independent sovereign states.[1] Given the vastness of the theme and its varied dimensions, this paper provides a synoptic, albeit not a comprehensive, survey of the issues raised by scholars,

1. Chandra, Bipan (1979). "Colonialism and Modernization", in *Nationalism and Colonialism in Modern India*. Hyderabad: Orient Longman. p.2. For a discussion on the development thesis, see Chandra, Bipan (1968). "Reinterpretation of Nineteenth Century Indian Economic History", *Indian Economic & Social History Review* 5(1): 35-75, March.

and the historiographical frames within which we can understand their scholarship.

Defining Colonisation

"Until the lions have their own historians, the history of the hunt will always glorify the hunter."[2]

If colonialism can be the analogue of the hunt, scholars within Western historiography have tended to privilege the Empire and have seldom sought to engage with the scholarship emerging from the perspective of the colony. Chinua Achebe, Nigerian litterateur, mentions an Igbo proverb that tells us about a man who did not know where the rain began to beat him, and hence could not say where he dried his body.[3] The efforts by scholars in the erstwhile colonial contexts to study and analyse colonialism outside the colonial frames of history mark the attempts to identify where the rain beat down on the metaphorical man and how he gained the agency to dry his body. On the other side, the hegemonic hold of imperialist histories has often diverted attention from the structures of colonialism and has presented narratives of the triumph of European colonisers, the inferior political and economic development of the colonies at the time of colonisation, the presence of the collaborators or compradore, etc. The emphasis in the last half century in both perspectives has been on the economic roots of colonialism, its political dimensions, the social transformations that emanated as a result of it, its cultural aspects, etc.

Long-distance Trade and the Making of Colonial Empires

Ian Morris in his splendid long-term view of historical processes across the world argues that there has been a tendency to construct long-term lock-in theories and short-term accident theories of global history, to understand the growth of imperialism and colonialism from the 16th century onwards, which resulted in a monolithic

2. African proverb cited by Chinua Achebe, *http://www.theparisreview.org/interviews /1720/the-art-of-fiction-no-139-chinua-achebe*
3. Achebe, Chinua (2012). *There was a Country: A Personal History of Biafra*. London: Allen Lane. p.1.

positioning of the East and the West in historical imagination.[4] In his analysis, we need to seriously grapple with this question because "in the last hundred years or so Westerners have shipped armies to Asia not the other way around. East Asian governments have struggled with Western capitalist and Communist theories but no Western government has tried to rule on Confucian or Daoist lines. Easterners often communicate across linguistic barriers in English; Europeans rarely do so in Mandarin or Japanese...The West has maintained a global dominance without parallel in history."[5] This, for Morris, justifies the title of his work about the contemporary rule of the West across the globe. For the lock-in theorists, the roots of this Western dominance lay in the inherent nature of the Western and Eastern societies. The latter were insular, centralised and self-sufficient, and required no additional challenges for economic growth and social development. On the other hand, Europe was singularly beset with various epidemics, economic downfalls because of the harsh environment and political strife—there was strong motivation for moving out of their insular social world to seek fortunes and a better life. In fact, Karl Marx's writings on Orientalist states can be seen as drawing upon this dualism—the East almost saw the stopping of the flow of history because of the nature of its fossilised society, whereas the West saw a linear progression from one kind of social formation to another.[6] Andre Gunder Frank, on the other hand, propounds the accident theory by placing the East more favourably *vis-à-vis* the West in the 15th century, with its flourishing agrarian economy, trading networks, monetised economy, etc. poised on the brink of an industrial revolution. However, the acute silver shortages in China, essential for currency, were balanced by the European pillaging of precious metals from Peru and Mexico after the discovery of America by Columbus, and thus "silver, savagery and slavery bought the West a third-class seat on the Asian economic train."[7]

4. Morris, Ian (2010). *Why the West Rules For Now: The Patterns of History and What they Reveal About the Future.* London: Profile Books. pp.11-18.

5. Ibid.: 11.

6. Ibid.: 15-16.

7. Ibid.: 19

Findlay and O'Rourke in a *longue duree* understanding of world trade over the second millennium look at the intertwining of political power and economic resources, literally and figuratively, across the seven macro-regions of Western Europe, Eastern Europe, North Africa, Southwest Asia, South Asia, Southeast Asia and East Asia.[8] Although there was contact between different regions with the Mongols and the Arabs providing crucial links, the major transformation in world trade occurred between 1500 and 1650 with Christopher Columbus "discovering" the Americas, paving the way for the first major "globalisation" in what is popularly known as the "Age of Mercantilism" between 1650 and 1780.[9] During this period, the seven geo-political regions mentioned above were directly connected to each other. Of greater significance was the fact that the volume of Europe's trade with the rest of the world grew during this period.[10] Most importantly, the coercive power exercised by European states was directly related to the increasing accruing of benefits of transoceanic trade to these countries.[11] For Findlay and O'Rourke, the transition to economic modernity occurred because of the subsequent Industrial Revolution in 19th century Europe, which saw growth in key sectors such as metallurgy and cotton textiles, growth in population without a major decline in living standards, and technological changes, particularly in the textile sector and transportation.[12]

But how do we explain the colonisation of Asian countries by Asian imperial powers within this framework? It is again within the long-term theory supporting the dualism of the West and East discussed by Morris that the Japanese imperial ambitions are sought to be explained: the process of getting on to the "civilisation and enlightenment" bandwagon, following arrival of the American fleet under Commodore Perry in Tokyo Bay, brought home to the Japanese

8. Findlay, Ronald and Kevin H. O'Rourke (2007). *Power and Plenty: Trade, War, and the World Economy in the Second Millenium*. Princeton and Oxford: Princeton University Press.

9. Ibid.: 106-08, 142-43.

10. Ibid.: 305.

11. Ibid.: 310.

12. Ibid.: 313-21.

that the Chinese, whom they always looked up to, were a decaying power and that the Western model of industrialisation, democracy and gender equality would help Japan become "civilized", on a par with the Western powers.[13] David Landes, in his well-known essay "Why are we so rich and they so poor?" also includes the Japanese in the set of "we" as "honorary Europeans".[14] However, it has been argued that Japanese colonialism cannot be compared to that of the Europeans because, first, it occurred well after the European scramble for colonies and the entrenched colonial interests of these nations became visible.[15] Japanese history reveals its confrontations with the powerful Chinese empire, on one hand, and its own failed expansionist ventures, on the other, which led to a deliberate policy of national isolation and seclusion pursued by the Tokugawa Shogunate between 1640 and 1854. It has been argued that precisely because of this stymieing of growth of the merchant, the artisan and the peasant, and the economy in general; Japanese colonialism developed certain peculiar characteristics.[16] The second half of the 19th century saw the Japanese shocked out of their isolation with the naval-diplomatic mission of Perry in 1853, the Meiji restoration in 1868 and expansionist policies aimed at maintaining national security.[17] Hyman Kublin's analysis seems to suggest an almost accidental element in the emergence of Japan as a colonial power. The colonisation of Formosa, after the Sino-Japanese war of 1894-95, has been identified as the moment when Japan arrived on the scene as an imperial power. While Kublin presents an apologist's view of Japanese colonialism, what is very clear even from the sketch of its colonisation of Formosa (modern Taiwan) is the nature of its primitive accumulation as demonstrated by the Europeans from the 16th to the 18th centuries in their colonies in the New World, which

---

13. Morris *op. cit.* no. 3: : 14-15, 522-24.

14. Landes, David (1990). "Why are we so Rich and They so Poor?", *American Economic Review* 80: 1-13.

15. Kublin, Hyman (1959). "The Evolution of Japanese Colonialism", *Comparative Studies in Society and History* 2(1): 68.

16. Ibid.: 71.

17. Ibid.: 71-73.

contributed to its own arrival on the world capitalist stage. In fact, it has been argued by Bipan Chandra that India and Japan in the pre-modern period were not very different in terms of social conditions, but that the difference between the two was that India had been colonised, whereas Japan was able to undertake the capitalist path with rapidity because of its political survival as a non-colony.[18] A variant of Kublin's argument can be found in the work of Mark Peattie, who sees Japan's vulnerability *vis-à-vis* Western colonial powers at work in its own colonial forays.[19] In fact, the regional dimension of the Japanese colonial empire is attributed to this pragmatic effort by Japan to compete on the world stage. According to James Nakamura, Japan had an advantage despite its late advent on the scene because of its colonisation of Asian societies based on agrarian rice-producing economies like its own, thereby allowing it to integrate more effectively the colonies with the metropole, unlike the European ones, which were primarily export-oriented enclaves.[20] Marius Jansen studies the Meiji period to understand the nature of subsequent Japanese imperialism, and argues that there was a strong opinion in Japan in favour of emulating the Western imperial powers by establishing colonies as a diplomatic and strategic counter-offensive to perceived Western interests in the region.[21] In our analysis, the economic dimensions of the imperialist tendencies remain under-emphasised, although it is acknowledged in various studies that industrial growth accompanied imperial expansion

---

18. Chandra, Bipan (n.d.). *Karl Marx*. pp.368-69.

19 Peattie, Mark R. (1984). "Introduction", in Ramon Hawley Myers and M.R. Peattie (eds.), *The Japanese Colonial Empire: 1895-1945*. Princeton University Press. pp.3-52.

20. Nakamura, James (1974). "Incentives, Productivity Gaps, and Agricultural Growth Rates in Prewar Japan, Taiwan, and Korea", in Bernard Silberman and Harry Harootunian (eds.), *Japan in Crisis: Essays in Taisho Democracy*. Princeton: Princeton University Press. p.350. Cited in Ibid.: 8.

21. Jansen, Marius B. (1984). "Japanese Imperialism: Late Meiji Perspectives", in Ramon Hawley Myers and M.R. Peattie (eds.), *The Japanese Colonial Empire: 1895-1945*. Princeton University Press. pp.64, 71, 75-76.

and that the colonies were profitable to Japan.[22] Peter Duus points out that although the oligarchs who designed the modernisation and capitalist development of Japan placed the profit motive below service to the state, "they recognized that the economy revolved around the entrepreneurs, financiers, and managers who lived by its commands."[23] Elsewhere, he refers to a Japanese report written in 1870, where Korea was described as a gold mine, its agricultural surpluses of rice and wheat extolled, and the potential of its human, mineral and other resources was recognised.[24] There was, in fact, a clear understanding by the 1870s itself that trade interests required Japan to exercise military force. In the course of its drawing upon Western imperial strategies, the Japanese attempted by the turn of the 20th century to cater to its industries by importing raw materials from outside and exporting its industrial products.[25] Certainly, the argument that has conventionally been made about Japan's incidental economic gains and primary strategic impulse for colonising seems suspect, and we need to see political economic reasons, similar to that in Europe, for its imperialist policies, which were kick started in the 19th century.

Capital Accumulation and the Rise of the West

To understand colonialism, it is necessary to look at the growth of capitalism, for scholars from differing perspectives have organically linked the growth of the former to the rise of the latter. The works of two major scholars who have shaped the manner in which both colonialism and capitalism have been understood will be undertaken here.

---

22. Ibid.: 78. For a discussion of the Japanese expectations from Korea and other colonies, see Peattie, M.R. (1984). "Japanese Attitudes Towards Colonialism, 1895-1945", in Ramon Hawley Myers and M.R. Peattie (eds.), *The Japanese Colonial Empire: 1895-1945*. Princeton University Press. pp.80-127.

23. Duus, Peter (1984). "Economic Dimensions of Meiji Imperialism: The Case of Korea, 1895-1910", in Ramon Hawley Myers and M.R. Peattie (eds.), *The Japanese Colonial Empire: 1895-1945*. Princeton University Press. p.131.

24. Duus, Peter (1995). *The Abacus and the Sword: The Japanese Penetration of Korea, 1895-1910*. Berkeley: University of California Press. p.35.

25. Ibid.: 245-46.

Adam Smith is considered the father of modern economics and his magnum opus *An Inquiry into the Wealth of Nations* has been described as "a manifesto for private property, free trade, and free markets."[26] In his discussion of how colonies have contributed to the wealth of Europe, he contrasts the 18th century colonies in America and the West Indies with those of the ancient Greeks and Romans.[27] Although the major states of the ancient world possessed small territories, they did not interfere in the direct control of these: "the mother city, though she considered the colony as a child, at all times entitled to great favour and assistance, and owing in return much gratitude and respect, yet considered it as an emancipated child, over whom she pretended to claim no direct authority or jurisdiction."[28] In the 15th and 16th centuries, the explorations of Europeans led them to new lands, and while their expectations of instant riches were not fulfilled, they paved the way for a new kind of colonisation, one in which the mother country was neither so liberal nor indeed saw the colony as a child to be left alone. Indeed, Smith lauds the colonies "of a civilized nation which takes possession either of a waste country, or of one so thinly inhabited that the natives easily give place to the new settlers, advances more rapidly to wealth and greatness than any other human society."[29] Among the many advantages Smith enumerates of colonisation of the New World by Europe, he gives importance to two—the increase of enjoyment of Europeans because of imports from the colonies; and the augmentation of Europe's industries. In the context of England, Smith sees monopolistic trade as forcing Great Britain to venture its capital into "a foreign trade of consumption" with a distant country. Secondly, this capital was mobilised into a round-about trade of consumption, for many of the commodities coming in via this trade exceeded the demand and

26. Otteson, James R. (2006). "Book Review of Samuel Fleischacker on Adam Smith's "Wealth of Nations": A Philosophical Companion", *The Independent Review: A Journal of Political Economy* 10: 3, Winter.

27. Smith, Adam (n.d.). *An Inquiry into the Nature and Causes of the Wealth of Nations.* Chapter VII, Part I. p.447. *www2.hn.psu.edu/faculty/jmanis/adam-smith/wealth-nations.pdf*

28. Ibid.: 448.

29. Ibid., Part II: 455.

consumption within the mother country, thereby being exported to other countries from Great Britain.[30] Smith argues against the monopoly trade of the Europeans on the grounds that it hindered industry in the long run and, more importantly, it restricted the accumulation of capital, which ultimately would lead to the wealth of nations.[31]

Karl Marx's two-volume *Capital* remains the landmark when it comes to the analysis of capital accumulation and the rise of the West; indeed, Engels mentions that it was referred to as the Bible of the working class.[32] For Marx, "Capital consists of raw materials, instruments of labour and means of subsistence of all kinds, which are employed in producing new raw materials, new instruments, and new means of subsistence... Capital also is a social relation of production. It is a bourgeois relation of production... Capital consists not only of means of subsistence, instruments of labour, and raw materials; it consists just as much of exchange values. All products of which it consists are commodities. Capital, consequently, is not only a sum of material products, it is a sum of commodities, of exchange values, of social magnitudes."[33] Colonialism for Marx was the means through which non-capitalist societies would be integrated into the world capitalist system; in other words, capitalism would be imposed from above.[34]

It is along these two tracks that studies on capitalism and Western dominance have been undertaken. The first represents a benign approach that provides an explanatory model for the fact of the rise and dominance of European nations between the 16th and 18th centuries, with a prescription for the development

30. Ibid., Part III: 487-88.

31. Ibid.: 495.

32. Engels (1886). "Preface to the English Edition", *Capital*, Volume One, *www.marxists.org/archive/marx/works/1867-cl/p6.htm*

33. Marx, Karl (1847). *The Nature and Growth of Capital. www.marxists.org/archive/marx/works/1847/wage-labour/ch05.htm*

34. Chandra, Bipan (2012). "Karl Marx, His Theories of Asian Societies and Colonial Rule", in *The Writings of Bipan Chandra: The Making of Modern India From Marx to Gandhi*. Hyderabad: Orient Blackswan. p.367.

of capitalism. The second attempts to analyse and critique the growth of capitalism as a universal system, with the growth of free trade and industries in the 19th century context, to underscore its complexity and contradictions.

Reversing the Gaze: Colonialism in the Eyes of the Colonised

Among the major critiques of the narratives of imperialist expansion that clearly eschewed the word colonialism, Eric Williams focuses on an aspect that even apologists of Empire find difficult to defend. In his path-breaking work *Capitalism and Slavery*, he argues that the slave trade in actuality financed the Industrial Revolution in England.[35] He critiques Adam Smith, feted in 18th century Europe and thereafter as the father of modern economics, for arguing that slavery originated and was sustained because the slave took pride and indeed loved the power exercised by his master (although Smith was opposed to slave labour as uneconomical as compared to free labour). As Williams puts it: "When slavery is adopted, it is not adopted as the choice over free labor; there is no choice at all." The reasons for slavery, wrote Gibbon Wakefield,[36] "are not moral, but economical circumstances; they relate not to vice and virtue, but to production." With the limited population of Europe in the 16th century, free labourers needed to cultivate the staple crops of sugar, tobacco and cotton which in the New World could not have been supplied in quantities adequate to permit large-scale production. Slavery was necessary for this, and to get slaves the Europeans turned first to the aborigines and then to Africa." Williams further criticises the assumption that slavery may be identified with the Negro; he argues that what was essentially an economic exploitation was given a racial twist, and that rather than see slavery as born of racism, we must recognise racism as a consequence of slavery.[37] Williams draws attention to the expansive triangular trade between

35. Williams, Eric (1944). *Capitalism and Slavery*. Chapel Hill: The University of North Carolina Press.
36. Wakefield was a British politician who wrote *A View of the Art of Colonization*. Cited in Ibid.: 6.
37. Ibid.: 7.

England-France, colonial America and Africa in the 17th and 18th centuries, where the first two regions supplied the exports and ships and the last provided the human merchandise essential to this trade.[38]

In another exceeding insightful work, Walter Rodney discusses how Europe underdeveloped Africa (this is the title of his book):

> The question as to who, and what, is responsible for African underdevelopment can be answered at two levels. Firstly, the answer is that the operation of the imperialist system bears major responsibility for African economic retardation by draining African wealth and by making it impossible to develop more rapidly the resources of the continent. Secondly, one has to deal with those who manipulated the system and those who are eager agents or unwitting accomplices of the said system. The capitalists of western Europe were the ones who actively extended their exploitation from inside Europe to cover the whole of Africa.[39]

In the Indian context, the pioneering work of Bipan Chandra brought to the fore the misplaced and Eurocentric conceptualisation of colonialism in the academic record. His critique of Karl Marx and Frederick Engels as neither providing a theoretical understanding of Asian societies nor being based on authentic sources has not been disputed even by the most ardent Marxists.[40] However, while there was a tendency to reject Marx's views on pre-colonial Asia, many scholars appeared to accept his formulations on colonialism, which were based on the understanding of the rise of capitalism and its impact on non-capitalist societies.[41] In a series of articles written in 1853, Marx identified three distinctive features of Asian societies, namely, Oriental Despotism based on irrigation, absence of private property in land, and cohesive village communities.[42] For Marx, the unchanging and stagnant Indian/Asian society received its first major

38. Ibid.: 51.

39. Rodney, Walter (2012, 1972). *How Europe Underdeveloped Africa*. Cape Town: Pambazuka Press. p.27.

40. Chandra *op. cit.* no. 33: 292.

41. Ibid.: 294.

42. Ibid.: 296.

stimulus for change in the form of British rule.[43] In this sense, British colonisation was seen as having a double impact of annihilation (of the old Asiatic society) and regeneration (modernisation through colonisation).[44] Further, the negative aspects of colonialism, or annihilation as Marx terms it, were equated with those of capitalism in the colonising country, the assumption being that capitalism would create its mirror image in the colony.[45] Chandra rejects this idea and formulates the concept of the "colonial mode of production":

> Colonialism did mean the intrusion of capitalism into India but not the development of capitalism or of productive forces. It did not prove to be, like capitalism, an advanced stage of social development...It was its negative image, its opposite side. Capitalism developed the forces of capitalism, colonialism obstructed them. Capitalism developed society, colonialism retarded and regressed it, i.e. underdeveloped it. Capitalism is driven by its inherent character to revolutionize the forces of production, colonialism possesses no inner potential for development.[46]

Again, rejecting the idea that modernisation in India was intrinsically linked to colonisation, Chandra points out that the contention "whatever industrial development occurred in India in the past occurred as a result of the integration of the Indian economy with the world capitalist system through trade and capital investment, is disproved by the very interesting historical phenomenon that the major spurts in industrial development took place precisely during those periods when India's colonial economic links with the world capitalist economy were temporarily weakened or disrupted."[47] It is in this sense that he talks of colonialism as a distinct historical period in modern India, which represented "a distinct social formation or sub-formation in which the basic control of the economy and society is in the hands of a foreign capitalist class which functions in the colony (or semi-colony) through a dependent and subservient economic,

43. Ibid.: 312.
44. Ibid.: 316-21.
45. Ibid.: 319, 324.
46. Ibid.: 372.
47. Chandra *op. cit.* no. 1: 8.

social, political, and intellectual structure whose forms can vary with the changing conditions of the historical development of capitalism as a world-wide system."[48]

Irfan Habib, one of the doyens of Indian history, also analyses colonialism through a critical appreciation of Marx's understanding of the Indian case.[49] He discusses the effect particularly of the Charter Act of 1813, which changed the character of trade of Britain with India, which was earlier focused on export and now became part of an import system as well. However, Habib raises a simple theoretical problem that has ramifications for the understanding of both capitalism and colonialism: "All surplus value is produced by the worker. Thus, surplus values of manufactured goods exported from Britain to India represented the exploitation of the English worker, not the Indian. Yet, these very exports caused vast unemployment and artisans' distress in India."[50]

Korea's economic exploitation under colonialism has been the subject of some important studies. Kyong Ju Kim focuses on the various interpretations of capitalist development in Korea, which tends to follow similar paths as in other colonised contexts, including India.

> Through the debates over the development of colonial society, there arose a 'colonial perspective' that portrayed the Choson society as economically stagnant. A Marxist perspective challenged this, linking Choson society as a stagnant structure to imperialism and semi-feudalism. This perspective was superseded by a nationalist position, which reformulated the relation of stagnation and progressive tendency in Choson society. In this view, it was the colonial rule that created uneven and distorted development and disarticulation.[51]

Dae-oup Chang argues that while the colonial state dominated the process of primitive accumulation in Korea's capitalist development,

---

48. Ibid.: 26.

49. Habib, Irfan (1995). "Marx's Perception of India", in *Essays in Indian History: Towards a Marxist Perspective*. New Delhi: Tulika. pp.14-58.

50. Habib, Irfab (1995). "Problems of Marxist Historiography', in Ibid.: 9.

51. Kim, Kyong Ju (2006). *The Development of Modern South Korea: State Formation, Capitalist Development and Nationa Identity*. Oxon: Routledge. p.104.

it did not build up a well-organised body of the state apparatus.[52] We come back here, then, to the vexed question of colonialism providing a path towards capitalist growth, which would then seek to trace the emergence of Korean capitalist development, after its independence from Japan, to the colonial period.[53]

Anti-Colonial Movements

> Colonial domination, because it is total and tends to over-simplify, very soon manages to disrupt in spectacular fashion the cultural life of a conquered people. This cultural obliteration is made possible by the negation of national reality, by new legal relations introduced by the occupying power, by the banishment of the natives and their customs to outlying districts by colonial society, by expropriation, and by the systematic enslaving of men and women.[54]

Fanon's evocative reading of the toxicity of colonisation and the need to invoke nationalism for its destruction is a stark example of anti-colonialism. Given the degradation posed by colonialism, Fanon argues that the colonised is driven,

> More and more to open, organized revolt. The necessity for an open and decisive breach is formed progressively and imperceptibly, and comes to be felt by the great majority of the people. Those tensions which were hitherto non-existent come into being. International events, the collapse of whole sections of colonial empires and the contradictions inherent in the colonial system strengthen and uphold the native's combativity while promoting and giving support to national consciousness.[55]

For Benedict Anderson, nation/nationality/nationalism was a cultural artifact that came into existence in the 18th century due to:

> The spontaneous distillation of a complex 'crossing' of discrete historical forces; but that, once created, they became 'modular,'

52. Chang, Dae-oup (2009). *Capitalist Development in Korea: Labour, Capital and the Myth of the Developmental State*. Oxon: Routledge. p.82.

53. See Kohli, Atul (2004). *State-Directed Development: Political Power and Industrialization in the Global Periphery*. Cambridge: Cambridge University Press. pp.27-61.

54. Fanon, Frantz (n.d.). "Reciprocal Bases of National Culture and the Fight For Freedom", *www.marxists.org/subject/africa/fanon/national-culture.htm*

55. Ibid.

capable of being transplanted, with varying degrees of self-consciousness, to a great variety of social terrains, to merge and be merged with a correspondingly wide variety of political and ideological constellations.[56]

For him, nationalism does not represent the emergence of self-consciously held political ideologies but needs to be understood in terms of the larger cultural systems within which it emerged.[57] In his reading, anti-colonial contexts provide a replication of European nationalism(s) through the spread of colonial education and thereby Western Renaissance ideals.[58] John Breuilly, on the other hand, advocates a political understanding of nationalism as a conscious expression of intellectuals and as representing the interests primarily of the political entity vested with power, namely the state.[59] He sees anti-colonial nationalism as providing a counter-force to the ideology of Western imperial/colonial powers by taking recourse to specific cultural signifiers. However, he refrains from drawing any direct or essentialist lineage of this cultural signification from pre-modern traditions, for he sees the possibility of the nation emerging as "a project, a unity to be fashioned out of the fight for independence and in the new era of freedom."[60] Ernest Gellner, Breuilly's mentor, also draws the genealogy of nations from certain pre-modern traits but strongly advocates a modernist parentage for these.[61] He focuses on transition from pre-industrial/agrarian society to the industrial one in the 18th century to argue for nations and nationalism as an intellectual articulation of a new social form.[62] While he does see

---

56. Anderson, Benedict (1983). *Imagined Communities: Reflections on the Origins and Spread of Nationalism.* London: Verso. p.4.
57. Ibid.: 12.
58. Ibid.: 120.
59. Breuilly, John (1993). *Nationalism and the State.* Manchester: Manchester University Press. p.1.
60. Ibid.: 7.
61. Gellner, Ernest (1983). *Nations and Nationalism.* Blackwell. pp. 55-6.
62. See, Breuilly, John (1983). "Introduction", in Ernest Gellner, *Nations and Nationalism.* Blackwell. p. xxii.

European nationalism as implicated in colonialism, surprisingly, the rise of anti-colonial nationalism is peripheral to his concerns.

In definitive terms, the specific instances of political struggles of colonised people against their colonial rulers broadly constituted anti-colonialism, and were often articulated in terms of violent revolution and liberation.[63] The Chinese revolution in 1918-19/1937-1945, the Algerian anti-communist movement, the Ghanian struggle and others in Africa and Latin America have been studied as truly revolutionary movements against colonial and neo-colonial/imperialist yokes. Most Marxist interpretations of anti-colonial nationalisms have tended to deprecate those struggles, which did not have violence as their backbone. However, in the context of India, Bipan Chandra argues against this kind of reductionism, and places the Indian national movement since the 1880s within the rubric of anti-colonialism because of its clear "critique of colonialism and colonization of the Indian economy, a pro-poor orientation and a basic commitment to political and economic independence, modern economic development, secularism, democracy and civil liberties, and internationalism and independent foreign policy."[64] Chandra, on one hand, rejects the left-wing criticism of nationalism as a bourgeois ideology, and, on the other, disagrees with the proponents of the view that nationalism in colonial contexts replicated/borrowed from Europe, the USA or Japan.[65]

In the Korean context, it has been argued that colonialism resulted in extreme exploitation of the peasantry, which in turn led to their mobilisation for revolution.[66] While Gi-Wook Shin criticises this as a very simplistic view, he also focuses on strategies used by peasantry to counter colonial dominance and the sustained efforts towards throwing off the mantle of the colonial

63. Ashcroft, Bill, Gareth Griffiths and Helen Tiffin (eds.) (2000). *Post-Colonial Studies: The Key Concepts*. Oxon: Routledge. p.16.

64. Chandra, Bipan (2012). "The Long-Term Dynamics: Gandhiji and the Indian National Movement", in *The Making of Modern India*. p.9.

65. Ibid.: 74, fn. 143.

66. See, Shin, Gi-Wook (1996). *Peasant Protest and Social Change in Colonial Korea*. University of Washington Press. p.6.

power.[67] Elsewhere, Shin argues that Korean nationalism must be understood as a product of historical embeddedness, geo-political contingency, contestation against colonial/imperialist dominance and modernity.[68] However, what is curious is that the colonial context and economic underpinnings of the nationalist ideology in the making have been glossed over in his work.

Conclusion

What is very apparent from the limited discussion above is that colonialism cannot be understood simply as a phenomenon without placing it in the wider context of the growth of worldwide trade networks, capital formation in the West, and politico-economic domination and exploitation of colonies by the European powers. Although the nature of colonisation depends on the context and geo-cultural region, the experiences in West Africa, South America and South and East Asia do allow us to engage with questions beyond the descriptive understanding of coloniser and colonised, to see how the slave trade, bullion trade, export of raw materials, import of finished products, etc. formed a part of the wider movement of capital and industrial development.

67. Ibid.

68. Shin, Gi-Wook (2006). *Ethnic Nationalism in Korea: Genealogy, Politics and Legacy.* Stanford University Press. pp.8-12.

PART I

Historiography In Precolonial India and Korea

1

R. MAHALAKSHMI

Historiography of the Pre-modern State in India

Introduction

India is a vast country that has often been described as a continent of cultures. Despite the variations and disparities, historically there have been points of convergence across regions and contexts. Further, what can distinctly be termed an Indic civilisation is also discernible in the pre-modern period, which continues to lend relevance to the concept of India as a unitary, albeit not homogeneous, whole. Karl Marx had referred to the state as an excrescence of society[1] and consonant with this understanding historians have preferred to analyse the state as rooted to economic and social processes. Most of the historical studies on India, irrespective of context, have linked the growth of agrarian economies to the rise and consolidation of state power. The study of the state has consequently received significant attention in the early historical Indian context. From R.S. Sharma's seminal work, which attempted to locate the forces of production that led to the growth of early states in the early historical period in north India predicated on limited slave labour and other forms of servitude,[2] to the non-Marxian analysis of the transition from lineage-based society to state in early historical India,[3] the evolution

1. Skalník, Peter (1981). "Some Additional Thoughts on the Concept of the Early State", in H. J. M. Claessen and Peter Skalník (eds.), *The Study of the State*. The Hague: Mouton. p.341.

2. Sharma, R.S. (1983). *Material Culture and Social Formations in Ancient India*. New Delhi: Macmillan.

3. Thapar, Romila (1984). *From Lineage to State: Social Formations in the Mid-first Millenium B.C. in the Ganga Valley*. New Delhi: OUP.

of political institutions and the concomitant growth of class society were key elements to understanding the state in early India.[4]

Emergence of Political Institutions in India

Vedic literature, comprising the *Rig*, *Sama*, *Yajur* and *Atharva* Vedas and the Brahmanas, and later texts called the *Upanisads* throw light on the nature of political organisation in north India across a vast time span between c. 1500 BCE and 500 BCE.[5] In the earliest period, there is evidence of clan-based tribal organisation, with the term *raja* being used to denote the leader of the clan (*raja* = to shine/ to lead). It is said that he was selected by the *vish* or people because of his ability to protect the clan and be the leader of his people in the cattle raids and wars that were the mainstay of that society, and different markers of the *raja's* suitability were considered. It is obvious from the contexts in which the term appears that we are not talking of the *raja* as a king ruling over a monarchical state but as a warlord tied through kinship affiliation with his people. Often the ruler was addressed as *gopati* or *gopa*, indicating the pastoral tribal social organisation.[6] The *raja* was assisted by a group of functionaries. The *senani* was the military commander, while the *purohita* was the priest. The latter particularly appears to have played an important role in legitimising the *raja* and composed poems lauding heroic deeds of the rulers. In return, they were given fantastic rewards that included cattle and women.[7]

On the other hand, the clansmen were organised into assemblies that acted as a check and balanced the power wielded by the *raja*. The *sabha* was an assembly with restricted membership, presumed to be select and exclusive, although women were known to be members.[8]

---

4. Jha, D.N. (1971). "Land Revenue in the Maurya and Gupta Periods", in R.S. Sharma (ed.), *Land Revenue in India: Historical Studies*. Delhi: Motilal Banarsidass. p.1–19.
5. Thapar, Romila (2002). *Early India: From Origins to AD 1300*. Great Britain: Penguin. pp.117-122; Sharma, R.S. (2005). *India's Ancient Past*. Delhi: OUP. pp.110-12.
6. Singh, Upinder (2009). *A History of Ancient ad Early Medieval India: From the Stone Age to the 12th Century*. Delhi: Pearson.
7. Sharma *op. cit.* no. 5: 111.
8. Ibid.

The *samiti* was more open and possibly had representation from all families belonging to the clan. The *vidatha* also appeared to be an exclusive gathering where primarily wealth acquired from war and cattle raids were redistributed.[9] Very interestingly, there are no references to any formal office for collecting taxes. The redistributive mechanism in this primarily pastoral society with some agricultural influence was through a kin-based system. Conceptually, *dana* and *daksina* appear as terms denoting two more types of redistribution. *Dana* was gift and part of the evolving patronage structures, where the priests were given gifts in return for their praise of the ruler. *Daksina* emerged gradually as fee for the ritual performance of a sacrifice. In both instances, it tied the ruling class in a symbiotic relationship with the priestly classes.[10] The *raja* himself received gifts in the form of *bali* from his clansmen. *Bhaga* was used to refer to a share of the war booty, while *shulka* was a term referring to the value of an item. At this stage, there is no indication that these were terms used for taxation.

Later Vedic society saw a transformation of the *raja* from a mere military leader into a personage who acquired superior social status as the performer of elaborate sacrificial rituals. The significance of the priests, who made these 'truth-claims' on behalf of the ruler, also increased considerably. The protector of the people was now also responsible for the settlement's security, and while the idea of firm territoriality had not emerged as yet, there was a ratification of the *raja's* rule beyond his kinship base and within a *rashtra* or region.[11] The office of the *raja* was increasingly seen as hereditary, and emphasis was laid on primogeniture. This process of the *raja* becoming distanced from his kin group is best seen in the expression *vishamatta* used for the *raja*, which signifies the eating of the people by the ruler. Towards the end of the later Vedic period, the *raja* was also known as *janapadin*, a settled region, indicating growth of the idea of fixed territoriality.

---

9. Thapar *op. cit.* no. 5: : 119.

10. Ibid.

11. Singh *op. cit.* no. 6: : 200-01; Thapar *op. cit.* no. 5: 120-22.

This gradual expansion of the power of the *raja* can be seen in the receding importance of the assemblies. The *sabha* and *samiti* continue to be mentioned in the *Brahmanas*, but they appear to be more of appendages to the political authority of the *raja*. Only the rich and those with military might were mentioned as members of these assemblies.[12] The *vidatha* is not known in this period, and women did not have access to the assemblies anymore. Ritual performances of the *rajasuya*, *ashvamedha* and *vajapeya* sacrifices reinforced the *raja's* right to rule. The pastoral economy of the earlier period gave way to an agrarian one. The *bali* or offering made by the clansmen to the *raja* in an earlier period came to be accepted as a tribute. This was still not understood to be tax in the sense of a formal structure or category.

The use of iron technology in the transformation of pastoral society to an agrarian, settled one in the early historical period has been attested to by archaeological and literary sources.[13] It is also argued that agrarian surpluses could be generated and conceived of as not merely economic but social products because of the transition from lineage-based societies to settled state societies, and that the role of social organisation and political authority was also important in this process.[14] The significance of iron technology may also be seen in its engendering transformations in social values, and the roots of ideological ferment in the 6th century BCE, marked by the growth of philosophical systems spurning elaborate rituals and the rise of Buddhism and Jainism, is linked to the material transformations occurring at this point in north India (Shrimali, 2007).

Towards Monarchy

The growth of monarchy in early India was a result of the *raja* or king emerging out of the *vish* or lineage group, and needing

12. Sharma *op. cit.* no. 5: 122-23.
13. Kosambi, D.D. (1956). *An Introduction to the Study of Indian History*. Bombay: Popular Book Depot; Sharma, R.S. (1958). *Sudras in Ancient India: A Social History of the Lower Order Down to Circa A.D. 600*. New Delhi: Motilal Banarsidass; Shrimali, K.M. (2007). *The Age of Iron and the Religious Revolution: c. 700–c. 350 BC*. New Delhi: Tulika Books.
14. Thapar *op. cit.* no. 3.

to negotiate not merely with other *vishpati*, but also at the local level with heads of households.[15] There were many parallels drawn between the *raja* and the *grihapati* or householder in the post-Vedic sutra literature: both were lords of their ritual and social spaces; both ensured production, distribution and reproduction; both were constituted within patrilineal kinship structures. The rituals of sacrifice in the public domain and those within the home were legitimising devices used in the proliferation of the concept of patrilineal kingship as well as patrilineal, patriarchal households.[16]

It is with the growth of *janapadas* and *gana sanghas* or oligarchies from the 6th century BCE that features of the state as an organisation with a standing army, regular taxation system, territorial power and administrative structure can first be seen. The *raja* appeared to have extraordinary powers and the unquestioned right to property. The ruler was referred to as *ekaraja* in the monarchies, and *samgha* or *anekaraja* in the oligarchies.[17] Some of these kingdoms grew into *mahajanapadas* such as Kashi, Koshala and Magadha. These were states that had elaborate bureaucracies, with *mahamatras* or officials such as *mantrin*/ministers, *senanayaka*/commander, judge, accountant, etc.[18] With the growth of urban centres as a concomitant of the flourishing agrarian economy of the times, there was a distinction between the urban and rural systems of government. The latter particularly was of considerable importance as agriculture continued to be the mainstay of the state.[19] Terms known in Vedic literature such as *bhaga, bali, kara* and *shulka* now took on new meanings as specific taxes.

The seizing of power by Chandragupta Maurya in c.321 BCE and the establishment of the Mauryan dynasty in Magadha are momentous events in the annals of the state in early India. This is the first instance of the evolution of an imperial state, with

15. Roy, Kumkum (1994). *The Emergence of Monarchy in North India, Eighth–fourth Centuries B.C.: As Reflected in the Brahmanical Tradition*. Delhi: OUP.

16. Ibid.: 280–82, 294.

17. Sharma *op. cit.* no. 5: 166.

18. Sharma *op. cit.* no. 5: 163.

19. Sharma *op. cit.* no. 5: 165.

its vast apparatus of government, institutional structures and integration of different types of pre-state and state polities into the larger empire.[20] It is primarily through the edicts of Ashoka, who ruled from 268 BCE to 231 BCE, that we have an understanding of the extent of the Mauryan empire, territorially as well as in terms of structures of governance. The text exemplar on political economy, *Arthashastra*, authored by the legendary figure Kautilya, provides a lucid account of the nature of state authority, its various institutions, the resources of the state and patterns of mobilisation, the colonisation of new areas for agricultural purposes, etc. There were new forms of taxation, such as labour dues, taxes for creating and maintaining irrigational facilities, tolls and customs duties and the levies on guilds referred to as *shreni* and *puga* in the sources.[21] The king was the nucleus of the empire, and Ashoka appears to have introduced a paternal kingship strategy. He was assisted by a council of ministers, and two key offices of the treasurer and chief controller oversaw the financial arrangements of the state. The treasurer maintained an account of the income available both in cash and kind, while the controller looked after the revenue registers. There were separate departments to oversee different economic activities such as agriculture, crafts of various kinds, trade, forests, armed forces of different kinds, the city and even prostitutes.[22] There was a differential system of administration in the metropolitan state of Magadha, and the core areas that were strategic areas in different parts of the sub-continent that possibly experienced state formation through influence of the Mauryan state apparatus. The former state as known in Magadha is referred to as having experienced primary state formation, while the latter are seen as undergoing secondary state formation.

20. Thapar *op. cit.* no. 5: 174-208.

21. Thapar *op. cit.* no. 5: 188.

22 Thapar *op. cit.* no. 5: 194-95.

Proliferation of State Society

For regions outside the Gangetic core then, the transformation from pre-state to state society is attributed to the Mauryan expansion into peripheral regions such as the Deccan and Kalinga.[23] However, there have been contestations of the idea of any simplistic separation of 'primary' and 'secondary' state formations.[24] The Satavahanas, who were a small pre-state tribal polity[25] in the 1st century BCE, emerged and grew as a political power establishing a state society. One of the primary arguments in favour of internal processes of change is the wide prevalence of pre-Satavahana coins, ranging spatially from those of the Kuras with the appellation Mahārathi in Brahmapuri (Kolhapur) to that of the Simhagosthis in Bhattiprolu (Andhra), known from the relic casket inscription of the *pramukha* Kuberaka, some of which continue to appear during the Satavahana period as well.[26] What this coinage and the ability of the local polities to mobilise sufficient resources to issue these coins indicate is that the process of state formation was well under way before the Mauryan state intruded into these regions.[27] In the context of the Deccan, despite archaeological evidence from sites like Adam indicating agrarian practices, its intensification and seasonal cropping, largely it is the megalithic culture that predominates.[28] The local polity seems to have played a role in the expansion of agriculture, and inscriptional records attest to trans-local merchants

23. Seneviratne, Sudarshan (1981). "Kalinga and Andhra: The Process of Secondary State Formation in Early India", in H.J.M. Claessen and Peter Skalník (eds.), *The Study of the State.* The Hague: Mouton. pp.317–38.

24. Gurukkal, Rajan (1995). "The Beginnings of the Historic Period: The Tamil South (up to the end of the fifth century A.D.)", in Romila Thapar (ed.), *Recent Perspectives of Early Indian History.* Bombay: Popular Prakashan. pp.246–74.

25. Parasher-Sen, Aloka (ed.) (1993). *Social and Economic History of Early Deccan: Some Interpretations.* New Delhi: Manohar.

26. Chattopadhyaya, B.D. (2003). *Studying Early India.* New Delhi: Permanent Black.

27. Ray, H.P. (1986). *Monastery and Guild: Commerce under the Sātavāhanas.* New Delhi: OUP's. Morrison, Katheleen D. (1995). "Trade, Urbanism, and Agricultural Expansion: Buddhist Monastic Institutions and the State in the Early Historic Western Deccan. *World Archaeology* 27(2): 203–21.

28. Ibid.

and these polities building reservoirs and wells.[29] However, it is with the emergence of the *Satavahana* polity in the 2nd/1st century CE that for the first time a clear-cut state apparatus with a monarchical form of government is known from the region.

In the context of the Tamil region in peninsular India, literary evidence dated between the 3rd century BCE and the 3rd century CE, anthologised as the Sangam corpus, throws valuable light on the society of the times.[30] The widespread presence of iron artefacts in the archaeological records is known from megalithic burials in this region; however, there was no indication that there was any corresponding technological innovation or application that would transform pastoral societies into agrarian ones capable of producing surpluses to sustain more complex stratified societies.[31] In the Tamil region, it appears that there were three levels at which political power could be located in the early historical period: that of the *vēntar* or kings, *vēlir* or tribal chiefs of the hilly regions, and *kilār* or local elites.[32] However, while an incipient state structure with a class of producers and a class of non-producing elites is apparent, the lack of institutional means through which resources could be harnessed, redistributed, and channelised for further investment, and the emphasis on war and cattle raids, and the loot and plunder generated therein, saw the accumulated wealth redistributed to the tribal community through pre-station and for services rendered.[33]

Regionalisation of State Society

It is primarily in the context of early medieval India that major historiographical debates in relation to the understanding of political

29. Ray *op. cit.* no. 27.
30. Zvelebil, Kamil V. (1973). *The Smile of Murugan: On Tamil Literature of South India*. Leiden: E. J. Brill; Narayanan, M.G.S. (1988). "The Role of Peasants in the Early History of Tamilakam in South India", *Social Scientist* 16(9): 17–34.
31. Veluthat Kesavan (1997). "'Into the "Medieval' and Out of it: Early South India in Transition (Section II, Medieval India: Sectional President's address)", in *Proceedings of the Indian History Congress: 58th Session, Bangalore*. Aligarh: Indian History Congress. pp.168–205; Gurukkal, Rajan (2010). *Social Formations of Early South India*. New Delhi: OUP.
32. Mahalakshmi, R. (2009). "Cankam Literature as a Social Prism: An Interrogation", in B.D. Chattopadhyaya (ed.), *A Social History of Early India*. New Delhi: Pearson Education. pp.29–42.
33. Ibid.

economy have occurred. Nationalist narrative histories,[34] continuing in the vein of the colonialists,[35] categorised Indian history broadly as Hindu, Muslim, and British. This period was treated largely as the dark ages, and the latter part of it was seen as marking the transition from the ancient to medieval period, a time when the 'Hindu' kingdoms were making a last ditch effort to preserve their sovereignty *vis-à-vis* the invading Muslim rulers. The interrogation of inscriptions and other sources and analysis of the increasing references to land grants, agrarian expansion, and rural settlements, particularly in the post-Gupta period in c. 6th–13th centuries CE, led to a radically different understanding of the period.[36] What were the implications of land grants for an understanding of the nature of rural society and questions of control over the forces of production? The debate has carried on in the decades with emphasis on the quantification of evidence (1970s) and interrogation of categories such as serfdom (1980s).[37] From the 1980s, the emphasis has been on integrative frameworks, with stress on the horizontal spread of rural settlements concomitant with the growth of local polities into supralocal powers, in an apparent bid to move the debate outside the centralisation *versus* fragmentation and feudalisation conundrum.[38]

---

34. Jayaswal, K.P. (1924). *Hindu Polity: A Constitutional History of India in Hindu Times.* Calcutta: Butterworth & Co.; Majumdar, R.C. (1918). *Corporate Life in Ancient India.* Calcutta: Surendra Nath Sen; Ghoshal, U.N. (1929). *Contributions to the History of the Hindu Revenue System.* Calcutta: University of Calcutta.
35. Mill, James (1817). *The History of British India.* 3 vols. London: Baldwin, Craddock and Joy; Smith, Vincent Arthur (1904). *The Early History of India from 600 B.C. to the Muhammadan Conquest: Including the Invasion of Alexander the Great.* London: The Clarendon Press.
36. Kosambi, D.D. (1969). "Indian Feudalism", in A.R. Desai (ed.), *Rural Sociology in India.* 4th ed. Bombay: Popular Prakashan. pp.148–49; Sharma, R.S. (1965). *Indian Feudalism: c. 300–1200.* Calcutta: University of Calcutta.
37. Sharma, R.S. and D.N. Jha (1974). "The Economic History of India up to AD 1200: Trends and Prospects" in *Journal of Economic and Social History of the Orient* 17(1): 48–80; Jha, D.N. (1979). "Early Indian Feudalism: A Historiographical Critique (Section I, Ancient India: Presidential Address)", in *Indian History Congress: Proceedings of the Fortieth Session,* Andhra Pradesh University, Waltair. New Delhi: Sumit Sarkar. pp.15–45; Shrimali, K.M. (1993). "Reflections on Recent Perceptions of Early Medieval India", *Social Scientist* 21(12): 25–39.
38. Kulke, Hermann. (1982). "Fragmentation and Segmentation *versus* Integration?: Reflections on the Concept of Indian Feudalism and Segmentary State in Early India" in *Studies in History* 4(2): 237–63; Chattopadhyaya, B.D. (1983). "Political Processes and Structure of Polity in Early Medieval India: Problems of Perspective", *Proceedings of the Indian History Congress* 44: 25–63.

The system of land grants was indicative of the scale of control over the primary resource by the state in a predominantly agrarian society.[39] Textual sources indicate that the king was considered the ultimate owner of the land and in this capacity he had the right to parcellise his control over land and the resources he extracted by means of taxes. While there was no indication of the peasant cultivator's alienation from the means of production, he was not the ultimate beneficiary of the productive process. It is interesting to note that not only were lands granted but increasingly communal agrarian resources were also given away to the donee.[40] The Gupta period saw forces of change that subsequently led to the growth of two important elements in the economy: the growth of landed intermediaries, and the expansion of agriculture and rural society.[41] Related to the first, the presence of a category of titleholders called *samanta*—who received their position and privileges from the king and were instrumental in alienating actual producers from the fruits of their labour—was seen as reflecting a decentralised polity.[42] The conceptual shift in significance of the *samanta*—from someone who was a neighbour[43] to a neighbouring king in the classical political treatise *Arthashastra*[44] to feudal baron—has led scholars to, in fact, equate feudalism with *samantavād*.[45]

In the context of the expansion of agriculture, inscriptional records provide ample evidence of the grant of lands—waste, fallow, and cultivated—to individuals and religious institutions.[46] The

39. Sharma, R.S. (1984). "How Feudal was Indian Feudalism", *Social Scientist* 12(2): 16–41.
40. Ibid. Jha, V.M. (2008). "Economy of North India", in R.S. Sharma and K.M. Shrimali (eds.), *A Comprehensive History of India* 4(2): 261–310. New Delhi: Manohar.
41. Chattopadhyaya, B.D. (1994). *The Making of Early Medieval India*. Delhi: OUP.
42. Sharma, 1965; Habib, Irfan (1963). *The Agrarian System of Mughal India, 1556–1707*. Bombay: Asia Publishing House; Yadava, B.N.S. (1973). *Society and Culture in Northern India in the Twelfth Century*. Allahabad: Central Book Depot.
43. Gopal, L. (1965). *The Economic Life of Northern India: c. A.D. 700–1200*. Delhi: Motilal Banarsidass.
44. Kosambi *op. cit.* no. 13.
45. Chattopadhyaya *op. cit.* no. 41; Shrimali *op. cit.* no. 37.
46. Sharma, R.S. (2001). *Early Medieval Indian Society: A Study in Feudalisation*. Hyderabad: Orient Longman.

importance of agriculture can be seen in the production of treatises such as the 11th century CE *Krsi Parashara*, which details different agricultural processes and throws light on the cropping patterns and crops grown in eastern India at this time.[47] Evidence from such texts has been corroborated with epigraphic evidence to show the cultivation of a variety of grains, pulses, oil-seeds, and cash crops, revealing a vibrant agrarian economy.[48] A significant analysis of rural society draws our attention to the changing topography of the agrarian landscape by focusing on inscriptions from north Bengal, south Karnataka and the Marwar region of Rajasthan, which in turn affected the nature of the village settlement itself.[49] While there is no dearth of evidence to show that agriculture was the mainstay of the early medieval economy, prevalence of agro-based craft production—the *cakrika* or oil press—presents one kind of evidence for this—the inscriptional references to corporate trading bodies such as Manigramam and the Nanadesis, the development of ports such as Kulottungapattanam and collection of tolls and taxes at these sites, and the flourishing of urban centres referred to as *nagaram* and *pattanam* in various sources, indicate a vibrant trading network across the sub-continent with specific regional patterns as well.[50] It has been argued that rather than move between the perennially oscillating centralising and decentralising forces theories, emphasis on the growth of regional formations in the early medieval period, based on the study of records from Orissa, central India, and Rajasthan, indicates the transformation of essentially tribal polities into expanding state societies as lineages moved outside their local bases.[51] The importance of ideological structures in providing

47. Gopal *op. cit.* no. 43; Chakravarti, Ranabir (2008). "Agricultural Technology in Early Medieval India (c. A.D. 500–1300)", *Medieval History Journal* 11(2): 229–58.

48. Jha *op. cit.* no. 40.

49. Ibid.

50. Chattopadhyaya *op. cit.* no. 41; Chakravarti *op. cit.* no. 47; Abraham, Meera (1988). *Two Medieval Merchant Guilds of South India*. Delhi: Manohar; Hall, Kenneth R. (1980). *Trade and Statecraft in the Age of the Cōlas*. New Delhi: Abhinav Publications; Champakalakshmi, R. (1996). *Trade, Ideology and Urbanization: South India 300 BC to AD 1300*. Delhi: OUP.

51. Kulke *op. cit.* no. 38; Chattopadhyaya *op. cit.* no. 38.

legitimacy to the state is seen in the change of nomenclature of dynasties and cults with a decidedly tribal flavour into Brahmanical ones.[52] Contesting the idea of ritual sovereignty (propounded by Burton Stein), scholars have stressed the socio-economic and political dimensions of religious institutions, as the state is seen as expanding its resource base by its land grants to temples and *brahmanas*.[53] The proponents of the feudal view have focused on the nature of land rights, the growth of the land-holding class, and subordination of the rights of cultivators. On closely scrutinising the role of the intermediate level of political authority, it has been found that the Chola state, for instance, attempted to centralise power by drawing local elites belonging to various sub-regions into the power structure at different time periods and using different mechanisms.[54] Trade and urbanisation developed around the nuclei of exchange, *nagaram*, in the agrarian regions called the *nadu*,[55] and the state also is shown to have played a prominent role in this by the development of political and religious centres.[56] Through the statistical analysis of inscriptions,[57] it has been possible to study the frequency of political titles and revenue terms in Tamil inscriptions.[58]

---

52. Chattopadhyaya *op. cit.* no. 26.
53. Karashima, Noboru. (1984). *South Indian History and Society: Studies from Inscriptions, A.D. 850–1800*. Delhi: OUP; Singh, 1994; Champakalakshmi, 1996; Jha, 1979; Nandi, R.N. (2000). *State formation, Agrarian Growth, and Social Change in Feudal South India, c. AD 600–1200*. New Delhi: Manohar; Veluthat, Kesavan (1993). *The Political Structure of Early Medieval South India*. Hyderabad: Orient Longman; Stein, Burton (1980). *Peasant, State, and Society in Medieval South India*. Delhi: OUP; Tirumalai, R. (1987). *Land Grants and Agrarian Reactions in Cōla and Pāndya Times*. Madras: University of Madras; Chakrabarti Kunal (2001). *Religious Process: The Purānas and the Making of a Regional Tradition*. New Delhi: OUP; Kapur, Nandini Sinha (2002). *State Formation in Rajasthan: Mewar during the 7th-15th Centuries*. New Delhi: Manohar.
54. Subbarayulu, Y. (1973). *The Political Geography of the Chola Country*. Madras: Tamilnadu State Department of Archaeology; Heitzman, James (1997). *Gifts of Power: Lordship in an Indian State*. New Delhi: OUP.
55. Hall *op. cit.* no. 50.
56. Champakalakshmi *op. cit.* no. 50.
57. Karashima *op. cit.* no. 53; Subbarayulu *op. cit.* no. 54.
58. Karashima *op. cit.* no. 53; Heitzman, 1997.

'Modes of Production': Tools for Writing History

In a long-term analysis of the characteristics of the Indian peasantry, Irfan Habib has pointed out that rather than look for disruptions with dynastic changes, or simplistically attribute social transformation to establishment of the Delhi Sultanate in the 13th century, we needed to scrutinise literary sources for the descriptions of rural society and particularly the peasant.[59] Carrying forward the arguments made by scholars studying the early medieval period, who focused on the caste system to understand the position of peasant and artisanal classes, Habib argues that the 13th century did not see any respite for the subjected castes. He also argued that the relations among different elements of rural society remained the same—the menial castes were subjected in much the same manner to the caste peasantry; the difference lay in the new structure within which these social relations were embedded. The Ghurid rulers brought with them a new system of territorial revenue assignments to military commanders—the *iqta* system during the period of the Delhi Sultanate and the *jagir* in Mughal times.[60] The *iqta* was understood to be in lieu of salaries, and the *muqti* or assignee did not hold it in perpetuity but to be passed on to his heirs.[61] Land revenue or *kharaj* was the main source of income for the state, and the significance of the revenue as a share of the produce and not as rent on land is seen from sources. Land was divided into the state lands—*khalisa*—and the revenue assignments or *iqtas*. It has been argued that in the 13th century, land revenue was largely in the form of tribute, and it is only from the time of Alauddin Khalji (1296–1316 CE) that a systematisation occurred through proper collection from the khalisa particularly, which now extended throughout the fertile Doab region.[62] Realising the significance of agriculture for the state, a 14th

59. Habib *op. cit.* no. 42.

60. Ibid.

61. Habib, Mohammad, and K.A. Nizami (eds.) (1970). "A Comprehensive History of India", *The Delhi Sultanat: A.D. 1206–1526*. Vol. 5. New Delhi: People's Publishing House.

62. Chandra, Satish (1997–99). *Medieval India: From Sultanat to the Mughals*. Pts. 1–2. New Delhi: Har Anand.

century ruler is believed to have established a department to extend cultivation and determine cropping patterns. Among the changes introduced, reduction of the area of wheat under cultivation and extension of crops such as sugarcane, grapes, and dates is known, although we are also told that these were not successful measures.

Satish Chandra has argued that the Delhi Sultanate has to be understood in terms of the lack of political consolidation of north India and the presence of numerous small kingdoms that lacked 'strategic consciousness.'[63] While some scholars had argued that the caste system may have hampered the mobilising of sufficient military manpower,[64] Chandra refers to later sources indicating the presence of Jats, Meenas, and the generic *kuvarna* or lower castes in the armies of the local rulers. Some scholars have attributed the establishment of the Sultanate to superior military technology of the Turks,[65] particularly the use of the crossbow and horses.[66] Chandra, Habib and other scholars have focused on the centralising authority of the state as seen in adoption of the *iqtadari* system, where the recipient of the grant was dependent totally on the largesse of the sultan. Attention has been drawn to the deliberate evocation of a unified identity of the new elites across the five dynasties of the Delhi Sultanate, where Turk *versus* non-Turk symbolised the new relationship between the ruler and the ruled.[67] While some have focused on the pull and push factors that allowed

---

63. Ibid.

64. Habib, Mohammad (1952). "Introduction", in Mohammad Habib, Abdur Rashid, and Khaliq Ahmad Nizami (eds.), *Elliot and Dowson's History of India: As Told by its Own Historians*. Vol. 2 (Rep. with introduction, commentary, and supplement). Aligarh: Cosmopolitan Publishers. pp.1-102.

65. Digby, Simon. (1971). *War-horse and Elephant in the Delhi Sultanate*. Oxford: Orient Monographs.

66 Habib, I. (1983). "The Peasant in Indian History", *Social Scientist* 11(3): 21–64; Jackson, Peter (1999). *The Delhi Sultanate: A Political and Military History*. Cambridge: Cambridge University Press.

67. Kumar, Sunil (2006). "Service, Status, and Military Slavery in the Delhi Sultanate: Thirteenth and Fourteenth centuries", in Indrani Chatterjee and Richard M. Eaton (eds.), *Slavery and South Asian History*. Indiana: Indiana University Press. pp.83–114.

military commanders to negotiate their own political terms in some regions, undermining the authority of the sultan in Delhi,[68] others have emphasised the institutional measures—the organisation of the court, nobility, and army, as well as experiments in the *iqta* system—that reveal the entrenched authority structures.[69] Scholars working on south India have looked at the processes of integration in the Andhra region during the 11th and 12th centuries under the Kakatiyas, and the Sultanate incursions into the region as not affecting the processes of agrarian expansion and regional power consolidation.[70] The consolidation of political authority across disparate linguistic regions of peninsular India in the Vijayanagara period and the process of feudalisation that occurred in the Nayaka period in the 16th century have been understood through the study of inscriptions and literature composed in Sanskrit, Telugu, Kannada, Tamil, and Persian.[71] Philip B. Wagoner has argued that the system of *nayakattanam* in medieval south India is modelled on the *iqta* system of the Delhi Sultanate.

The pioneering work of Habib led to new digits of analysis for medieval Indian history, outside the bracket of Islamic history, popular in colonial, nationalist, and neo-imperialist historiography. The publication of his doctoral thesis on the agrarian system of the Mughal period stemmed from the same impulse that drove Kosambi and Sharma to bring to the centre stage of history writing an understanding of the socio-economic structures and transformations that affected the lives of the mass of

---

68. Kumar, Sunil (2007). *The Emergence of the Delhi Sultanate, 1192–1286*. New Delhi: Permanent Black.

69 Ibid.

70. Talbot, Cynthia (2001). *Precolonial India in Practice: Society, Region, and Identity in Medieval Andhra*. New Delhi: OUP; Wagoner, Philip B. (1996). "Sultan among Hindu Kings: Dress, Titles and the Islamicization of Hindu culture at Vijayanagara", *Journal of Asian Studies* 55(4): 851–80.

71. Karashima, Noboru (2002). *A Concordance of Nāyakas: The Vijayanagara Inscriptions in South India*. Delhi: OUP; Talbot, 2001.

ordinary people living in those times.[72] In this analysis, the highly centralised Mughal state was dependent on revenue from agriculture, and as a result placed a heavy burden of taxation on the peasantry whereby the bulk of the peasantry lived on the barest minimum needed for subsistence. While trade and monetisation occurred, it resulted in hoarding rather than redistribution, obstructing the transformation of the structure of production and exchange.[73] A critique has been offered by scholars who see the growth of area under cultivation during these times as well as the introduction of new crops such as tobacco, maize and chilli, and growth of crops such as indigo, cotton, and sugarcane to cater to the expanding international networks of trade, resulting in the growth of portfolio capitalism,[74] mercantilist states,[75] and the proto-middle classes of the colonial period.[76] It has been countered that the mercantile activity and rise of institutional support for trade was neither sudden nor dissociated from state control.[77] Also, the premise that the putting-out system and development of merchant capital could automatically lead to industrial capital has been rejected.[78] Reiterating the position that the Mughal state was a highly centralised one, scholars have drawn attention to the nature of centralised bureaucratic structure, the composite nobility with its checks and balances, and the innovative theories of kingship that were established particularly during the time of Akbar.[79] In one

72. Habib (1963), *op. cit.* no. 42

73. Haider, Najaf (2011). "Once More Unto the Breach: Money Matters in the Writings of Irfan Habib", in P. Patnaik (ed.), *Re-envisioning Socialism.* Tulika Books. pp.173–86.

74. Ibid.

75. Stein, Burton (1998). *A History of India.* London: Blackwell.

76. Bayly, Christopher Alan (1983). *Rulers,Townsmen, and Bazaars: North Indian Society in the Age of British Expansion.* Cambridge: Cambridge University Press.

77. Ibid.

78. Habib, Irfan (1969). "Potentialities of Capitalist Development in the Economy of Mughal India", *Journal of Economic History* 29(1) :32–78.

79. Ali, M. Athar (2001). *The Mughal Nobility under Aurangzeb.* New Delhi: OUP; Moosvi, Shireen (2005). "The Pre-colonial State", *Social Scientist* 33(3/4): 40–53.

interpretation, drawing upon the Weberian notion of patrimonial authority as an extension of the personal familial patriarchal power exercised by a leader over a larger social group, it has been argued that the Mughal state was a combination of the pre-modern patrimonial and early modern bureaucratic state.[80] Thus, the text exemplar of the early Mughals, *Ain-i-Akbari*, is seen as reflecting the ruler and his household at the centre of all political and administrative activity. Still more recent scholarship engages with a Foucauldian interrogation of the truth claims of literary sources given the locus standi of the authors within the royal court,[81] and that there is an *a priori* assumption of the structure of the state which is belied when a processual analysis of political developments is undertaken.[82] In a bid to straddle the two poles of interpretation, it has been posited that a middle path of studying the imperial court and local politics engaging with political institutions as "units in action" would allow a view unto how structure and process constituted the Mughal state.[83] It has been pointed out by Shireen Moosvi in a rebuttal of these post-modern interpretations that anyone with a cursory awareness of the Persian sources in particular would find it difficult to ignore the extent of control of the Mughal state and its effect on different sections of society.[84]

In relation to the institutions of *jagirdari* and *mansubdari*, it has been shown that the ranking of nobility within the official hierarchy was dependent on the ability to maintain troopers and collect revenue to maintain them.[85] The *jagirdari* system depended

80. Blake, Stephen P. (1979). "The Patrimonial-bureaucratic Empire of the Mughals", *Journal of Asian Studies* 39: 77–94.

81. Ibid.

82. Alam, Muzaffar, and Sanjay Subrahmanyam (1998). "Introduction", in *The Mughal State, 1526–1750.* Delhi: OUP. pp.1–71.

83. Hasan, Farhat (2004). *State and Locality in Mughal India: Power Relations in Western India, c. 1572–1730.* Cambridge: Cambridge University Press.

84. Ibid.

85. Chandra, Satish (1959). *Parties and Politics at the Mughal Court, 1707–1740.* Aligarh: Aligarh Muslim University

on the assignee of the jagir exacting the income or *hasil*, with a realistic assessment of the revenue or *jama*.[86] In relation to the *mansabdari* system, it has been pointed out that while the system showed a measure of accommodation of different interests (Turani, Irani, Afghan, Shaikhzada and Rajput), there were attempts to reduce salaries and to optimise the benefits of the system without any corresponding increase in rank.[87] While the system of military ranking or *mansab* was shown to be particular to the Indian context, an innovation of the time of Akbar, it has been posited that despite the similarities of the land revenue assignment or *jagir* with the earlier *iqta* system, the specific modalities of its working reveals its origins in Akbar's time.[88] An insightful work on the evolution of the *zamindari* system has thrown light on the close nexus between the class of landed elites and the state, despite both seeking to appropriate a large share of the produce from the primary producer.[89] The responsibility of the primary and secondary *zamindars* in squeezing the peasant until he was barely left with subsistence has been identified as one of the main reasons for the crisis in the Mughal state in the 17th and 18th centuries.[90]

86. Chandra *op. cit.* no. 62.

87. Ibid.

88. Ali, M. Athar (2006). *Mughal India: Studies in Polity, Ideas, Society, and Culture.* Delhi: OUP; Moosvi, Shireen (2008). *People, Taxation, and Trade in Mughal India.* New Delhi: Oxford University Press.

89. Hasan, Syed Nurul (1964). "The Position of the Zamindars in the Mughal Empire", *Indian Economic and Social History Review* 1(4) :107–19.

90. Habib *op. cit.* no. 42; Hasan *op. cit.* no.83.

The focus on particular regions such as Maharashtra,[91] Bengal,[92] Tamil Nadu,[93] Andhra,[94] Punjab,[95] Rajasthan[96] and Gujarat[97] has elucidated some of the arguments related to the growth and influence of state structures discussed above.

Conclusion

In conclusion, the study of the state in ancient and medieval India clearly indicates its emergence, evolution and transformation over two millennia, in different parts of the sub-continent, and through differential processes. The colonial assumptions of a static society, lack of political stability or institutions, and the negation of the prospects of economic growth under such conditions is belied by the rich and diverse sources for this period. That the state forms were not merely exploitative, top-heavy 'Byzantine' monarchies can be understood from the various treatises and inscriptions that reveal elaborate structures of governance, challenges to state power and hegemony, and the engagement of various sections of society with

---

91. Fukazawa, H. (1982). "Maharashtra and the Deccan: A Note"', in Tapan Raychaudhuri, Irfan Habib and Dharma Kumar (eds.), *The Cambridge Economic History of India, c.1200–c.1750*. Vol. 1. Cambridge: Cambridge University Press. pp.193–202; Wagle, N.K. (1999). "Hindu-Muslim Interactions in Medieval Maharashtra", in Gunther-Dietz Sontheimer and Hermann Kulke (eds.), *Hinduism Reconsidered*. New Delhi: Manohar. pp.51–67; Kotani, Hiroyuki (2002). *Western India in Historical Transition: Seventeenth to Early Twentieth Centuries*. New Delhi: Manohar.

92. Chaudhury, Sushil (1995). *From Prosperity to Decline: Eighteenth Century Bengal*. New Delhi: Manohar; Eaton, Richard M. (1993). *The Rise of Islam and the Bengal Frontier, 1204–1760*. Berkeley: University of California Press.

93. Narayana Rao, Velcheru, David Shulman, and Sanjay Subrahmanyam (1992). *Symbols of Substance: Court and State in Nayaka Period Tamilnadu*. New Delhi: OUP; Karashima, 2001.

94. Talbot *op. cit.* no. 70.

95. Alam, Muzaffar (1986). *The Crisis of Empire in Mughal North India: Awadh and the Punjab, 1707–48*. Delhi: OUP; Grewal, J.S. (1990). *The Sikhs of the Punjab*. Cambridge: Cambridge University Press; Singh, Chetan (1991). *Region and Empire: Panjab in the Seventeenth Century*. Delhi: OUP.

96. Singh, Dilbagh (1990). *The State, Landlords and Peasants: Rajasthan in the 18th Century*. New Delhi: Manohar.

97. Hasan, Farhat (2004). *State and Locality in Mughal India: Power Relations in Western India, c. 1572–1730*. Cambridge: Cambridge University Press.

the state apparatus. Ultimately, the claims of 'unchanging India' existed more in the imagination than in reality, and appears to have provided justificatory claims to the coloniser that the colony was the beneficiary of colonial rule.

2

PANKAJ MOHAN[1]

Historical Texts on Early Korea and Modern Historiography

In the late 19th century when Japan began to resemble the imperialist powers of the West and 'Conquer Korea Policy' became a cornerstone of Japan's expansionist nationalism, Korea was divested of its significance as an actor of history as defined by the Western imagination. It was because the scientific study of Korean history commenced in Tokyo in an era of expansionist nationalism centred on the myth of Japan's axial position in ancient East Asia. Japanese writings on Korean history were now mostly intended to authenticate Japan's contemporary political imagination, parts of it influenced by Western theories of empire building.[2] Japanese historians formulated such theories about Korea as geographical determinism which meant that Korea being a peninsula wedged between bigger neighbours, the course of Korean history was determined by political developments in China, Manuchuria or Japan. Japanese historians gave credence to the legend of Kija, first

---

1. *Acknowledgement:* Material for this paper has been adapted from my paper published in the Korean journal *DonggukSahak* (June 2011).

2. Foucault's thesis of linkage between power and knowledge, and although the pun of "Enough Said" is not without its merit, orientalism's parameters of understanding are relevant to our discussion. Romila Thapar's essay, "Ideology and Interpretation of Early Indian History," in her *Interpreting Early India*. Delhi: Oxford University Press. 1992. pp.1-22 and Snodgrass's book on Buddhism in Meiji Japan look at the same question in different contexts. Also see Bhatia, Nandi (1994). "Kipling's Burden: Representing Colonial Authority and Constructing the 'Other' through Kimball O'Hara and Babu Haree Chunder in Kim", *Sagar* 1(1). *http://asnic.utexas.edu/asnic/sagar/spring.1994/sagar.intro.toc.may1994.html.* And quite significantly, this colonial knowledge functioned as true not only in Japan, but also in some quarters of Korea and the West. There are innumerable English language publications of the colonial era which echo the Japanese propaganda about Korea as a nation deficient in innate drive, and about Japan as an agent of modernisation and reform in Korea.

mentioned by Sima Qian in his *Shiji*. Kija (Chinese: *Jizi*), a prince of Shang Dynasty is believed to have escaped to the Korean peninsula and spread civilisation amongst its so-called barbarian inhabitants. Ken Gardiner has correctly noted that Sima Qian himself doubted the historical authenticity of this story, because he did not mention it in the actual account of Choson, the state Kija is believed to have founded in approximately 10th century BCE, and which continued to exist in the living memory of this grand historian of China. Japanese historians of the Meiji era and in the subsequent period of Japan's colonial occupation of Korea (1910-1945) looked at the latter's indigenous tale of state-formation, the so-called Tangunlagend as an interesting folk-tale devoid of any historical element. This tale appears in the Samgukyusa, a 12th century text and describes how the son of God descended to the earth, and encountering a tiger and a bear who wanted to marry him, gave them a magic formula that could transform them into a woman. The bear followed the instruction faithfully, duly assumed the body of a woman, and as a consequence of his union with the Son of God gave birth to Tangun (Lord Sandalwood)—Tangun is believed to have established a state in 2333 BCE.

In this paper, I attempt to demonstrate how Korean historians during the colonial period used history as an instrument to construct a nativist cultural space and weave the fabric of an imagined community in response to the Orientalist theories about Korean history formulated by Japan. It is apparent that Japanese treatment of Korean historical subject was reduced to the category of *bunshohokoku* (writings in defence of the state), and in the hands of Korea's nationalist historians the practice of historical writing became a conduit to spread nationalist ideology. However, before discussing the rise of nationalist historiography of ancient Korea during the colonial period, it is important to look at the historical texts on ancient Korean history that were transmitted to the modern times.

Historical Texts on Early Korea

The principal source that sheds light on the beginning of history-writing in the ancient three kingdoms of Koguryo, Paekche and Silla is the *Samguksagi*, composed by a Koryoliteratus Kim Pu-sik in the 12th century. According to this text, Koguryo compiled its first history soon after the state was established. In the beginning of the kingdom when Chinese writing was first used, events (of the state) were recorded in 100 chapters, and the book was known as *yugi*. The *Samguksagi* further states that the ancient historical texts of Koguryo were revised in 600 CE; and a condensed version in five chapters, titled *Sinjib*, was prepared. *Samguksagi* records in the entry of King Kunch'ogo (of Paekche) that Paekche did not have any historical text until the arrival of Ko Hung who introduced the tradition of compiling history in that state. Ken Gardiner has correctly identified Ko Hung as a Chinese who migrated to the Korean peninsula after fall of the colonial outpost of Lolang in the middle of the 4th century.[3] To quote Gardiner, "Ko Hung is not mentioned in any other book, nor is it known who he was. The Weishu mentions two men with the surname Kao (Korean: *Ko*) who fled to Koguryo during the disorders in China at the beginning of the fourth century; if Ko Hung really existed—and the terms in which the *Samguksagi* mentions his name to suggest the recalling of an almost forgotten piece of information –then he was almost certainly a Chinese." Silla, according to the *Samguksagi*, started compiling history in 545 CE when King Chinhung established a bureau of history.

It is obvious that the genre of history-writing in Korea is closely associated with the introduction of Confucianism and the related Chinese ideas and institutions to the Three Kingdoms. Commencing from the 4th century, Koreans started compiling historical texts based on the Confucian framework and the model of Shiji,

---

3. I am grateful to Ken Gardiner (1987) for lending me his unpublished paper entitled, "The Beginning of History-Writing in Korea and Japan".

composed by Sima Qian. These historical texts, however, survive only in the form of brief quotations in *Nihongi*.[4]

Kim Pu-sik's *Samguksagi* (Ch.: *Sanguoshiji*) or History of the Three Kingdoms (Ancient Korean states of Koguryo, Paekche and Silla), compiled in the mid-12th century, is the oldest surviving text on early Korean history, and as is evident in its name , it is modelled on Sima Qian's s work, *Shiji*. Indeed, Kim Pu-sik was consciously opening a new chapter of Confucian historiography in Korea.[5] Ken Gardiner, notes that Kim Pu-sik filled out the early phase of Korean history by appropriating material from Chinese sources, which lent "an aura of historical authenticity to the legendary kings in whose reigns they have been placed."

Closely following the style and thematic structure of the Chinese dynastic histories, he divided his work into annals (*pongi*), tables (*p'yo*), treatises (*chi*) and biographical records *(yoljon*). Profoundly steeped as he was in Confucian principles and precepts, he gave a pronounced Confucian accent to the historical realities of early Korea.[6] Kim's Confucian outlook is evident even in the prefatory memorial about *Samguksagi* that he submitted to the King. He remarked that his intention to write the history of the three ancient kingdoms of Silla, Koguryo and Paekche was inspired by his conviction "that lessons from the records of the past revealing virtues and vices of rulers, loyalty and treachery of ministers, peace

---

4. It is also worthy of note that in the Japanese context the craft of Confucian historiography was adopted with a different kind of modification. The Yamato rulers who sponsored the first national histories in the early 8th century wished them to project the significance of Japan as a sovereign and independent political entity and not merely the satellite of the Chinese empire whose cultural forms, political institutions and norms of social relations were spun into the fabric of its statehood. Japan also aimed to emphasise its superiority over the Korean state of Silla at whose hands it had suffered a crushing defeat in the Battle of Paekch'on nearly half a century ago in 660 AD. The records on the early Korean states in the *Kojiki* and *Nihonshoki* are tainted with a Japan-centred outlook, and were in many instances, the back-cast projections of the concerns of Yamato administration in the late 7th and early 8th centuries. *Nihonshoki* contains material from the early Korean texts (now lost), but they were modified to achieve the objective of the Yamato administration, as is evident in the use of the term 'honourable country' for Japan by the ruler of one of the petty states on the Korean peninsula.
5. Gardiner, K.H.J. (1970). "The Samguk-sagi and its Sources", *Papers on Far Eastern History* 2: 11. Also see Rogers, Michael C. (1969). "Traditional Sino-Korean Relations", *Asia* 16: 8-10.
6. Ki-baek, Yi (1978). *"Samguksagi non"*, in *Han'guksahakuipanghyang*. Seoul: Ilchogak. pp.19-20.

and crises of the country and obedience and rebellion of commoners would impart moral lessons to future generations."[7] In the late 19th and early 20th centuries when Korea began to construct its national identity and search for ethno-symbolisms of the nation, Confucian historiography, representing Korea's ideological and cultural subordination to a foreign power, was challenged and a new framework of understanding history was developed. Indeed, the nationalist historiography of modern Korea privileged the Samgukyusa, which was composed by a Buddhist monk in the late 13th century and which distanced itself from the Confucian format and worldview.

Ethno-symbolism of Tangun in the De-Confucianised (Nationalist) Historiography

Korea's nationalist historiography developed at the end of the 19th century, initially under the aegis of the Independence Club and its offshoot, the Patriotic Enlightenment Movement, pioneered by Shin Ch'ae-ho. The Independence Club represented the first attempt in modern Korea to build a civil society and a forum for spreading modern ideas of civilisation and enlightenment. The founders of the Independence Club were well-versed in the writings of Fukuzawa Yukichi, the exponent of the theory of civilisation and enlightenment and author of the explosive thesis "De-Asianizing Japan". And like Fukuzawa Yukichi, they launched a vigorous campaign to de-centre China, exorcise the country of Confucian influence and mould the ideas and institutions of the country on the Western prototype. Editorial pages of *The Independent*, the mouthpiece of the Independence Club lauded the West, particularly the United States, as "the strongest, the wealthiest, the most civilized, the most enlightened country, the land where people obeyed the Gospel of the Lord."[8]

---

7. *Tongsŏnmun*, 44

8. Seo, Joong-Seok (2007). *Korean Nationalism Betrayed* (Co-translated with Do-hyun Han and Pankaj Mohan). Folkestone, Kent, UK: Global Oriental.

Shin Ch'ae-ho, arguably the founding father of Korea's nationalist historiography, was attracted towards the anti-Confucian emphases of the agenda of the Independence Club, but it is remarkable that he was not impressed by the model of Western or Christian civilisation which was proposed as the alternative to Confucianism by this organisation. Shin believed that the meaning of education lay in inculcating nationalist sentiments in the minds of the people and promoting a civilising process that stressed upon aesthetic dimension of the country such as folk traditions, customs and language.[9] Under the influence of German idealist Johann G. Fichte (1762-1814), who formulated the concept of ego and non-ego in his "First Introduction into the Science of Knowledge", Shin wrote that historically a nation or a national culture is in constant struggle with other or foreign nations or foreign cultural forces, and it either survives or perishes in this process.[10] For him, state, people and history formed an inseparable troika: "When you take away the people, history becomes meaningless; and if you take away history, people's enthusiasm for the state diminishes."[11]

The nationalist character of Shin became further consolidated when he joined the Taejonggyo, an indigenous religion centred on Tangun-worship and founded in 1909. Shin Ch'ae-ho and other historians belonging to Taejonggyo saw in the Tangun cult the possibility of pushing the boundary of Korean history to misty antiquity and expanding the territorial expanse on which Korean

9. Ibid.

10. Ch'ae-ho, Shin (2007). *Tanjae Shin Ch'ae-hochonjib* (Complete Works of Shin Ch'ae-ho). Vol.1. Ch'onan, Korea: The Independence Hall of Korea Publications. p.5.

11. Lee, Peter H. and Bary, Wm. Theodore de (eds.) (1990). *Sources of Korean Tradition*. Vol. 2. New York: Columbia University Press. pp.317-19. Some representative studies on Shin Ch'ae-ho in English are as follows: Robinson, Michael (1984). "National Identity and the Thought of Sin Ch'ae-ho: Sadaejuui and Chuch'e in History and Politics", *Journal of Korean Studies* 5: 121-42; Ryang, K.P. (1990). "Sin Ch'ae-ho and Modern Korean Historiography", *The Journal of Modern Korean Studies* 4: 13-52; Schmid, Andre (1997). "Rediscovering Manchuria: Sin Ch'aeho and the Politics of Territorial History in Korea", *Journal of Asian Studies* 56(1): 26-46; Em, Henry H. (1999). "Nationalism, Post-Nationalism, and Shin Ch'ae-ho", *Korea Journal* 39(2): 283-317 and Em, Henry H. (1999). "Minjok as a Modern and Democratic Construct: Sin Ch'aeho's Historiography", in Gi-Wook Shin and Michael Robinson (eds.), *Colonial Modernity in Korea*. Cambridge, MA: Harvard University Asia Center. pp.337-52.

history unfolded farther beyond the limits of the Korean peninsula. Sonia Ryang has correctly noted that Korean history was shaped on the basis of the subjective view and vision of the historians who pushed the date of the foundation of the state into remote antiquity, realising that "the earlier the better and the older a nation is, the greater that must be."[12] Shin Ch'ae-ho, for instance, argued in his book *Chosonsanggosa* (The Early History of Korea) that Tangun was not a legendary figure but a historical personage, and furthermore, he established a new framework of ancient history in which Tangun Choson, Puyo and Koguryo formed a line of continuity. Shin contended that Puyo inherited the territory, culture and population of Tangun Choson which in turn was passed on to Koguryo. In this book he traced the origin of the powerful Jurchen tribe of Manchuria from Ko Choson, noting that it represented one of the branches of that state.

In order to authenticate his theory about Tangun, Shin Ch'ae-ho traced the rituals and belief-system of the Samhan (that later developed into the early Korean states of Paekche, Silla and Kaya) on the southern part of the Korean peninsula to Tangun. He believed that the institution of Sodoi originated during the Tangun period. In fact, he called the Tangun age the "Sudu" period.[13] He further explained that dissemination of iron culture in the southern part of the Korean peninsula brought changes in political structure, and the domains of politics and religion were divided. These developments led to the change in the character of Sodo as a sanctuary for those who felt alienated by the new cultural and political climate of the state.[14]

Shin Ch'ae-ho's hypothesis is interesting, but problematic. The *Sanguozhi* account of the Dongyizhuan (Korean: *Tongyi-jon*), whose veracity has been partially confirmed by archaeology in the

12. Ryang, Sonia (1990). "Historian-judges of Korean Nationalism", *Ethnic and Racial Studies* 13(4): 503-26;

13. Ch'ae-ho *op. cit.* no. 10: 33-40.

14. Ch'ol-jun, Kim (1986). "The Formation and Development of Ancient Korean Culture", in *Introduction of Korean Studies*. Seoul: The National Academy of Sciences. p.45.

Japanese context, together with other archaeological data of the period, makes it clear that the Han areas had only an inchoate political structure in the third century, and there is no solid basis for assuming a sophisticated political structure of Han settlements in the 3rd century with an articulated distinction between sacred and profane domains (as claimed by Shin Ch'ae-ho). The undercurrent of Sinocentric bias is doubtless present in the *Sanguozhi*, but we do not have any reason to doubt its historical reliability, as it has the merit of having been written close to the point of its time. Its historical authenticity is also supported by archaeological findings. Shin Ch'ae-ho's interpretations of Korea's ancient past are, therefore, to be understood as the expressions of romantic nationalism. They are in sharp contrast with the record of the *Sanguozhi* that the Han tribes on southern part of the Korean peninsula lacked a sharply delineated political authority.

As an intellectual who witnessed the most humiliating event in the modern history of his country, Shin wrote particularistic history, charged with an intense realisation of Korea's unique national identity and collective memory. Shin's writing was, furthermore, specifically addressed to the challenges of Japanese theories about Korean history, and was intended as a means to promote national cohesion and build national strength. For instance, Shin's emphases on Manchuria as an integral part of Korea's geographical self-identity and on Tangun as the symbol of racial uniqueness was an articulation of a nationalist historical consciousness and represented a response to the challenges of the imperialist historiography. In other words, Shin's interpretation of Tangun Choson as marking the beginning of the Korean state that subsequently developed into Puyo and Koguryo was aimed at refuting the thesis of contemporary Japanese historians who traced the formation of the first state on the Korean peninsula to the migration of Kija, a sage-prince of Shang China.

Shin's belief that Koguryo epitomised the true spirit of the Korean people was consolidated when he climbed Mount Paekdu (where Tangun is believed to have descended) and visited Koguryo sites in Manchuria in 1914. He is reported to have said, "The relics testifying to the glorious past of our nation are scattered in Manchura, and are gradually disappearing. Thinking of this I fail to control tears that well up in my eyes."[15]

Ch'oe Nam-son, another pioneering scholar of the colonial era, sought to establish the Tangun legend as history by noting that the elements of miracle were a subsequent encrustation, and rather than understanding tiger or bear in its literal form, one needed to take a broad ethnographic look at the legend and interpret them as women of the tribes with tiger or bear totems. He also pointed out that *chongun* (Heavenly Lord) that appears in the Chinese historical text, *sanguozhi* was identical with Tangun, the shaman-king. Giving a philological perspective on the word *Tan* of Tangun, he pointed out that such phonetically similar Mongolian words as *tagri* and *tongol* meant both heaven and shaman. He also noted that *tanggul* and *tangurae* meant shaman in many local dialects in Korea during the bronze age, and the word *tegari* of modern Korean (meaning head) could be reckoned as a remnant of the ancient usages. He contended that *Tan* was a corrupt form of the words *taigari* or *tagar* meaning shaman or heaven in archaic Korean, and concluded that both Tangun and Cheongun referred to the same concept of shaman-king. It is also worth noticing that Roberte N. Hamayon, a scholar of Central Asian religions, has noted that the "cosmic category" *tengeri* (skies) figures prominently in the ritual and religious life of Mongolia, as is illustrated by the 33 *tengeri* in the Mongol epic of Gesar or the concept of *Mongketengeri* (eternal sky) associated with the emergence of Chinggis Qa'an's pan-Mongolian empire. He further writes, "The term tengerism is used precisely to refer to the fact that state formations among the Turco-Mongol societies of Inner Asia had the notion of 'sky' (heaven) as a privileged ideological support."[16]

15. Ch'ae-ho *op. cit.* no. 10: : 78.

16. See Hamayon, 1994: 87. Discussion on Ch'oe Nam-son's historiographical approach can be found in the following works: Takeuchi, 1988: 78; Takeuchi, 1990: 793-96; Sok, 1987.

Apotheosis of Koguryo as the Symbol of Korean Race

Shin wrote that seeing the ancient Koguryo sites once was 10 thousand times better than reading the history of Koguryo, as told by Kim Pu-sik in his *Samguksagi*. Kim Ch'ol-jun made an insightful comment on the impact of the trip to Koguryo sites in Manchuria on the shaping of Shin Ch'ae-ho's historical understanding:

> When Shin Ch'ae-ho saw King Kwanggaet'o stele of Koguryo or the huge tumuli of Koguryo rulers or heard various legends about Koguryo that were still transmitted from mouth to mouth in Manchuria, one can imagine the awe and excitement he must have felt at the character and essence of Koguryo reflected in those relics and monuments. One can also guess how sad he might have felt at the decline of the nation.[17]

Under the pen of Shin Ch'ae-ho, the so-called 'villains' that appear in the pages of Confucian history become the role-models of the nation, the archetypal exemplar of valor and virtue. One such hero is Yongae Somun.[18] Shin wrote that because of the loss of indigenous historical texts on Koguryo, people's understanding of Yongae Somun as a villain was based on the accounts of historians from hostile lands. Korean historians immersed themselves in slavish Confucian and Sino-centric cultural traditions, denouncing his character and undermining his achievements. Their sole yardstick to judge Yongae Somun was the China-centred ethical code embodied in such precepts as "loyalty to the ruler" and "fear of Heaven by following the rules of hierarchy". When Shin found out about the great military strategy and unflinchingly strong spirit of the Koguryo hero, Ulji Mundok, he was overwhelmed with a sense of pride in the nation's past: "My spirit surged and my boldness leaped. Raising my face to heaven, I shouted, 'This! This is the nature of our nation!' ...Nothing in either the past or the present rivals such a great figure and such a great deed."[19]

---

17. Ch'ol-jun, Kim (1979). *Hangukmunhwasaron* (Essays on Korean Culture). Seoul: Chisiksanopsa. p.173.
18. Ch'ae-ho *op. cit.* no. 10: 143-57.
19. Schmid, Andre (2002). *Korea Between Empires, 1895-1919.* New York: Columbia University Press. p.63.

Indeed, Shin's historiography is important in understanding Korean sensitivity to Koguryo and their response to the challenges of Chinese nationalism. Shin played a seminal role in shaping the Korean understanding of the past and sustaining nationalist consciousness during the colonial era.[20] In the post-liberation era, Shin's methodology was challenged and new approaches were developed, but his framework of ade-Confucianised Korean history which privileged Koguryo as "self" and the essence of the ancient race was not forgotten. During the era of President Chun Doo-hwan (1980-1987), in particular, the legacy of Shin was revived and an intensely nationalist version of history gained unprecedented credence due to the government's projection and promotion of an ultra-nationalist historiography as "state ideology". As historian Han Yong-u has noted, "(During this period) history textbooks written by the ultra-nationalist historians of the Taejonggyo in the early 1900s spread like wildfire, resulting in the dissemination of fantastic notions of Korea's ancient history that had little basis in facts."[21]

Korguryo and China: Fact and Fiction

The birth of Tangun is the national holiday in Korea, celebrated as the Day of the Opening of Heaven (*Kaech'onjol*), and the year of his birth, 2333 BCE, the year Tangun is believed to have founded the first Korean state of Ko-Choson (ancient Choson) is recognised by conservative and amateur historians in Korea as the beginning of chronology and the basis of a calendar. It does not have, nonetheless, any value for a historian other than the folk-lore that may have circulated in the 13th century when monk-historian Iryon compiled the unofficial historical text, the *Samgukyusa*.

Tangun's linkage with Koguryo is a complete fiction. Koguryo's significance lies in the fact that it represented the first Korean kingdom to make a successful transition from a form of tribal polity

20. Kwon, Hui-yong (2005). *"Shin ch'ae-houisangosatamnon-kwaminjokjuui"* (Shin Ch'ae-ho's Discourse on Early Korean History and Nationalism), *Hangukkunhyondaeuisangosadamnon-kwaminjokjuui*. Songnam: Hangukhakchungangyonguwon.

21. Yong-u, Han (2010). *The New History of Korea*. Vol.3. Seoul: Kyongsaewon. p.240.

to an early state on the Chinese model, due primarily to geographical contiguity and close political interaction with China. Subsequent to the rise of Koguryo as a centralised monarchical state, the tribal leagues in the southern part of the Korean peninsula and on the Japanese archipelago developed their own political structures and cultural forms through the process of peer-polity interaction. As a result of diffusion of the advanced ideas and institutions of the continental provenance through contacts with Koguryo, the whole of East Asia adopted the Chinese model of a centralised state which included an officialdom loyal to the throne, a centralised fiscal administration, a standing army, a capital city, and the like.

Looking at the foundation of Koguryo as the early state, the original Chinese sources depict Koguryo as a weak tribal polity tied to the Xuantu Commandery. The weakness of Chinese sources is that they are written from a Sino-centric perspective, and tend to interpret Korean institutions in relationship to their success or failure in approximating the Chinese models.

It is clear, however, that over the centuries, the Chinese officials of the Han commanderies encouraged people living outside direct Chinese rule to provide gifts, interpreted as tribute, which could be forwarded to the Imperial Court. These gifts suggested that imperial rule was so beneficial that even those who lived beyond it wanted to express their appreciation of it, a type of propaganda which is by no means unique to China and which could be paralleled in the history of the other imperialist states such as Ancient Rome and to some extent Ancient India. In return for their gifts, the chieftains were given rank and status within the Chinese system, and no doubt some advantage derived from this.

There were also some disadvantages. The Chinese attempted to use the chieftains on whom they had bestowed status, to control and even exploit the people amongst whom these chieftains lived. For instance, in 12 CE the Chinese court attempted to recruit the Koguryo people to fight against Xiongnu which made the people of Koguryo so irate that they rebelled, raided and ransacked the Chinese settlements and killed the Chinese governor. Later when the

Chinese General Zhuang Yu enticed Chu, the Marquis of Koguryo, and assassinated him, popular anger against China resulted in widespread revolt that erupted on a large scale which Wang Mang was unable to repress. However, in various publications, sponsored by the project, one finds only a truncated version of the event. The Chinese authors just mention two facts: first, Koguryo was a vassal state and therefore, it was ordered to participate in a military expedition, and second, since the Koguryo chief defied the order of the Chinese ruler, he was killed. This is one of the many examples of very selective use of data.

Koguryo's ceaseless resistance against the military pressure of various non-Han rulers of the north in the post-Han era, including the devastating attack by Wei in 244-245 CE, testifies to the character of Koguryo as an independent political entity in Northeast Asia. Koguryo survived a series of fierce Chinese invasions, because they could not break its tributary structure that extended to Koguryo's own network of tributary states that included such tribal federations as Okcho, Ye and Maek in the lowland areas.

The Korean problem during the Sui was derived from the fact that during the latter part of the Sixteen-State Period, Koguryo had occupied Liaodong. Silla and Paekche sought to get relief from the growing military pressure of Koguryo by inflaming Chinese hostility towards this state. They projected Koguryo's incursion into Liaodong as an act of defiance against the Son of Heaven and the violation of the precepts and principles of the Confucian World Order. It was as a result of this incitement that Emperor Sui Wendi launched a massive attack in 596 CE as an act of retaliation against Koguryo's raid of Liaoxi. Although the expedition did not lead to the victory of Sui, Koguryo realised the need to submit to the power of the Sui Emperor. Needless to add, this act of submission was more a rhetoric than a reality.

When Sui collapsed and the Tang dynasty emerged, Paekche and Silla sent embassies to China complaining that Koguryo was blocking their route to that country. In 625 CE, Emperor Gaozu remarked that it was inappropriate for him to force Koguryo to submit as his subject just for the sake of glory and greatness of his empire, although Chief Minister Pei Ju disagreed with him, noting that the land of Liaodong (under Koguryo) was the land of Jizi (Kija) and subsequently one of the Han commanderies, and therefore, Tang could not be "placed on an equal footing with Koguryo."[22]

China sent an embassy to make peace. In 631 CE, a Chinese mission was despatched to Koguryo to collect the bones of those who had died in the Sui-Koguryo wars, and 10 years later when Chinese envoy Ch'en Dade returned from Koguryo he reported seeing many Chinese in that kingdom. Tang Taizong appears to have remarked that "the territory of Koguryo was once under the sway of the Han commandery, a part of China, and if the economy of the Northeast would pickup it could easily be made part of China again."[23]

In 642 CE, at the end of the year, Yon'gaeSomun seized power in Koguryo, killing King Yongnyu, and installing a puppet king, the latter's nephew Pojang. In 644 CE, Tang ordered Yon'gaeSomun to halt his hostilities against Silla, and on his refusal the Tang commenced its invasion. Operations were, however, halted in autumn due to the Liao flooding. In 645 CE, Tang recaptured Liaoyang and advanced towards the Yalu, but fierce resistance and early cold made the Tang army to retreat. In 647 CE, Tang resumed its raids, both by land and sea, though Koguryo sent princes in a vain attempt to negotiate. In 655 CE, 658 CE and 659 CE, Emperor Gaozong renewed attacks on Koguryo, and in 660 CE he attacked Paekche in a pincer movement. And finally in 668 CE, Koguryo fell to the joint Silla-Tang forces.

The independent political status of Koguryo *vis-à-vis* China is also evident in its worldview. The rulers of Koguryo claimed that they were the descendants of Heaven. In Koguryo's own historical annals, preserved in the work of Yi Kyubo, a Koryoliteratus, we notice that Chumong proclaims himself as 'the Grandson of the

22. Yi-hong, Pan (1997). *Son of Heaven and Heavenly Qaghan: Sui-Tang China and its Neighbors.* Bellingham, Washington:Western Washington University Press. p.121.

23. Ibid.: 210.

Emperor of Heaven, and King of the Western Realm.'[24] The motif of divine descent also figures in the foundation legend of Chu Mong[25] as it appears on the pages of the *Samguksagi* and Moduru and King Kwanggaet'o inscriptions.

This brief overview of Koguryo's relations with the various Chinese states makes it clear that Koguryo refused to recognise China as its suzerain in 12 CE, and in the subsequent centuries Koguryo established its position as a rival and formidable opponent of Chinese rule in the Manchurian region. Ken Gardiner has correctly noted that "Koguryo always took advantage of the period when China was weak, although it kept a low profile when China was a strong unified imperial state."[26] It is hardly surprising, therefore, that in the wake of the Northeast Project of China, books and television dramas celebrating the status of Koguryo as a relentless rival of China and a parallel imperial power in Northeast Asia gained immense appeal.[27]

Conclusion

Modern Korean historiography evolved in the late 19th century when Korea was faced with imperialist challenges. In the twilight

---

24. Gardiner, Ken (1970). "Beyond the Archer and His Son: Koguryo and Han China", in K.H.J. Gardiner, *Papers on Far Eastern History* 2. 57-82.

25. For an analytical perspective on the Koguryo legend, see Song (1974): 37-92; Gardiner (1982a): 60-69; Gardiner (1982b): 31-48 and Gardiner (1988): 149-93; So (1991): 157-91. Commonality of motifs in the foundation myths of various Korean kingdoms brings to mind the fascinating study of Campbell, Joseph (1949). *The Hero with a Thousand Faces*. New York: Bollingen Series, Pantheon Books.

26. Pankaj Mohan and Gardiner, Ken (2005). "Kenneth Gardiner: Indefatigable in Acquiring Knowledge, Tireless in Teaching Others", *Review of Korean Studies* 8(3): 93-112.

27. Some of the popular television dramas projecting Koguryo as a land of intrepid warriors and highlighting its victory over various Chinese states are: Chumong, Yon'gaesomun, Taewangsasingi, Tae Cho-yong (of Parhae). And the titles of patriotic history books include: *Koguryo: The Centre of the Universe; The History of Great Imperial Power Koguryo; Story of Our Ancestors who Jolted China; Ah, Koguryo; Valiant and Sovereign State in the History of Our Race; Koguryo, Silla and Paekche Ruled China; Koguryo, an Empire with its own Son of Heaven; Koguryo's Footsteps in Central Asia; Koguryo: The Centre of the Universe; Koguryo Fort Defying China; YongaeSomun, A Brilliant Hero of Koguryo; History of the Great Koguryo Empire; Clear the Way: Koguryo is Marching Past; UljiMundok: Hero of the Salsu Battle; Koguryo: The Land of War.* It is also interesting to note that numerous Korean citizens wore ancient armour characteristic of Koguryo warriors, while staging demonstrations in front of the Chinese embassy in Seoul.

years of the 19th century, Korea's Independence Club initiated a spirited campaign to shatter the shackles of Sinocentrism with which Korea was tightly bound for several centuries and exhorted the masses to embrace Western ideas and institutions. Confucianism was considered obsolete and irrelevant to the task of modernisation in which the country was engaged. Early Korean historians, notably Shin Chae-ho realised that the identity of the new nation could be built on the foundation of "common shared culture" and he defined the idea of national community and history in narrowly ethnic terms—Tangun as the progenitor of the Korean race and Koguryo, a state that defied China, as the proud symbol of the nation.

Korea's de-Confucianised nationalist historiography, on the other hand, is charged with an intense realisation of the country's unique racial identity and a sense of community. Sin's emphases on Manchuria (which was under the control of Ko Choson, Puyo, Koguryo and Parhae) as an integral part of Korea's geographical self-identity and on Tangun as the symbol of racial uniqueness were an articulation of a nationalist historical consciousness and represented a response to the challenges of the imperialist historiography of Japan.

Bibliography

Sok, Chi-yong (1987). "*Yukdang Choe Nam-son-ui yoksa insik: kodaesa yongu-rul chujungsim-euro*" (Historical Understanding of Choe Nam-seon: Focusing on his Studies of Ancient History), *Yidae sawon* 27: 91-138.

Takeuchi, Chizuko (1988). "Ch'oe Nam-son: History and Nationalism in Modern Korea". Unpublished PhD dissertation. University of Hawaii (UMI).

———. (1990). "Northeast Asia Centered Around Korea: Ch'oe Namson's View of History", *Journal of Asian Studies* 49(4): 787-806.

PART II

Colonial Process

3

SHRI KRISHNA

The Colonial State in India
Military, Legal and Administrative Structures

Modern colonialism was grounded in economic exploitation: a central reason for establishing colonial rule was that the colonies would supply raw materials to and provide captive markets for the metropolitan centre. In the early years, the British justified their rule based on the right of conquest; however, by the early 19th century the official discourse spoke of the civilising mission of British rule, which had brought to India a new political and moral order based on Western norms.[1] Colonial rule was necessary for the good of India, and the British flag came to signify progress for and care of the natives. The colonial army and police were the principal means through which the political authority of the colonial state was exercised while the judiciary and bureaucracy implemented laws framed by the colonial policymakers.

The Colonial Military Apparatus

The colonial army was the mechanism used by the colonial state to maintain its authority. Its emergence can be traced to the establishment of the Bengal army under command of the Bengal Presidency. Major Stringer Lawrence, who formed the first military units of the East India Company in Madras in 1748, is regarded as 'the father of the Indian Army'. He organised the East India Company's Army, which came under three Presidencies: Bengal, Madras and Bombay. The East India Company's increasing financial powers, derived from its monopoly over trade and supplemented by the diwani rights to collect revenue, enabled it to directly recruit

1. Dasgupta, Biplab (2003). "The Colonial Political Perspective", *Social Scientist* 31(3/4): 30.

and pay soldiers instead of hiring through indigenous chiefs. The British utilised the power of the infantry, organised on the basis of a strict command and training pattern. The collective, coordinated musket-fire required professionalism, which meant that the army had to be separated from civil society for a long time so as to train and discipline soldiers as professionals who could act in a cohesive and coordinated unit on the battlefield. This professionalism required not only regular military parade and close-order drill but also payment and, in time, a system of rewards and security, such as a promotion system linked to the length of service and performance and a pension system for long-serving sepoys. The military logistics were also professionalised by routine purchase and stockpiling of non-perishable goods so as to attain mobility without resource problems and without resorting to plunder.

The linguistic and the caste-divisions of Indian society were used by the British to create a socially segregated inward-looking community, thinking only in terms of their own regiment and divorced from civil society. Soldiers were grouped into companies and battalions and were commanded at the lower unit by Indian officers from the sepoy's own social group. The East India Company's Army consisted of the Bengal Army, and that armies of the Bombay and Madras Presidencies each with a different type of internal organisation and level of professionalism. The sepoys of the Bengal Army generally hailed from the high-caste (Brahmin and Rajputs) Hindu families of Awadh and Bihar.[2] They maintained the caste and village community ties even in their 'military villages' or camps. Such ties were slackened, but not lost entirely. The Bombay and Madras Army recruits, on the other hand, belonged to the Punjab, Awadh and Rajputana and hailed from different castes. There was a large influx of Maratha soldiers also after the Anglo-Maratha wars. These mixed armies with supra-caste, supra-class and supra-religious composition, with a pride in their regiments, came handy in the days of the 1857 revolt. The colonial state also took special

2. Alvi, Seema (1995). *The Sepoys and the Company: Tradition and Transition in Northern India 1770-1830*. Delhi: Oxford University Press. pp.39,45-46,49

care to deny the Indian rulers access to resources to prevent them from organising and mobilising similar professional armies. The system of subsidiary alliance with Indian rulers was initiated with the aim of liquidating the indigenous military and even quasi-military forces and thus achieve a complete de-militarisation of the indigenous ruling powers.[3]

The British Indian army was the strong arm of the British Raj. Its main purpose was to quell internal disturbances and to counter external aggression in the subcontinent. However, the mutiny of the Bengal Army in 1857 exposed its weaknesses. This resulted in its complete change and reorganisation. The recruitment pattern changed and became linked to the notion of martial races.[4] Before 1858, though each Presidency had its own army, the Bengal Army (being the largest) had a distinct position as its Commander-in-Chief was also the head of the Company's other armies. He was supposed to exercise supervisory control over them. Prior to 1886, he had no authority over the Punjab Irregular (later Frontier) Field Force—known as the "Piffers"—on the North-West Frontier, which was controlled by the Lieutenant-Governor of the Punjab.[5] Also, of course, he had no direct control over armies of the princely states. In fact, no officer exercised control over all of the Indian land forces.[6] In August 1858, the British Government introduced a major shift in its organisational setups. For such drastic changes, the Peel Commission (1859) and the Eden Commission (1879) played a major role. The Commission reports stressed the need to maintain a disciplined, professional and loyal trained army. All three armies were retained, but the position of the Commander-in-Chief was

---

3. Menezes, S.L. (1993). *Fidelity and Honour: The Indian Army from the Seventeenth to the Twenty-first Century.* New Delhi: Viking. pp.124-143; Farewell, Byron (1989). *Armies of the Raj: From the Mutiny to Independence, 1858-1947.* New York: W.W. Norton & Company Inc. pp.15-19 and 57-64 and Rosen, Stephen P. (1996). *Societies and Military Power: India and its Armies.* Ithaca: Cornell University Press. pp.173-77.

4 Roy, Kaushik (1997). "Recruitment doctrines and the colonial Indian Army", *The Indian Economic and Social History Review* 34(3).

5. Menezes *op. cit.* no. 3: 76.

6. Farewell *op. cit.* no. 3: 27.

braced with more powers. The strength of the British troops was raised to 80,000, of which 50,000 were for Bengal, 15,000 for Madras, and 15,000 for Bombay. They were also given total control over the artillery and some other branches of the army. Additionally, according to the Peel Commission, the native forces were not to far outnumber the Europeans in the cavalry and infantry. The ratio should not be more than two to one for Bengal, and three to one for Madras and Bombay respectively. The homogeneous nature of the Bengal Army was one of the factors that contributed to the outbreak of the mutiny. Hence, later, the British maintained a distinction and separateness of caste and class in the army. No single caste or class was allowed to dominate or command another caste or class. To preclude unity among native soldiers, the Peel Commission Report recommended that the Native Army should be composed of different nationalities and castes, and as a general rule, mixed promiscuously through each regiment. In the year 1895, all the three armies were amalgamated to create the Indian Army, headed by a Commander-in-Chief. Under the Commander-in-Chief, there were four commands: the Madras Command, the Bombay Command, the Bengal Command and the Punjab Command, each headed by a Lieutenant General. The Indian Army became one of the marvels of modern times, and for which the people of the subcontinent used to say:

Khalk-i-Khuda

Mulk-i-Sirkar

Hukm-i-Sahiban Alishan

(Mankind belongs to God, the land to the Government,
and power to the powerful Sahibs).[7]

The recruitment of soldiers, 1857 onwards shifted to the north and north-western regions of India (present-day Pakistan) at the expense of other regions, especially Bengal. As a result, during first half of the 20th century, the army was dominated by soldiers from the north and north-west of India. Gurkhas from Nepal, and the Punjabis and the Pathans were preferred. The number of Punjabis

7. MacMunn, George F. (1911). *The Armies of India*. London: Adam & Charles Black. p. 220.

increased gradually. The main martial races of the west Punjab recruited were the Tiwanas, Noons, Gakkhars, Janguas, Awans, Baluchis, Khattars, Khokhars and Sials.[8] The British Army's senior officers believed that certain classes and communities in India were warrior races—martial races. Such classes and communities were believed to prove better and braver soldiers and to be more suitable for army service. The Eden Commission reported in 1879 that the Punjab was the "home of the most martial races of India" and that it was "the nursery" of the best soldiers. The martial race theory helped to bring about an end to the Peel Commission recommendation that "the (regional) armies must balance each other". According to Field Marshal Frederick Sleigh Roberts, the so-called "balance" was discarded in the 1880s. The "mutiny" brought about a search for a martial race which would not turn against the British once again. The crux of the matter was that some races were superior to others. All natives were not equal in soldierly qualities. Roberts boldly asserted that "no comparison can be made between the martial values of a regiment recruited amongst the Gorkhas of Nepal or the warlike races of Northern India (Punjab and the NWFP [North-West Frontier Punjab]), and those recruited from the effeminate peoples of the South". This ideology of martial race was clearly an attempt by the colonial state to utilise ethnicity for promoting imperial interests. The territorial nomenclature of the armies was changed as the Bengal Army was reorganised by absorbing soldiers from the so-called martial races such as the Sikhs, Jats, Pathans, Dogras and Nepali Gorkhas.[9] The indigenous soldiers were to be recruited on the basis of distinction between warrior and effeminate social groups, who were seen as loyal and proud but with no competence to lead or command. In fact, they were envisaged as dirty, savage and unintelligent. The colonial medical authorities were, therefore, perplexed and at pains to explain the low rates of venereal diseases

---

8. Ibbetson, Denzil (1916). *Punjab Castes. A Reprint of the Races, Castes and Tribes of the People.* Lahore: Superintendent, Government Printing, Punjab. pp.166-67.

9. Streets, Heather (2004). *Martial Races: The Military, Race and Masculinity in British Imperial Culture (1857-1914).* Manchester: Manchester University Press.

among indigenous soldiers. It was explained in terms that did not put at risk the alleged superiority of the British soldiers. Factors held responsible for the low incidence of venereal diseases among Indian soldiers were: lack of drinking habits, absence of commercial sex among Indian soldiers due to caste obligations, ability to come across less unsafe sexual encounters, older age-composition of Indian soldiers, their less stimulating diet and the practice of sending payments to support families at home, thus, leaving them with less money for self-pleasure and keeping of their wives in regimental bazaars, etc.[10]

These peasants-turned-soldiers, who until now were malnourished, under-paid and maltreated by the rich feudal class, were more committed, hardworking and disciplined, and willing to take up assignments with more rigour and vigour. The army provided everything: salary, uniform and prestige, as they were working directly with the colonial rulers. Indeed, military service provided a guaranteed salary while the peasant class working in the fields was faced with poverty and an uncertain source of income. The new recruitment policy aimed at exploiting the socio-economic life of Punjab.[11] Granting rewards in return for loyalty was a very traditional and old tool of British domestic and international policy. This contrivance was applied in the north. Those who joined the British Indian Army were previously peasants. For them the best and the biggest reward was allotment of land. The British used to allocate land to soldiers in return for loyalty and gallantry on their retirement. Such land awards made army service an attractive profession. The policy of granting agrarian land as a reward for military service also encouraged recruitment. The British Indian government began constructing a network of canals and their branches and distributaries in the plains of Western Punjab. This process was initiated in 1885 and continued intermittently until

10. Levine, Philippa (2003). *Prostitution, Races and Politics: Policing Venereal Diseases in the British Empire. New York: Routledge. pp.283-84.*

11. Omissi, David (1994). *The Sepoy and the Raj: The Indian Army, 1860-1940.* London: Macmillan. pp.49-52.

the end of British rule, during which period large tracts inhabited by semi-nomadic peoples were brought under cultivation. There were nine such areas, called the Canal Colonies, where land with sufficient canal water became available. The British Indian government distributed this land mainly on political considerations, that is to reward people and communities for services to the Raj.[12] Substantial tracts of the colony lands were allotted to ex-servicemen, both officers and of other ranks. Land was also granted for keeping breeding-horses, camels and other animals for the supply to the army and taking care of them. Substantial allotments of land were made to the veterans of World War I.[13] However, the regional recruitment shift was about to repeat the same mistake that was committed in the case of the Bengal Army—a vast homogeneous fusion of soldiers of the Punjab. Therefore, to avoid a repetition of Bengal of 1857, the British divided Punjab. In 1901, Viceroy Lord Curzon, adopting and modifying an idea of Lord Lytton, carved the North-West Frontier Province (NWFP) out of Punjab. The NWFP was administered by a chief commissioner with headquarters in Peshawar and responsible directly to the Government of India (GoI).[14] Now the chemistry of conscription was such that in Bengal there were 7,117 combatant recruits out of a total population of 45 million, whereas Punjab offered 349,689 out of a total population of 20 million.[15]

Troops were employed in the country many times a year to prevent internal disorder and sometimes to quell it. The use of army for the purpose of maintaining or restoring order was always on the increase. Even after its preponderant position was firmly established, the army regularly undertook internal security duties to foil any bid

12. Ali, Imran (1988). *The Punjab under Imperialism, 1885-1947*. Princeton: Princeton University Press. pp.109-126.

13. Ali, Imran Anwar (2003). "Business and Power in Pakistan", in Anita M. Weiss and S. Zulfiqar Gilani (eds.), *Power and Civil Society in Pakistan*. Karachi: Oxford University Press. p.104.

14. Collen, Edwin Henry Hayten (1907). *The Indian Army: A Sketch of its History and Organisation*. Reprinted from the third edition of the 'Imperial Gazetteer'. Oxford: Clarenden Press. pp.19, 347-53.

15. *Report of the Indian Statutory Commission*, Vol. 1, Survey, RCIO. Calcutta: Official publication of the Government of India. 1930. p.61.

to challenge the British authorities. Among the situations that the colonial rulers needed to prepare for were violent attacks, guerrilla activities, banditry, peasant revolts, lockouts, labour unrest and Hindu-Muslim communal riots.[16]

The Police Organisation

The colonial state in its early phase used the indigenous institutions for controlling crime. Warren Hastings retained the post of *fauzdar* and utilised the policing functions of the *zamindars*. But finding the arrangement inadequate, he also appointed magistrates in districts and each district was sub-divided into units, each under a *darogah*, who headed a group of 20-30 policemen and supervised village watchmen. The *darogahs* functioned under overall control of the magistrates. Under the system evolved by Lord Cornwallis, district collectors combined the duties of revenue collection and police duties as magistrates. These functions were separated briefly on recommendations of the Bird Committee (1808-12). However, in 1844, the duties of the collector, the magistrate and the police officer were again combined.

The real police organisation as an autonomous organ of the state emerged in the NWFP in the 1840s as a quasi-military instrument for maintaining order. Sir Charles Napier was instrumental in its evolution in Sind, which was on the pattern of the Irish Police Organisation of 1836. Easy mobility, a clear and firm hierarchy of command, direct and formal links with the army and centralisation of command were some of its main features. *Thanedars* or the commissioned officers of the mounted police were in charge of each division of a district. By 1859, a complete network of 245 *thanas* was in place in Sind. This type of police organisation was later recommended by the Police Commission (1860) and adopted in the Police Act of 1861. This system of policing was applied almost in every province except Bombay and Madras, for which separate Police Acts were passed. Although the colonial government gave the responsibility of maintaining law and order to the police, the

16. Omissi *op. cit.* no. 11: 216.

army was frequently deployed to curb disturbances. The military, rather than a civilian model of police, influenced even the colonial perception of crimes and violations of law. The police were less for the prevention and detection of crime and more for maintaining political stability.[17]

The lack of financial resources and political will compelled the police to rely on selective controls, i.e., identifying particular social groups, especially the so-called criminal tribes, as their prime targets. The police remained poorly armed, inefficient, corrupt and lacking in proper training. In the 1920s, an armed contingent of police was established to avoid over-deployment of the military in a period when nationalist mobilisation was becoming more intense.

Judiciary and Legal Machinery

The colonial state found that the indigenous legal system in India punished criminals in accordance with their caste status. After an initial recognition of caste hierarchy, the colonial state tried to incorporate the element of formal equality in its legal system. The idea of imperial law also travelled to colonies, where its arrival required translation, negotiation and domestication, and sometimes all-out war. The processes of travel and domestication changed law itself: its content, its meaning, its scope and its ultimate effects. The colonial rulers, as they attempted to define criminality, private property and social order, negotiated the content, scope and meaning of law with local powerful social groups. The colonial state's concerns for stability, private property, order and justice required accommodations with some local powerful social groups, which saw opportunities to further their own varied interests. The process of transporting British law to colonial sites was not only contentious, but also creative of new struggles over authority, legality and power. Law in the colonial period was not merely an instrument of colonial rule: it was an arena of conflict, and these conflicts re-defined local social hierarchies, state authority and the relationship between

17. Das, Dilip K. and Arvind Verma (1998). "The Armed Police in the British Colonial Tradition: The Indian Perspective", *Policing: An International Journal of Police Strategies & Management* 21(I): 354-67. pp. 354-67.

subjects and state. The British saw their mandate extending only to matters of economy and order, and so explicitly left the domains of religion, culture and "private law" under the control of social groups that are local and powerful. In India, this meant that for the first time the Muslims were to be governed by "Muslim law" and Hindus by "Hindu law", according to British understanding of these laws, based upon ancient and classical texts and not local practice.

The colonial legal system was also based on racial discrimination and racial privilege. Although the British subjects could be tried in the same courts as the Indians in civil matters, an Indian judge could still not try them in criminal cases. The famous Ilbert Bill Controversy (1882-83) reflected the racial prejudice of European administrators in India. The Bill was based on the liberal principle of equality before the law and sought to empower Indian magistrates in rural areas to try British subjects. The British opponents of the Bill argued that India's social and legal institutions were different from those of Europe, hence such legal equality could not be granted.

The early Company courts followed the principle of fusion of executive and judicial powers. Warren Hastings established two types of courts at the district level: *diwani adalat* (civil courts) and *nizamat adalat* (courts for criminal cases). The British collector enjoyed both revenue and judicial powers in the district, whose boundaries followed the pattern of pre-existing revenue units called *Sarkars*. *Pandits* and *moulvis* were associated with these courts to assist European judges. The Governor-in-Council acted as the court of appeal in both criminal and civil cases. In India, the laws were generally based on memory and customs embedded in a variety of usages. Hastings believed that the knowledge of Indian laws as embodied in the textual traditions was relevant for developing the judicial system in India. The traditional Indian legal interpreters, the *pandits* and *moulvis*, were seen as the upholders, expositors and interpreters of the Indian legal tradition and hence were associated with courts as experts.[18] The British, however, distrusted Indian subordinates due to their own racial inclinations. They wanted

18. Bhatia, H.S. (2001). *Justice System and Mutinies in India.* New Delhi: Deep and Deep Publications. pp.299-320.

to acquire a complete knowledge of the authoritative legal texts. This could be done by codifying the Indian laws, for which Indian assistants were needed but their integrity the British doubted. NB Halhed's *A Code of Gentoo Law* (1776) and HT Colebrooke's *The Digest of Hindu Law on Contracts and Succession* (1798) were early attempts to codify the laws concerning property, inheritance, marriage, succession, etc. The utilitarian ideology emphasised the need to remove the vagueness and diversity in legal practices in order to dismantle the "despotic" rule in India. The Indian Penal Code (1860) codified the laws and the Codes of Criminal Procedure (1872) settled the question of the quality and quantity of evidence required for proving or disproving facts related to the offences. The Indian Penal Code (1860-1862) was put in place in India as a result of debates in England over the criminal justice system, debates which did not result in a criminal code in England but which stimulated the desire to put British justice into effect in India. The Code attempted to create in India a rule of law which could be an ideal in England.[19] The myth of origins runs deep and continues to affect Indian law, even though the Indian Penal Code did not draw exclusively from English law, and even though its drafter, Thomas Babington Macaulay (1800-1859), inserted new elements based on supposed "Indian" realities such as criminal castes, *thuggee* (ritual murder) and dacoity (banditry).[20] The Indian laws were seen as changeless and immutable, whereas the English was based on historical precedents, and hence responsive to historical change and flexible in nature. The element of flexibility and principle of multiple interpretation were reintroduced in workings of the high courts, which were established in 1861 in Calcutta, Madras and Bombay and later in a few other places as they took cognition of earlier judicial decisions. The colonial state could, thus, easily use the principle of non-interference to justify existing oppressive practices under the pretext of continuing customary practices or modifying the

---

19. Wright, Barry (2010). "Macaulay's Indian Penal Code: Historical Context and Originating Principles", in Wing-Cheong Chang, Stanley Yeo and Barry Wright (eds), *Codification, Macaulay and the Indian Penal Code: Legacies and Modern Challenges of Criminal Law Reform*. Farnham and Burlington: Ashgate Publishing Limited. pp.19-58.

20. Singha, Radhika (1993). "Providential' Circumstances: The Thuggee Campaign of the 1830s and Legal Innovation", *Modern Asian Studies* 27(1): pp. 83-146.

existing laws or enacting laws to protect the rights of specific social groups. The example of such enactment was the tenancy acts and land alienation acts.

Foucault points out that function of the penal system in Europe at the end of the Middle Ages to the 18th century was to stamp out rebellion. Therefore, the penal system was aimed, very specifically, against the most mobile, the most excitable, and the "violent" and "dangerous" elements who had to be isolated so that they could not spearhead popular resistance.[21] The British penal system similarly was directed against the rebellious tribal people who had waged wars for territories, prior to 1857, on many occasions in different parts of the country. Through surveillance and other mechanisms of social control, it defined certain social groups as beyond the bounds of civility. The colonial strand of anthropology and anthropometry contributed to the notions of hereditary criminality. A number of groups and communities were stigmatised as "criminal tribes". The colonial state defined these groups as criminal by reference to their caste identity, which rendered crime as an inborn trait of their group.[22] According to Susan Bayly, the construction of entire castes by the British as "criminal" was part of a larger discourse in which caste determined the occupational profile as well as social and moral characteristics of all its members.[23] The various ethnographic texts prepared after 1860 and subsequently the emergence of anthropometry or measurement of physical indices like average height, weight, the size and shape of the skull, the relation of head size to body size, etc. were aimed to identify such groups and communities so as to make social control easier.

---

21. Foucault, Michel (1980). "On Popular Justice: A Discussion with Maoists" in *Power/Knowledge: Selected Interviews and Other Writings; 1972-1977*. Sussex: Brighton. pp.14-15.

22. See, Yang, Anand A. (ed.) (1985). *Crime and Criminality in British India*. Tuscan: University Of Arizona Press; Simhadri, Y.C. (1979). *The Ex-Criminal Tribes of India*. New Delhi: National Publishing House; D'Souja, Dilip (2001). *Branded by Law: Looking at India's De-notified Tribes*. New Delhi: Penguin and Radhakrishna, Meena (2001). *Dishonoured by History: 'Criminal Tribes' and British Colonial Policy*. New Delhi: Orient Longman, for this type of stereotyping of these social groups and communities.

23. See Bayly, Susan (2000). Caste, Society and Politics in India. New Delhi: Cambridge University Press. pp.119-43.

There were penal settlements in the Straits, Penang, Malacca and Singapore before the revolt of 1857 with a considerable number of Indians in them.[24] After 1857, the British authorities started the new penal settlement in the Andaman and Nicobar Islands[25] and it came to be known as "kala pani" in popular imagination and was inhabited by "unmitigated savages".[26] Captain Henry Mann, who had headed settlements in the Straits, was appointed temporary superintendent of the new settlement with instructions to follow the rules and regulations of settlements in the Straits. These new techniques, rationales, targets and sites of segregation were imported by the colonial state,[27] imparting a new meaning to cultural practices of isolation in the sub-continent especially after 1857. The "carceral archipelago" of the Andamans was developed just immediately after the events of 1857. The geographical and physical features of the island were fused with the upper-caste fear of crossing the kala pani or the black waters and subsequently its meaning and representation were further transformed in cultural production, story-telling and nationalist memories. While the colonial practices of architectural design and interior partitioning to further segregate the prisoners were imported, other elements of prisoners' sufferings such as feelings of indignation at the crossing of the black waters and unfamiliarity with some aspects of prison life such as common mess facility and public common bathing in prison were related to high-caste perceptions of many political and nationalist prisoners.[28]

---

24. Newbold, Thomas John (1839). *Political and Statistical Accounts of Settlement in Straits.* Available on Google from New York Public Library.

25. Temple, R.C. (1996). *Provincial Gazzetteers of India: Andaman and Nicobar Islands.* New Delhi: Asian Educational Services (Reprint). pp. 56-57

26. Russel, William Howard (1860). *My Diary in India, in the Year 1857-59* (Available on Google.) p. 133.

27. See Anderson, Clare (2003). "The Politics of Convict Space: Indian Penal Settlement of the Andaman Islands", in Carolyn Stranger and Alison Bashford (eds.), *Isolation: Places and Practices of Exclusion.* New York: Routledge. pp. 40-56.

28. See, Arnold, David (1994). "The Colonial Prison: Power, Knowledge and Penology in 19th Century India", in D. Arnold and David Hardiman (eds.), *Subaltern Studies.* Vol. VIII. New Delhi: Oxford University Press. pp.148-87, for an analysis of colonial jails.

The Bureaucracy as the Steel Frame of the Raj

Apart from the armed forces, police and legal machinery, the colonial state created a centralised bureaucracy. The colonial bureaucracy maintained its racial exclusiveness, although Indians occupied the lower rungs of administration. The structure and logic of this bureaucracy guaranteed the unquestionable dominance of the British. Cornwallis framed rules to guide its actions. Initially, the Company's civil servants, were paid in the form of commission on the amount of revenue collection. The system of appointment was based on patronage and nomination by the Court of Directors. In 1800, the College of Fort William was established to train the Company's civil servants, but it was soon abolished and the training shifted to Hertfort in 1805 and to Haileybury in England in 1809. The Haileybury College provided training in oriental languages, literature and history. The Charter Act of 1853 abolished the system of patronage and started recruitment through competitive public examination. The Haileybury College for training civil servants was abolished in 1858 and recruits for the civil services were affiliated to various colleges and universities. In 1892, the Covenanted Civil Service was the higher administrative service dominated by Oxford and Cambridge graduates, who generally had a "public school" background. However, there was a fair representation from Irish universities too. There was also a provincial civil service recruited in India itself.[29]

The bureaucracy provided the steel frame to support the Raj. It was dominated largely by the British. Educated Indians demanded a simultaneous examination in India but despite its acceptance in principle, it came to be conducted in India only after World War I. Even then the selected Indian candidates were excluded from a particular category of posts, especially in the judicial services. The Indian recruits also received lower pay and allowances. The nationalist leaders demanded an end to racial discrimination but

29. Puri, B.N. (1982). *History of Indian Administration (Modern Period)*, Vol. III, Munshiram Delhi: Manoharlal Publishers.

the pace of Indianisation intensified only after World War I.[30] By the time of the Quit India Movement in 1942, half of the civil servants were Indians. Since education in India was skewed in favour of the upper castes and upper classes, even such representation was not truly Indian.

Conclusion

Thus, the colonial state had certain features that distinguished it from the state in Europe and the post-colonial state in developing countries. First, it was an instrument of control and oppression over the local inhabitants. To this end, it established strong bureaucracies, the police and military forces. Hence unlike Europe, it was an authoritarian state and not a liberal democratic one. Secondly, it was expected to protect and further economic and political interests of the European colonial rulers and their home countries and not those of the local inhabitants. Thirdly, the colonial rulers also believed they had a civilising mission to perform and attempted to transplant their culture and values in the colonies. Hence, they saw colonialism as a white man's burden. It is difficult to measure the degree of the colonial state's reliance on the consent of people and the ideological precepts for justifying its rule in India. It did to some extent try to legitimate its rule as a public authority responsible for maintaining social order and justice. But although the rhetoric of the "rule of law" and "individual freedom" decorated its claims to legitimacy, in practice the colonial state maintained its domination by demonstrating its use of force, which reflected the very nature of the colonial state in India.

30. Sharma, Malti (2001). *Indianisation of Civil Services in British India*. Delhi: Manak Publishers. p.219.

Bibliography

Callahan, Raymond A. (1972). *The East India Company and Army Reforms 1783-1798.* Cambridge, Mass: Harvard University Press.

Das, S.T. (1969). *Indian Military: Its History and Development.* New Delhi: Sagar Publications.

Heathcote, A. (1974). *The Indian Army: The Garrison of British Imperial India, 1822-1922.* New York: Hippocrene Books.

4

VISALAKSHI MENON

Aspects of Colonial Education in India

Introduction

In modern times, for any new regime seeking to establish itself, control over education and devising a coherent educational policy are an imperative. It was the case for the British too, when it became clear that they would be playing an important role in India—not just as a trading company but administratively too. This enlargement of their role from merchant to ruler took place in the last decades of the 18th century. At the same time, they began to acquaint themselves with legal institutions of the Indians, their languages and literature, their scriptures, etc. This period, which we refer to as the phase of Orientalism, was one in which they were trying to familiarise themselves with the Indian reality. They were impressed by what they saw and learnt and felt that Indian culture and civilisation was easily comparable to that of ancient Greece and Rome, perhaps even superior. (William Jones on the sublimity of the Sanskrit language.)

Colonial Attempt to Know India: The British Initiative for Education

In order to promote traditional learning, they gave grants for setting up a madrasa in Calcutta in 1781 and a Sanskrit College in Benares in 1792. The Calcutta *madrasa* had a curriculum comprising philosophy, Islamic theology and law, grammar, geometry and arithmetic, and logic. The medium of instruction was Arabic. The Sanskrit College was intended to preserve and cultivate the laws, literature and scriptures of the Hindus. Quite obviously, here the medium of instruction was Sanskrit. The students were not charged fees in either case. Instead, they received stipends from the government and the costs maintaining the institutions were met through assigning the revenues of certain villages.

What needs to be noted, however, about these early efforts of the British colonial state is that their educational interventions reflected their somewhat incorrect way of perceiving Indian social reality, which they saw as comprising two distinct religious groups—the Hindus and the Muslims—each with its educational systems that had nothing to do with each other.

They later realised that matters were not so simple. In the early decades of the 19th century, they began surveying, on a regular basis, the schools and higher institutions in different parts of the country. While in the cases of Madras and Bombay these surveys were undertaken by the governors themselves, in Bengal, a missionary named William Adam did the work. Adam's report, which is extremely well-known and oft-quoted, is an eye-opener. It recorded an impressive network of elementary schools in the rural areas of Bengal. Adam put the number of such schools at around 100,000—or roughly two schools to every three villages. The most striking feature of the *pathshala* system was its diversity—there was no uniform pattern. *Pathshalas* evolved in response to local needs and the curriculum was drawn up by the teacher or guru. For instance, a moneylender's son would be taught *mahajani* accounts while a landlord's son would be taught *zamindari* accounts. The timing of these *pathshalas* was in accordance with convenience of the local, rural population and the agricultural calendar. There were no standard textbooks and most knowledge would be transmitted orally and by the rote method.

Besides *pathshalas*, there were *tols* or *chatuspathis*, which were institutions of higher learning as well as the *madrasas*. But what was interesting was that even Hindu students could go to *madrasas* and all children of the village, irrespective of their religion, would attend *pathshalas*. The gurus in the *pathshalas* could be Hindu or Muslim, upper- or lower-caste (Kazi Shahidullah, *Pathshalas into Schools*, p.20). Women were not educated. Social prejudices against educating girls were very strong.

The findings for Bengal were not unique. Thomas Munro, who surveyed the Madras Presidency, and Mountstuart Elphinstone in Bombay had similar findings. Munro, for instance, found that there were 12,498 schools in the Madras Presidency with 1,88,650 pupils. In fact the Madras system of schooling so impressed the British educationists that it was replicated in England as a cheap and efficient method of education.[1]

Things began to change with the advent of missionaries in the second decade of the 19th century and here we can take up one or two examples. Eric Stokes in his *English Utilitarians and India* vividly describes the views of the Clapham sect—Zachary Macaulay, Charles Grant, William Wilberforce and others. The religions of India, their laws, arts, agricultural practices and handicrafts were all viewed with contempt. To prepare the Indian mind to receive the Christian truth, it had first to be cleared of all error and superstition. Education was the least obtrusive method of evangelising, the least likely to create social or political disturbance. This, they argued, would also benefit commerce. To quote Charles Grant: "In every progressive step of this work, we shall also serve the original design with which we visited India, that design is still so important to this country—the extension of its commerce."

By the 1820s and 1830s, to cite Stokes again, a new spirit characterised British administrative policy. There was a new feeling of self-confidence: a growing conviction that the British government should stand forward as an English government, instead of masquerading as the feudal subject of the Mughal emperor in Delhi.

Viceroy William Bentinck, legal member of his council Thomas Macaulay and political secretary Charles Trevelyan enthusiastically promoted this new spirit. A quote from Trevelyan's pamphlet *Education of India* would be appropriate here:

> The political education of a nation is a work of time and while it is in progress, we shall be as safe as it will be possible for us to be. The natives will not rise against us. We shall stoop to raise them... the national activity will be fully and harmlessly employed in acquiring

1. Ghosh, S.C. (n.d.). *The History of Education in Modern India*, p.9.

> and diffusing European knowledge and in naturalizing European institutions. The educated classes, knowing that the elevation of this country on these principles can only be worked out under our protection, will naturally cling to us.

"Cling to us", yes, but for how long? What Trevelyan did not anticipate was that their political education would enable Indians to see the "un-British" nature of British rule in all its starkness and clarity.

It is customary to date the advent of Western education in India and its steady expansion from Macaulay's famous "Minutes on Education" of 2 February 1835, wherein he declared the objective to be the creation of "a class of persons, Indian in colour and blood but English in tastes, in opinion, in morals and in intellect". But gradually the whole onus of education was shifted on to the shoulders of Indians. In fact this was inherent even in Macaulay's diffusionist theory, whereby the British confined their efforts to educating the upper crust and left the much more challenging task of educating the masses to this upper crust. Wood's Despatch of 1854, the next milestone in British educational policy, came up with the Grants-in-Aid Scheme, whereby the responsibility of running institutions would be handed over to local notables. The British were unwilling to spend more than a small fraction of their budget on education.

Social Reform Movement Helped the Cause of Women's Education

As the 19th century drew to an end and the new century unfolded, education for girls became one of the most prominent issues in the public arena. But as will be discussed in the following section, through a case study of north India, it was an initiative of Indians that created an impressive network of women's educational institutions.

Karuna Chanana has suggested that the demand for women's education arose as a concomitant of the social reform movement. There was also a fear of the challenge posed by Christian missionaries, who were apparently proselytising while imparting education. Since they had already taken the initiative in setting up girls' schools, there was a fear that the girls who attended these schools might be converted to Christianity.[2] The only option was to set up parallel schools either under the auspices of the Arya Samaj or other such organisation, so that the girls would not need to go to schools run by Christian missionaries. The story of Lala Munshi Ram's decision to start a girls' school in Jullundur in 1888 typically illustrates this anxiety. One evening on his return from court, his daughter Vedakumari came running to him with her newly learnt knowledge: "Christ is the Prophet. No price is required to mention his name. Christ is my anchor. He is my Krishna..." It was then that he resolved to start an Aryan Girls' School. And by 1890, the Jullundur Arya Samaj had succeeded in opening the Arya Kanya Path Shala.[3] Eleven students and a staff of three teachers constituted the academic corpus of the institution. Funds for the school were raised in an interesting variety of ways. There was the atta fund, wherein housewives were asked to set aside a handful of atta every day for the cause. "Accordingly, in every house a 'Dharm Pot' was kept, in which ladies of the household used daily to put a handful of flour."[4] This method had first been employed in Lahore to generate funds for Arya Samaj work and had subsequently become popular throughout the Punjab. Another method was street begging and it must have been a curious sight indeed to see respectable lawyers and merchants of the town standing on the streets and begging for money to start a girls' school![5]

What was it that drove people like Ishwar Chandra Vidyasagar in Bengal, Jyotirao Phule in Maharashtra, Lala Munshi Ram, Lal Dev Raj and others in Jullunder, Sayid Karamat Husain in United Provinces (UP) and Lala Jugal Kishore in Delhi to work against the odds, divert their hard-earned money or their ancestral riches and even compromise their dignity to set up schools for girls? Obviously it must have been the same spirit that drove many others to start

2. Chanana, Karuna (1988). "Social Change or Social Reform The Education of Women in Pre-Independence India, in Karuna Chanana (ed.), *Socialisation, Education and Women: Explorations in Gender Identity*. New Delhi. pp.100-01.

3. Jones, Kenneth (n.d.), *Arya Dharm*. pp.104-05.

4. Jambunathan, M.R. (ed.) (1961). *Swami Shraddhanand*. Bombay. p.78, cited in Ibid.: 83.

5. Lala Dev Raj, the manager of the Kanya Pathshala, apparently took to begging in the streets to raise funds for the school. Ibid.: 105.

newspapers, which they knew would have a precarious existence and could lead them to financial bankruptcy. Or later still, to resign their government jobs and lucrative legal practice on hearing the appeal of Gandhi. Or even to stand on the streets with a measuring rod in hand and sell *khaddar*. All these people and countless others were public-spirited and had an overwhelming desire to work for the common good and an ability to act on their convictions and beliefs.

Another reason offered by the colonial authorities for the move to set up girls' schools was the influence of Western ideas on the male section of the Indian population. The 1921 Census Report, in its chapter on literacy, observed:

> ...there is little doubt that the women of India owe the growing facilities offered them for acquiring literacy to the influence on the male section of the community of foreign standards and ideals....It is only, or at least chiefly, when the general advance of male culture has reached well beyond the stage of vernacular literacy that the atmosphere becomes favourable to real progress in the instruction of women...[6]

Sayid Karamat Hussain's Story

Sayid Karamat Husain was a lawyer from the UP, passionately committed to the cause of girls' education. In the closing decade of the 19th century and opening decades of the 20th, he went around starting one girls' school after another. In the course of his own studies in England, Husain had been greatly impressed by the position of women in British society. He became convinced, like several others of his time, that the best way for a country to progress was for its women to be educated. Of course, he too believed that a woman's duty was to manage the household and that education would enable her to discharge this duty better. But what made him different from others of his time was his insistence on sending girls to school. He felt, he argued and he insisted that school education was far superior to the practice of employing tutors at home because a school could offer better teachers and a broader curriculum than

6. *Census of India*, 1921, Vol.1, Part 1, pp.179-80.

any home could. To give shape to his ideas, he first set up a girls' school in Allahabad in the late 1890s, followed by a similar one in Aligarh in 1906 and yet another in Lucknow in 1916. In his endeavour to set up the Allahabad school, which came to be known as the Crosthwaite Girls School, he got the support of several fellow lawyers and administrators—"members of a growing Indian middle class, both Hindu and Muslim"—and together they created a fund for the school.[7] The Crosthwaite Girls School took off and became an important landmark in Allahabad's educational history. Among its alumni were well-known figures like Mahadevi Varma and Subhadra Kumari Chauhan. So continuous was Karamat Husain's involvement with the school that, throughout his stay in Allahabad, notwithstanding his busy schedule as a teacher of law and then a judge at the Allahabad High Court, he would find the time to drop in at the school on his way back home in the evening.

Husain's ideas were at variance with those of Sir Syed Ahmed Khan, who was a powerful force in Aligarh in the late 19th century. Sir Syed had never been too enthusiastic about education for girls, since he felt that it was more important to educate boys first. When Husain first raised the issue of women's education at the annual meeting of the Muhammadan Educational Conference in Allahabad in 1890, the other members of the Conference were horrified. Nevertheless, at the following session of the Conference in Aligarh, he, along with some others, succeeded in getting a resolution in favour of women's education adopted. Seven years later, he was instrumental in creating the women's education section of the Muhammadan Educational Conference, which in turn began working towards setting up the Muslim Women's Normal School in Aligarh. Here, he had the active support of Shaikh Muhammad Abdullah, who had been his student when he had taught law at Aligarh College. Sheikh Abdullah and his wife set up the Aligarh Girls' School in 1906. The school later went on

7. Minault, Gail (1997). "Sayyid Karamat Husain and Education for Women", in Violette Graff (ed.), *Lucknow: Memories of a City*. New Delhi. p.159.

to become the Women's College of Aligarh University.[8] This trajectory bears close resemblance to that of the Indraprastha School and College.

The story of Husain's efforts in Lucknow was even more interesting. This city, more feudal and conservative in its outlook, had not responded positively to his initial attempts at setting up a school for girls. But when he returned to the city after his retirement from the Allahabad High Court in 1912, the Raja of Mahmudabad, a leading *taluqdar* of Awadh, approached him to start a girls' school in the city. What was significant was that the same notable had been vehemently opposed to Husain's attempts at opening such a school in the 1890s. The Raja was now favourably impressed by the Crosthwaite Girls School example and admitted that he had been wrong. Now he wanted a school, but was insistent that it should be exclusively for Muslim girls. He even assigned the revenues of several villages, amounting to ₹600 a month, for expenses of the school.[9] Besides this financial help, Husain set up a waqf based on the income from his own land, to the tune of ₹1,25,000, the proceeds of which were for expenses of the school. Lady Meston, wife of the lieutenant governor of the province, inaugurated the Muslim Girls' School in March 1916. The first principal of the school was Anima (Ethel) Pope, an Englishwoman who had converted to Islam and had been superintendent of the girls' boarding house at the Crosthwaite Girls' School.[10]

Husain's story testifies to the importance of private, indigenous efforts in the area of women's education. It also shows how, at the turn of the century in Northern India, despite all the deterrents, women's education could be promoted if there was determination for it. This was precisely what was lacking in British policy. In any case, the colonial government considered women's education to be of low priority. In the 1880s, throughout British India, only 4.6 per cent of the educational budget was allocated to women's education.[11]

8. Ibid.
9. Ibid.: 160-61.
10. Ibid.
11. Bhattacharya, S. *et al.* (2001). *The Development of Women's Education in India: A Collection of Documents 1850-1920*. New Delhi. p.xiii.

The allocation for the UP was even less, only 3.8 per cent. Punjab fared somewhat better with an allocation of 6.4 per cent.[12] What is also noteworthy is that the discourse on education revolved around education for boys. Girls were hardly in the picture.

Barriers to Women's Education

A variety of excuses would be offered for not setting up schools for girls or for closing down the existing ones. So much so that Henry Sharp, in his "Report on the Progress of Education in India" in 1914, remarked: "It is customary to commence any discussion on the education of Indian girls and women by a recital of its difficulties." He then went on to say: "There is no reason for departing from this practice; for the topic, if monotonous, is the key-note to the whole subject."[13] The "customs of the people" and the lack of adequate female teachers were the most oft-repeated excuses. The rigid seclusion of women under the purdah system and the practice of early marriage of girls were the frequently cited social impediments. The former practice, i.e., *purdah*, was more prevalent in Northern India than in the South. Besides, there was also apparently a fear among "Indian gentlemen" that the education of girls would lead to a "loosening of social ties, the upheaval of customary ways and ... prolonged and severe domestic embarrassment".[14] True, in the 19th century, Krishna Mohan Banerjee, who had been part of the Young Bengal movement and had taught at Calcutta University, had stated that many an Indian male, though "desirous in the abstract", would be unwilling to educate his wife and daughters because "female improvement would materially increase their expense". Such women would "disrelish the drudgery of the house" and hence more servants and handmaids would have to be employed![15] But this statement was made in the 1880s and things had changed considerably by the second decade of the 20th century. For, as will be evident in

12. Ibid.
13. Ibid., Document No.80: 376-77.
14. Ibid.: 377.
15. Ibid.: xxiii.

this study, in the sphere of women's education, there was no stasis. Rather, the speed at which changes occurred and mind-sets altered was almost unbelievable.

Another excuse trotted out frequently was the paucity of women teachers. The inspectress of schools in the UP observed:

> ...the difficulty in establishing a school is not to fill it with children, but to supply the staff; given a good teacher the children will come and the parents will not object.[16]

But what was the definition of a "good teacher"? Here, there was apparently a peculiar problem. Parents were said to prefer married women as teachers for their wards. Unmarried women or widows were not very favourably looked upon as an ideal choice for a teacher. But married women who had received some sort of teacher training were few and far between. Even these exceptional individuals were often unable to overcome family disapproval and step out of their homes to earn a livelihood. Society was, at that time, still unwilling to accept the idea of a working woman. (Of course, this also meant that those few women who were in a position to come out and work as schoolteachers had a better bargaining position and could actually earn a better salary than their male counterparts!)

All this was to change rapidly in the opening decades of the 20th century, when more and more women came forward for teacher training and some institutions preferred to have unmarried women as teachers because they believed that such women would be more dedicated to their work. Thus, the IT College in Lucknow, for instance, had a rule that only unmarried women could teach in the institution. As soon as they decided to get married, they had to resign their job.

It was also felt that setting up a school for girls was economically unviable since the number of girls who would be able to come to the school was extremely small. Was it then worthwhile to incur the cost of acquiring land, constructing a building, employing teachers—all for the sake of a handful of students? Quite often the answer would be "no" and for a cash-strapped government this kind of a negative answer came all the more easily. In 1915, a memorial on women's education

---

16. Quoted in Henry Sharp's report, Ibid.: 378.

was submitted to the secretary of state, pointing to the enormous disparity in the number of girls and boys under instruction in British India and asking for "every possible facility for the training of Hindu, Muhammadan, and Buddhist women teachers and inspectresses." The reply of Austen Chamberlain, secretary of state, was typical:

> The times are not propitious, either in India or here, for a great additional outlay or for large new schemes; nor do I think that the moment of a great war in which the Empire itself is at stake and that British rule in India or here stands for is threatened—I do not think that such a moment is the best to choose for a calm and careful study of a vast problem of this kind.[17]

It is not surprising then that whatever schools for girls did exist came largely through private endeavour. Often setting up such a school also meant establishing a hostel, especially if the distance between home and school was considerable. If it was not, escorts would have to be provided for the journey to the school and back. Besides all these, often freeships had to be provided as an incentive to parents to send their daughters to school.[18] All these compounded the overhead costs considerably.

Some of Munshi Premchand's stories dwell upon the predicament of idealistic, public-spirited men who tried to set up schools for girls. In *Rahasya*, for instance, we have Vimal Prakash, who set up Sevashram, a school for poor girls in Benares. He was constantly struggling for funds to keep the school going. The year was not half over and the ashram already owed ₹12,000. This would rise to ₹20,000 by the time the year had ended. What was he to do? If he raised the fees by one rupee per month, the ashram's income would increase by ₹500. And if each girl's fee for the hostel were raised by ₹2, that would bring in another ₹500. But then what would happen to his grand scheme of giving education to girls of poor families? As Vimal Prakash saw it, the only solution was to find women teachers

17. Ibid.: 389-97.

18. Chanana *op. cit.* no. 2: 105.

who would share the same idealism and be willing to work for nothing more than their room and board.[19]

Another option was to have co-educational institutions and this was also tried. Co-education, it was found, would work at primary level but most parents were unwilling to send their daughters to study alongside boys once they had attained puberty.[20] However, the pattern varied from region to region. Punjab had one of the lowest figures of girls enrolled in co-educational schools. From 5.4 per cent in 1922, it went up to 8.1 per cent in 1927, 11.2 per cent in 1932 and 10.7 per cent in 1937. The UP figures were higher, but by and large remained static: 36.7 per cent in 1922, 33.3 per cent in 1927, 35.8 per cent in 1932 and 38.7 per cent in 1937.[21] By 1930, almost all the provinces were in favour of introducing co-education at primary level, separate schools at the secondary stage and again reintroducing co-education in the universities.[22]

Against All Odds: Revolution in Women's Education

Despite all these drawbacks, by the 1920s in a tentative way and in the 1930s with greater conviction, there was a revolution taking place in the sphere of women's education. No longer were schools anxiously waiting for pupils. Instead, it was the other way around. Girls were flocking to schools and colleges and the existing institutions were finding themselves unable to cope with this rising demand. The statistics testify to this. According to the 1921 Census, while increase in the number of literate males during the decade had been 16 per cent, that in the number of literate females was 71 per cent.[23] In the 1931 Census, the increase in female literacy was put

19. Adapted from Rubin, David (1998). *Widows, Wives and other Heroines: Twelve Stories by Premchand (Translated)*. Delhi. pp.19-20.

20. Even as late as in 1946, the Minister of Education in the U.P., Dr Sampurnanand, referred to this as being a very real problem to reckon with. UP Legislative Assembly Debates, 26 July 1946, Discussion on the Budget 1946-47, Discussion on Demands for Grants for Education, p.569.

21. Cited by Chanana *op. cit.* no. 2: 115.

22. Ibid.: 116.

23. *Census of India, 1921*, Vol.1, Part 1, p.179.

at 50 per cent, but the figures in the 1941 Census were staggering. There was a 150 per cent increase in female literacy! The most remarkable region in this respect was Punjab, where there was an overall increase in literacy of 140 per cent, with 110 per cent increase for males and 390 per cent for females! The UP figures were much less impressive—80 per cent overall, 70 per cent for males and 170 per cent for females.[24] Quite clearly, these were the decades of women's education, part of the impetus for which came from the growing participation of women in the national movement.

Anybody who studies the participation of women in the national movement, as this author has, would be struck by the fact that the thirst for education and involvement in the nationalist struggle often went hand in hand. Margaret Cousins, the Irish Suffragete leader who spent some time in India, observed in her book *Indian Womanhood Today:*

> Education is a liberating influence of the greatest importance. A trained and well-furnished mind gives its owner self-confidence, discrimination...and independence...Ignorance is weakness, knowledge is power.[25]

One of the favourite pastimes of women who had been arrested for their political activities was to learn to read and write. In the case of those who were already literate, the jail period was an ideal one to pursue their studies and some even went ahead to take their degree examinations while behind bars.[26] Durga Devi Vohra, whom we referred to at the beginning of this article, was married to Bhagwati Charan Vohra, the well-known revolutionary. As the wife of someone who was always on the move, evading the police, she led a very unsettled life. Yet, she was able to pick up the threads of her schooling and even became a schoolteacher in Lahore in the late 1920s. In 1939, nine years after the death of her husband, she went

---

24. *Census of India, 1931,* Vol.1, Part 1, p.328 and Census of India, 1941, Vol.1, p.31.
25. Cousins, E. (1947). "Margaret", *Indian Womanhood Today.* Allahabad. Revised Edition. p.51.
26. Thus Purnima Banerji, a U.P. Congresswoman, took her BA degree while in jail. For more information, see Menon, Visalakshi (2003). *Indian Women and Nationalism.* New Delhi. p.154.

to Madras and obtained training in the Montessori system, following which she set up the Lucknow Montessori School in 1940.[27]

A case for educating women was also very powerfully made through women's journals that were brought out during this period. By way of example, let us look at some of the writings in Stree Darpan, a women's journal published from Allahabad by Rameshwari Nehru in early decades of the 20th century. The 1 March 1919, issue carried a poem titled *Sachhi Holi*, in which women were exhorted to celebrate Holi with a difference. One of the stanzas ran as follows:

Vidya ka aabhushan pehno, seva maang bharo ri
Deshbhakti ki sari odho, phir bharat gaan karo ri[28]

Most of the women's journals of the period gave prominence to the issue of women's education in their editorials. Special articles and short stories on this theme would also be frequently carried.

Conservative India also Strove for Women's Education

What is significant is that the campaign for women's education was noticeable not just in cities like Allahabad, which was considered progressive and liberal, but also in the more conservative Lucknow, Aligarh and Benares. In Benares, the first move had been made by Annie Besant in 1904, when she started the Central Hindu Girls' School, following upon her earlier success in setting up the Central Hindu College for Boys in 1898. This would have served as a model for subsequent efforts by others, and those, interestingly, were on a community basis. The Agarwal Samaj, founded in 1896, set up a Kanya Pathshala in 1918. It ran for many years "with half a dozen girls, one teacher and no building."[29] There was also the Arya Mahila School, set up in Benares in 1926 by Vidya Devi, a widow from Bihar, who had a remarkable ability to raise funds. Begun initially as a primary school, it was recognised as a high school six years later.[30]

27. Oral History Transcript of Durga Devi Vohra, Nehru Memorial Museum and Library.
28. *Stree Darpan*, 1 March 1919, p.119.
29. Kumar, Nita (1994). "Oranges for the Girls, or the Half-Known Story of the Education of Girls in Twentieth-Century Banaras", in Nita Kumar (ed.), *Women as Subjects*. Calcutta. p.214.
30. Ibid.: 220.

A third institution was the Durga Charan Girls' School, founded by Krishnabhamini, a widow of means, with the purpose of providing free education for Bengali widows. By 1931, it had become the Anglo-Bengali Lower Middle Girls' School and was probably more nationalistically inclined that the other two schools.[31]

Gradually, a distinction between girls' schools, which were loyalist, stoutly resisting political involvement, and those nationalistically inclined was beginning to emerge. The Crosthwaite Girls School, for instance, with its "large compound enclosed on all the four sides by high walls", where "strict purdah is and can be observed" and where all the teachers were "ladies", was nevertheless "uncompromisingly nationalistic".[32] At the time of the Civil Disobedience Movement of the 1930s, Uma Nehru, a fiery participant in the boycott of foreign cloth and the manufacture of salt, was a member of the managing committee of the Crosthwaite School. She had offered her resignation to the committee but it was not accepted. Consequently, the UP government decided to stop its grants to the school and the very existence of the institution was in danger.[33] Appeals were made to public-spirited individuals to keep the institution going. On the other hand, the other well-known girls' school in the city, St. Mary's was clearly on the side of the British government. But it is likely that the students of this institution, as with several others of its kind, had been affected by the prevailing nationalist spirit and defied the authorities or tried to subvert the restrictions in an interesting variety of ways! The most common gesture was silence when the English national anthem was being sung.

In the 1920s, Benares Hindu University had established a Women's College with a separate hostel in which a hundred women students could reside. The University acted as a magnet, drawing

31. Ibid.: 224.

32. Schomer, Karine (1983). *Mahadevi Varma and the Chayavad Age of Modern Hindi Poetry.* California. p.170.

33. *The Leader,* 28 September 1930, p.7.

women teachers as well as students from neighbouring provinces as well.[34]

The 1941 Census recorded that while there was an overall increase of 80 per cent in literacy for the decade in the UP, female literacy accounted for a 170 per cent increase.[35] The story of the Prayag Mahila Vidyapith, which went a long way in filling the gap, bears recounting here. Set up in the 1920s by Babu Sangam Lal Agarwal, a public-spirited Allahabad lawyer, the institution was originally intended only as an examining institution. Those who had passed the vernacular lower-middle examination could pursue higher studies through this institution, which had a prescribed syllabus for each level. The Vidyapith could confer degrees corresponding to the Middle School Leaving Certificate, the High School Matriculation, the BA and the MA, and these degrees were known as the *Praveshika*, the *Vidya Vinodini*, the *Vidushi* and the *Saraswati*, respectively. Until 1937, these degrees had no official recognition but thereafter, under the popularly elected Congress ministries, recognition was accorded. What was amazing was the overwhelming response to the Vidyapith's examinations. Students took the examination not just from the UP, but all the neighbouring provinces as well as from southern India. From 1932, to make the system more efficient, the Vidyapith became a teaching institution, even providing hostel accommodation for students. It flourished under the able guidance of Mahadevi Varma, who was its principal for several years.[36]

And yet the UP was considered to be more backward in this respect than Punjab, where, largely due to Arya Samaj efforts, the ground had been better prepared. We have the story of Lado Rani Zutshi, wife of a cousin of Jawaharlal Nehru, who chose to leave her husband's home in Allahabad in 1917 and return to Lahore, so that her three daughters could have a better education, much to the consternation of her husband who opposed her. Undeterred, she then went to Motilal Nehru, who was the uncle of her husband—the

34. Sundaram, V.A. (ed.) (1936). *Benares Hindu University 1905-1935*. Benares. p.474.

35. *Census of India, 1941*, Vol.1, p.31.

36. Schomer *op. cit.* no. 32: 221.

same Motilal Nehru who was indifferent to the education of his own daughters. Interestingly enough, he told her to go ahead and take the girls to Lahore. One of the daughters, who went on to study at the Government College, Lahore, has given us a rather vivid description of what it was like to be a girl student in college in those days, when there were very few girls in colleges:

> There was no common room for the girls and since co-education was in its beginning, we were very careful not to mix with the boys. We just tagged ourselves on to the lecturers, sitting in their room and when the lecturer went to the class-room, we walked behind him and when he came out, we walked out. We never used libraries. We never participated in any of the students' activities.[37]

Notwithstanding all this, Manmohini went on to become the first woman president of the Lahore Students' Union! In the meantime, her elder sister had become a lecturer at the same college. In 1930, when Manmohini Sehgal and her younger sister wanted to go for a meeting near the banks of the Ravi river for breaking the Salt Law, the elder sister was angry with them. It was examination time and she felt that they should be studying instead of attending political meetings. Manmohini's reply to her sister was: "Look here, if we fail we will appear next year, but what we will see today, breaking of Salt Law and launching of the movement, we will never see in the rest of our lives."[38]

Lahore was where Hajra Begum and her five sisters, including the irrepressible Zohra Sehgal, were sent for education in the 1920s. They belonged to the princely state of Rampur but their father had moved to Saharanpur, where he was a *tahsildar*. The girls went to the Queen Mary's College school in Lahore, a boarding school where they mingled with the daughters of well-known political figures like Liaqat Ali Khan and Sikandar Hayat Khan. She recalls that it was "a purdah school", where no boys were allowed to enter. "We were not allowed to mix with boys or young men. But the day-scholars who came would

---

37. Sehgal, Manmohini (n.d.). *Oral History Transcript*. NMML. p.8.

38. Ibid.: 18.

"secretly tell us what was happening outside in the bazaar." Those were the days of the Khilafat Movement and they sang songs like:

> Charkha kaato to beda paar hai
> Charkha Swadeshi Talwar hai
> and
> Boliye Ma Mohammad Ali ki,
> Jaan Beta Khilafat Mein De Do.[39]

The Content of Girls' Education

While by the beginning of the 20th century there was a growing consensus on the need to educate girls, some questioning of the received wisdom on what subjects a girl should be taught in school was also beginning to take place. The generally accepted norm was to have a separate curriculum for girls, with emphasis on the development of household skills such as hygiene and domestic economy, child-rearing, cooking and sewing, with painting and music thrown in for good measure.[40] Sometimes there would be instruction in Puranic and other religious literature as well. Subjects like geography and natural sciences were considered beyond the level of comprehension of the average girl student and were therefore to be soft-pedalled. The evidence submitted by the Lahore Arya Samaj before the Indian Education Commission in 1882 may be cited to illustrate the prevalent attitudes:

> That they should not be made to swallow history and geography indiscriminately. The bare principles of the geography of India, and a little detailed information of that of the Punjab, together with a general knowledge of the geography of the world, will be sufficient for all purposes. Under the subject of history, an elementary history of the Punjab and India will answer all their objects. Big books containing detailed lists of the names of kings and battles, and of lakes and capes, are not only unsavoury to them but perfectly useless.[41]

39. Begum, Hajra (n.d.). *Oral History Transcript*. NMML. pp. 9-10.
40. The Indian Education Commission of 1882, perhaps giving in to local pressure, recommended a differentiated curriculum for boys and girls.
41. Cited in Bhattacharya *op. cit.* no. 11: 86-87

But by the 1930s, women educationists and others were speaking out against this stereotyping. Hannah Sen, the first principal of the Lady Irwin College for Women in Delhi, wrote around 1937 in an article titled "Education for Women and Girls":

> It seems paradoxical that while the progress of higher education has reduced the inevitability of marriage as the only career for women, greater stress is being laid on the study of domestic subjects. The present attitude is but a reaffirmation of the age-old principle that, whether women marry or follow other pursuits, on them will devolve the main task of managing the home, at least for decades to come.[42]

Ironically though, the institution she headed was itself dedicated to the teaching of home science.

Rameshwari Nehru, wife of a cousin of Jawaharlal Nehru and who had worked closely with Mahatma Gandhi, emphasised that the objective of education should not be just the creation of a good wife or good mother. Education should help a woman to evolve as a good human being and good citizen. It was important that girls should be equipped to earn a livelihood as well and should therefore be given the same kind of education as boys.[43]

Curiously, F. McDougall, principal of the Women's Christian College, Madras, had, as early as in 1917, articulated some of these ideas forcefully. She urged the need for a thorough mental training for women beyond the idea of "a good wife and mother", and insisted on an agency for women in deciding what the content of their education should be: "Education will not make much progress if a woman is to be confined to such learning as the men of her locality think suitable for her."[44] In fact, as has been shown by Meena Bhargava and Kalyani Dutta in their work on Delhi's Indraprastha College, there was an active debate on the curriculum for girls in the Madras Presidency at this time. Despite this area being very progressive in these matters, when it came to implementation, the tendency was to fall back on the

42. Nehru, Shyam Kumari (ed.) (n.d.). *Our Cause: A Symposium.*

43. Speech at Kanya Gurukul, Dehradun in 1939 and at the RSD College in Ferozepur, Rameshwari Nehru Papers, NMML, S.No.4, pp.2-5, 32-33.

44. Bhattacharya *op. cit.* no. 11: xxiv.

more conservative position. Hence, when the government set up an intermediate college for women, it could choose only from the arts courses for their optional papers, the reason given being that science subjects were more difficult for girls.[45]

The Indraprastha College for Women was, however, more liberal in its approach. From the very beginning, it offered a more "radical mix of subjects". While there was no getting away from needlework, health, hygiene, domestic science fare, equal stress was laid on history, mathematics and science. Economics was added as a subject in 1928 and philosophy a few years later.[46] Slowly, the mindset was changing. Girl students were going on to higher education and in the MA and MSc classes of the Universities of Allahabad and Lucknow, a few girl students could be found by the 1930s. Their numbers increased by the 1940s and they also figured on the merit lists, which were duly published in the leading newspapers of the period.[47]

All this is not to say that large sections of women had access to education even by the 1940s. The fact that schools for girls were still largely an urban phenomenon and that the rural population had practically no access to even the barest level of literacy was realised by many of the women nationalists of the time. This was why the Kasturba Memorial Trust, set up in memory of Mahatma Gandhi's wife who had passed away in February 1944, and headed by Sucheta Kripalani, devoted itself to training women for teaching in rural areas.[48] It held training courses for women, usually of one year's duration. Those "with an aptitude for village works" and with a knowledge of reading and writing at least up to the primary standard, could enrol for these camps. After training, they would be paid salaries ranging from ₹30 upwards to go and teach in the villages.

---

45. *Women, Education and Politics: The Women's Movement and Delhi's Indraprastha College*. New Delhi. 2005. p.47.

46. Ibid.: 48.

47. The Lucknow University MA results for 1946, published in the National Herald, revealed that girls were doing reasonable well. To take the MA English results for instance: while Deoki Devi Pande, had secured the 2nd position, 3 out of 10 who had obtained 2nd division were girls and so were 4 out of the 34 in the 3rd division. National Herald, 18 May 1946, p.3.

48. *National Herald*, 17 October 1946, p.2.

Apparently, there was a good response to these programmes. The women of Northern India had come a long way indeed! No longer was unwillingness of women to come forward as teachers an impediment to setting up schools for girls.

Conclusion

This article traces the course of women's education in one of the most backward parts of the country. The story is all the more remarkable because of this handicap. The role of pioneering figures like Annie Besant, Lala Jugal Kishore or even the widows of Benares is undoubtedly of great significance. They provided the initial impetus, which set the process of women's education in motion. As the 20th century unfolded and the nationalist movement entered the phase of mass politics, the campaign for educating women dovetailed into the anti-imperialist struggle. What we have suggested is that this factor gave the educational effort greater urgency. It also provided opportunities for women to educate themselves in the most unconventional of ways. However, the issue of the curriculum for girls remained an unresolved one. There was a division of opinion on whether there should be a separate curriculum for girls or whether they should be allowed to study the more difficult subjects that were considered to be more suitable for boys was hotly debated. This dispute was part of a larger debate about the role that women were to play in the public arena.

5

R. VENKATARAMANUJAM

Religion and Empire in India

Introduction

The paper is an attempt to explore the approaches of three empires towards religion in India. Broadly it deals with the Portuguese, the Dutch and the British. Their approaches towards religion and missionary activities varied in accordance with their domestic experiences and their relative position in the colony.

The missionaries themselves had reached the shores of India even before the colonial empires arrived. The earliest reference to missionary activity is to the Syrian Christians, who claimed to have been converted by St. Thomas in the 1st century AD. Further to that, we have the Catholic missions established in Madura, to which Beschi and other popular missionaries belonged.

Portuguese Empire and Religion

In 1498, Vasco da Gama reached India and discovered a sea route to India from Europe. The discovery laid the foundation for establishment of the Portuguese empire. Under Albuquerque, Goa became the headquarters of the Portuguese settlements in India and the east.

According to K.M. Panikkar, the first 50 years of the Portuguese were able to maintain themselves with little or no military power because of their friendly relations with the Hindu empire of Vijayanagar, both of which looked at Muslims as the common enemy.[1] Missionary activities were rather moderate in the early years.

---

1. Panikkar, K.M. (1959). *Asia and Western Dominance: A Survey of Vasco da Gama Epoch of Asian History, 1498-1945*. Kuala Lumpur: Malaysia: The Other Press. p.43.

There was a distinct lack of force or coercion. They adopted methods that would entice the natives to the new religion for benefits and accommodation rather than enforcing their religion forcefully as would happen later. The adoption of orphans, accommodating the interests of the natives by including traditional customs, providing jobs, etc., were strategies adopted by the Portuguese rulers in the early phase of their colonial experience in India. Co-option was the order of the day.

The moderate phase soon gave way to an aggressive one which was to characterise the nature of the Portuguese colonial state in India for the most part of their years of occupation in India. The period witnessed the destruction of temples, mosques and other places of worship. Conversions by force took place. A number of laws aimed at the Hindus in general and the upper caste *gauncars* in particular were enacted. To add to these, the threat of inquisition was also used as a tool. As a result, about 800 people fell victim to the Inquisition during the period 1600 to 1773.

> In one of his letters, Albuquerque wrote to the King of Portugal, 'I leave no town or building of the Mussalmans. Those who are taken alive I order them to be roasted...' All the Hindu temples on the island of Goa were demolished by 1540. In 1560, the year the Inquisition was set up, 13092 Hindus were forcibly converted. In 1578, the Paulist group of missionaries pulled down 350 temples and converted 100,000 people.[2]

This aggressive attitude and approach fizzled out by 1700s. It was more or less a lukewarm phase. By this time, no important large-scale conversions took place in the newly acquired territories.

The answer to the Portuguese approach to religion in India could be traced to its own experience at home in Europe. It was deeply involved in the crusades against the Muslim 'infidels.' The period also witnessed Counter Reformation in the Catholic Church. Portugal was a strong Catholic country and Counter Reformation activities were intensified, especially in the use of the Inquisition. The Inquisition was used to exterminate hundreds of those accused of heresy.

---

2. Rao, R.P. (1963). *Portuguese Rule in Goa, 1510-1961.*Bombay: Asia Publishing House. p.44

The nature of the Portuguese colonial state was the product of its experiences at home where it encountered the Muslims with crusades and heresy with Counter Reformation and inquisition and the condition of the colony where the ruling classes were the Muslims who were their traditional enemies. Religion was used as a tool for colonial domination by the Portuguese. It used a combination of accommodation and force towards conversion. It accommodated Hindu interests by allowing the incorporation of local customs into Christianity. A good example is the caste system. On the other hand, the Muslims were crushed ruthlessly. Ruthless suppression was the norm in cases of rebellion. A significant example of ruthless suppression was the way the revolt in Cuncolim Village was suppressed in 1583. According to R.P. Rao, "From the time of Albuquerque religion was the main instrument of Portuguese domination, except perhaps for a short period after the proclamation of the new republic in 1910."[3]

Further, even by design the Portuguese colonial state in India was a missionary state. The archbishop enjoyed powers rivalling those of the viceroy. There are several instances when archbishops had been named viceroy.

> For the Portuguese viewed themselves as a mercantile and maritime empire cast in a military and ecclesiastical mould. Every male Portuguese who went out to the East did so in the service of the Crown or that of the Church. [Religious] 'mission' was never different from mercantilism, or conversion from commerce. Missionary activity under the Portuguese must be seen as being linked very closely to the establishment of military and political rule in Goa and in other regions taken over by them.[4]

Danish-Halle Mission

The Danish people had a small settlement in Tranquebar, in present-day Tamilnadu. It was close to Thanjavur, under the control of the Marathas. The Danish king, driven by missionary

3. Ibid.
4. Robinson and Clarke, 2003.

zeal, wanted to send missionaries to Tranquebar and recruited two German missionaries trained in pietism. Those two young men—Bartholamous Ziegenbalg and Henri Plutschau—were the pioneering protestant missionaries to India. They arrived in India much before the celebrated protestant missionary William Carey. The Danish king's missionary zeal was neither shared by his subjects nor by his viceroy in Tranquebar. The young missionaries were made to stand the whole day on the beach of Tranquebar before given entry into the colony. On a different occasion, Ziegenbalg was even imprisoned. All the events point to the dislike of the colonial government for activities of the missionaries, who were looked upon as rivals to their power.

Ziegenbalg's method was in sharp contrast to that of the Portuguese. He stressed a proper understanding of the local language and literature, and Hinduism. His understanding of the local language and religion could be to a great extent understood from his book *Malabarican Heathenism*. It is to the credit of Ziegenbalg that he did not engage in a mindless ridicule of the native practices and religion. In fact, his mastery of the Tamil language and literature enabled him to concede that, "God had shown some light in this part of the world even before the missionaries arrived as an appreciation of local ethics and practice." Ziegenbalg's missionary efforts leaned on informed and learned debates with the scholars and custodians of native faith. He also believed that education was an effective tool towards changing the heart of the people.

In this case, the Danish state was weak. Missionary zeal was a wistful thinking of the state. It was more of an individual effort without backing of the colonial authorities of Tranquebar. This probably accounts for the more ideological approach to missionary activity rather than force or accommodation. In fact, the missionaries of the Danish-Halle mission engaged the native rulers, *viz.*, the Marathas of Thanjavur. One of the missionaries, Schwartz, was the celebrated teacher of Serfoji II.

British Colonial State and Religion

The British followed an official policy of religious neutrality until 1813. There was a ban on missionary activities in British India. Further, during this period, the Orientalists were dominant and the influential William Jones established the Asiatic Society of India and he, along with H.H. Wilson and others, translated a number of Sanskrit works like *Mahabharata, Bhagvad Gita* and *Abhijnanashakuntalam*.

The English East India Company, which took over the administration of India, soon began to don the role of a successor to the Indian states. It brought large-scale modification and changes in revenue administration. However, it kept up the pretence of the Mughal sovereign alive. With regard to religion and society, it allowed the pre-existing state to continue. That the East India Company became a successor state is evident from numerous instances when Indian religious disputes were brought before the Company authorities for resolution. Of the numerous instances, one such case was the Vadakalai and Tenkalai conflict in Triplicane, Chennai. The contending parties approached the East India Company for peaceful settlement.

Another case is when Lionel Place, collector of Madras, took an active interest in functioning of the temples.

> It is said that he went so far as to present offerings at the shrines of the idols, and to this day the Brahmans exhibit what they describe as the votive gifts of the good collector. His representations to the government were successful; and in 1796 the temples were placed under his charge, and he undertook willingly enough, the due appropriation of what he called the 'Church Funds'.[5]

During the early period of the colonial era, the Company gave precedence to trade over religion. They were more interested in extracting revenue rather than imposing the Christian faith or bringing about social changes in the light of utilitarian developments at home. In fact, temples, mosques and religious institutions were

5. Kaye, John William (Sir) (1859). *Christianity in India: An Historical Narrative.* London: Smith, Elder & Co. p.381.

looked upon as an important source of income. When the Board of Revenue was created, those religious institutions were brought under its control. Temples, in particular, were huge sources of revenue. Hence, they wanted to maintain the existing socio-religious set-up and supplanted themselves as a successor state to native rule to continue to enjoy the revenue from temples and religious institutions. Consequently, they assumed responsibility for the repair and general maintenance of temples and mosques, etc.

In the words of R. Suntharalingam:

> The early policies of the British in south India did not directly impinge on the fabric of religious and social life of the Hindus. By proclaiming at the outset the policy of religious neutrality, the Company's officials gave cover to all established faiths in India, even to the extent of tolerating some archaic social usages. Obstacles that lay in the way of the free exercise of religious and cultural activities were largely removed. To an extent, the British even usurped the role of earlier Indian regimes by assuming supervision of Indian religious institutions and by keeping a tight rein on the entry and free movement of Christian missionaries.[6]

The control of the colonial regime over temples and religious institutions was strengthened through legislation. The earliest of the legislation in this regard were the Bengal Regulation XIX, 1810 and Madras Regulation VII, 1817.

> From 1817 onwards, consequently, the Government of Madras took direct responsibility for the daily exercises of 'Hinduism'. All ceremonies being conducted within all the temples under its sway... came under direct management of the imperial state. Not only did the state take control over the revenues and supervise temple repairs; but also enforced entrenched local customs and practices in which it otherwise have never been involved.

The period saw the growing influence of the Utilitarians and the missionaries in England. The missionaries attacked the colonial government in India for patronising heathen religion

---

6. Suntharalingam, R. (1974). *Politics and National Awakening in South India, 1852-91*. US: Association for Asian Studies, University of Arizona Press. p.32.

and its institutions. They accused the colonial government of supporting idolatry and other heathen practices. At about the same time, the English East India Company was greatly under the influence of Charles Grant and William Wilberforce. They argued for discontinuance of English support for the heathen religion and practices, and for the entry of missionaries into British India.

> The public debated around charter renewal, much of it generated by missionary publicists, worked to focus public attention on spectacular examples of 'barbarism' in India. Now when scandal was associated with India, it was attached to Indian customs rather than British activities. Indeed, India became a land of scandal in an entirely new way, with scandal now a feature of generic Indian custom rather than personal English excess. Under new missionary pressure, it became a scandal that the Company allowed the continuation in British territory of the barbaric practices of sati (widow burning) or thugee (highway robbery and murder with cultic overtones) or ritual such as 'hookswinging' (a form of devotion involving hooks embedded in the back).[7]

As a result of that crusade against promoting Indian religious institutions, the colonial government disengaged itself from such activities between 1833 and 1867. All the temples were handed back to the natives.

Lord William Bentinck, under utilitarian influence, introduced a number of reforms affecting native socio-religious practices. His key reforms included abolishing *sati* and female infanticide, and suppressing human sacrifice, particularly in Orissa, where wild tribes performed human sacrifices to please their gods and goddesses. He not only brought about many reforms but also introduced English as a medium of instruction in 1835.

These bits of legislations were supported by the progressive section of Indian society. However, the bulk of Indian society viewed it as attempts to modify local practices in the mould of English and Christian practices. Some acts were vehemently contested. One such law was the Lex Loci Draft Act. According to the Act, a person

7. Dirks, Nicholas B. (2008). *The Scandal of Empire: India and the Creation of Imperial Britain*. USA: Harvard Universtiy Press. p.23.

converted to Christianity would still retain the right to ancestral property. This was considered to be a way of promoting Christianity and interfering in Indian religious practices. As a result of the opposition, the controversial clauses were removed. However, a few years later, another law incorporating the controversial clauses of the Lex Loci Draft Act was passed as the Caste Disabilities Removal Act of 1850.[8]

Missionary activities increased by the middle of the 19th century. It led to an inevitable confrontation with the local community. Communal clashes resulted as a consequence of the activities of the missionaries. In November 1845, communal clashes took place in Tirunelveli in Tamilnadu. Official support became evident when about 100 Hindus were charged by the local police and convicted by the local court. However, there was also the rule of law. On special appeal to the Sadr court, many of those convicted in the local court were acquitted. The then Governor of the Madras Presidency, Tweeddale, called for the record and eventually dismissed a judge.[9]

Those problems and the doctrine of lapse, adopted by Lord Dalhousie, which again interfered in Indian socio-religious and political practices, eventually led to the 1857 revolt. The revolt led to the change of administration when the British Crown directly took over from the English East India Company.

The warnings of the 1857 revolt were sufficient for the British Raj to take a relook at the question of religious issues, particularly activities of the missionaries. While missionaries continued to operate, the officialdom distanced itself from such activities. Further, with the British Crown taking over the mantle of administration, it was resolved that the Indian subjects would be treated on a par with British subjects. The Queen's Proclamation of 1858 expressly mentioned that there would be no imposition of the Christian faith on the Indian subjects.

However in practice, there were ways in which missionary activities continued. An effective tool in this regard had been

8. Suntharalingam *op. cit.* no. 5: 40-41.

9. Ibid.: 43.

provided by Bentinck in the form of education. Missionaries used education as an instrument of both proselytisation and colonial subjugation.

The curriculum framework was designed to promote the Christian faith. Especially, English literature and the writing of the likes of William Shakespeare were used to inculcate the Christian faith and principles. According to Andrew Porter,

> Most missionaries had devised as system which incorporated Christian instruction while avoiding the appearance of directly imposing Christian belief on their pupils and they had learned to live with the occasional exodus of pupils to the 'secular' private or government schools in reaction against religious offence. Both missions and government found they could accommodate the sporadic public protests sparked off by occasional conversion.[10]

The British also continued to legislate on religious institutions in a bid to bring them under their control, for laws bestowed legitimacy on them as well as brought revenue. Some of the legislation that brought the temples and religious institutions firmly under their control were the Act XX of 1867 and Madras Hindu Religious Endowment Act of 1927. Consequently, they established the Hindu Religious Endowments Board.

Conclusion

Unlike the Portuguese empire, which relied more on force, or the Danish, under which independent intellectual efforts were made to counter the Indian religious and social practices, the British colonial state effectively used education and legislation to exercise control over Indian religious and social practices, while at the same time promoted the cultural superiority of English culture and the Christian religion. At the same time, the British colonial state was successful in masking the real intentions with a veneer of the English sense of justice and fair play, and religious tolerance. It is also significant that despite the colonial project, when it came to extracting the resources

10. Porter, Andrew (2004). *Religion versus Empire? British Protestant Missionaries and Overseas Expansion, 1700-1914*. UK: Manchester University Press. p.177.

in temples and religious institutions, it distanced itself from the missionaries. However, the distance was more than bridged by the missionaries' control of education.

6

ALOK BAJPAI

Science in Colonial India
An Overview with Some Reflections

Introduction

Before embarking upon the subject, we need to comment on the science-technology (hereafter ST) paradigm in the context of history. Science and scientific knowledge is simply more than technology-related activities. Science, or scientific temperament, connotes scientific knowledge, urge and distinct methodology for deriving truths with capital 'T', i.e. unveiling the mysteries of universe and nature including life. The spread and propagation of science in all walks of life is a modern phenomenon and is chiefly responsible for the advancement of rational society. Science has a universal character and appeal. Technology is the application of some bits of scientific knowledge and is intricately related to materialistic interests of the holders of that particular technology. Obviously technology is not without value and it has concrete socio-cultural political dimensions. Deepak Kumar, a distinguished historian of the subject, reflects on this complex historical situation in colonial India in these words:

> Technology—whether as tool or form of knowledge is not value-free; it always manifests political qualities. In colonial conditions, it naturally acquired the contours of the colonial power, both commercial and administrative. Technical change in colonial India was mostly effected as a by-product of economic activities. Conscious innovation in order to bring about a new combination of processes or products was a rarity.[1]

1. Kumar, Deepak (2000). "Science and Society in Colonial India: Exploring an Agenda", Sectional President's address, Indian History Congress, 1999, Calicut Session, in *Proceedings of the Indian History Congress.* p.442. For full address see pp.434-55.

Often these two salient features of modernity function interdependently but these are very distinct in their orientation and purpose in a colonial society and context.[2]

Background

The establishment of British rule in India was not a smooth or peaceful transfer of power from native rulers to the East India Company. It involved many long battles and violent struggles. Of course, on the political front, the main actors were the East India Company and other European companies and native rulers; but on popular fronts also, there were rebellions, uprisings and continuous violent struggles. Ultimately the East India Company emerged the winner, and this culminated in establishment of the British empire.

The nature, methods and motives of the British were different from their predecessors. Unlike the Mughals or other regional native rulers, India remained foreign to the British.[3] The British (as the ruling class) kept themselves aloof. Simultaneously, their main objective was to rule India perpetually. So, they made every effort to transform India into a viable colony, because until India professed certain dominant features of a colonial economy and society, it was almost impossible to keep hold over such a vast land. To meet this end, the British gradually introduced an exhaustive political-administrative structure whose primary concern was to facilitate and safeguard the colonial interests of the empire. This

2. The Indian national movement dealt with this complex and peculiar situation with a lot of maturity and promise. On the one hand, it opted for a modern scientific society and fought against colonial rule; on the other, it remained cautious about a blind adaptation of technological lures created by colonial structures.

3. R.C. Dutt, one of the first intellectual giants in the world to authoritatively analyse the mechanism of colonial structures, with reference to India wrote about the basic difference between British rule and pre-British rule in simple language. "But a change came over India under the role of the East India Company. They considered India as a vast estate or plantation, the profits of which were to be withdrawn from India and deposited in Europe." in Dutt, R.C. (2006). "Preface", in *The Economic History of India*. Vol. I. First published 1901. New Delhi: Publication Division.

colonial structure was semi-hegemonic and semi-authoritarian in orientation and functioning.

Related to this colonial need for hegemony was the Pax-Britannica rhetoric, whose main logic was that British rule was for the benefit of the Indians. The basic component of this "civilising mission" was the "modernisation promise" to colonial India. By this rhetoric, it was easy for colonialism to hide its real face. The prime concern or "common sense" of British conquest in India was profit. The role of ST in empire building was well recognised by the British because it was one of the main tools for getting sanction for domination.[4] Ultimately it was the modern ST paradigm that gave moral legitimacy to colonialism.[5] So in this historical background, ST drives got activated in colonial India.[6] Thus emerged the phenomenon of "colonial science" or science in colonial India.[7]

Genesis and Causation

From the mid-18th century, the East India Company gradually got control of small territories in coastal areas. With it emerged a crucial need and demand to know the geography, geology, botany, natural resources and native people's culture. As the territories and control over colonial land increased, more scientific knowledge was thought to be necessary and this got reflected in ST-related interventions.

4. Kumar *op. cit.* no. 1: 442.

5. From hindsight, we can say that British officials and colonial policy makers were well equipped with the emerging modern science technology paradigm and they applied it to consolidate the colonial empire.

6. Here it is not to suggest that all activities of British officials were consciously regulated by keeping in view the colonial interests only. In fact, many British officials contributed in individual capacity to promote and popularise science in India. But these individual sporadic efforts should not be construed as basic colonial policy of the modernisation drive.

7. It is important to point out that the rise of new ST in Europe coincided with capitalism as a system, colonial expansion and industrialisation. A complex interrelationship among these salient features developed in colonial intellectual discourse and it was ideologically put forward by the colonial authorities for the colonised people. It was reflected in colonial policy for science-technology propagation in India.

The beginnings of scientific explorations took place in the shape of scientific surveys.[8] For obvious colonial reasons, these surveys were done primarily in the areas the British colonialists were interested in. Renell (Bengal region), Colonel Kelly (Carnatic region) and Major Lambton (from Coromandel to the Malabar Coast area) are some major names in land measurement surveys from the mid-18th century. Later was created the Great Trigonometrical Survey of India. Marine surveys were also encouraged and in 1809 a Marine Survey Department was established in Bengal.

After land surveys, it was the geological surveys and explorations that were important for natural resource extraction. Coalfields and other mineral reserves had to be searched for. The colonial authorities enthusiastically invested in this. Many geological departments were established at local and provincial levels. The Geological Survey of India was established and it did some remarkable research not only in mining but also pure science.[9] Botanical surveys and investigations were also done by creating botanical gardens and agriculture-based departments. Here plantation research was emphasised more and commercial crops like cotton, indigo, tobacco and tea were promoted in a focused manner. These items were sent to Britain to aid the industrial revolution.

From the late 18th century, scientific societies were formed. They were formed by British officials in an individual capacity and their purpose was to create a platform or meeting point for discussing various fields of knowledge including science. Undoubtedly the Asiatic Society in Bengal, established by Sir William Jones in 1784, and other societies under its inspiration did some basic foundational

8. For a detailed and perceptive description of Scientific Surveys, see Kumar Deepak (2011). "Scientific Surveys in British India: A Survey, 1760-1900", in Uma Das Gupta (ed.), *Science and Modern India: An Institutional History, c 1784-1947*. Volume-XV, Part 4 of D.P. Chattopadhyaya (General Editor), *History of Science, Philosophy and Culture in Indian Civilization*. pp.3-21. PHISPC, Center for Studies in Civilizations. Delhi: Pearson Longman. (Hereafter Science and Modern India.)

9. This paradoxical situation of colonial scientist has been referred as "dual mandate". On one hand, they had to serve the colonial interests even in ST-related activities; on the other hand, they had a relative autonomy and freedom of limited scope to work independently on their own.

work in propagating scientific knowledge.[10] These societies covered many areas of science and knowledge. For example, Agricultural Horticultural Society of India (1817), Calcutta Medical and Physical Society (1823), Madras Literacy and Scientific Society (1818) and the Bombay Branch of the Asiatic Society (1829) contributed in diffusing scientific methods of investigation, though in a limited sense.

It is interesting to investigate the colonial assertion of introducing modern ST in colonial India. Some points need to be stressed.

First, British officials of the East India Company participated in the initial phase. So ultimately they had to serve the colonial interests. Moreover, they were not professional scientists; rather, they may be called multi-task officials who discharged various duties. These "colonial scientists would try their hand at several fields simultaneously and each scientist was, in fact a botanist, geologist, geographer and educator—all rolled in one."[11] They worked as data gatherers whose main task was to send their information to the colonial headquarters. Analysis and interpretation were done in Britain. There were no attempts from early colonialists to establish basic research centres in colonial India. So, in a way, all this exercise culminated in strengthening the colonial grip over India as these data provided not only raw material to colonial ideology[12], but an upper hand in military operations and revenue extractions.

Second, these surveys had little to do with the conditions of Indian people. The subjects that primarily dealt with the Indian people—agriculture, zoology, medicine and diseases—were tackled

---

10. For detailed information on the work and functioning of Asiatic Society, see Sen, Srabani (2011). "The Asiatic Society and the Sciences in India, 1784-1947," in *Science and Modern India op. cit.* no. 8.

11. Quoted from IGNOU, Unit 7 "Science in Colonial and Modern India", p.44.

12. These gathered data were studied by those professional scientists of Great Britain who had scant knowledge of India. They would not correlate their scientific studies with concrete social realities of India. Obviously the studies based on this data exercise had a deep tinge of colonial ideology. It helped immensely in formulating colonial policies. Deepak Kumar makes an interesting and highly debatable remark that "colonial science did help to develop what a recent work calls the 'core culture' of imperialism". See Kumar, Deepak (2011). *Science and the Raj.* New Delhi: Oxford. p.17. He referred to Chakravarty, Suhash (1991). *The Raj Syndrome: A Study in Imperial Perceptions.* New Delhi. p.8, 40, 44.

sporadically and selectively.[13] In the health sector, only epidemics were dealt with because they affected the British too.

Third, and most important, these survey activities were principally done not for the welfare and constructive transformation of the Indian people towards modernisation. Obviously these drives lacked coherency, administrative coordination and involvement of the Indian people. The imperialist notion of the British being the introducers of modern science in India is inappropriate as far as the promotion of higher education in science is concerned. Figures given in later pages show the opposite picture.

Finally, it is interesting to note that the individual efforts of colonial scientists and officials in creating scientific societies and investigation bodies were not in confrontation with the colonial interests of the empire. It was feasible to do so because these were individualistic and sporadic in their approach and functioning. So, there was no danger of permeating scientific knowledge and temperament among the Indian people in a broader way. On the other hand, these activities added to the colonial stereotype of the civilising mission and thus enhanced the prestige of colonial rule.

The colonial state in India never engaged in a concerted effort to promote fundamental science and research in India, because it was not strategically feasible as far as the colonial ideological discourse on the colonised people was concerned. Any scientific modern consciousness would lead to anti-imperialist, anti-colonial instincts and ideologies. The colonial think tanks knew this.

The Condition of ST Higher Education

PC Ray, a renowned chemist and great man of science in modern India, narrated the pathetic condition of ST in the colonial period from the national platform of the Indian Science Congress in 1920 as its president:

> While Europe, America and Japan have taken to the field of Science with singular vigor and activity, how does the land lie about us in India? The situation fills our mind with sorrow and shame.... It is now

13. As unemployment, poverty, food availability and education were never a priority for the colonial government, no inclusive approach was adopted in this direction.

> becoming abundantly clear that the fate of a nation will henceforth depend more upon the achievement of its students of science than upon the skill of its generals or the adroitness of its diplomatists and statesman.[14]

Now a brief sketch of ST-related higher education in colonial India will suffice to put the perspective correct.

During the first 50 years or so of colonial rule, India witnessed very few engineering-industrial education efforts undertaken by the colonial state. Only two efforts are worth mentioning, one in 1824 in Bombay and the other in 1840 in Madras. Even these were of a limited scope and range. It is interesting to remember that this was the period of Indian history when indigenous industries of colonial India were being forced to die. Dadabhai Naoroji and R.C. Dutt, two nationalist economists, have graphically described the process of de-industrialisation.[15] In the absence of any technological alternative, Indian society was doomed to depend upon agriculture.

The example of Roorkee College of Engineering is very interesting. It was established in 1847 and touted as an excellent engineering centre. A comparative analysis with its contemporary institutions speaks otherwise. Tokyo Engineering College was established in 1873 and Massachusetts Institute of Technology (MIT) in 1865. Tokyo Engineering College, within 30 years of its existence, had 24 professors, 24 assistant professors and 22 lecturers. MIT had 306 teachers within 40 years of its inception. Roorkee had a different story of growth. Even after 100 years of existence, it had three professors, six assistant professors and 12 lecturers.[16]

Prospects of higher education and research in science (like other subjects) were almost absent in 19th century colonial India. It was in 1906, after nearly 150 years of colonial rule, that chairs were

---

14. Ray, Prafulla Chandra (2007)., "Dawn of Science in Modern India", quoted in Rakesh Batabyal (ed.), *The Penguin Book of Modern Indian Speeches, 1877 to the Present.* New Delhi. pp.176-77, 180. For full edited speech, see pp.176-89.

15. Bipan Chandra refers to early nationalists as perhaps the first—and certainly before Hobson or Lenin—who evolved a detailed economic critique of colonialism. See Chandra, Bipan (1988). *Indian National Movement: The Long Term Dynamics.* New Delhi. p.7.

16. The source of this information is IGNOU, Unit-37, "*Technology, Science and Empire*". pp.61-62.

created in government and private colleges to give special impetus to science education. It is difficult to believe that till 1917, there were no post-graduate classes in subjects like physics, chemistry, applied mathematics and experimental psychology. If we look at the scientific and technical manpower strength in 20th century pre-independence India, we find that the average annual number of post-graduate scientists during 1910-1914 was 77, which increased to 588 during 1935-1939. And at its best, it reached its highest point of 901 during 1945-1947. Similarly, the average annual number of engineering degree holders' figures during 1915-1919 was 114, which increased to 1,057 during 1945-1947. The average production of engineering diploma holders was 340 during 1915-1919, which increased to 1,513 during 1945-1947. Without doubt, these statistics, even if not 100 per cent accurate, show the gloomy picture of ST education in colonial India.[17]

British rule had evolved a colonial structure that prevented any organic shift from indigenous technology-based manufacturing to modern technology-based industrialisation. Bipan Chandra has authoritatively argued that under colonial rule India witnessed a massive de-industrialisation.[18]

Stereotyped logic for the poor state of ST has been given by colonial sympathisers, who attribute it to the "spiritual mould" or inherent cultural backwardness of the Indians. From the Indus Valley days to the later Mughals, Indian society and its people, like any other society, progressed and transformed themselves in different spheres of materialistic life. Even in 18th century pre-British India, which is assumed to be a period of chaos and anarchy, a whole spectrum of

17. These statistics are from *The Gazetteer of India, History and Culture*, Vol-II, p.697. New Delhi: Publication Division.

18. It was the work of Bipan Chandra that recognised colonialism as a distinct structure established primarily against the interests of the colonised Indian people. Some of his works in this direction are Chandra, Bipan (1979). *Nationalism and Colonialism in Modern India*. New Delhi: Orient Longman; Chandra, Bipan (1966). *Rise and Growth of Economic Nationalism in India*. New Delhi: PPH; Chandra, Bipan (1999). *Essays on Colonialism*. New Delhi: Orient Longman.

economic activities including vibrant internal and external trade are evident.[19]

As argued earlier, British ST policy functioned within the framework of colonialism, so it obviously discriminated against Indians from all possible ways to hinder their progress.[20] Indian scientists had to face many odds and difficulties in pursuing their science research work in the colonial period. P.C. Ray, in the speech referred to, said:

> A signal proof of what can be done by Indians, when they are allowed to work under a healthy and free atmosphere, is afforded by the University College of Science, Calcutta. This College grew out of the magnificent and princely gifts of Sir Rashbihari Ghosh and the late Sir T. N. Palit, and was established in 1916; but owing to limitation of funds, the laboratory and the workshop could not be properly organized. In spite of these discouraging conditions, it is the only institution which has shown anything like life and activity as evidenced by the output of original contributions published in the leading scientific journals of England and America. During the academic year 1918-19, there were 17 original contributions from the departments of Applied Mathematics, 24 from the Physics department, and 21 from the Chemistry department. Yet this promising institution is treated like a charity boy by the Government and has had only miserable doles ladled out to it.... It is, therefore, necessary that steps should be taken to allow Indians to stand on

19. The arrival of European companies as traders is itself a historical indicator of a dynamic Indian society. For a detailed and perceptive analysis on the state of pre-colonial science, See Kumar *op.cit.* no. 8: 18-31.

20. Even early nationalists like Dadabhai Naoroji criticised the discriminatory policy of appointing the British and avoiding Indians. "Whenever any question of reform arises, the only remedy that suggests itself to English officials' minds is, 'Apply more European leeches, apply more European leeches!'" Furthering his argument he again attacked it by saying "the Commission suggests the institution of an Agricultural Department, and a very important suggestion it is. But they soon forget that it is for India this is required, that it is at India's expense it has to be done... and that India cannot afford to have more blood sucked out of her for more Europeans while depriving so much her own children... No; prostrate as India is and for which very reason the Commission was appointed to suggest a remedy, they can only say, 'More Europeans,' as if no such thing as a people existed in India.... Were any Englishman to make such a proposal for England, that French or German youths be instructed at England's expense, and that such youths make up the different public departments, he would be at once scouted and laughed at." Naoroji, Dadabhai (1969). *Poverty and Un-British Rule in India.* Delhi. pp.211-12.

> their own legs. This policy which has hitherto been the guiding principle is that everything should be done 'for' them and nothing 'by' them, and this goes to explain their virtual ostracism from the higher responsible post in the various scientific services. A vast amount of ability and potential energy is thus allowed to run to waste.[21]

In a similar vein, Dr BC Roy, who later became chief minister of West Bengal, spoke about the discriminatory policy of British colonialism in his presidential address to the All India Medical Conference in 1929: "The process of exclusion has been so carefully, may I say shamelessly, planned and manipulated that even an Indian of established repute has no chance of getting into the group."[22]

Despite this, not only colonial ideologues, enlightened early nationalists believed in the slogan of "benefits of British Rule."[23] Early nationalists like Naoroji, Dutt and M.G. Ranade, though convinced about the exploitative nature of colonial rule, believed that modern ST would accrue from that. Dutt wrote:

> They have introduced western education, bringing our ancient and civilized nation in touch with modern thought, modern sciences, modern institutions and life ... these are the results which no honest critique of British work in India regards without high admiration.[24]

Here I may suggest that the early nationalists did question and even criticise the Pax-Britannica rhetoric. For example, Naoroji in 1880 mocked the colonial claim of modernising India:

> The English rulers boast, and justly so, that they have introduced education and Western civilisation into India; but, on the other hand, they act as if no such thing had taken place, and as if all this boast was pure moonshine. Either they have educated, or have not. If they deserve the boast, it is a strange self-condemnation that after

21. Batabyal *op. cit.* no. 14: 185-86.
22. Ibid.: 200. For full edited speech, see pp.197-201.
23. The rhetoric of 'benefits of British rule' could not be contested with the rigour and far-sightedness it deserved. Of course, the force of modernisation logic was so formidable that the thinking people of India could not develop an authentic and constructive critique of British policies in the realm of science and technology and culture.
24. Dutt *op. cit.* no.3.

> half a century or more of such efforts, they have not yet prepared a sufficient number of men fit for the service of their own country. Take even the Educational Department itself. We are made B.A.'s and M.A.'s and M.D.'s etc., with the strange result that we are not yet considered fit to teach our countrymen.[25]

Conclusion

To understand this "belief" of early nationalists, it is necessary to point out that they were basically the initial representatives of modern scientific consciousness and it was not for them to distinguish between techno-centric interventions and the propagation of science as scientific knowledge.[26] It was for another generation of nationalist leaders who from experience sensed that colonialism was not for grounding science knowledge among Indians. They understood that colonialism only lured the Indian people with some techno-centric sporadic fragmentary interventions within a colonial perspective. Mahatma Gandhi was the foremost to recognise this colonial rhetoric of modern civilisation based on ST. Even at the risk of being called medievalist or anti-modernist, he strategically argued against technology-based modernity. The Indian national movement, being a counter-hegemonic movement against colonial hegemony, evolved a competent leadership on the science front too. Indian scientists argued in favour of both aspects of ST in an independent enlightened manner, which in certain ways was a departure from colonial science. With this vision they combined the concerns of Indian society and its people, understanding the crucial needs of institutionalising science knowledge in Indian society. Their dream came true to a larger extent in post-independence India.[27]

---

25. Naoroji *op. cit.* no. 19: : 197.
26. Deepak Kumar *op. cit.* no. 1 comments "the distinctions between pure and applied science appeared only in the late 19th century and are still unclear."
27. P.C. Ray, B.C. Roy, J.C. Bose, C.V. Raman, S.N. Bose, Meghnad Saha, Mahendra Lal Siran and others of similar calibre were those giants of science who immensely contributed in making the road map for post-independent India. For briefest but most perceptive description of these Indian scientists, see Batabyal *op. cit.* no. 14: 175-76.

7

NEERJA SINGH

Aspects of Social Change and Social Perspectives

Issues of Women in 19th Century India

The intellectual movement in the 19th century was a responsive one to the impact of Western cultural, social, political and economic structures, institutions and value systems. The colonial impact triggered the process of self-introspection by intellectuals of the 19th century. Reacting to the virulent criticism of native culture, tradition and value system by the colonialist, the early writings on the 19th century social and cultural conditions by Indian intellectuals reflected on the critically debated and recorded social behaviour, customs, traditions, cultural and religious patterns of authority and control. The movement critically examined and reviewed the patterns of authority and control exercised through structural institutions existing during the period.

The heterogeneous intellectual awakening in India in the 19th century was marked by a high degree of sensitivity to the question of women. Intellectuals took up the issue from various standpoints—humanistic, rationalistic and even nationalistic. The deplorable condition of women—characterised by their inferior status, lack of independence, illiteracy, poverty and the denial of property rights—constituted the core of reform ideas and endeavours during the period. The prevalence of debilitating social practices such as child marriage, polygamy, enforced widowhood and disfigurement and infanticide came under scathing intellectual attack. Marriage on puberty, monogamy, widow remarriage and the end of infanticide were advocated as options for the healthy wholesome growth of society and country, though degrees in intensity and articulation differed from one region to another due to somewhat varying contextuality.

A very significant feature of pre-British India was the absence of a stratified social order depending on occupational and educational diversification. Land economy and limited education were both obstructive and destructive to the social stratification and proliferation of social groups. But more important were the backwardness of technology and the existence of a domestic system of production from which no stratified order could emerge. Small-scale handicraft production afforded little scope for a multiplicity of economic activities. Thus, pre-British society was divided into fixed status groups. In such a Brahmin-dominated social organisation, women with regard to property rights were relegated to a secondary position. They had no right of inheritance to the property of their father, even in the absence of brothers. Whatever property rights a woman was entitled to lay entirely in the property of her husband. Even these rights were limited. Wives enjoyed only a right to maintenance in their husband's property.

The 19th century, therefore, was a very significant phase in the history of modern India. It was during this period that the country witnessed the emergence of myriad of intellectual currents for national regeneration, in all its aspects—social, cultural, economic and political. Although the intellectual endeavours were aimed at organic improvement, their emphasis was on women-related issues. In other words, issues such as illiteracy, monogamy, early widow re-marriage, child marriage, sati and dowry formed one of the major planks of the 19th century Indian intellectual movement. This is, however, not to mention that in terms of programme and perspective, they were not fundamentally one-dimensional: in fact, multi-dimensionality of vision constituted an important facet of the 19th century Indian intellectual ideas.

There were two main areas of intense intellectual activity in the country—Bengal and Maharashtra. Bengal was the first to herald the beginning of the movement for women's emancipation in India. Rammohun Roy spearheaded the movement against the practice of *sati* (the burning of the wife on the funeral pyre of her husband). His efforts resulted in the abolition of this practice in 1829. He also raised the question of women's property rights.

What happened in Bengal was often taken as an all-India phenomenon and it would be a truism to say that it represented the beginning of the intellectual awakening which reached its zenith during the Indian national movement and afterwards. It was no denying that the spark of this intellectual revolt in 19th century India was first led in Bengal, but the movements in Maharashtra, Punjab and another parts of the country during the period had their own intensity and character. They were influenced by Bengal but were not merely an extension of it. Therefore, to understand the intellectual awakening during the 19th century and its translation into movements, focusing on women's emancipation with all its complexities, one has to focus on other areas too—that is western India.

Western India too during the period witnessed the onset of powerful literature and orature on the questions of women and the need for their immediate amelioration. A host of reformers such as Lokahitawadi, Mahatma Jyotirao Phule, M.G. Ranade, N.G. Chandavarkar, G.G. Agarkar and Pandita Ramabai raised their voice against the injustice and cruelty inflicted upon women as a social category in the patriarchal structure of society. They denounced the pernicious practices for being not only unjust and irrational but also inimical to national unity and strength, denoting civilisational deficiency. Phule and Pandita Ramabai, in particular, raised the fundamental questions of human equality, freedom and dignity, and tried to liberate woman from the centuries-old hold of the male-dominated social structure, which allowed little voice or choice to them. Therefore, the issue of subjugation of women cannot be understood without contextualising it within the intellectual reform movement.

During first half of the 19th century, the movement remained a feeble force. It was a very small affair of an extremely limited number of individuals whose passion for fighting social obscurantism and other evils could not be transformed into an open challenge at the level of practice. The movement, however, maintained its momentum and reached its peak during the second half of the 19th century. The period of four decades between the 1840s and the 1880s saw the movement in its most vigorous form. The fraternity of intellectuals during the period considerably expanded with a galaxy of other enlightened individuals joining the fray. The movement now could no longer be ignored by the orthodox sections, which, realising its growing strength, launched a multi-pronged attack on the intellectuals. In fact, the intellectual movement, both in Bengal and

Maharashtra, faced its severest opposition only during second half of the 19th century. Thus, second phase of the movement constituted a curious blending of ardent reform, and blind as well as enlightened reaction; for example, when in 1869 intellectuals of Maharashtra arranged a widow remarriage in Pune, the orthodox sections struggled very hard to prevent its consummation. The marriage, the first of its kind in the presidency, was however successfully celebrated. The event marked the beginning of active and strong orthodox opposition to the movement and its leaders. A joint debate of the orthodox and the intellectuals on legality of the marriage was held at Pune in 1870. The numerical preponderance of the orthodox enabled them to pass a resolution of *prayaschita* (penance) on those who had participated in the marriage. The Pune meeting also passed a resolution of ostracisation of all those who had attended the dinner. This was more severe punishment because dining was viewed by the orthodox to be a graver crime than participating. Moreover, jeering at intellectuals was a regular phenomenon and the instances of their being beaten up were known.

Non-conformism was the underlining theme of the movement. It was, however, not confined merely to its non-conformist behaviour. Its non-conformism was inseparably mingled with the notion of social reformism. In other words, the 19th century pioneers were not merely social critics but, more importantly, social reformers and intellectuals. To clarify, their interest about the problems of society was not merely academic. Moreover, their criticism of society and culture was not directionless; they had the vision and a model for the socio-economic development of India and all their ideas and activities were geared to the attainment of that goal.

One of the characteristic features of the early phase was that while in Bengal the movement had begun on a religious and philosophical note, in Maharashtra strictly social issues came to occupy a prominent place. The movement was initiated not from the pulpit of philosophical abstraction, but from the very ground of the perception of concrete social conditions. Their approach to the understanding of Indian problems was a matter of fact, much down to earth in nature. So much so that under its impact during the latter half of the 19th century to the middle of 20th century, the notion of empowerment of women gained a wider connotation as a social movement with an ideology focusing on freedom of choice in occupation, education, health, housing and social relationships. It also implied enabling the marginalised and discriminated sections of society to gain self-respect by acquiring self-generating power to be equal partners in the process of development, removing vulnerability to exploitation and preventing violence and injustice.

Women's empowerment meant women's power of self-organisation, their capacity for self-reliance by rejecting relationships of subordination on account of gender, social and economic status, and the role in family and society. It implied their ability to make choices, control resources and enjoy participatory relationship within family and community.

The re-generation of Indian society was the central theme of the intellectuals' initiative in 19th century Bengal and Maharashtra. The concern of the intellectuals centred largely on social and cultural questions. Identification of the socio-cultural evils constituted an important starting point of their attempt at social renewal and women's empowerment. A host of social customs and religious practices such as the low position of women, child marriage, polygamy, enforced widowhood, illiteracy, *sati* and other kinds of injustice came under severe intellectual attack in the 19th century. They were highlighted as denoting all-round social decay and degeneration. In an attempt to renovate the social order, the intellectuals advocated the uplift of the position of women, marriage only after puberty, monogamy, widow remarriage, eliminating caste distinctions, monotheism, spiritual worship and the end of social bigotry and superstitions. The underlying concern was the all-round progress of Indian society on the foundations of a reformed socio-cultural system.

The social thinkers viewed the existing socio-cultural scene of the country and came to the conclusion that the condition of women in India was deplorably bad and wretched. The question of women was, therefore, given special attention in the 19th century scheme of social transformation. Nearly every social thinker was concerned with this. The existing practice of child marriage, *sati*, enforced widowhood, female infanticide, female seclusion and prostitution were some of the major issues the reformers were concerned with. G.H. Deshmukh in 1850 wrote: "Child marriage is a crime against half of our beloved humanity. Its monstrousness lies in the fact that it opens the flood gate of other corruptions."[1] R.G. Bhandarkar wrote: "Child marriage of girls to a full-fledged man is a human sacrifice. It, therefore, deserves greater condemnation."[2] According to N.M. Parmanand[3], child marriage was thought to be at the root of other social evils and injustice. It was believed to result in early widowhood and promoted polygamy. Polygamy was viewed as the fertile source of evil, moral as well as physical, and a relic of barbaric and primeval necessity.

Enforced widowhood was regarded as murder. They saw it as butchering young daughters in cold blood. To R.G. Bhandarkar, enforced widowhood denoted barbarity and low level of a social development. According to him,

> The society which allows men to marry any number of times, even up to the age of sixty while it strongly forbids even girls of the age seven or eight to have another husband after one is dead—a society which sets very little value upon the life of a female human being, and places women on the same level with cattle, is in an unsound condition, disqualified for a successful competition with societies with a more healthy constitution.[4]

Ishwar Chandra Vidyasagar, Balshastri Jambhekar, Phule, Pandita Ramabai and others condemned the practice of hiring girls to dance and sing during weddings and other ceremonies. In the *Bombay Darpan* of 11 September 1832, Jambhekar wrote that this system signified the humiliation and helplessness of women or girls. The amelioration of the condition of Indian women was emphasised as a matter of utmost urgency and necessity in the social reformers' intellectual scheme of social change. The intellectuals held that social and national progress could not be achieved unless women were liberated from social tyranny and corrupt practices. Rammohun Roy in 1818 published "A Conference Between an Advocate for and an Opponent of the Practice of Burning Widows Alive". In this, he bitterly criticised the practice and cited scriptural sources to justify his contention that sati was an aberration and degeneration of Hinduism. He relied on the

1. Deshmukh, G.H. (1963). *Lokhitwadinchi Shatrapatren*, No.30. N.R. Inamdar (ed.). Poona: Deshmukh Prakashan. p.213.
2. Bhandarkar, R.G. (n.d.). *Collected Works*. Vol II. p.490.
3. N.M. Parmnanda (n.d.), Letter No. III, pp. 25-26.
4. Bhandarkar *op. cit.* no. 2: 488.

Vedas, *Upanishads* and *Vedanta-sutra* for defending his rational and humanistic beliefs.

Diagnosis of disease was one aspect; the search for its cure was another. The intellectuals of the time cogitated over the means so as to remedy the social ills. They sought alternative solutions to women's problems by generating awareness through debates and speeches regarding *sati* and widow remarriage. The question of widow remarriage and *sati* received greater attention. Although the Indian government outlawed *sati* in 1829 and legalised the marriage of Hindu windows by the Act of XV of 1856, passed by the legislative council, it made little progress on account of popular feeling against the reform. It was, therefore, found highly desirable, especially in the Bombay Presidency, to drive this issue to the people's conscience. It should however be emphasised that the intellectuals of Maharashtra, unlike in Bengal, never advocated compulsory widow remarriage; what they wanted was the elimination of social obstacles in the way of realising voluntary widow remarriage. N.G. Chandravarkar, one of the protagonists of widow remarriage, said the aim of the reform was only to remove the obstacle enforced by custom, and not to compel every widow to marry, but to allow a feeling to grow in society that it was permissible for a widow to marry if she decided.

To garner support for their attempt to improve the position of women, the intellectuals during second half of the century sought the support of the scriptures. Rammohun Roy to Vishnu Shastri Pandit, they all profusely quoted the scriptures to prove that *sati* abolition and widow remarriage were religiously sanctioned. M.G. Ranade wrote: "[T]he writings of Manu and Vajnavalkya show and the Itihaas and Puranas confirm that monogamy is the natural concern of Aryan life, and that polygamy and polyandry are disreputable excrescences."[5] In short, most of the intellectuals, with a very few exceptions like Agarkar, tried to justify the reforms by quoting from the scriptures. Balshastri Jambhekar[6] clarified that "all reforms must grow slowly

5. Ranade, M.G. (1915). *Miscellaneous Writings.* Ramabai Ranade (ed.). Bombay: Manoranjan Press. p.72.

6. Jambhekar, Balshastri (1950). "Memoirs and Writings", in G.G. Jambhekar (ed.), *Centenary Memorial Volumes.* Vol. 1. Poona. p.69.

from within, on evolutionary lines, conforming where desirable to the best thought of Hindu Shastras and traditions." This is, however, not to suggest that the intellectuals played according to the tune of the religious scriptures. It was not the scriptures that influenced their opinions; it was they who moulded the scriptures in accordance with their ideas. They were highly selective in their choice. They cited only those passages that supported their ideas of reforms. They did not quote portions that supported conservative opinions. For example, idol worship, pilgrimage and temple building were dominant features of the *Bhagwat Dharma*, but they did not cite them.

Nor were the intellectuals guided by the commands of religious dispensation. The search for scriptural sanctions was simply an afterthought, and not the starting point of the intellectual endeavour. K.T. Telang stated:

> Some allege that the 'reformers' have raised the shastrical question in support of their view on the age of consent question. But it is not the 'reformers' that are relying on the shastras... They are merely answering what the opponents of the Age of Consent Bill have been arguing on the basis of the Shastras. The supporters of the Bill base their support on the claims of humanity not on the Shastras at all. The Shastric argument is an afterthought of the opponents of the Bill, not its supporters.[7]

Significantly, the intellectuals tried to reinterpret the Shastras in support of what they advocated. The scriptures were interpreted as promoters of change in society. N.G. Chandravarkar wrote:

> The Hindu Shastras are wide and comprehensive enough to include any measure of reform...They have given us a free hand in changing with the time by agreeing upon the point that custom or usage can supersede the injunctions of the Shastras. The whole history of the Hindu society has been a history of tumultuous departure, whenever the departure was rendered necessary or expedient, from the laws laid down in the Shastras. Every custom marks the beginning of such a departure; and if the Shastras themselves say that we can make customs, I do not see why the social reformer should confine himself to Shastras alone...The Shastras have been more liberal than we care to be, by giving us free hand to deviate from them when necessary.

7. Telang, K.T. (1916). *Selected Writings and Speeches.* V.N. Naik (ed.). Bombay. p.473.

> The Shastras are valuable means of showing that our history has been a history of change.[8]

According to the reformers, society had evolved to its present form bypassing the scriptural regulations. Hence, deviation from the scriptural authority was not a new phenomenon in the history of Hindu society. K.T. Telang wrote:

> The Shastras have silently seen changes occurring in the society against their regulations. As to the caste system, we have departed from the rule of our own old scriptures. They (scriptures) recognised only four castes at first. In our present circumstances, the number of castes into which the Hindu community is divided is four thousand more than four.[9]

Thus, we see that the scriptures had a utilitarian value for them. They used them and discarded them, depending upon the gravity of the issue. "A custom arises at its inception out of some necessity and it becomes stereotyped for ages. The principle underlying the custom is forgotten; the form remains. If a society wishes to advance these customs are to be continuously corrected to meet new challenges."

Vidyasagar and Vishnu Shastri Pandit were among a few who were staunch advocates of widow remarriage. Vidyasagar was the main influence in proposing and processing the Widow Remarriage Act XV of 1856. Shastri provided leadership to the Widow Marriage Association of 1865. The objective of the association was to encourage such marriages and to create favourable public opinion. Concerned at the problem of widowhood, Vishnu Shastri Pandit set an example by marrying a widow in 1875. To most of the intellectuals, the daring deeds and ideological commitments of Vidyasagar and Vishnu Shastri Pandit to women's emancipation were the source of inspiration and courage. R.G. Bhandarkar, facing stiff opposition from conservative forces, which involved a threat to excommunicate him, allowed the remarriage of his daughter in 1891. However, the sincere attempt of the thinkers failed to achieve any significant progress on this issue.

It is intriguing to note that most of the intellectuals emphasised monogamy and widow remarriage. Rammohun Roy, Balshastri

---

8. Chandavarkar, N.G. (1911). *Speeches and Writings*, L.V. Kaikini (ed.). Bombay: Manoranjak Grantha Prasarak Mandali. p.66.

9. Telang *op. cit.* no. 7: 305.

Jambhekar and G.H. Deshmukh stood distinct from the others on the question of solutions to women's problems. They sought a permanent solution, not just in matters of monogamy and widow-remarriage, but in equal rights for women. G.H. Deshmukh wrote in 1849:

> The sub-ordination of women has emanated from the absence of equal rights to them. The country which does not give equal rights to women and thus keeps them in sub-ordination to man is dead society, it cannot prosper.[10]

Balshastri Jambhekar wrote the lasting solution to women's problems was equal rights to women, something required for the prosperity of the nation also. These thinkers regarded the denial of property rights to women to be the root cause of their subordinate position.

The intellectuals and reformers of the 19th century were equally concerned about the means by which social transformation could be effected. The debate, centred around the means of social transformation, focused mainly on the question of whether the method of reform should be only educational or both educational and legislative. On one hand, there were those who strictly advocated "reform from within", and on the other, was a group of individuals who approved of the "reform from without". V.N. Mandlik and B.G. Tilak were the great exponents of the "reform from within" tactic—"we agree with public opinion that government should not interfere with the custom," wrote B.G. Tilak.[11] V.N. Mandlik's view was:

> I am opposed to the enactment of the governmental laws on social matters unless the people want them—the government would do well to refrain from interfering in social matters which are quite outside the pale of government interference, and which the Hindu community consider as peculiarly the province of their own religious constitution, the violation of which by the state would be regarded as an evil of vast magnitude.[12]

10. Deshmukh *op. cit.* no. 1: 213
11. Wolpert, S.A. (1962). *Tilak & Gokhale: Revolution and Reform in the Making of Modern India.* University of California Press.
12. Mandalik, V.N. (1896). *Writings and Speeches.* N.V. Mandalik (ed.). Bombay Archives. pp.156-79.

Rammohun Roy and Vidyasagar from Bengal and M.G. Ranade and N.G. Chandavarkar from Maharashtra were the important leaders who saw no reason why state help should be rejected for implementing reforms. M.G. Ranade wrote:

> The initiation is to be our own...dictated by our responsible sense, and all that is sought at the hands of foreigners is to give to this responsible sense the force and sanction of law. In the matter of social reform legislation, the distinction of foreign and domestic rulers is a distinction without difference.[13]

The method of reform was determined by the merit and urgency of social issues. The practice that was regarded as most heinous and regressive was to be abolished "with one stroke". It was precisely in such cases that legislation was advocated. Chandavarkar wrote: "The state has a function to regulate and minimise the evil, if the evil can be minimised better than the individual effort. On this principle alone can state action be justified."[14] M.G. Ranade too emphatically pointed out:

> The history of the suppression of Infanticide and Sati shows that these institutions...were checked, and could be checked, only by the strong arms of Law, and once they were denounced as crimes, they disappeared from the face of the country—The diseased corruptions of the body cannot and should not be dealt with in the same way as its normal and healthy developments. The sharp surgical operation, and not the homeopathic infinitesimally small pill, is the proper remedy for the first class of disorders and the analogy holds good—also in dealing with the parasitical growth of social degeneration.[15]

The intellectuals of both Bengal and Maharashtra were not very sharply divided on the question of the means by which social change was to be brought about. Nearly all of them held education to be the most effective agent of social change. It was only through the spread of knowledge that reformation could be effected and social salvation realised. Therefore, education and legislation were regarded

13. Ranade *op. cit.* no. 5: 80.
14. Chandravarkar, G.L. (1981). *A Wrestling Soul: Story of the Life of Narayan Chandavarkar.* Bombay: Popular Book Depot. p.42.
15. Ranade *op. cit.* no. 5: 82.

as the most desirable alternatives to actualise the goal of women's emancipation.

The intellectuals of the 19th century, through their writing, strongly conveyed the fact that only women's education could largely minimise the asymmetry in gender relations prevalent in society. There was, however, no unanimity among the reformers on the issue of equality in education between man and woman. Most of the mainstream intellectuals viewed domesticity to be the principal domain of women as a social category. Higher education for them was, therefore, viewed to be not as pressing as in the case of men. Education for women was seen more as a tool to equip them to refine the home environment and provide enlightened companionship to men rather than for their own independent growth. Some reformers, however, went beyond such boundaries and stood for equal educational opportunities for both men and women. Rammohun Roy, Vidyasagar, Parmanand Agarkar, Phule and Pandita Ramabai were in the forefront. The intellectuals not only advocated women's education but also attempted to translate it into actual practice. Some of them started schools for them. Vidyasagar, Phule and Pandita Ramabai did pioneering work in this field. They opened schools and training institutions for women. Phule and Savitribai Phule opened schools for girls belonging to the most marginalised sections of society, i.e., the Shudras. Pandita Ramabai opened a shelter called the Sharda Sadan in Pune in 1889.

The social psyche, however, limited the extent of lessening gender-related rigidities. Legislation as mentioned earlier was another method advocated for correcting social ills. Rammohun Roy, Vidyasagar, Bhandarkar, Ranade, Chandavarkar and Behramji Malabari were prominent proponents of state action in social matters during the period. Malabari spearheaded the movement for a rise in the age of consent for the consummation of marriage, and the consent controversy virtually galvanised the intellectual fraternity of the time. The Age of Consent Bill was finally passed in 1891, raising the age of consent of wife from 10 to 12 years. Legislative action was however advocated as the second option and was deemed essential only in cases where surgical solutions were called for, particularly in a situation where there was hardly any social readiness for initiating reform.

The currents of thought in the period played an instrumental role in reorienting rigidities. One of the indices of its effects was discernable in the unprecedented increase in the number of girls going to school in the 19th century. The gradual decline in the instances of child marriage was another indicator of the winds of change set in motion by the reform movement during the period.

However, during the national movement and post-national movement, the effort at the empowerment of women and the ideology sustaining it has undergone a significant differentiation in India. The period threw up a leadership among women and also deeply influenced their role perception over the following decades. Commensurate with these objectives, many legislative changes were introduced. The past 60 years reflect some basic changes in the status and role of women in society. They have now become increasingly conscious of their discrimination in several areas of public life and family. The establishment of the National Commission for Women to monitor their status achieved, and demand for reservation of 33 per cent of seats in political institutions of the country (village councils, assemblies and parliament) through a constitutional amendment testify to the increasing recognition of their role in the power structure. Therefore, the movement for empowering women was in ideological terms co-optional and generalised, but in the contemporary period it has become more particularistic. It focuses entirely on the condition of women as a separate entity. Studies have shown that during the post-colonial and post-industrial era, attempts at empowering women succeed only when attention is invited by women through their self-managed and self-sustained organisational and movement-oriented activities and not when the agenda of empowerment has been made part of the general development plan of society.

Nevertheless, it should be kept in mind that whatever may be the nature of initiatives taken by women's organisations for empowering themselves, it was the 19th century social reform movement that prepared the ground for their activities. Several groups started during the social reform movement and the national movement are even now doing very effective work.

8

VLADIMIR TIKHONOV

China and Chinese in Colonial Korea

Discourses on China and Chinese in 1920s: Early 1930s Prose Literature and Journalism

Prologue: China as a Hope and as Reality

There hardly was a country—perhaps besides the colonial mother country, Japan—that was more important for colonial Korea (1910-1945) than China. Chinese residents in Korea were the second largest group of resident non-Koreans after Japanese, their economic prominence far exceeding their numerical strength. In 1930, before the start of the Japanese invasion of Northeastern China (Manchuria), 67,794 Chinese citizens lived in Korea—almost one-eighth of the number of Korea-based Japanese residents.[1] The Chinese migration to Korea was amply reciprocated. By 1945, almost a million Koreans resided in China, including its Northeastern provinces. In the 1920s and 1930s, the latter group was harbouring perhaps the most radical armed anti-colonial movement by foreign-based Korean residents, after the one by Russia-based Koreans. By 1924, the Japanese police estimated the number of armed Korean radicals in the Chinese provinces bordering Korea at 3,438—and was greatly alarmed by the radicalisation of the Northeastern China-based Korean diaspora.[2] Shanghai, one of East Asia's most vibrant international cities, was home to hundreds of Korean émigré radicals,

1. Jun, Yang and Wang Qiubin (2006). *Zhongguo yu Chaoxian Bandao quanxishi lun* (On the History of Relationship between China and the Korean Peninsula). Beijing: Shihui Gexue Wenxian Chubanshe. pp.206-07.

2. Hyonju, Yi (2009). *1920nyŏndae Chaejung hangil seryŏk ŭi t'ongil undong* (The Movement for the Unification of the China-Based Independence Struggle Forces in the 1920s) Ch'ŏnan: Tongnip Kinyŏmgwan. pp. 207-08.

both of nationalist and more radical (anarchist or Communist) persuasions. And China's ongoing revolution—in which a good number of China-based Korean émigrés actually participated—was a hot topic in the colonial press, mostly viewed in very sympathetic tones. Indeed, it was seen as a most realistic hope for Korea's own eventual liberation. To a large degree, the interest was reciprocated. Korea's independence movement was widely covered in republican China's periodicals, and often depicted with sympathy in the works of fiction. For example, Chinese press gave perhaps the most detailed coverage of Korea's 1 March 1919 movement in the world. This coverage, often explicitly sounded as a rebuke to the Chinese who "could not rise up like Koreans", often identified as being among the inspirations for China's own 4 May 1919 movement.[3]

At the same time, the treatment of the resident Chinese in Korean colonial prose literature—and largely in mainstream journalism as well—was mostly hostile. They were seen as competitors against both Korean workers and entrepreneurs, actual and potential criminals, and ultimately, as a source of social 'pollution'. This view was instrumental in bringing about the tragic events of 1931, when a large-scale anti-Chinese pogrom occurred in Korea, accompanied by a massive loss of life and property. The present chapter looks at the factors instrumental in igniting the mood of anti-Chinese hostility in the colonial-time discourse on the resident Chinese. Further, it will contrast the antagonistic attitude towards the Korea-based Chinese diaspora with much more sympathetic treatments of the Chinese revolution in Korean periodicals, ultimately attempting to understand the range of meanings that "China" and "Chinese" represented for 1920s–early 1930s Korean intellectuals. Beginning with the images of Chinese in the colonial Korean prose literature—and taking Ch'oe Sŏhae (original name—Ch'oe Haksong, 1901-1932) as an example of hostile literary treatment of the Chinese—I will then look at the historical roots of the colonial-time Sinophobia, and contrast it with much more positive attitudes towards the Chinese

3. Daily *Minguo Ribao* only published 20 articles on Korea's independence movement between 12 March and 6 May 1919. Jun and Qiubin *op. cit.* no. 1: 211.

revolution, which was often directly linked to the issue of Korea's own liberation.

Ch'oe Sŏhae and the "Boundary Experiences"

Ch'oe Sŏhae was perhaps the colonial-time prose writer with the largest experience of "China" and "Chinese". The best definition of Ch'oe Sŏhae, whose meteoric rise to prominence was one of the defining events of the literary scene in 1920s colonial Korea, would be a "boundary personality". First and foremost, he managed to transcend the boundaries between different classes of the colonial society: a son of a poor tenant family and a native of Sŏngjin in the distant Northern Hamgyong Province, he entered the literary circles mostly populated by wealthier middle-class graduates of prestigious schools inside and outside of Korea. By contrast, Ch'oe's own education was limited to elementary knowledge of classical Chinese and some years of elementary school,[4] from which he eventually had to drop out without ever formally graduating. Instead of studying abroad, his formative experience was that of a migrant manual labourer living in dire poverty in Manchuria, where his family settled in 1917. Painfully aware of his inferior status, the constant urge to compare himself to his social betters became almost ingrained in Ch'oe's consciousness. In an autobiographical essay,[5] he vividly describes the trauma left by the experience of social inferiority, portraying his old elementary school friends who succeeded in getting further education and became local officials, and then allowed themselves to assume haughty airs and openly despise Ch'oe as a hapless loser.

For Ch'oe, who was strongly motivated to raise his status but lacked the material or cultural capital for doing so from the very start, the gap between different classes and strata of the Korean society was the pivotal point of social reality as he perceived it. For him—a less than well-educated son of a poor family from a distant province—socialising in the literary circles of Kyŏngsŏng (Keijō, today's Seoul),

4. Kor. *pot'ong hakkyo,* Jap. *futsu gakkō.*

5. Sŏhae, Ch'oe (1927). *Chŏn'asa* (On Sending Off and Meeting), *Tonggwang* 9: 29-42.

consisting mostly of well-educated scions of predominantly middle-class families, was a "boundary experience" akin to emigration abroad. It was not merely a paranoid feeling of inferiority stemming from his background and lack of educational credentials. It was, in fact, how he was routinely perceived by some of his luckier peers in Kyŏngsŏng's literary milieu. See, for example, an obituary written about him by Kim Tong'in (1900-1951):[6]

> His upbringing differed from that of older writers. He was a person who experienced countless difficulties and bitterness from the days of his childhood, spent under dire circumstances. He's gone through all sorts of ordeals. As a poor, pitiable creature faced with starvation, he experienced the life of a monk, a vagabond, an opium addict, and an unskilled worker. Thus the society he described differed from the society which Korean writers were used to depict up until then. The society he described was one of darkness. It was a society where hunger, disease, pain, sin, brutality and fear were all mixed up. The Korean readers, who had so far seen only the life of the well-to-do in the novels, regarded Sohae with astonishment, and the reason they applauded him was the fascination with the novelty of the society described in his novels. And that was the reason the Proletarian Association [of writers] accepted Sŏhae as a leader.

This obituary by Kim Tong'in, a son of a wealthy family, who could boast of studying abroad in Tokyo,[7] shows that the mainstream Kyŏngsŏng writers and literary connoisseurs obviously perceived Ch'oe's novels as "exotic and outlandish" tales, of which "normal" colonial gentlemen of means hardly ever had any experiences . As an exotic object to be observed and gazed at by wealthy connoisseurs, Ch'oe had no reason to share the lofty ideas about "sublimity" or "special role" of the *belles-lettres*. For him, writing was first and foremost an economic activity inside the framework of the capitalist system—he was a "manuscript-producing worker" rather than an

---

6. Tong'in, Kim (1932). *Aedosa: Sosŏlka rosŏŭi Sohae* (Condolatory Address: Sŏhae as a novelist), *Tonggwang* 36: 97-98.
7. In 1914-1917 (Tokyo Gakuin and Meiji Gakuin) and 1918-19 (Kawabata Art School). For Kim's biography, a standard (albeit somewhat outdated) work is Ch'ŏl, Paek (1989). *Kim Tong'in Yŏn'gu* (Research on Kim Tong'in). Seoul: Saemunsa.

"author". He might have regarded it as a "degradation of talent" of sorts, but reality remained:

> I wrote a manuscript. On completion, I sent it to the newspaper's or journal's editorial office. How can I describe in detail all the humiliating scenes which took place after I sent it? When it was first requested, they were doing their best to curry favour with me; but then, after it was completed and sent, they became supercilious and even delayed the payment of a meagre honorarium they owed me. Since I could not fight them over these things, I could only be racked with worries and indignation in solitude. (...) Since I've written for profit alone, unable to even think about any artistic impulses, every time I thought about my manuscripts, I've thought of money. Thus, I had to write almost against my will, barely able to mobilize sufficient emotion for the sake of writing. It is of no small pain."[8]

Supposedly a 'writer', Ch'oe was in reality just a non-permanent employee of various Kyŏngsŏng publishers—in other words, a small-time literary entrepreneur producing and selling fiction. Proclaimed a 'new star of the literary circles', a fashionable author who managed to fascinate his middle-class readers with stories of poverty and pain, in reality he stood somewhere on the 'boundary' between being a 'worker' and a 'writer'.

"Poor" Koreans, "Evil" Chinese.

Another and also crucially important defining moment in Ch'oe's 'boundary' experience was his life in Southern Manchuria, in the region known as Jiandao to the Chinese and Kando to Koreans. Pioneering the 'narrativisation' of Kando experiences was in fact one of the chief merits of Ch'oe's novels. Kando, with its conflict-ridden complex mixture of Chinese, Korean and Japanese populations, was a multiethnic and multicultural space—a complexity which Ch'oe could hardly allow himself to ignore. However, his view of the Chinese populace of Kando—one of the main 'heterogeneous elements' for the Koreans living there—is surprisingly negative. This fact should be given consideration, especially in the light of Ch'oe's

---

8. Sŏhae, Ch'oe (1927). *Chŏn'asa* (On Sending Off and Meeting), *Tonggwang* 9: 29-42.

affiliation (albeit temporary) with the Socialist "New Tendency School" (*Sinkyŏnghyangp'a*). The socialist writers, while mindful of the 'national contradictions' of colonial Korea, were also keen to emphasise their 'internationalist' commitments and the importance of transnational class solidarity for achieving the eventual objectives of socio-political transformation. Thus, they tended to be strict in distinguishing between the (oppressive and exploitive) Japanese Empire and the 'Japanese' as a whole—the latter also including the class of exploited, a potential ally of the Korean radicals. However in Ch'oe's works, especially the novel *Hongyŏm* (Red Flames),[9] it is not specifically 'class enemies' and 'exploiters' but 'the Chinese' as such who were described in the most negative way. The chief villain in the novel is a Chinese landlord with the surname Yin, but rest of the Chinese personages are hardly presented in a better light. The conflict between the 'evil, immoral and exploitive' Chinese and their Korean victims constitutes the centre of the novel's plot.

However, the conflict between Koreans and the evil and exploitive Chinese as an important element of the literary *sujet* is just a peculiarity of Ch'oe's work. Poor Korean tenant/servant oppressed by evil, sex-obsessed and cunning Chinese exploiter was a popular subject-matter in colonial Korean fiction as a whole. One well-known example by Ch'oe's literary patron, Yi Kwangsu (1892-1950), is narrated in his novel *Sambong'inechip* (Sambongi's Family).[10] It's a story of a Chinese landlord, Mr Hu (K. Ho Roya), who's seemingly interested in seducing Ŭlsuni, a sister of the main protagonist Sambong, Hu's honest servant. Sensing this and burning with jealousy, Mr Hu's junior wife falsely accuses Sambong of "banditry" and hands him over to the Chinese police. As a result of Mr Hu's sexual lust and his wife's jealousy, Sambong's faithful service as a pig shepherd undeservedly ends in tragic ruin for the whole family. In a

9. *Hongyŏm* (Red Flames), *Chosŏn Mundan* 18 (1927). A recent republication: Sŏhae, Ch'oe (2001). *T'alch'ulgi, Hongyŏm* (Record of an Escape, Red Flames). Seoul: Pŏmusa.

10. Serialised in *Tong'a Ilbo*, 29 November 1930–24 April 1931. Republished in *Yi Kwangsu Chŏnjip* (Collected Works by Yi Kwangsu). Seoul: Samjungdang. 1966. Vol. 2.

similar vein, in Kang Kyŏngae's novel, *Sogŭm* (Salt),[11] an evil Chinese landlord, Fang Deng, rapes the female protagonist Pongyŏm in the absence of his own wife, and then in a completely inhuman fashion, expels the pregnant Pongyŏm from his land. So, the 'sex-obsessed, immoral Chinese exploiter' seemed to have been a rather typical personage of colonial Korean fiction. Apart from sex, the 'Chinese exploiter' was thought to be, naturally enough, obsessed with greed—to the point of becoming an unrepentant serial murderer. In a novel by Kim Tong'in, *Pulgŭn San* (Red Mountain, 1932), a "Manchurian landlord" first beats to death his Korean tenant Song Ch'ŏmji, accusing him of failing to pay adequately for his tenancy, and then beats to death another Korean protagonist, a village hooligan nicknamed "Wolf" (*sak*), who—his habitual antisocial behaviour notwithstanding—tried, as a fellow Korean, to take the evil landlord to account for the murder of Song.[12] In a word, "victimization by an evil Chinese landlord"—economic, sexual or social—was one of the stereotypical plots of the Korean colonial novel.

However, the conflict in *Hongyŏm* can't be reduced to its class dimension—the victimisation of a poor tenant family of Korean provenance by a rich and powerful Chinese landlord. The Korean protagonists—as well as the author himself—make critical, sometimes disparaging, remarks about all Chinese, not necessarily only those with whom they found themselves in a direct socio-economic confrontation. "The *toenom* who do not even know their parents", "barbaric *toenom*", "do the *toenom* possess any ethics?", are usual remarks that the Korean protagonists exchange between themselves when referring to the Chinese. And, as if approving of their remarks, the author intervenes with direct words of his own:

> In Kando, when the Chinese are either taking forcibly or consensually buying Korean women, they usually do not allow them to leave their houses. Even the parents' requests for meetings with their daughters

11. Kyŏngae, Kang (1934). *Sogŭm* (Salt), *Sinkajŏng* 5 : 224-30 (May); 6: 225-32 (June); 7: 181-88 (July); 8: 200-06 (August); 9: 88-96 (September); 10: 200-16 (October). Republished in Sanggyŏng, Yi (ed.) (1999). *Kang Kyŏngae Chŏnjip* (Collected Works by Kang Kyŏngae). Seoul: Somyŏng. pp. 491-549.

12. Tong'in, Kim (1932). "*Pulgŭn San*" (Red Mountain), *Samch'ŏlli* 4(4): 114-17.

are often rejected. People say that the Chinese behave in such a fashion since they are full of suspicions [*Hongyŏm* (Red Flames), *Chosŏn Mundan* 18 (1927)].

Together with the author's own direct remarks, the coarse, broken Korean the landlord Yin speaks in the novel, as well as the descriptions of his residence, were to emphasise both the "barbaric rudeness" of the "Chinese other" and the atmosphere of a frightening "strangeness" around him. Yin's house is depicted as old, with the walls frighteningly blackened by smoke, the ceilings covered by cobwebs and the eyes of the historical figures on the antique wall-pictures glittering in the tobacco smoke as if they were hungry demons. The chief Korean protagonist, Mun *sŏbang*, is shivering with fear when he visits the residence of his Chinese patron. And while the latter is clearly associated with "hungry demons", Mun—who kills him with an axe in the finale and liberates his daughter who was forcibly taken by inhuman "Chinese enemy"—assumes the aura of a demon-fighter. While it is not impossible to characterise Mun's—and the author's—hostility to the "Chinese exploiter" as class enmity, it should also be noted that none of the non-privileged Chinese (servants of Yin etc.) were given even the semblance of a positive treatment in the novel. In the final analysis, the novel depicts a clash of "our/Korean goodness" with "their/Chinese evilness", ending with a cathartic revenge of "our hero" against "their evil anti-hero". Of course, *Hongyŏm* is somewhat unique among Ch'oe's novels in that the "national antagonism" between the Korean and Chinese was made a pivotal element of the plot. However, the "otherness" of the Chinese is also emphasised in Ch'oe's other novels, albeit without giving it such a crucial role in the development of the story. In Ch'oe's famed *T'alch'ulgi* (Record of an Escape),[13] for example, the protagonist describes the conditions of Kando in the following fashion:

> I was searching for land to cultivate, but there was no empty land there. I could not even get my hands on one *p'yŏng* of land before paying for it. Otherwise, I had to rent the land owned by the Chinese, and either to pay half of the harvest as rent, or make individual

13. *T'alch'ulgi* (Record of an Escape) , *Chosŏn Mundan* 6, 1925. A recent republication: Sŏhae, Ch'oe (2001). *T'alch'ulgi, Hongyŏm* (Record of an Escape, Red Flames). Seoul: Pŏmusa.

> sharecropping arrangements. If you enter into a tenancy agreement while also borrowing the foodstuffs from the Chinese, your share of the crops at the end of the year would not be sufficient even to cover the amount of the foodstuffs owed; and in any case, nobody was willing to accept such an inexperienced fellow like me as a tenant. Alien nature, alien people—here then, should I head for?"

This description is undoubtedly realistic—in the early 1920s, Chinese nationals indisputably constituted majority of the landowners in Kando. By the end of the 1920s and beginning of the 1930s, Koreans represented around 75 per cent of the Kando population, but only 7 per cent of the Korean populace were landlords, while 44 per cent of the ethnic Chinese in the region were landlords. In principle, Koreans could also own land on the condition that they became naturalised Chinese citizens. However, the process was hindered by bureaucratic procedures on the Chinese side and the Japanese insistence on Koreans being "imperial subjects" without any right to choose another nationality. The Chinese efforts to speed up the naturalisation of Koreans and the measures taken against non-naturalised Koreans were seen as "anti-Korean persecution" by the mainstream public in Korea proper: newspapers reported that some Korean activists were also urging associations of the resident Chinese in Korea to join the petitioning campaign against such persecutions, thus implying that the resident Chinese of Korea too were co-responsible for the fate of Koreans in China.[14] But in any case, according to Japanese reports, the majority of the Korean migrants to Southern Manchuria in the early 1920s were too poor even to buy the seedlings for farming, let alone land.[15] Regardless of the realism in the description of conflict between the Chinese landlords and Korean tenants, the striking feature of Ch'oe's rhetoric is the deliberate attempt to further "ethnicize" the ethno-class conflict in Kando's agrarian society. The Chinese—a majority of whom were poor and exploited too—were fully identified with the

---

14. *Tongp'o ongho ŭi taeundong: panpang kokkok ŭi sŏngwŏn sosik* (A Great Movement to Help the Compatriots: News of the Petitioning Campaign Everywhere), *Tong'a Ilbo*, 27 December 1927.

15. Park Hyun, Ok (2005). *Two Dreams in One Bed: Empire, Social Life and the Origins of the North Korean Revolution in Manchuria*. Durham: Duke University Press. pp.78-123.

"exploiters" in Ch'oe's work, and, moreover, reduced to the "negative other" directly in contrast to "us Koreans".

Most typically, nationalism of the colonial and semi-colonial peripheries of the capitalist world-system tended to describe the world in terms of the dichotomy between Euro-American colonisers and their non-Western victims. Korea, victimised by the Japanese instead of Europeans, stands apart from this general trend. The Chinese, who were victimised by both the Western and Japanese imperialists, were commonly depicted in a strongly negative light by Korea's literary nationalists. In fact, it is difficult to find even one positive Chinese hero in colonial Korean fiction—the stereotypical Chinese being lazy, sex-obsessed, unscrupulously exploitive and dirty. A good example of an extremely negative portrayal of the Chinese in Korean prose of the 1920-1930s is Kim Tong'in's masterpiece, *Kamja* (Potato), published in 1925, the same year as *T'alch'ulgi*. In this 'model work' of the Korean colonial naturalism, a licentious and shameless diaspora Chinese, Wang *sŏbang*, sexually violates the main female protagonist, Pongnyŏ, and then causes her death. And Wang is not the only Chinese villain in this novel—Yuk *sŏbang* and rest of the male members of the resident Chinese community in Pyongyang are also shown as habitual abusers of the Korean females. The author's direct speech in the novel emphasises the 'otherness' of the Chinese: "The flock of the Chinese was playing some strange instruments and singing a strange melody, producing lots of noise."

In 1925, more than half a century after the beginning of modern settlement of the Chinese on the Korean Peninsula, they were still "strange", exotic "others" for a representative prose writer of colonial Korea. Uncommonly oversexed, lustful Chinese males remained a stereotypic feature of the colonial prose literature well into the 1930s—Yi Hyosŏk's well-known novel, *Punnyŏ* (1936), features a Korean female protagonist being seduced by yet another Wang *sŏbang*, a Chinese lecher possessing both money and powers of seduction. Description of the resident Chinese as eroticised and ultimately inimical "others" may well be termed "orientalisation" in the Saidian terms—the difference being that it was Korea, represented by the females seduced and abused by the Chinese males, which was taking the symbolical role of the passive, feminine victim.

The Historical Roots of Enmity

What were the historical roots of inimical perception of the resident Chinese so visible in Korea's modern literature? In the historical perspective, the origins of such a perception may be traced to the historical overlap between the emergence of the resident Chinese community in Korea and the imperialist onslaught against the country. The first Chinese traders—around 40 people—came to Korea together with the Chinese (Qing) troops despatched to put down the Imo Soldiers' Mutiny in June-July 1882. In the wake of the Chinese-assisted suppression of this rebellion, Korea became a *de facto* semi-protectorate of China, and the resident Chinese, allowed to build their settlement in Inch'ŏn (Chemulp'o), settled in Hansŏng (Seoul) and a number of other cities, were soon placed under the special protection of China's supreme representative at the Korean court, Yuan Shikai (1859-1916). The special protection ended with China's defeat in the Sino-Japanese War (1894-1895) and consequent withdrawal from Korea, but despite all attempts of the now-powerful Japanese to stem the size and commercial influence of the Chinese diaspora, the numbers of resident Chinese continued to grow there were ca. 2,300 Chinese traders in Hansŏng alone by 1907. The rich opportunities to raise capital through familial networks and the exclusive nature of the Chinese enterprises (they tended to hire Chinese only, usually relatives or people hailing from the same locality) made them powerful, and often distrusted, competitors of the nascent Korean bourgeoisie—and rather unpopular competitors. Already in pre-colonial modern Korea, the anti-Chinese sentiment was palpable.[16]

The numbers of resident Chinese in Korea grew quickly during the colonial period, first and foremost because of the large-scale influx of Chinese manual workers. They were considered both "reliable"

16. Uyong, Chŏn (2003). *Han'gŭk kundae ŭi hwagyo munje* (The Problem of the Resident Chinese in Modern Korea), *Han'guksa Hakpo* 15: 377-409.

and "cheap"—by 1931, the average daily wage of a Chinese worker was 1 yen 63 sen, lower than the "Korean wage" (1 yen 76 sen) and almost twice lower than the "Japanese wage" (almost 3 yen).[17] One reason for cheapness of the Chinese labour was its abundant supply: the "coolies" were arriving in increasing numbers from the Chinese provinces torn apart by violence of the local warlords after the 1911-12 Xinhai revolution failed to build a stable and strong republican government, endemic warfare, epidemics and general abject poverty. By 1920, the Japanese Government-General registered approximately 16,000 Chinese workers in Korea, roughly half of them being low-qualified or non-qualified. By the end of 1925—the year when Ch'oe's *T'alch'ulgi* was published—the number had reached 21,000.[18]

Many of them worked on the construction sites; others were employed at Korea's pioneering factories, mines of the northern regions of Korea, and even commercial agriculture. There was widespread belief among the Korean workers that the Chinese 'competed' with them for the jobs, and the hostility was strengthened by cases when the Chinese workers were used as strike-breakers—notably, during the strike on postal ships in Pusan in 1919. The most notorious case was the use of ca. 500 Chinese workers to break up the general strike in Wŏnsan in 1929—although this strike was simultaneously supported by a number of labour bodies in China, and gave an example of solidarity between the Korean and Japanese workers, the latter also joining the dispute.[19] Chinese workers sometimes were striking too—fighting for higher wages and better working conditions,[20] but their image as 'easy-to-use strike-breakers' was already solidified by the late 1920s.

17. Cited in Kyŏngsik, Pak (1986). *Ilbon Chegukchuŭi ŭi Chosŏn Chibae* (The Japanese Imperialist Rule over Korea). Seoul: Haengji. p.297.

18. *Noŭn Yuch'ul Pangji Kanggu* (Research on the Ways to Prevent the Outflow of Money Paid as [Chinese] Workers' Wages), *Chosŏn Ilbo*, February 11, 1926.

19. Kim Kyŏng'il (1989). *1929nyŏn Wŏnsan Ch'ongp'aŏp e taehaesŏ* (On the 1929 Wŏnsan General Strike), *Ch'angjak kwa Pip'yŏng* 17(1): 301-39; Uyong, Chŏn (1989). *Wŏnsan esŏ ŭi singminji sut'al ch'eje ŭi kuch'uk kwa nodongja kyegŭp ui sŏngjang* (Formation of the Colonial Exploitation System in Wŏnsan and Growth of the Working Class), *Yŏksa wa Hyŏnsil* 2: 21-57.

20. See, for example, an account of a strike by the Chinese workers employed at a relatively small iron goods factory by a Japanese owner: *Shinajin Shōkō Yongsan de Higyō* (Chinese Workers Striking in Yongsan), *Chōsen Shimbun*, 2 August 1929.

The 'divide-and-rule' tactics by the employers and Japanese administrations sometimes were successful in leading the Korean workers' organisations to publicly protest the use of Chinese labour.[21] Japanese newspapers took a lead in voicing support for the protests, sometimes describing the entry of large groups of Chinese 'coolies' as a 'threat' to the colony's job market.[22] By 1931, as the preparations for an onslaught on Manchuria were in full swing, the Japanese colonial administrations were making full use of the anti-Chinese sentiments, and posed as 'protectors' of the colonial labour market, often by ordering wholesale firings of the Chinese workers, to be substituted by Koreans.[23] Competition for jobs between the two subaltern groups was in the end to be exploited for legitimising imperialist policies among the ethnic majority of the colonial subalterns.

The economic conflict exploited by the colonial power was complicated by the daily-life tensions. Since many of the resident Chinese were eventually going to return to their homes in China, they often did not bring the female household members with them to Korea. Especially for the manual workers, bringing spouses to Korea would be in most cases economically impossible. Thus, the Chinese community in colonial Korea was predominantly male: in 1922, there were, all in all, 30,826 resident Chinese registered by the colonial Government-General. Only 3,203 of them, however, were women—around 10 per cent of the total.[24] The spouseless Chinese were often looking for relations with local women—and were often described by the local press as "lecherous", over-sexed or abusive. Whether the sexual misbehaviour was more typical of the resident Chinese than of the local males, is hard to verify now; it is undeniable, however, that the "abuse of our women" by the "foreigners in our midst"

---

21. Yuguang, Jin (1983). *Luhan Liushinian Jianwenlu* (The Record of Sixty Years' Sojourn in Korea). Taibei: Zhonghua Minguo Hanguo Yanjiu Xueguan. pp.37-54.

22. See, for example: *Rōdō Shijō no taikyōi: Shinajin koryoku no taikun* (Great Threat to the Labour Market: a Large Group of Chinese Coolies), *Chōsen Shimbun,* 10 March 1931.

23. *Chunggugin inbu nŭn haego, chosŏnin man ch'aeyong* (Firings of the Chinese Workers; Exclusive Employment of Koreans), *Maeil Sinbo*, 8 August 1931.

24. Yuguang *op. cit.* no. 21: 25.

attracted much more attention of the nationalist press than similar misconduct by the locals.

The newspaper stories on the "Chinese abusing our girls" proliferated in the 1920s,[25] and were giving abundant material to creative writers of the Ch'oe Sŏhae, Kim Tong'in, and Yi Hyosŏk's calibre. Aside from simple "abuse", the transnational Chinese networks were also often accused of human traffic—that is, of selling bought or kidnapped Korean girls abroad (mainly in China).[26] Selling girls to brothels into a sort of indentured slavery was a widespread practice in Korea, and it was condoned by the colonial authorities.[27] However, the human traffic by the transnational, transborder actors was understood, in nationalist terms, as a "foreign threat" against "our women". In a paradoxical twist, the Japanese policemen—normally seen as part of the repressive colonial administrative machine by the nationalist press of the 1920s, and (justly) criticised for all sorts of rights violations[28]—were presented as "saviours of the Korean girls" by nationalist newspapers emphasising the nefarious role of the Chinese network in the international "trade in human flesh".

---

25. See, for example, *Chunggugin yangmyŏng i punyŏ rŭl nŭngyok* (Two Chinese Abused a Married Woman), *Tong'a Ilbo*, 19 November 1929, dealing with two Chinese employees of a racing club who had been accused of raping the wife of their Korean colleague (who seriously injured one of them in the subsequent fistfight); *Chosŏn Sonyŏ Nŭngyok* (A Korean Girl Abused), *Tong'a Ilbo*, 15 August 1927, a brief account of a Chinese silk trader from the vicinity of Kwangju who reportedly bought a 13 years-old Korean girl and made her his sex slave; *Sobu Nŭngyok Misu* (An Abortive Attempt to Abuse a Small Girl), *Tong'a Ilbo*, 23 June 1927, on a Kongju-based Chinese owner of a bakery, "notorious for his abusive behaviour with the Korean girls", in whose house another Chinese, a vegetable trader, unsuccessfully tried to kidnap and rape a 15 years-old Korean girl servant.
26. See, for example, *Hobyŏng ŭro sonyŏ yuin* (Enticed a Girl with a Chinese Rice Cake), *Tong'a Ilbo*, September 30, 1924, on a Shandong Chinese who lived in Korea for seven years and was professionally involved in kidnapping girls and illegally sending them to China; *Chungguk manyo* (Chinese Witch), *Tong'a Ilbo*, 23 April 1925, on a Seoul-based Chinese woman who had been involved in the business of buying, raising and re-selling Korean girls for 6-7 years, etc.
27. Yŏngae, Yamasida (1997). *Singminji chibae wa kongch'ang chedo ŭi chŏn'gae* (The Colonial Rule and the Development of the Licensed Brothel System), *Sahoe wa Yŏksa* 51: 143-81.
28. Sangŭi, Yi (2010). *Ilche ha Chosŏn kyŏngch'al ŭi t'ŭkching kwa kŭ imiji* (The Special Features of the Korean Police under the Japanese Colonial Rule and its Image), *Yŏksa Kyoyuk* 115: 165-85.

In addition to being a potential threat to the Korean women, the Chinese (men) were also routinely accused of opium smuggling and generally trade in drugs.[29] The quick growth in the number of drug addicts in the 1920s Korea was a proven fact—some journalists estimated the addicts' number at ca. 70,000 in 1926, and most observers agreed that it was rapidly increasing. The real reasons for this most likely were the lax enforcement of prohibitions against the illicit drug trade by the Japanese police, a general gloomy mood of helplessness in the educated strata of the colonial society, and the desperate poverty of colonial workers, artisans and small-time traders, coupled with a lack of informed perspectives.[30] It was easier, however, for the nationalist media to accuse the "alien" Chinese of spreading evil than to analyse the complicated reasons behind socio-cultural crises in the colony.

One reason why the nationalist media outlets tended not to lose any opportunity to blacken the image of the resident Chinese was the position of the Korean bourgeoisie which owned the mainstream Korean press and exerted decisive influence on editorial policies. From the viewpoint of colonial Korea's ethnic Korean entrepreneurs, the Chinese were competitors—and, unlike the Japanese capitalists, they were relatively easy targets for an inimical campaign, since they were not protected by the colonial administration. According to the Japanese colonial statistics, in 1922, the "merchants" constituted 51.8 per cent of the resident Chinese population in Korea (the rest being either workers or peasants mostly specialising in production of vegetables). Certainly, the absolute majority of individual Chinese "merchants" hardly owned more than a Chinese restaurant (Chinese cuisine gained popularity in the urban areas of Korea from the

29. Drug addiction was understood to be a "Chinese disease"—China's national disaster which caused the country's "national degradation". An editorial in *Tong'a Ilbo* (justly) ascribed the prevalence of drug trade in China to the collusion of local militarists and criminals: *Ap'yŏn Chungdok* (Opium Addiction), *Tong'a Ilbo*, 1 June 1925. Simultaneously, however, the nationalist newspapers were emphasising the role of the resident Chinese in the drug trade in Korea: Uyong, Chŏn (2003). *Han'guk kŭndae ŭi hwagyo munje* (The Problem of the Resident Chinese in Modern Korea), *Han'guksa Hakpo* 15: 377-409.

30. Kang, Pak (2008). *20 Segi Chŏnban Tongbug'a Han'in kwa Ap'yŏn* (Northeast Asia's Koreans and Opium in the First Half of the Twentieth Century). Seoul: Sŏn'in. pp.106-19.

late 1910s), a barber shop, a textile workshop, or a small retailing company selling imported textiles. However, some of the resident Chinese capitalists were famously rich—typically, Tan Jiesheng (1853-1929), a Guangdong native who came to Korea in 1885 and made a fortune in the import of British and Chinese goods already before the colonisation. By 1922, Tan still was Kyŏngsŏng's top taxpayer, and paid in taxes 213 per cent more than the richest Japanese taxpayer therein.[31]

Tan's case was somewhat exceptional, but economic position of the affluent top stratum of Korea-based Chinese merchant community was generally strong enough to be envied by the local competitors. According to anecdotal evidence from a Korea-residing Chinese trader, in the mid-1920, around three of five stalls at the biggest urban markets there were owned by the resident Chinese, who controlled the prices of the (mostly imported) textiles, in addition to those of chilli peppers and garlic.[32] An important basis of the economic prominence of the diasporic Chinese in colonial Korea was their control over the trade with China, the amount of which grew seven times by 1927 as compared with 1913.[33] Much of this trade was in textiles, and was seen by the Japanese trading community in Korea as undermining their position. To protect the position of the Japanese businessmen, the colonial authorities enacted a number of protectionist measures—for example, levying in 1924 a prohibitive 100 per cent customs duty on the import of (mostly British-produced) cottons and (mostly Chinese-produced) silks from China.[34] These measures also benefitted the local

---

31. Ŭn'gyong, Pak (2002). *Han'gugin kwa pihan'gugin—tan'il hyŏlt'ong ui sinhwa ga namgin ch'abyŏl ui nolli* (Koreans and Non-Koreans: the Logic of Discrimination Generated by the Myth of a Single Bloodline), *Tangdae Pip'yŏng* 19: 272-87; Ryōta, Ishigawa and Kim Nakki (2007). *Tongsunt'ae wa Inch'ŏn Hwagyo Muyŏk* (The Tongshuntai Company and the Inch'on-centered Chinese Diaspora Trade). Inch'ŏn: Inch'ŏn Munhwa Chaedan.
32. Guanjun, Lu (1956). *Hanguo Huaqiao Jingji* (The Chinese Diaspora Economy in Korea). Taibei: Haiwai Chubanshe. pp.53-54.
33. Zhaoquan, Yang and Sun Yumei (1991). *Chaoxian Huaqiao shi* (The History of the Korea-residing Chinese). Beijing: Huaqiao Chuban Gongshi. pp.191-92.
34. Yongsin, Kim (2005). *Ilche sigi Chaehan hwagyo (1910-1931)* (The Resident Chinese in the Japanese Colonial Period, 1910-1931), *Inch'ŏnhak Yŏn'gu* 4: 207-44.

producers of textiles, both Korean and Japanese—including, for example, the brothers Kim Sŏngsu (1891-1955) and Kim Yŏnsu (1896-1979), who held the majority stake and managed both the premier Korean-run textile factory, Kyŏngsŏng Pangjik, and the most influential local newspaper, *Tong'a Ilbo*.[35] The interests of the local and Japanese business elites clashed on many issues, but overlapped to a certain degree in a common rivalry with the Chinese entrepreneurs. Small wonder that the *Tong'a Ilbo* was one of the newspapers regularly printing the Sinophobic stories, while the *Maeil Sinbo*, run by the colonial authorities, took the lead in accusing the resident Chinese of smuggling, drug trade, violent misbehaviour, and drug abuse, and in emphasising the "persecutions" against Koreans in China, especially in the Northeastern areas of China.[36] The modern "print capitalism", both local and colonial, served as an important agent in the process of articulating the anti-Chinese prejudices and embedding them in the masses of newspaper-reading urban public.

The smouldering conflict between the locals and Chinese immigrants ended up in the 1931 anti-Chinese riots in Korea. The pretext for the riots was—in this case, largely imagined—"anti-Korean persecutions" in Manchuria; the immediate impulse for rioting was in reality given by largely exaggerated reports of the local press, which was consistently demonstrating its anti-Chinese bias. The alleged reason for the rioting was clashes between the Korean tenants and Chinese peasants in the locality of Wanbaoshan (in the Northeastern vicinities of Changchun, today's Jilin Province). There, in June-July 1931, a group of Koreans protected by ca. 40 Japanese consular policemen tried to build an irrigational waterway against the opposition of the local Chinese peasants whose fields were thus threatened by flooding. The clashes claimed no lives and eventually ended up in favour of the Korean side, but an influential

35. On their business empire's history and its relations with the colonial authorities, see: Eckert, Carter J. (1991). *Offspring of Empire: The Koch'ang Kims and the Colonial Origins of Korean Capitalism 1876-1945*. Seattle: University of Washington Press.

36. Sŭnghoe, Son (2009). *1931 nyŏn singminji Chosŏn Paehwa P'oktong kwa Hwagyo* (The anti-Chinese Riots in Colonial Korea in 1931 and the Resident Chinese), *Chungguk Kŭnhyŏndaesa Yŏn'gu* 41: 141-65.

Korean newspaper, the *Chosŏn Ilbo*, claimed in a series of "reports" printed between 2-4 July that "two hundreds of our compatriots" were injured in the clashes amidst a large-scale conflict between the Japanese and Chinese police forces. While the anti-Chinese rioting had already started in Inch'ŏn on 3 July, the *Chosŏn Ilbo* on 4 July published a new editorial appealing for "rightful action" in the name of "love toward our compatriots tied to us by blood". Basically the newspaper was fanning up the pogroms, obviously allowed to do so by the Japanese colonial administration (which had censorship powers over the Korean press) which was interested in heightening the anti-Chinese animosity in Korea on the eve of the military invasion of Manchuria. While 5 July onwards the *Tong'a Ilbo* tried to cool down the anti-Chinese hysteria, its articles for 2-4 July also mentioned the (non-existent) "violence by the Chinese peasants."[37]

The Sinophobic agitation in the media ended up in serious bloodshed. The anti-Chinese riots in a number of Korean cities in early July 1931 claimed 142 lives (with 91 resident Chinese missing, presumed dead). About 44 per cent of the Koreans arrested as the perpetrators of anti-Chinese violence were classified as "workers" by profession. In most cases, they regarded the Chinese as their competitors in the labour market, and were additionally provoked by misleading reports of the "anti-Korean atrocities" in China. The *Chŏson Ilbo*, whose reporting ignited the bloodshed, did not seem to have changed its basic editorial line even after the pogroms—it continuously viewed the Chinese, both inside and outside of Korea as an 'other', either potentially hostile or involved in a Darwinian "competition for survival" against the Koreans. However on 5 July 1931, the *Chŏson Ilbo's* editorial manager, well-known nationalist thinker An Chaehong (1891-1965), published an article in which he appealed for "calm"—in the name of safety of the Manchurian Koreans, who might be harmed in revenge.[38] It looks as if in the

37. Tugi, Min (2002). *Sigan kwa ŭi Kyŏngjaeng* (Competition with the Times). Seoul: Yonsei University Press. pp.185-92.

38. T'aeung, Kim (2009). *1920-1930 nyŏndae Han'gugin taejung ŭi hwagyo insik kwa kungnae minjokchuŭi kyeyŏl chisigin ŭi naemyŏn segye* (The Mass Perception of the Diasporic Chinese by the Koreans in the 1920-1930s, and the Internal Worlds of the Domestic Nationalist Intellectuals), *Yŏksa Kyoyuk* 112: 93-131.

mental world of the nationalistic intelligentsia, lives of the resident Chinese mattered only as the issue of safety of "our compatriots in China" was also at stake. Mostly negative reporting on the resident Chinese community—whose economic weight drastically dropped after the start of Japan's all-out aggression in China in 1937—continued throughout the 1930s, gradually merging with the denigrating view on the "pre-modern, inept, effeminised and lazy" Chinese produced by the mainstream official discourse as Japan was preparing to launch a full-scale onslaught against China.[39]

Chinese Revolution and the Possibilities of Solidarity

It is undeniable, however, that a sizable stream of sympathy and positive interest towards China also existed in the colonial literary and intellectual discourses. For example, in Chu Yosŏp's novel, *Illyŏkkŏkkun* (Rickshaw),[40] the roles are reversed—wealthy Koreans are shown as exploiters of a poor Chinese rickshaw driver. In the intellectual life outside of the literary circles, a colonial thinker famed for his eccentric paradoxes, Pyŏn Yŏngman (1889-1954), used to call China, where he spent several years in exile, his "second motherland" and considered Zhang Binglin (1868-1936), China's great modern philosopher, his teacher.[41] The *Tong'a Ilbo's* Chinese correspondent, Sin Ŏnjun (1904-1938), who was deservedly called colonial Korea's "China hand", actively tried to achieve reconciliation between the Koreans and the Chinese after the 1931 Wanbaoshan incident and the subsequent anti-Chinese pogroms in Korea.[42] An interesting example of rather positive—albeit romanticised and

39. Uyong, Chŏn (2003). *Han'guk kŭndae ŭi hwagyo munje* (The Problem of the Resident Chinese in Modern Korea), *Han'guksa Hakpo* 15: 377-409.

40. *Illyŏkkŏkkun* (Rickshaw), *Kaebyŏk* 58: 8-19, 1925. Republished in Yosŏp, Chu (2000). *Kurŭm ŭl Chabŭryŏgo* (To Catch the Clouds). Seoul: Choŭn Ch'aek Mandulgi. pp.457-45.

41. Yŏngman, Pyŏn (1931). *Chunggug'in ŭi Saenghwallyŏk* (The Life Energy of the Chinese), Tong'a Ilbo, 7 May 1931. Republished in Yŏngman, Pyŏn (2006). *Pyŏn Yŏngman Chŏnjip* (Collected Works of Pyŏn Yŏngman). Seoul: Sŏnggyun'gwan Taehakkyo Taedong Munhwa Yŏn'guwŏn. Vol.3. pp.187-88; Yŏngman, Pyŏn (2006). *Chang T'aeyom kke* (To Zhang Binglin), Pyŏn Yŏngman Chŏnjip (Collected Works of Pyŏn Yŏngman). Seoul: Sŏnggyun'gwan Taehakkyo Taedong Munhwa Yŏn'guwŏn. Vol.1, pp.319-20.

42. Tugi *op. cit.* no. 37: 193-205.

sketchy—portrayal of China is colonial Korea's prose literature is the novel *Hŭkp'ung* (*Black Wind*; serialised in the *Chosŏn Ilbo*, 9 April 1935–4 February 1936) by the celebrated Buddhist reformer and poet, Han Yong'un (penname Manhae; 1879-1944). The novel's main protagonist is a "romantic outlaw" of the late Qing times—a poor peasant's son from the Hangzhou area who begins by taking revenge against the rich landlord (who had previously blackmailed his tenant father into sending him his daughter as a concubine) and ends up joining the anti-Qing revolutionaries and going to the USA in search of "new knowledge".[43] While the "Chinese revolutionaries" were obviously an allegory for Korea's own militant nationalists whose courage Han greatly admired, the novel is peppered with descriptions of late Qing period historical events and Chinese cities (Hangzhou, Shanghai etc.)—which Han himself never visited anytime in his life. It is obvious that for Han, China was a part of the same civilisational and historical space as Korea itself, and the Chinese historical time was moving in sync with Korea's own, both countries being pregnant with national revolutions.

The Chinese revolution was, indeed, a hot topic for the 1920s–1930s Korean intellectuals, indicating for many of them the possibility of a mass upheaval which would put an end both to colonialism and capitalism in East Asia. Sun Yatsen's activities, seen as crucial to the success of a democratic revolution in China, were widely covered by the Korean press—both by China-based émigré publications and newspapers and journals in Korea proper. A 1920 contribution by Sun to a Japanese daily suggesting that Japan's occupation of Korea was a threat to China's interests, was quickly translated and reprinted both by Korea's leading liberal daily *Tong'a Ilbo* and the émigré *Tongnip Sinmun*, the mouthpiece of Shanghai-based Korean Provisional Government.[44] Sun, hard pressed to seek

43. The novel is included in *Han Yongun chŏnjip* (Complete Works of Han Youngun). Seoul: Sin'gu Munhwasa. 1974. Vol.5. pp.17-309. See also Chinhong, Ch'ae (2004). *Han Yongun ŭi Hŭkp'ung yŏn'gu* (Study on Han Yongun's Novel, Black Wind), *Kugŏ Kungmunhak* 138: 369-402.

44. Yatsen, Sun (1920). *Shinajin no Nihonkan* (The View of Japan by the Chinese), *Taishō Nichinichi Shimbun*, 1 January; *Son Ilsŏn ssi ŭi Ilbon'gwan* (Sun Yatsen's View of Japan), *Tongnip Sinmun*, 17 January 1920; *Chosŏn Munje wa Chungguk* (The Korean Question and China), *Tong'a Ilbo*, 11 August 1920.

support in Japan in his confrontations with China's warlords, was hardly in a position to actively support Korea's independence even if he wanted to do so; Korea's intellectuals, however, were keen to discern even the slightest signs of possible support for Korea's cause by the man seen as the Chinese revolution's most prominent leader. Thus, Sun's famed Kobe speech (28 November 1924) which emphasised the roles of both China and Japan as Asia's "natural leaders" in its struggle against "Western hegemonism"—while not mentioning at all Korea's plight under Japanese control—could not but produce a tremendous disillusionment among Korea's educated stratum. Typically, the *Tong'a Ilbo* briefly covered the speech expeditiously, just two days after it took place,[45] and then published a lengthy English editorial with detailed criticisms of Sun's positions—targeting also the foreign readership.[46] Sun's flirting with their imperialist mother country opened the eyes of Korea's colonial intellectuals to the complexities of East Asia's international power politics. China's revolution, with all the possibilities it seemed to bring, still did not mean an immediate aid for Korea's cause from its giant western neighbour.

Still, the interest in perspectives that the Chinese revolution was opening persisted, and was not necessarily limited to Sun's towering personality. When Feng Yuxiang (1882-1948), the "Christian warlord" who later joined ranks with Guomindang and eventually came to be on friendly terms with Communists, took Beijing, changed the governmental system, invited Duan Qirui (1865-1936) to the presidency, and hosted Sun Wen in Beijing in 1924-25, Korea's representative intellectual monthly, *Kaebyŏk* published a lengthy, unabashedly optimistic piece on the possibilities of China "turning red" (*chŏkhwa*). Viewing China's presumed ancient system of government under the legendary "sage emperors" (Huangdi, Yao, Shun, Yu, etc.) as "proto-Communism" of sorts, the editorial writers of the journal dwelled both on Feng Yuxiang's pro-Soviet

45. *Ilbon Sinho si e chaehan Son Mun ssi yŏnsŏl ŭi naeyong: Taeaseachuŭi rŭl kojo* (The Content of Mr. Sun Wen's Speech in Kobe, Japan: Emphasis on Pan-Asianism), *Tong'a Ilbo*, 30 November 1924.

46. "Dr. Sun Yatsen's Speech", *Tong'a Ilbo*, 6-7 December 1924.

stance and on the potential of China's radicalised trade unions and Guomindang's own radicals—still seeing the Guomindang as a Soviet ally. The possibility of an imperialist intervention in the imminent revolution in China was the *Kaebyŏk* writers' worst fear, China being seen by them, on par with Korea itself, as imperialism's foremost victim in East Asia.[47]

It has to be noticed here that 'victims' solidarity', in a broader sense of the word, was also the viewpoint from which Chinese revolutionaries of different shades considered Korea's colonial plight. Empathy was visibly mutual; however, unlike the majority of Korea-based modernist Korean intellectuals who tended, in a good nationalist spirit, to view China as a potentially helpful and friendly but still distinctly foreign state, some of the more conservative Chinese republicans still looked at Korea through the old Sino-centric lens, mixing the age-old perception of Korea as a "faithful tributary" with modern racialist rhetoric. The Guomindang officially cited Korea's "time-honoured position as China's tributary" and the putative "descent of Koreans from Yin and Zhou" as the historical reasons for its decision to support the China-based Korean émigré nationalist movement.[48] Sun Yatsen, while meeting the Shanghai-based Korean Provisional Government's foreign minister and long-term friend of the Chinese republicans, Sin Kyusik (1879-1922) in October 1922, pointed out to the "commonality of letters (i.e., culture) and race between the brotherly countries of China and Korea, as well as their long history of mutual ties as close as lips and teeth" as the reasons why the Guomindang was "morally obliged" to accept at least some requests of the Korean independence activists.[49]

The figures to the left of Guomindang were, however, much less tradition-bound in appreciating Korea's struggles. Chen Duxiu (1879-

47. *Chungguk hyŏngmyŏng undong u ichiban un yŏha* (What is the Basis of China's Revolutionary movement), *Kaebyŏk* 65: 30-43, 1926.

48. Cited in Kim Han'gyu, *Hanchung Kwan'gyesa* (The History of Korean-Chinese Relations). Seoul: Arŭk'e. 1999. Vol.2. p.923. The decision was taken in March 1920, after the Shanghai-based Korean Provisional Government was formed.

49. Sŏngnin, Min (1942). *Chunghan Oegyo Sahwa* (Tales of Sino-Korean Diplomacy). Chongjing: Dongfang Chubanshe. p.26; cited in: Wanmin, Xu (1999). *Chunghan Kwan'gyesa* (History of Sino-Korean Relations: Translated by Chŏn Hosŏk *et al.*) Seoul: Ilchogak. pp.299-300.

1942), soon to co-found the Chinese Communist Party, evaluated Korea's 1 March 1919 independence movement as a major world historical event. He even expressed his hope that post-independence Korea would preserve the spirit of non-violent, unarmed resistance amply shown during the mass anti-Japanese demonstrations in March 1919, and pioneer the way towards a disarmed, post-militarist world. Closer to home, he shamed his compatriots for their inability to do what Koreans did, despite the utter failure of democracy in post-Xinhai China and complete alienation between the rulers and the ruled. Unlike Korea, where "students and Christians" rose up and demonstrated, China's "students and Christians" were "seemingly dead in their spirit".[50] In view of China's own 4 May 1919 movement, which was to happen little more than a month after Chen's pessimistic remarks on Chinese students saw the daylight, Chen evidently was excessively critical of his younger Chinese contemporaries. What is important here for us, however, is the fact that admiration of the neighbour's revolutionary prowess between China and Korea was by 1919 rather mutual. China's revolutionary intellectuals also could find reasons to admire their smaller eastern neighbour and its denizens' ability to perform such rituals of modern democratic citizenship as mass demonstrations, often at great risk to their life.

The Guomindang's 1925-1928 Eastern and Northern expeditions were closely covered by the Korean newspapers, interested in both the historical and world-political meaning of China's reunification and in its revolutionary potential. While it was not widely reported in the colonial Korea, a good number of Koreans did participate in these crucial military campaigns. The Guomindang's Whampoa Military Academy enrolled 34 Korean students by 1928, and even employed some Korean teachers (a Korean, O Song'yun, taught Russian there).[51] Its Korean graduates, famed for their military exploits in 1925-1928, included Yang Rim (1898-1936), a youthful activist of

---

50. *Chaoxian Duli Yundong zhi Ganxiang* (Impressions of Korea's Independence Movement), *Meizhou Pinglun* 14, 22 March 1919. Reprinted in: Duxiu, Chen (1987). *Duxiu Wencun* (Duxiu's Remained Works). Hefei: Anhui Renmin Chubanshe. pp.404-05.

51. Wanmin *op. cit.* no. 49: 306.

the Northeastern China-based anti-Japanese armed struggle who distinguished himself as a battalion commander in both campaigns. A Chinese Communist Party member from 1925, he fought on the Communist side against the Guomindang in the 1930s and heroically died during the Long March.[52] Not unlike Yang Rim, the majority of Whampoa Koreans were leftists of different sorts. At least 24 Korean students were followers of Kim Wŏnbong (1898-1958), the legendary leader of the Korean Heroic Corps (*Ŭiyŏldan*, founded in 1919), an anarchist-leaning armed resistance organisation which was actively seeking cooperation with Communists in mid- and late 1920s.[53] The Republican revolution as such did not imply an immediate and sure boost for Korea's anti-colonial liberation efforts. As Sun Yatsen's lukewarm attitude towards the Korean cause showed, China as a conventional nation state had its own interests, which did not necessarily coincide with Korea's. Communism or anarchism, by contrast, were much more explicitly internationalist, the Communist revolution in China being seen by many émigré radicals as a possibly crucial factor in Korea's liberation.

For commentators in colonial Korea, many of them standing to the left of the centre too, China's political unification by the Guomindang's military was not the only object of interest. What happened in China was regarded as first and foremost a revolution from below. Thus, the conditions and attitudes of China's "masses" were of primary interest. In 1927-1929, Sin Ŏnjun, for example, serialised in the *Tong'a Ilbo* a number of high-quality articles on China's working class, socio-economic situation and revolution, focusing largely on what China and Korea had in common. As in Korea, much of the workers' radicalism in China could be explained by the nationalist anger against mostly foreign entrepreneurs, with their openly racist attitudes. According to Sin's statistics, 75 per cent of all strikes during 1927 in Shanghai were related to the foreigners' abuse of Chinese workers. More generally, China was suffering from

52. Sangdo, Han (2004). *Chungguk Hyŏngmyŏng sok ŭi Han'guk Tongnip Undong* (The Korean Imdepepndence Movement amindst China's Revolution). Seoul: Chimmundang. pp. 200-04.

53. Yingji, Piao (2001). *Kŭnhyŏndae Chunghan Kwan'gyesa Yon'gu* (Research on Modern and Contemporary Relations between China and Korea). Seoul: Kukhak Charyowon. pp. 90-96.

the foreign capital-led industrial development, the subsequent downfall of traditional artisanship and agrarian overpopulation, which the underdeveloped urban industry was in no position to ameliorate. While Korea is not explicitly mentioned in these articles, an educated and socially aware Korean reader could easily see that China's problems were in fact also Korea's.[54]

Amidst the wave of a generally heightened interest in contemporary China, a Korean translation of Lu Xun's (1881-1936) seminal *Kuangren Riji* (A Madman's Diary, 1918) was first published in 1927 (it was later republished in 1935).[55] The translation is somewhat abridged, and done in a quite unnatural, heavily accented Korean. In fact, the translator, China-based émigré militant Yu Kisŏk (1905-1980)—who respected Lu Xun to such a degree that he took the latter's original name, Shuren, and made it into his penname, Suin, in Korean)—was brought to China as a 10 years-old boy by his nationalist parents, and spoke Chinese, rather than Korean, in his everyday life. Initially a Christian nationalist, he, as many other younger émigré Koreans, became radicalised in mid-1920s, turning into an anarchist militant.[56] Lu Xun, in his turn, was coming closer to the Communists in his last years—and the news of his "left turn" were duly reported by the Korean press,[57] further strengthening the association between "China" and "revolution". Another reason for Lu Xun's considerable popularity in colonial Korea was actuality of the topics he dealt with, for the Korean readers of his translated works. His well-known short story, *Zai Jiulou Shang* (*In the Drinking*

54. *Chungguk Nodong Undong ŭi Yurae wa Kyŏnghyang ŭi Kwanch'al* (The Origins of China's Labour Movement and Observations on its Tendencies), *Tong'a Ilbo*, December14-15, 1927; *Chungguk Hyŏngmyŏng ŭi ponjil kwa kŭ Ch'use* (The Essence of the Chinese Revolution and its Tendencies), *Tong'a Ilbo*, 5-17 June 1929. See also Tugi, Min (ed.) (2000). *Sin Ŏnjun Hyŏndae Chungguk Kwan'gye Nonsŏl Sŏn* (A Selection of Sin Onjun's Articles on Contemporary China. Seoul, Munhak kwa Chisŏngsa. pp.201-32.

55. Xun, Lu (1935). *Kwang'in Ilgi* (A Madman's Diary), *Tonggwang* 16: 52-58; *Samch'ŏlli* 7(5): 292-99, 1935.

56. Kisŏk, Yu (2010). *30 nyŏn Pangnanggi* (The Story of 30 Years-long Wanderings). Seoul: Kukka Pohunch'ŏ.

57. *Chungguk Mun'in Insanggi: Kodok kwa P'ungja ŭi Sangjing'in Chigŏm Chwagyŏnghan No Sin ssi* (Impressions of Chinese Writers: Mr. Lu Xun, the Symbol of Loneliness and Satire, who has now turned Left), *Tong'a Ilbo*, 3 May 1935.

House, 1924), translated and published in Korean in 1933,[58] dealt, for example, with the issue of the continuous ideological hegemony still exercised by the outdated Confucian canon—an issue which Korea's modernists and radicals could easily recognise as their own.

After the Guomindang's counter-revolutionary turn in 1928, the foremost interest of the Korean leftist writers was the status and perspectives of the Chinese Communist movement. The Guomindang, apart from being counter-revolutionary, was also perceived as too weak to achieve the revision of the "unequal treaties" with the Westerns powers and make China genuinely independent. Sun Wen was regarded as a "utopian socialist" of sorts, but the post-1928 Guomindang was seen as having betrayed Sun Wen's legacy. The Communists, by contrast, were waging both class and national struggles, being the only authentically anti-imperialist force.[59] The Soviet movement in China was another fascinating issue for the colonial radicals; in 1932, one author estimated that Soviet zones existed in 8 out of 18 provinces of China, controlling a territory twice as large as Korea's. Their future was seen as dependent on the Soviet Union's ability to come and aid them in removing the Guomindang government and, more generally, on the "overall situation in the worldwide class war."[60]

A very special category of colonial Korea's "China watchers" were the Korean intellectuals who went to China either to live in exile or to study. Most of them were usually connected with either nationalist or socially radical (anarchist or Communist) movements. One of the best known examples is Pak Ŭnsik (1859-1925), who, after going into Chinese exile in June 1911, contributed both to Chinese and Korean periodicals—furnishing them, among others, with opinion pieces and analytical articles on contemporaneous China's status and perspectives. Initially, in 1912-1916, he appeared to basically

58. Xun, Lu (1933). *Chae Churu sang* (In the Drinking House: Translated by Kim Kwangju), *Cheilsŏn* 3(1).

59. Nam, Sok (1931). *Yŏlgang Kŭktong Chŏngch'aek kwa Chungguk ŭi Kŭmhu Chŏnmang* (The Far Eastern Policies of the Powers and China's Future), *Hyesong* 1: 12-15.

60. Yangmyŏng, Hong (1932). *Chungguk Ssobet'ŭ Undong ui Changnae* (The Future of the Chinese Soviet Movement), *Samch'ŏlli* 4(5): 10.

support the Xinhai revolution. While being critical of Yuan Shikai's dictatorial rule,he supported the republican revolutionaries.[61] At the same time, his articles and editorials in the rather conservative, Shanghai-based daily *Shiminbao* (October 1921–August 1922) are focused on what he seemed to have considered China's worst problem, namely the proverbial "warlord rule" of the post-Yuan period. In one of his articles, for example, he contrasted the pacifist tendencies of the post-First World War world with the endless clashes between China's warlords, the "public enemies" of peace as Pak called them, and appealed for a pan-national anti-warlord movement based on the citizenry's democratic participation.[62] Pak openly pinned his hopes on the popular movements following the famed 4 May 1919 student demonstrations in Beijing, which he termed "the beginning of people's awakening". Unless the popular democratic movements were to win control over the warlord oligarchies, China's international position was destined to remain "lower than that of Europe's smaller states".[63] In a word, Pak, the erstwhile champion of statist self-strengthening and reforms from above in the pre-colonial Taehan Empire,[64] turned into a sort of democrat in the highly charged atmosphere of post-4 May China. Given his Confucian background and close ties to such conservative reformists as Kang Youwei (1856-1927), this turn may be best explained by his hope that mass-based popular movements—such as Korea's own 1 March movement of 1919—would be instrumental in the process of Korea's future decolonisation. Pak's other hope was an anti-Japanese alliance between Korean and Chinese nationalisms and

61. Kyŏnghan, Pae (2007). *Ssun Wŏn kwa Han'guk* (Sun Yatsen and Korea). Seoul: Hanul Ak'ademi. pp.157-88.

62. *Pinghua shidai zhi naizheng* (The Civil Wars of a Peaceful Epoch), *Shiminbao,* 19 February 1922. Reprinted in: Chŏnjip, Paeg'am Pak Ŭnsik (ed.) (2002). *Paeg'am Pak Ŭnsik Sŏnsaeng Chŏnjip P'yŏnch'an Wiwŏnhoe* (Collected Works of Paeg'am Pak Ŭnsik). Seoul: Tongbang Midio. Vol.5. p.511.

63. *Guomin sixiang zhi jinbu* (The Progress of People's Ideas), *Shiminbao*, 16 May 1922. Reprinted in Chŏnjip, Paeg'am Pak Ŭnsik (ed.) (2002). *Paeg'am Pak Ŭnsik Sŏnsaeng Chŏnjip P'yŏnch'an Wiwŏnhoe* (Collected Works of Paeg'am Pak Ŭnsik). Seoul: Tongbang Midio. Vol.5. p.529.

64. On Pak's ideas in the 1900s, see, for example, Yongha, Sin (1986). *Pak Ŭnsik ŭi Sahoe Sasang Yŏn'gu* (Research on Pak Ŭnsik's Social Ideas). Seoul: Soul Taehakkyo Ch'ulp'anbu.

Soviet "anti-imperialism". In this spirit, he proposed that Koreans might join Chinese in boycotting Japanese goods by choosing to buy local wares, thus undermining Japan's continental trade; this would help bring Japan closer to impoverishment and, hopefully, lead to a "peasant and workers' revolution," which would then result in Korea's liberation.[65]

Pak's most representative piece on post-Xinhai China, published in the colonial-era Korean monthly, *Kaebyŏk*, in 1923, was however written in much less optimistic tones. Seeing China as East Asia's natural centre, traditionally self-sufficient ideologically and economically, Pak at the same time subscribed to the modernist criticisms of "old China", lamenting the supposed lack of public spiritedness and the "corrupt customs" of the contemporaneous Chinese—"too egoistic", from his point of view. He gave a detailed description of China's internal conflicts and warlord warfare during 1912-1922, and made some rather pessimistic conclusions for his Korean readers. Being critical of the "federalist" projects—which envisioned China as a union of very autonomous provinces—Pak hoped for China's re-unification but estimated the chances of peaceful re-unification as extremely slim. While some warlords, notably Shanxi's Yan Xishan (1883-1960), were trying to "civilize" their provinces, a majority of them were cruel exploiters whose incessant warfare was ruining people's livelihood. The only way to unify China was to eliminate them by force—but the party of the strongest potential unifier, Sun Yatsen, was plagued by internal squabbles and lacked money and arms, despite its pan-national character.[66] Pak's ultimate Sinophilic attitude is visible in this piece too; he called upon his readers not to disdain China's temporary

65. *Uri do Chungguk Kakkye ŭi Undong kwa Ilch'iro haja* (Let Us Coordinate with China's Various Movements), *Tongnip Sinmun*, 14 March 1923. Reprinted in Chŏnjip, Paeg'am Pak Ŭnsik (ed.) (2002). *Paeg'am Pak Ŭnsik Sŏnsaeng Chŏnjip P'yŏnch'an Wiwŏnhoe* (Collected Works of Paeg'am Pak Ŭnsik). Seoul: Tongbang Midio. Vol.5. pp.546-48.

66. *Hyŏngmyŏmg hu 12 nyŏn kan ŭi Chungguk* (China in 12 Post-Revolutionary Years), *Kaebyŏk* 39: 25-28, 33-34, 1923. Partly reprinted in Chŏnjip, Paeg'am Pak Ŭnsik (ed.) (2002). *Paeg'am Pak Ŭnsik Sŏnsaeng Chŏnjip P'yŏnch'an Wiwŏnhoe* (Collected Works of Paeg'am Pak Ŭnsik). Seoul: Tongbang Midio. Vol.5 pp.552-54.

weakness, and emphasised China's "natural" greatness. However, as a practicing émigré activist, Pak implicitly appealed to his Korean readers to be realistic. A unified China, as a potential sponsor of Korea's own independence movement, was not going to emerge easily any time soon.

All in all, "revolution", "masses" and "anti-feudalism" were the main code words associated with "China" in the Korean nationalist and left-wing journalism of the 1920s and early 1930s. There seemed to be a wide cleavage between perceptions of the Korea-based resident Chinese—seen as either "competitors" or "threat" or both—and those of a more abstract, detached "China", with which diverse hopes for social and national liberation were easily associated. While the resident Chinese were eagerly regarded as extraneous and ultimately threatening or "polluting" the Korean "national body" they permeated, "China"—as long as it was seen as essentially a foreign place politically and spatially detached from Korea—represented a generally positive world-historical development which was believed to benefit Korea too in the long run. "Revolution" was a common code of Asia's radical post-First World War intelligentsia, influenced as it was by the events in post-1917 Russia and the worldwide "left turn." Korea's anti-colonial mass movements were highly appraised on the Chinese side too, but for understandable reasons, Korean interest in Chinese developments was incomparably stronger and deeper. As the nationalist limitations of mainstream republican revolutionaries were becoming clearer—and especially after the 1927 break between the Guomindang and the Chinese Communist Party—the interest and sympathy of a large number of Korea's radical intellectuals naturally enough went to the movements associated with the latter, notably the Chinese Communist Party (CCP)'s Soviet movement. However, a rather critical analysis of Guomindang's strength and weaknesses can be found even in Pak Ŭnsik's writings from the early 1920s on, suggesting that illusions about the Guomindang's "progressive" or "revolutionary" nature were not quite dominant even before 1927. China, in a nutshell, was Korea writ large—it was a fellow victim of national and social injustice, and the necessity of a revolution there would make clear that Korea too was in need of similar developments.

The supposed commonality of "tradition" or "race" between the two countries—often emphasised by the more conservative Guomindang figures—was of little or no significance to the Korean radicals, since they clearly perceived an all-important new commonality of historical perspective between themselves and their great western neighbour.

In Place of Conclusion

The interest in and sympathy for China's revolutionary struggles was palpable among the Korean intellectuals, especially in view of the former's assumed importance for the prospects of Korea's own decolonisation. China's radical movements—first the Guomindang in its capacity of a Soviet ally, and then China's Communists—were the most important source of hope for Korea's own leftist intellectuals besides the Soviet Union. As a prominent Communist activist, An Kwangch'ŏn, puts it in his well-known May 1929 piece (published under the pseudonym Sagong P'yo in the Beijing-based émigré Communist periodical, *Leninchuŭi*, Vol. 1) on Korea's political situation and the Communists' tasks:

> China and Korea are closely related to each other, as both are being exploited by Japanese imperialism. (...); Japan's China investments, even if only the important investment cases before 1925 are considered, amount to 1.443.610.7000 yen. Japan cannot sustain itself without the raw materials for heavy industry imported from China, China's enormous market being of life-and-death importance for Japanese businesses. That is why Japan has to necessarily intervene in China's revolution. As I have shown, China is of cardinal importance for the very existence of Japanese imperialism, and China and Korea are closely related in their struggles against the Japanese imperialists. The whole process of China's liberation is destabilizing capitalism worldwide and accelerates a world revolution.

Then, An pointed out that China's revolutionary struggles were also accelerating Korea's own revolutionary movement, raising Koreans' awareness of the necessity of a world revolution, giving them concrete revolutionary lessons to learn, and allowing the China-based émigré militants to participate in a real-time revolutionary fight.[67] The Soviet Union represented the future for the colonial-period Korean Communists; the Chinese revolution represented the way to this future under these given, rather onerous, circumstances.

However, tragically enough, the leftist intellectuals' quest for Sino-Korean solidarity did not seem to influence colonial Korea's mainstream literature to any significant degree, as far as its treatment of Chinese was concerned. While China's revolution was mostly seen as ultimately beneficial for Korea's national destiny, the presence of the Chinese diaspora in Korea was regarded rather as a national problem. In the nationalist consciousness of the colonial-period intelligentsia, China as a potential foreign ally of Korea was wholly acceptable; "Chinese in our midst", however, were much more difficult to tolerate. The "stars" of the colonial prose literature—Ch'oe Sŏhae, Yi Hyosŏk, Kim Tongin and others—were continuously producing stereotypically antagonistic descriptions of the Chinese in their rather popular literary works, thus reproducing and reinforcing the negative image of the Chinese peddled by the colonial press, both Japanese and Korean-owned. While most modern nationalists typically tend to produce and spread the images of "negative others", in colonial Korea's case, it happened to be Korea's closest neighbour and oldest partner in the cultural exchange that came to be negatively stereotyped and "otherized". One of the reasons for such a development was an acute commercial rivalry between Korean and Chinese entrepreneurs, which was often reported in the press as a "trade war" of sorts, where economic "survival" of the whole Korean community was at stake. Incensed by the (often exaggerated) reports of conflicts between the Chinese authorities and Korean immigrants in Manchuria, a number of colonial intellectuals came to perceive the Chinese as an inferior and inimical group, against which all the inferiority complexes forced upon the Koreans by Japanese colonialism could be safely vented out, in a sort of "vicarious compensation" for the indignities and humiliations of colonial life.

67. P'yo, Sagong (1987). *Chosŏn ŭi Chŏngse wa Chosŏn Kongsanchuŭija ŭi Tangmyŏn Immu* (Korea's Political Situation and the Imminent Tasks of the Korean Communists), Reprinted in Sŏngch'an, Pae (ed.) (n.d.), *Singminji Sidae Sahoe Undongnon Yŏn'gu* (Research into Theories on the Colonial-Period's Social Movements). Seoul: Tolpegae. pp.68-69.

The Sinophobic discourse of the intellectuals created and spread by the "print capitalism" and the modern Korean prose writings overlapped with the sense of competition against the Chinese labour, which already existed among a significant portion of the urban workers. A tragic result of this unhappy combination was the 1931 anti-Chinese riots in Korea.

9

RAKESH BATABYAL

Colonialism and Communalism in India

Introduction

Communalism is a modern consciousness and a set of beliefs that the communities are defined only on religious grounds and that the non-religious interests of individuals within the communities "thus defined" are often antagonistic to the similar interests of individuals in other similarly defined communities. This came to be part of the consciousness of sections of the Indian people during the 19th and 20th centuries as a result of the political, social and economic restructuring of Indian society.[1]

Historical discourse, politics and statecraft during the last two centuries have made this consciousness a part of India's modern political culture, while at the same time a deeply contested battle against communalism has also come to define the political sensibilities in politics, society and culture in modern India.

Communalism: A Colonial Product

Communalism as an ideology has been the product of colonial rule in India. Quite often this fact has been trivialised by colonial apologists by indicating features of communalism which were

---

1. One of the finest treatments of the issue is by Bipan Chandra, whose book *Communalism in Modern India* was the first to treat communalism as an ideology and therefore treat all variants, i.e., Hindu, Muslim and Christian, of communal ideology quite penetratingly. See Chandra, Bipan (1984). *Communalism in Modern India*. Delhi: Vikas. Smith, W.C. (1945). *Modern Islam in India*. Lahore, has been the work that provided an intellectual basis for many of the works including this one. A good historiographical treatment can be found in Batabyal, Rakesh (2005). *Communalism in Bengal*. Sage. The post-Independence Hindu communal challenge has been treated in Batabyal, Rakesh (2011). "Hindu Communal Challenge 1964-1984" in *Centenary History of Indian National Congress*. Vol. V. New Delhi: Academic Foundation. pp.347-74.

products of the Indian socio-cultural milieu and where colonial rule or the state seemed to have no role to play, i.e., communalism had always been there even before colonialism.[2] A critical and slightly intelligent reading of Indian history, however, easily indicates that it was the advent of the colonial powers that created the socio-cultural as well as economic context in which communalism came to be a political ideology defining the existing communities in a new way. The new definitions of communities as Hindu or Muslim seemed to be exclusive definitions and went on to change the inter-community relations too. Colonial rule foisted itself on an evolving society—its polity and economy—and instead planted a colonial state with its interests and priorities to oversee local society.

In fact, many of these changes in the 18th century remained a matter of deep contest between those who see colonialism bringing a rupture in society and the economy and those who argue that colonialism did not bring any fundamental change.[3] The latter, in many ways, anticipated the valorisation of colonialism in today's global discourse by suggesting that colonialism brought tremendous benefits to the host societies.[4] The claims however have always been strongly refuted by historians in India.[5]

While the colonial powers gradually created an administrative and political frame to rule the country, the emerging new intelligentsia from the mid-19th century, most often the product of new English education, particularly in the latter, i.e., 1850-1900, part of the 19th century began to realise that there existed a basic cleavage between

2. Bayly, C.A. (1985). "The Pre-history of 'Communalism'? Religious Conflict in India 1700-1860", *Modern Asian Studies* 19(2): 177-204.

3. Habib, Irfan (1998). "Eighteenth Century in the Indian Economic History", in L. Blusse and F. Gaastra (eds), *On the Eighteenth Century as a Category of Asian History: Van Leur in Retrospect*. Aldershot. pp.217-36.

4. In the Indian case, the colonial administrators in the 19th century began the trend but the intellectual defence came also from the historians and economic historians, particularly those located in Cambridge and Oxford.

5. Sen, Sunanda (1992). *Colonies and Empire*. Calcutta: Orient Longman; Habib, Irfan (2010). *Economic History of India 1858-1914*. Delhi: Tulika; Chandra, Bipan (1999). *Essays on Colonialism*. Orient Blackswan; Mukherjee, Aditya (2008). "The Return of the Colonial in Indian Economic History: The Last Phase of Colonialism in India", *Social Scientist* 36(3/4): 3-44.

colonial rule and welfare of the people in India.[6] A consciousness of this basic divide made many of them work for enlarging the community of people with an argument for self-rule. This self-rule was demanded to a nation, a modern political and ideological community which invoked a large mass of people to galvanise itself into a nation, transcending smaller and narrower and parochial affinities. Raja Rammohun Roy, one of the founders of India's modern political discourse, had asked the people as early as in the 1820s to shun caste differences; otherwise, he argued, "national consciousness" would be difficult.[7] Attempting at creating a "national community" to contest the colonial constructs of society and the polity, the intelligentsia embarked on a painstaking effort to reconstruct and provide a rather correct and scientific understanding of the past, present and possible future of society and its economy.

In the new colonial context, a new public space was emerging with novel political articulations and desires. Not only were modern political formations emerging, the state itself was a deeply entrenched party in this politics. Therefore, where the colonial state wanted on its terms to move the politics, the dividing lines of the communities were sought to be found and magnified. It is in this context that there were deliberate as well as accidental conflations of religion and society. Groups and communities were given exclusive identification along with religious denomination they were found to be affiliated to. The fuzzy domain and fluidity of social lives were now closed by a new state that had its own interests in exclusive definition. The nascent intelligentsia was hard placed to extricate society from this entanglement, which they thought was the reason for society to have fallen behind and colonised.

---

6. Chandra, Bipan (1965). *Rise and Growth of Economic Nationalism in India*. People Book House.

7. Collet, Sophia Dobson (2009). *Life and Letters of Raja Rammohun Roy*. Delhi: General Books. Originally published in 1914. See also Batabyal, Rakesh (2007). *Penguin Book of Modern Indian Speeches: 1877 to Present*. Penguin Books; Chandra, Bipan (1989). *India's Struggle for Independence*. Penguin; Chandra, Bipan (2009). *History Modern India*. Orient Blackswan. (Originally published in NCERT, 1971).

Nationalism and Communalism

There were signs of a new political sensibility emerging during the second part of the 19th century, i.e., nationalist sensibilities. Nationalism in the colonies was seen all over the world as a natural movement of the people against colonial rule. The emergence of an intelligentsia and its articulation of a nationalist cause against colonial presence, however, were not viewed sympathetically by the colonial state and its intellectual defenders. It was described as an "artificial and unnatural reaction" of a "petty English-educated middle class" or "upper-caste men". The saga of condemning nationalist urges against colonialism continues even today in the writing mainly emerging from the erstwhile centres of colonial defence.[8]

It has been seen as anti-peasant, anti-worker, anti-woman, anti-depressed caste, and so on. The colonial claims of benevolence were invoked to show how nationalism, as was claimed by the nationalists, was devoid of any positive vision and grand ideas, and how it would be a disaster in managing inter-community relations, which only colonial rule, being a benevolent and honest arbiter, was capable of.

In its bid to create this colonial anti-nationalist narrative, to portray nationalism as unnatural, an entire sociology of India was developed. Society in the subcontinent was now read and shown to be essentially fragmentary and hierarchical. Any talk, therefore, of a unity like the one espoused by the nationalists was shown to be ahistorical.

This newly created sociology was soon given a respected academic place in colonial anthropology and later on in the historical works beginning to come out of universities like Oxford and Cambridge in

---

8. Nationalism, in this reading, is deprived of any grandeur or positive agenda. It is deprived to be anti-poor and anti what is being termed as subaltern. It has been conjured up as anti-peasant. With the emergence of gender studies as a global discourse, there have also been efforts to align the sectarian political critique in India to the general (western) feminist critique of nation as a male construct, and therefore an essentialist argument that Indian nationalism, which was different from communalism (which is being referred to in these writings as Hindu nationalism or Muslim nationalism to make its western readers more comfortable), was anti-woman. The evidence, on the contrary, suggested that the movement created the largest space in Indian history for women to come out of their household domain and use the political space for their own emancipation. See Menon, Visalakshi (2000). *Gender and Nationalism: The UP Story*. Delhi: Har-Anand.

the post-imperialist phase.[9] India was called merely a geographical expression, which, it was argued, the British administration had brought under one unit. There was nothing elevating found in the social realm except cleavages and disharmony—it had remained a geography of tribalism of the worst kind. The new nationalism was in fact shown to be the reflection of such trite tribalism devoid of benevolence and magnificence.[10] The Indian intelligentsia, since the late 19th century, had engaged itself against such an argument. It pointed out that though India presented circumstances unlikely to be called a nation in the modern sense, it was trying to make it one. This nation in the making became a political as well as socio-intellectual effort for the intellectuals.

Communalism entered the mindscape of people at this juncture of history. The newly crafted Indian history, a reoriented state power instrumental in heightening social divisions, and an emerging socio-economic life in a colonial economy bringing economic distress, were all contributing to a new public sphere. The colonial state's attempts to treat communities differently in matters of jobs and patronage also did not go unnoticed. While the minuscule clerical jobs were available to the English-educated section, it was the Hindu literati that had most of them as it had embraced English education early. The entry of

---

9. Later-day historians have added sophistication to this reading of society. India, in these works, remains a congeries of groups, castes, communities and nothing much. This, therefore, is against the tenor of the politics of the nationalist and also the Marxists, whose efforts have been to create a larger unity of people based on existing or presumed channels of unifying links in society. It is, thus, significant that at the core of the historiographical contest remains the idea of society and of politics in that society. See Bayly, C.A. (1990). *The Local Roots of Indian Politics: Allahabad, 1880-1920.* Oxford University Press; Seal, Anil (1968). *The Emergence of Indian Nationalism: Competition and Collaboration in the Later Nineteenth Century.* Cambridge University Press; Tomlinson, B.R. (1976). *The Indian National Congress and the Raj, 1929-1942: The Penultimate Phase;* Washbrook, D.A. (2008). *The Emergence of Provincial Politics: The Madras Presidency, 1870-1920.*

10. An example of depriving any lofty ideal in Gandhi's movement is Brown, Judith M. (1977). *Gandhi and Civil Disobedience: The Mahatma in Indian Politics, 1928-1934.* London: Cambridge University Press; Brown, Judith M. (1972). *Gandhi's Rise to Power. Indian Politics, 1915-1922.* Cambridge University Press. Gandhi devoid of any lofty ideals becomes a simple peddler for power in these works. The later day products from Oxford has taken the work forward by arguing that Gandhi was primarily a product of rumour, myth and concoctions, see Amin, Shahid (1995). *Events, Metaphor and Memory: Chauri Chaura 1922-1992.* Princeton University Press.

the Muslim youth, therefore, also came with the idea of competition with the Hindu youth. With the colonial economy not raising the levels of employment, the scarce opportunity would soon make this competition quite stiff. The new history and the new sociology began to provide a completely new prism to locate the issues at hand now, i.e., whether jobs in government or representation in the legislative assemblies was seen through the prism of the community. Thus, when competition among individuals for limited positions became very acute, the colonial state could then convert this to show how one community profited at the cost of the others. Religiously defined communities, therefore, meant that the cause of deprivation or even maladies could now be pointed at the other religious community. Communalism was thus born. The nationalist intelligentsia wanted to help people transcend this attribution of cause at doors of the other community by pointing to the larger malady, i.e., colonial rule. Anti-colonial rule in some sense was the true ideology as against a false explanation of communalism that the other community was the cause for some malady. The national community they invoked was a sum of all religious, linguistic and political affiliations.

It is here that the classic contest between the nationalist idea of a nation and communalism began to take shape. There have been efforts in recent times to conflate (and also reduce) the concept of communalism with nationalism for either academic convenience or political camouflage. Communal groups and phenomena have been referred to as religious nationalists or religious nationalism, i.e., Hindu nationalism or Muslim nationalism. This is contrary to the historical evolution of concepts and politics behind the ideology called communalism. It any way wants to replace nationalism, which the nationalists have resisted, but academics want to give away easily.

The Real and Imagined Boundaries: Colonial Historical Project and Communalism

The newly recruited colonial administrators were taught the history of India in order to understand the people and rule over them. The history that came to be conjured up and written was modular history. The most famous and popular was James Mill's

History of India, which was written in 1815 and periodised the movement of Indian history in religious or what increasingly came to be seen as in communal terms, i.e., the Hindu period and Muslim period. The British period was called the modern period. The Hindu period coincided with ancient India and the Muslim with medieval. The periodisation was based on the spurious understanding that religion of the ruler decided the history of a people or the country. By the same logic, the third period should have been called the Christian period. However, the book and its propagation as a classic frame of reference by the colonial establishment and later by the universities had a tremendous negative impact on the understanding of not only Indian history, but also politics and society. It consolidated the idea that one community was the loser and another the winner. Secondly, the communal periodisation made the national imagining much more difficult as one was now required to overcome an understanding of the given history also.

New efforts against the colonial reading and imposition of Indian history required a counter history, which not only presented a rather correct picture but also an idea and politics different from the one given by the colonial rulers and its historians. It is here that one of the bitterest contests over history began to be fought. Nationalist historians, as they have been called, tried to reconstruct an Indian history and the glories or accomplishment of an Indian people in which they countered the colonial contention that India did not have history and that the history was full of battles between kings and between Hindu and Muslim kings. To counter the communal categorisation, historians tried to bring out facts of communities living together and in a spirit of give and take, and evolving Hindu-Islamic culture—a synthetic culture.[11]

Hindu and Muslim communal organisations, intellectuals and leaders, however, saw the British history of India as a model and they made their own contribution by magnifying the fragmentary and communal parts. For the Hindu communal historians, Hindus

11. See for present-day treatment of composite culture, Chandra, Bipan and Sucheta Mahajan (eds.) (2007). *Composite Culture in a Multicultural Society*. Delhi: Pearson Publishers and National Book Trust.

had all their glory destroyed by the Muslim invaders, while the Muslim communal historians saw the British destroying the glory of Islam and that the glory had to be regained. This was to be achieved by establishing Islamic rule. It is here the colonial state actively intervened. Once Indian nationalism emerged, the colonial state could be seen wooing Muslim public opinion makers to argue that the alliance of the British and Muslim leaders could bring glories. By the beginning of the 20th century, when demands for representations were conceded, reluctantly though, the state ensured that a core was maintained among the Muslim elite who would be opposing any larger democratisation of the representation principle by championing and demanding community representation. Therefore, in 1909, when the election principle was introduced, it was done by giving separate communal electorates, sowing the seed of sectarian politics.

From the beginning, one finds national opposition to colonialism has been constantly critiqued on various grounds. However, what has been quite instructive is to find no critique of communalism from the colonial authorities. On the other side, as though reciprocal, there was hardly any critique of colonialism developed by the communal leaders, intellectuals or the organisations. The Muslim League and Hindu Mahasabha in fact depended quite often on the colonial bureaucracy to help them. On many critical occasions during the 1940s, when the Indian National Congress objected to India being dragged into the World War without taking the consent of its people, it is the Muslim League that helped the colonial establishment to run the government and the Hindu Mahasabha was ready to join the ministry at any point. In fact Syama Prasad Mookerjee, president of the Hindu Mahasabha, was a minister in Bengal. The colonial policies more often than not supported communal demands. While it took years of agitation, for example, to give representation to Indians in the financial committee of the viceroy, it took no time to concede representation and separate electorate in the local and provincial assemblies based on religious and separate identities, ultimately dividing people.

While one communalism—Hindu communalism—defined the Indian nation as existing even before the arrival of the British, the other tried to define a monolithic religious community, Islam, as constituting the basis of a nation, Pakistan. Neither required a critique of colonial rule. Clash was always against the other community. Thus, the creation of a sense of the "other"—Hindu, Muslim, etc.—would give India its national identity. This was a product of a new history that came to be written by the British. While the Hindu period was a glorious one, the Muslim one was a dark age and the modern was a period of development under the British aegis.[12] When in the late 19th century the nascent nationalist leadership had a decidedly Hindu middle-class participation, the British position began to shift and now the Muslims were infected with a fear about the future. With publication of the Hunter Committee report, it began to be shown that the British would be the mentor and benefactor of the Muslims and in any arrangement, it would behove well for the Muslims to be with the Hindus. Increasingly, one could see that the regional differentiations were being given the go by and attempts to create a community of religious affiliation were given pride of place.

Early Indian nationalists tried to correct this and argued that India also had a glorious phase in the ancient period. So they agreed with the historiographical presuppositions of colonial historiography, and tried to counter them by applying the same presupposition. This created a problem, out of which we are yet to come out completely and this is the problem on which the Hindu as well as the Muslim communal historians bank to present their idea of history. The early nationalist historians argued against the colonial assertion that India never had a democratic experience or any sense of popular participation, science or technology. In sum, it was always a backward authoritarian society steeped in spiritualism. This was countered by saying that ancient India had democracy, democratic institutions, science and technology. It was a golden age of Indian history. Then the obvious question was how had it vanished. The trap was clear

---

12. The first detailed classic statement of communalism in Indian history has been Thapar, Romila, Bipan Chandra and Harbans Mukhia (1969). *Communalism in Indian History.* People's Publishing House.

and obvious. It was the Muslim period and the dark ages. Though the nationalist historians did not want to enter into this period, the linear understanding of history in this way entrapped them. The idea of a golden age of ancient India remained strong, and it became the cornerstone of many fabulous stories and concoctions—anything other than history.

Marxist historiography, beginning in the 1960s, was the first major breakthrough which tried to take Indian scholarship as well as historical understanding out of this morass into what one would call a processual history that tried to argue that history is of the people and not of kings and soldiers and that in this history what matter are larger historical processes. In these processes, what matters most is how people lived, etc. Here colonialism was found to be a major exploitative system, while at the same time the exploitative social systems of medieval and ancient India were seriously looked into. Their solid empirical research, backed by an understanding of the processes, made them argue that there is nothing like a golden age or a Hindu India or Muslim India. The notion of an all-India Hindu community is as much a construction of colonial historiography and other practices as such a notion of an all-India Muslim community. Thus, the Marxist scholars of the first generation fought not only against the colonial depiction but also its communal interpretations.

Political Mobilisation and Communalism

History, sociology and the way colonial rule worked its divisive politics, using all these knowledge-producing domains, increasingly created a landscape in which religious communities over time became a target of mobilisation in the emerging politics. The latter part of the 19th century saw efforts to mobilise Indians along organisations pan-Indian in character and also took up issues pan-Indian in shape. Increasingly the tenor of these organisations and the issues they took up, i.e., representations of Indians in the legislative councils, opposition to the use of Indians and the Indian military in the foreign lands, reduction of taxes and allowing Indians to enter the civil services, etc. showed them in an anti-colonial light. The colonial authorities began to show their opposition to leaders and organisations like the Congress. The opposition began to crystallise by 1888-89, when the annual session of the Congress was ridiculed by Viceroy Lord Dufferin, who called it a three-day spectacle. It was about this time that one saw the emergence of voices against the Congress from leading feudal landlords and people like Sir Syed Ahmed Khan, who was keen to educate Muslims and had set up the Mohammedan Anglo Oriental College. An anti-Congress set-up began to emerge and its active official patronage was also very visible.

Not long after this, a deputation of Muslim leaders led by Agha Khan waited on the viceroy in Shimla (Shimla was the summer capital of the empire) in 1906 to impress upon him issues related to the community. There was an indication that this had been organised indirectly by the Nawabs and elite, who had support of the bureaucracy. The result of the deputation was the formation of All India Muslim League. The League soon became the meeting point of the Muslim elite and pro-British elements among the Muslims. Through the next 40 years, it was destined to play the most crucial role in articulating a position which one may argue was the Muslim "communal position". It began by arguing that the Muslims required more representation in the official forum. By the 1930s, the extent of representation began to be pitched so high as to demand a virtual statutory majority in many parts of the country, such as Bengal and Punjab. It was very strange that the idea of a demographic majority, which went on to become the deciding factor in partition of the country in 1947, was used to give the Muslim representative almost a statutory majority, creating space to create what was called the hurt sentiments of the Hindus. The British authorities also pampered such Hindu groups to come up to occupy space from the nationalist Congress. The Congress and many nationalist intellectuals fought hard to counter the communal propaganda but they faced an immense hurdle as the British colonial authorities remained the final arbiter in dividing seats, etc. in the legislatures, which were used to divide people further.

However, the character of the political movement was changing. By the 1920s, with the arrival of Gandhi, the masses—peasants, workers, women and students—were joining the national movement under the aegis of the Congress and other parties like Peasants and Workers' Party and the communist parties. It is here that communal politics too was changing its profile. There was demand for more representation in the councils, which needed to be widened. It is here that communal slogans and negative politics began to be used. The Muslims were now to be brought under the Muslim League ambit by giving them the idea of their 'discrimination' and 'future marginalisation' at the hands of the 'Hindu majority', which 'controlled' the Congress. The Congress began to shape a democratic point of view and therefore democracy itself was attacked for paving the way for Hindu rule. In a similar vein, Hindu communal organisations like the Hindu Mahasabha too began to argue against the 'discrimination' of the Hindus in a possible democracy in which the Muslims will permanently rule with a demographic and statutory majority like that in Bengal. An idea of 'Hindu interest' came to be popularised.

The phase of the mass movement also transported the movement of ideologies: the 1920s saw the emergence of the Khilafat movement, which, for the first time, brought a huge number of Muslims into the larger political fold. Gandhi tried to forge a link between the national cause and the cause of the Khilafat as the Allied powers were humiliating the Ottoman Sultan after the First World War. The sultan was also the caliph, the religious head of the Muslims across the world, and through the agitation the Muslims in India wanted to get an assurance from the British government that it would not harm the sultan, as was promised to them before the War had begun. Gandhi felt that assuaging feelings of the Muslims would bring them to the national fold. It was a successful move as thousands came out and the Muslims now could make the anti-colonial nationalism their cause too. However, soon Kemal Pasha abolished the Caliphate, thereby removing the cause for the movement.

Gandhi had anticipated that political unity between the Hindus and the Muslims needed to be translated into social unity too. Here he saw that politics on the basis of a separate electorate would be damaging. He, therefore, tried to dissuade the Congress from entering the electoral arena. He was right and the faction that participated discovered that electoral politics was educating people on different lines. It was, therefore, no wonder that the 1920s was when some of the worst communal alignments and communal violence erupted in many places from Punjab to Bengal. These events, as we discuss later, further mobilised people communally.

This was the phase of liberal and constitutional communal politics, where the demands were about increased representation for a particular community in the councils, etc. articulated best by the demand for more seats for the Muslims in Bengal and Punjab. The colonial authorities demonstrated open support to Muslim communalists. It was strange that in Bengal, the Muslim majority was given a statutory majority in the legislative assembly. It was a skewed system as the minority here was increasingly denied any right. This placed the Congress in an awkward position as Hindu communal leaders attacked the party for being "anti-Hindu". There had been every effort by the colonial authorities and the post-imperial colonial historians to even now argue that the Congress was a Hindu party and Gandhi, Nehru and almost the whole leadership in some way masked their Hindu communal selves. It is surprising that even some Marxist scholars with abysmally poor knowledge of Indian history and politics now go along with the colonial historians in betraying prejudice against the independent stance that the leadership in the colonies took upon themselves to free not only from colonial rule, but also from intellectual hegemony.[13]

The national movement, however, remained steadfastly anti-communal. In fact, it adopted an extremely secular position. Not only were the British not attacked on religious grounds, the issues were determined not on the basis of their religious quotient. The Congress had already demonstrated that it represented all Indians, irrespective of caste, creed and religion. In 1931, during its annual session in Karachi, the party by passing the charter of fundamental rights, which came to be known as the Karachi resolution, forcefully indicated that in any constitutional arrangement it had committed

13. See, Broomfield, J.R. (1976). *Elite Conflict in a Plural Society, Twentieth century Bengal*. Berkeley and LA: University of California Press; Anderson, Perry (2013). *The Indian Ideology*. Delhi: Three Essays Collective.

itself to the minorities' constitutional safeguards and that the character of the state will be secular.

The colonial government, tried to fragment the movement by organising the Round Table Conference in 1930-1932 and representatives of all conceivable groups and sectional interests were invited to participate. The Congress was treated virtually as merely an upper-caste interest group and as if it vied with the Hindu Mahasabha for even that space. Years later this treatment has been sometimes legitimised by many scholars and historians by arguing historically that the Congress occupied the same ideological space as the Hindu Mahasabha did—both were interchangeable. The Congress leadership refused to participate, and rightly so, in the first conference. In the meantime, the Civil Disobedience Movement of 1930-31, launched with Gandhi's famous march from Sabarmati to Dandi on the Gujarat coast, saw millions, including Muslims, participating across the country and thousands, including all Congress leaders, going to prison. The movement was suspended after the Gandhi-Irwin pact and Gandhi agreed to attend the Second Round Table Conference. This time too the Congress was sought to be reduced to one interest group and Gandhi kept insisting that he represented all India and not merely a group or community. In a similar way, looking for more chinks in the Indian social body, the British government now decided to give a blow to Congress' claims to represent even the Hindus, leave aside all Indians. It now conceived to fragment the larger Hindu mobilisation by introducing separate electorates for the depressed castes as had been done for the Muslims and Hindus in 1909. The communal electorate of 1909 created a chasm and impediment in developing a common political space and programme. It was thereafter very difficult to undo the damage done by the separate electorate, by the rules of which a Hindu would vote for a Hindu and a Muslim for a Muslim. The same mechanism was now designed to be foisted upon the large Hindu society. The colonial state had been encouraging and supporting voices that demanded separate political treatment to non-Brahmin castes in South India and untouchables in the north. Now with the announcement of what came to be known as the MacDonald Award (after Prime Minister Ramsay MacDonald), the masterstroke was giving a separate electorate to the depressed castes. However, Gandhi understood the design, and he undertook a fast unto death. He argued that he would not let the social body to be divided by colonial machination. He said that the Hindu upper castes would have to be prepared to give more representation to the depressed caste but would have to negate the idea of a separate electorate. The final settlement came when the Indian leaders including one of the leaders of the depressed classes whom the British patronised, BR Ambedkar, agreed to let go the separate electorate. The whole episode awakened people to the designs of the colonial authorities as to how the idea of representation in the electoral bodies was not merely an extension of the principles of representation, but at the same time an extension of the idea of fragmenting society. The counter-point had to be devised by the anti-colonial forces—and as Gandhi had been arguing and before him the nationalist intellectuals and leaders, a larger unity of the people by ameliorating the social and economic conditions.

When the masses were mobilised in the 1930s and 1940s, politics was completely radicalised. The communal groups found it hard to go to the people with merely one agenda, i.e., representations in legislative assemblies. It is here that communal ideology was redesigned in a new phase where antagonistic interests and antagonistic politics began to define the communities. One saw the very rabid and aggressive anti-Congress and anti-Gandhi rhetoric in Hindu communal groups like the Hindu Mahasabha. It was during the early period that the Rastriya Swayamsevak Sangh was founded to counter the Congress and its secular nationalism. India was defined as a Hindu nation and its future was to be coloured as such.

The Muslim league too began to metamorphose itself. By the mid-1930s, it began to be stridently anti-Congress, which it defined as a caste-Hindu party. The Muslim League was defeated in many places, while the Congress had done well in many Muslim constituencies. This worried the Muslim League as well as the colonial authorities. The League began to attack the Congress and, during 1937-1939 in its annual meets, began to present reports like the Pirpur Report, narrating thousands of cases of Congress ministries' supposed atrocities on Muslims. These uninvestigated and quite often imaginary reports then created the basis for propagating the anti-Muslim character of the Congress and how in all future democratic set-ups the Muslims will fare badly. The Pirpur Report and other such attacks on the Congress came at a time when the Congress ministries, for example in UP, were launching anti-feudal moves and there were many big feudal lords who were Muslim. Similar was the case of Hindu feudal lords. This section was a support to the colonial state. Thus, the Congress was up in arms against the colonial system and it is here the communal parties and their agenda came to prevent any radical social and political policy by the Congress ministries.[14]

Communalism, Independence and the Colonial State

The colonial state was the apparatus of colonial policies. In the 1940s, when the Muslim League was moving ahead with its mass mobilisation programme, the colonial bureaucrats too were supporting it to the hilt against the Congress. In most of the deliberations, one could see that the British bureaucrats were providing the Muslim League a kind of veto over any concrete or positive proposal to solve the imbroglio. Gandhi, for example, understood it so well and wanted to bypass the bureaucracy and meet Jinnah directly. He met Jinnah 22 times in 1944 and presented a plan of participation without intervention of the British. Jinnah was non-committal and wanted everything and with British supervision. He was confident that the British would help him. However, it was more of maintaining the imperial hegemony as an honest broker between the warring communities and groups. So when the hegemony was over, the empire was naked and it publicly showed its unabashed antagonistic attitude to the people and was not intended to maintain even the veneer of civility and law and order.

14. There are some who very strangely and mistakenly argue that the Congress did not have any radical agenda for example in Bengal. The fact remains that Bengal had a Muslim League-supported Ministry with a sectarian agenda. See Chatterjee, Partha (1984). *Bengal: The Land Question, 1920-47*. Kolkata: KP Bagchi.

When the national movement was reaching a crescendo in 1946-47, there were tremendous expectations of the impending freedom all round. At the same time, the idea of having a free Pakistan, which the Muslim league had been demanding and mobilising support for, had also been agitating human emotions. Communalism, which had attacked a composite Indian nationalism, was coming centre stage and there were violent overtones of communal mobilisation.

By this time, the idea of Pakistan had been concretised in the popular mind. At the end of the elections of 1945-46, it was clear that the League had achieved some sort of a mandate of being the representative agency fighting for Pakistan. The League wanted people's support in its endeavour to realise Pakistan, a nation whose geographical contours were left to the popular imagination. Now the people who were mobilised since the 1930s and particularly after the League had adopted the Pakistan resolution in March 1940 were repeatedly told that the biggest roadblock to Pakistan was the Congress, which was an upper-caste Hindu party. Neither the Muslim League nor its leader, Jinnah, had ever espoused a critique of colonialism or envisioned a society without the colonial presence, so that the movement for achieving Pakistan could be galvanised by critiquing the colonial power. Instead, it was the Congress that the League argued was the representative of the Hindu population, which was constantly demonised. By the 1940s, it was not just the Congress but also the general Hindu population that was depicted as opposing the creation of Pakistan.

Therefore, in the last phase of the movement for freedom, when the colonial state and its bureaucratic apparatus were trying to harmonise its forced removal from India (with its public announcement of voluntary decolonisation), the Muslim League was its most powerful support through which it was able to veto any Congress proposal that went against colonial interests. By 1946, when it was clear that the days were numbered, the Cabinet Mission arrived to negotiate, and wanted the Congress on board. The Muslim League, realising that it now had to force its views, announced direct action against what it viewed as a Congress betrayal. On 16 August 1946, when the direct action was to take place, a riot broke out, leaving 6,000-7,000 deaths in the next six days. Within six weeks in a place called Noakhali in East Bengal, there were ferocious attacks on the Hindu minuscule minority and there were efforts to erase their religious symbols. Hindu women were married to Muslim men, and forced conversions took place. It was the triumph of Muslim communalists. The Noakhali riots were qualitatively different from the earlier communal riots including the Calcutta killings of August 1946, which immediately preceded them. This also was the field day for Hindu communal ideas and they became victorious when there were riots all across central Bihar, apparently to avenge the Noakhali riots. The narrative of Noakhali and Bihar gradually became part of the larger communal violence that took the share of partition killings in which millions were displaced from these villages in west and east Punjab and in east and west Bengal. India stood partitioned between India and Pakistan.

Conclusion

Communalism has been one of the most baneful of the modern political discourses in India. The communal riots and large-scale violence that India has witnessed over the last two centuries now have been not only a reminder of the divisive politics that colonial rule could create for its purpose, but that one if it comes to the surface it acquires its own life. Communal violence, which post-independence India has seen, may comfort the defenders of colonial attitudes that these were Third World or Asian realities, but the fact remains that they were the unnatural products of colonial rule. The colonial state, the knowledge it tried to produce and the politics it played to create or magnify fragments, produced a fragmentary public sphere that the nationalists tried to bridge with much difficulty. However, as long as colonial rule remained, the nationalist forces had to contend with the colonial state, which tried to block all politics of bridge building and unity as it monopolised the role of the arbiter in any such politics. Communal ideology destroyed a civilisational unity, which took a couple of thousand years to be made. Colonialism partitions: it partitions by producing fragmentary knowledge and fragmentary politics. All societies politically partitioned will testify to this rather simple fact obfuscated by what is called complex history writing.

Bibliography

Alatas, Syed Farid (1997). *Democracy and Authoritarianism in Indonesia and Malaysia: The Rise of the Post-Colonial State.* New York: St. Martin's Press.

Anderson, Perry (2013). *The Indian Ideology.* Delhi: Three Essays Collective.

Anderson, Walter K. and Shridhar D. Damle (1987). *The Brotherhood in Saffron: The Rashtriya Swayamsevak Sangh and Hindu Revivalism.* New Delhi: Vistaar Publications.

Banu, Zenab (1980). *Politics of Communalism.* Bombay: Popular Prakashan.

Batabyal, Rakesh (2005). *Communalism in Bengal: From Famine to Noakhali, 1943-47.* New York, London, Delhi: Sage.

Batabyal, Rakesh (2007). *Penguin Book of Modern Indian Speeches.* Delhi: Penguin.

Batabyal, Rakesh (1997). "Communalism, the Noakhali Riot and Gandhi", *Studies in Social Sciences and Humanities* IV(2): 135-70. Shimla: IIAS.

Bayly, C.A. (1985). "The Pre-history of 'Communalism'? Religious Conflict in India 1700-1860," *Modern Asian Studies* 19(2): 177-203.

Bayly, C.A. (1988). *Indian Society and the Making of the British Empire.* New York: Cambridge University Press.

Bhambhri, C.P. (1990). "State and Communalism," *Social Scientist* 19(.207-208): 22-26. Delhi.

Broomfield, J.R. (1968). *Elite Conflict in a Plural Society, Twentieth Century Bengal.* Berkeley and LA: University of California Press.

Chandra, Bipan (1984). *Communalism in Modern India.* Delhi: Vikas.

Chandra, Bipan, Mridula Mukherjee and Aditya Mukherjee (2009). *India Since Independence.* Delhi: Penguin.

Chandra, Bipan and Sucheta Mahajan (eds.) (2007). *Composite Culture in a Multicultural Society.* Delhi and National Book Trust: Pearson Publishers.

Chatterjee, Partha (1986). *Nationalist Thought and Colonial World: A Derivative Discourse.* London: Zed Books.

Chatterjee, Joya (1994). *Bengal Divided: Hindu Communalism and Partition, 1932-1947.* Cambridge: Cambridge University Press.

Dasgupta, J.N. (1970). *Language Conflict and National Development: Group Politics and National Language Policy in India.* Berkeley: University of California Press.

Dixit, Prabha (1974). *Communalism: A Study in Power.* Delhi: Orient Longman.

Engineer, Asghar Ali (1995). *Communalism in India: A Historical and Empirical Study.* Delhi: Vikas.

Feldman, Herbert (1969). "The Communal Problem in the Indo-Pakistan Subcontinent: Some Current Implications," *Pacific Affairs* 42(2) (Summer): 14563 Vancouver.

Gallaghar, John, Gordon Johnson and Anil Seal (1973). *Locality Province and Nation: Essays on Indian Politics 1870 to 1940.* London: Cambridge University Press.

Graham, B.D. (1990). *Hindu Nationalism and Indian Politics: The Origins and Development of the Bharatiya Jana Sangh.* Cambridge (Massachusetts): Cambridge University Press.

Habib, Irfan (2006). *Indian Economy, 1858-1914.* Aligarh: Aligarh Historians Society.

Kumar, Pramod (ed.) (1992). *Towards Understanding Communalism in India.* Chandigarh: CRIID.

Mahajan, Sucheta (1999). *Independence and Partition: Erosion of Hegemony in Colonial India.* New York, London, Delhi: Sage.

Menon, Visalakshi (2003). *From Movement To Government: The Congress in the United Provinces, 1937-42.* Delhi, Thousand Oaks and London: Sage Publications.

Misra, Salil (2001). *A Narrative of Communal Politics.* New Delhi, Thousand Oaks, London: Sage Publications.

Mukherjee, Aditya (1991). "Colonialism and Communalism", in S. Gopal (ed.), *Anatomy of a Confrontation, The Babri Masjid-Ram Janmabhumi Issue.* Delhi; Viking. pp.164-78.

Mukherjee, Aditya *et al.* (2003). *History in the New NCERT Text Books: A Report and an Index of Errors.* Indian History Congress.

Mukherjee, Mridula and Aditya Mukherjee (ed.) (2002). *Communalisation of Education, The History Textbook Controversy.* Delhi: Delhi Historians' Group.

Mukherjee, Mridula, Aditya Mukherjee, and Sucheta Mahajan (2008). *RSS, School Texts and The Murder of Mahatma Gandhi: The Hindu Communal Project.* New Delhi, Thousand Oaks, London: Sage Publications.

Shakir, Moin 91983). *Khilafat to Partition: A Survey of Major Political Trends among Indian Muslims during 1919-1947.* Delhi: Ajanta Publications.

Shakir, Moin (1970). *Jamat–E-Islami Hind: Theory and Practice.* New Delhi: Kalamkar Prakashan.

Tambiah, Stanley (1996). *Levelling Crowd: Ethnonationalist Politics and Collective Violence in South Asia.* Berkeley: University of California Press.

Thapar, Romila, Bipan Chandra, and Harbans Mukhia (1969). *Communalism and the Writing of Indian History.* Delhi: People's Publishing House.

Vanaik, Achin (1997). *Communalism Contested: Religion, Modernity and Secularization.* London: Verso.

Vorys, Karl von (1976). *Democracy Without Consensus: Communalism and Political Stability in Malaysia.* Singapore: Oxford University Press.

PART III

Colonialism and its Impact

10

SHIN YONG-HA

The Incipient Phase of Modern Korean Nationalism

Korean nationalism is a product of Korea's rich and complex historical experience, and the Western world has yet to understand this issue adequately and insightfully. There are primarily two ways of interpreting the emergence of nationalism. The first one is primordialism, referring to a force arising naturally from pre-existing differences of language, culture and ethnicity, and the second is modernism that connotes forces and factors generated by such modern processes as capitalism, including print capitalism or modern media and communications, rise of new classes and the political, economic, social and cultural policies of modern states.

Modern Korean nationalism developed as a response to challenges of modernisation, but its origin can be traced to the pre-existing shared identity that assumed a distinct shape in the aftermath of the wars with Japan and Ch'ing China of the late 16th and early 17th centuries respectively. Historically, Korea faced numerous threats and invasions from foreign powers, but the crisis of the late 16th and 17th centuries led to the re-evaluation of Korean traditions by a group of scholars, knows as the Practical Learning School (*Sirhak*). The crisis of the Choson dynasty (1392-1910) became acute in the mid-19th century when it had to wage a relentless struggle against powerful and aggressive imperialist powers of the West and Japan. In other words, modern Korean nationalism, representing collective consciousness and will of the Korean people, was formed and matured when the Choson dynasty had to grapple with the challenges of foreign powers in the late 19th century. This essay, therefore, would delineate the process of nationalism's rise by providing a discussion of the *Sirhak*, representing the initial glimmers of ideological modernity and national identity, and proceeding to the Enlightenment Faction or the Progressives whose ideology was nurtured in the cradle of *Sirhak* thought.

Sirhak: The Initial Stirring of Modern Nationalism

The initial stirrings of modern nationalism are evident in the *Sirhak* thought that challenged the China-centred worldview of Hwa-yi (civilised *versus* barbarian) in order to establish the uniqueness and independence of Korean culture *vis-à-vis* China. According to the Hwa-yi thought, China was the Middle Kingdom, the source and repository of civilisation, and Korea, along with other states located on the Chinese borders, was a barbarian state. The Confucianists of the Choson dynasty regarded their country as "Little China", and claimed that after the fall of Ming China and establishment of the Ch'ing dynasty which was Manchu in its origin, the centre of civilisational gravity had shifted to Choson, because Choson was superior to Manchus in terms of Confucian learning, values and virtues. They also claimed that Choson, "the Little China" was the only state on the Chinese border that preserved the Chinese tradition. Such an assumption was very subjective in nature, and was undergirded with the spirit of ideological subordination to China. It is remarkable that the Chinese viewed Korea unambiguously and consistently as a barbarian state. *Sirhak's* radical doubt regarding the thought of Hwa-yi, which was held as sacrosanct and served as the cornerstone of the edifice of Sino-centric world order, became the strongest ideological pillar of modern nationalism in Korea. Representative scholars who challenged Hwa-yi are Hong Tae-yong (1731-1783), Park Ch'i-won (1737-1805), Chong Yak-yong (1762-1836) and Yi Kyu-kyong (1788-1856).

Hong Tae-yong used his knowledge of astronomy to dispute the validity of the Hwa-yi thought and the attendant centrality of China in the universe. He argued that the earth was neither flat nor static, and pointed out that based on the scientific fact of the earth's rotation, it was absurd to claim that China was the Middle Kingdom. In his view, the West that had a difference of 180 degree latitude with

China also occupied a central position, and it was also civilised. He wrote:

> The Chinese consider their country as the centre and the West as a periphery. On the other hand, Westerners regard the West as the centre and China as periphery. In fact, there is the same sky above and the same earth below all over the world. There is no justification, whatsoever, in the binary construction of civilised and barbarians.[1]

It is obvious that Hong Tae-yong possessed ascientific temper, and his worldview was anchored in his knowledge of modern science. According to this new perspective, Korea was as advanced as China and Korean rulers were as virtuous as the Chinese 'Son of Heaven'. He was a pioneer scholar who generated a new force that swept away the China-centred outlook and paved a path for the emergence of an independent and self-reliant spirit.

Chong Yak-yong, known by his pen name of Tasan, also launched a vitriolic attack on the civilised-barbarian binary that sustained the myth of China as the Middle Kingdom. He wrote:

> When the sun shines over our head at mid-day, the very place where I stand represents the centre of the East and the West. Moreover, iflatitudinally, the arctic and antarctic zones equally divide the earth, the place where I stand is the middle of the South and the North. It is obvious that China is not perennially located at the centre of East, West, North and South. Needless to add, there is no justification in affixing the title of 'Middle Kingdom' to China.[2]

Chong Yak-yong also argued that since time immemorial, various Korean states imported the teachings of such Chinese sages as Yao, Shun, Yu, Tang, Confucius and Mencius, and produced works of insightful scholarship on Confucian learning. Korean culture also deserved an axial position in the ideological universe of Confucianism. Chong Yak-yong emphasised the need to study both Chinese and Korean history, because he had deep faith in the innate resilience and strength of Korean culture. He lamented the fact that

1. Hong Tae-Yong cited in Shin Yong-Ha (1989). *Formation and Development of Modern Korean Nationalism*. Seoul: Dae Kwang Munwhasa. p.19.

2. Chŏng Yak-yong cited in Shin Yong-Ha (1989). *Formation and Development of Modern Korean Nationalism*. Seoul: Dae Kwang Munwhasa p.20.

the Korean literati took pride in their knowledge of classical Chinese language and Chinese history and culture and looked down at their indigenous tradition. To quote him, "If people are not familiar with the wisdom bequeathed by their ancestors, they are ignoramuses, however learned they are in the intellectual and cultural tradition of China."

Pak Chi-won, another major exponent of the *Sirhak* tradition, criticised the gentry of his time for fostering and promoting a ritually obsequious relationship with China. He called the time-cherished doctrines such as 'Serve and Respect the Great Ming' or 'Learn from Civilised China and Reject the Barbarian West' as not only meaningless but also harmful to the interests of Korea. He called for the accommodation of science and technology of the so-called barbarian countries of the West, and emphasised the need to promote utility and welfare. He wrote that the empty rhetoric of Confucianism was obsolete, and the need of the hour was to create a militarily strong and economically prosperous country. In his view no knowledge is 'barbarian' knowledge, which implied that Koreans needed to learn from the experiments and experiences of Manchus who occupied the dragon-throne (of China) at the time and whom the Confucian literati of the Choson dynasty looked down upon as 'barbarians'.

Park was also one of the pioneer historians to underscore the need to develop a new framework of historiography that was anchored in native Korean impulses and distanced itself from Chinese cultural sensibility. He criticised Kim Pu-sik, the author of the *Samguksagi* (The History of the Three Ancient Korean States), the oldest existing work on ancient Korea, for the China-centred perspective and parameters with which he looked at Korean history, leading to a distortion of historical facts and undermining of the strength of Korean history. He pointed out that the territorial expanse of early Korean history extended to Manchuria, but under Kim Pu-sik's pen Korean history loses its range and richness.

Yi Kyu-kyong praised the Korean writing system, known as *Hunminchongum* (Proper Sounds to Instruct the People), invented by King Sejong in the mid-15th century. He called it one of the great wonders of mankind because combinations of vowels and consonants facilitated transliteration of all the sounds of the Korean language. He also deplored the fact that the Korean literati were enamoured of classical Chinese and looked down on their own writing-system. In addition, he provided a fresh perspective on Korean history by rejecting various China-centred interpretations. He disputed the notion that a Chinese Lord, Kija established the early Korean state of Ko-Choson, and he also played a seminal role in appropriating the legacy of Parhae and establishing its identity as an ancient Korean state. China-centred historian that he was, Kim Pu-sik did not mention this state in his *Samguksagi*.

It is evident from the above-mentioned account of *Sirhak* scholars that their ideas represented the first glimmers of the spirit of independence and a sense of national identity. It is worthy of note in this context that the spirit of national identity, espoused by *Sirhak* scholars, served as the seed of modern Korean nationalism. *Sirhak* set in motion the process of ideological modernisation and exerted an immense influence on the future generations of intellectuals who sought to assert the independent national identity of Korea and overcome ideological challenges posed by the imperialist powers. Their adoption of empirical or evidential learning and their criticism of Sinocentric history, propagation of nativist values and assertion of Korea's distinct racial identity *vis-à-vis* China, emphasis on the Korean language and ascientific understanding of the geography and topography of Korea were of particular relevance as 'ethnies' ethno-symbolisms and contributed significantly to the construction of Korean national identity. 'Ethnies' created shared cultural meaning and experience enabling the Korean people to consolidate their belief in a collective self, and became the basis for the nation's social and political norms and programmes.

The Legacy of *Sirhak*

The legacy of *Sirhak* was not recognised universally, but its influence is clearly evident in the mainstream of the intellectual history of modern Korea. In the late 19th century, a newschool of thought, known as *Wijongch'oksa* (Protect Orthodoxy and Reject

Heterodoxy), appeared in response to the challenges of the times which repudiated the legacy of *Sirhak*. It demanded expulsion of all foreign powers, acomplete ban on foreign ideas, and maintenance of the orthodox Confucian tradition. Yi Hang-no, the leader of the movement, wrote that the dividing line between right and wrong in the world was co-terminus with distinction between Chinese culture and barbarism and difference between the Confucian kingly way and despotism. He called the former orthodoxy that was to be maintained and cherished and the latter as heterodoxy to be rejected. The *Sirhak* scholars were Confucian scholars, but they explored a new world of intellectual inquiry beyond the Neo-Confucian Li-Qi (Principle-Material Force) debate, but the exponents of Protect Orthodoxy and Reject Heterodoxy views considered Neo-Confucianism as sacrosanct. It is interesting to note that even in 1876,[3] the year when Korea was forced by Japan to sign an unequal treaty and open its doors, a Korean literatus outlined Neo-Confucian values as the sole guiding ideology of the state. To quote:

> For the last five centuries our country has adhered solely to Zhu Xi Neo-Confucianism. Those who violate the principles of Zhu Xi are condemned by the state as criminals, and if a member of the gentry demonstrates inclination towards the teachings of Buddha or Laozi, he is dismissed from office and exiled to the provinces.

Such figures regarded Korea as "Principle" and Japan and the West as "Material Force", and their rejection of the West and Japan was informed by the belief that Chinese culture was the sole repository of wisdom and the only guide to construct an ethical and humane society. They attacked Japan because they believed that Japan had lost its Eastern, Neo-Confucian character by imitating Western ways and adopting the ideas and institutions of Western provenance.

Tonghak (Eastern Learning), founded by Ch'oeChe-u in 1960, represents one of the most popular responses to the challenges of the 19th century, but it is remarkable that was not equipped with a

3. *Kim Kisu, Ildongkiyu* Vol.2, (1876) Quoted in Kwon Hi-yong *Hwayironesomun-myongkaehwaroneuro* (From Civilised/Barbarian Binary to the Theory of Enlightenment), South-North Korean Scholars Conference Proceedings, Yanbian University. 15 October 2009, p.94

modern concept of nation-state, and also falls in the category of pre-modern nationalism. It is difficult to establish a direct relationship between *Sirhak* and *Tonghak*, but it is worthy of note that both the currents of thought emphasised "de-centreing China" and the consequent Korea-centred worldview. The spirit of *Sirhak* was inherited by the Enlightenment Faction, which launched an abortive coup d'état in 1884 in order to drive the country on the path of modernisation.

Kaehwa (Enlightenment) Thought

Kaehwa thought, formulated by a handful of intellectuals during 1853-1860s before the opening of Korea, radiated immense influence on the minds of Korean intellectuals in the late 19th century. Pak Kyu-su and O Kyong-sok, who acted respectively as ambassador and interpreter for Korean missions frequently dispatched to China, had seen that China was subdued by the overwhelming military might and technological prowess of the Western powers, and concluded that a similar fate would befall Korea. With a view to prepare for this eventuality, they brought back many new books from China introducing Western civilisation. One of O's friends, Yu Tae-ch'I, read the books and agreed on the need to provide the wherewithal to meet any crisis to come. These men of foresight felt that they should infuse a new thought in the young generation to take the helm of state in the future and instruct them in things Western. They opened a class for reading *Sirhak* (Practical Learning) classics of the late Choson dynasty and books on Western civilisation. They enrolled talented youths from *yangban* families.

Among them were Kim Yun-sik, Kim Hong-jip, O Yun-jung, Pak Yong-hyo, Kim Ok-kyun, Pak Yong-kyo, Hong Yong-sik, So Kwang-bom and Yu Kil-jun. Through reading new books and examining internal and external conditions, they developed a new thought which was called *kaehwa* thought. They found the challenge from the Western powers in a new social system founded on advanced technology and advocated a new way of response different from New-Confucianism. *Kaehwa* thought had the following characteristics.

First, it called for the introduction and adoption of advanced technology of the West. They well recognised the technological lag of Korea and the Orient and believed that learning and adopting Western technology was necessary to make the nation strong and prosperous.

Second, it ascribed the technological lag to the defects in social institutions and called for an overall reform and the introduction of a modern capitalistic social system free from such defects.

Third, it called for a political transition from the old authoritarian to a constitutional monarchy and establishment of a modern nation-state.

Fourth, it called for the growth of industry and commerce by putting Western technology to economic use. It called for efforts to enhance productivity and introduce capitalistic institutions.

Fifth, it sought to realise freedom and equality of the people through abolition of the absolute *yangban* system. Its adherents believed that recruitment of men should be made on merit of the person and the entire people should be effectively mobilised for the defense and development of the nation. They demanded that modern schools should be immediately established to give new education to youths.

Sixth, they urged that Korea should embrace many cultures of the West, other than the Chinese culture, and thus develop and enrich Korea's own unique culture, language, arts and history.

It is apparent that *kaehwa* thought held that the national crisis could be overcome, if and when Korea adopted not only the technology but also the good social institutions of the West. The *kaehwa* faction worked for sweeping reforms as the country was opened to intercourse with the Western world. The reforms included:

1. administrative reorganisation such as the creation of *T'ongnigimuamun* (Foreign Office);
2. despatch of students to China for technical training;
3. despatch of an observer mission to Japan;
4. establishment of modernised schools;
5. publishing of a modern newspaper;

6. inauguration of a customs house;
7. establishment of an agricultural experimental station;
8. introduction of a modern postal system;
9. publishing of new books;
10. introduction of Western technology and promotion of industry.

The military riot (*Imogullan*) of 1882 brought Chinese troops to Korea under the command of Yuan Shih-k'ai who attempted extensive intervention in the internal affairs of Korea and also attempted to put down modernisation policies of the early *kaehwa* faction and indeed rid the government of this faction.

At this juncture, radical members of the faction launched a coup d'état in order to take over the government and introduce general reforms. But the coup d'état lasted only three days, and while a small number of the extremists exiled themselves to foreign countries, the rest were captured and executed by the Chinese army and the conservative faction. Thus, the modernisation bid was foiled.

Kapshinchongbyon, or the coup d'état of 4 December 1884, staged by the Progressives served as a channel to articulate their demand for the nation's autonomy from China's suzerainty and for commercial and trade relations with the outside world. They seized power through this coup from the Conservatives led by Queen Min, but they were driven out of power by the Chinese troops then stationed in Seoul. However, many historians attach importance to this coup and the ensuing short-lived Progressive government. This is because the thought underlying this coup and the policy the Progressives called for, are considered to be underpinned with the epoch-making aim of building a modern nation-state in Korea.

But all historians do not necessarily agree on the historical significance of the coup d'état of 1884. Rather they are more sharply split on the evaluation of this coup than on other issue of modern Korean History. At one extreme are those who see the coup simply as a power struggle between the pro-Chinese faction and the pro-Japanese faction that had nothing to do with the will to modernise the country. At the other extreme are those who praise the coup as the first modern civil revolution in Korean history.

One way to settle the disputes on pros and cons of the coup d'état of 1884 is to analyse and review the thought this coup pursued. The Progressives who launched the coup harbored the thought of enlightenment that the nation could become rich and strong only by opening the country to the outside world, and after having seized power in the coup they proclaimed progressive policy guidelines based on this enlightenment thought.

I will briefly discuss the course of development the enlightenment thought took in the later 19th century in order to bring to light the historical characteristics of the coup d'état of 1884, and then deal in more detail with the platform the Progressives announced after the coup.

Development of Enlightenment Thought

In the middle of the 19th century, Western powers made inroads into Northeast Asia, and in the latter half of the 1860s the enlightenment thought arguing for opening the country to the outside world was developed chiefly by O Kyong-sok (1831-1879), Pak Kyu-su (1807-1876) and Yu Hong-gi (1831-1884). The enlightenment thought had two origins, one is *Sirhak* (Practical Learning) developed in the 18th century, and the other the Western thought introduced to the country by way of China in the 19th century.

Pak Kyu-su, took over the academic traditions and ideas of the *Sirhak* titan Pak Chi-won (pen name Yonam, 1737-1805) who was his grandfather. In 1860 when Pak Kyu-su was working in the government, an allied force of British and French troops occupied Peking, the capital of Ch'ing dynasty China. This incident was a great shock to the Choson dynasty government which had believed that China was the most powerful country of the world. In January 1861, the Korean government sent a consolatory mission to Peking. Pak Kuy-su was deputy head of this mission, and he observed Peking exposed to danger under the influence of Western powers. Anticipating that Korea would also come under Western influence, he felt keenly the necessity of studying the Western world. He brought home many books on geography, history, politics, economy, culture and military affairs of the Western nations. China opened its ports to the West in 1842 and this prompted many Chinese scholars to publish books on the West. Pak Kyu-su developed the enlightenment thought on the basis of his grandfather's thought of *Sirhak* and his study of the books on the Western ideas and ways that he brought from Peking.

In 1872, Pak Kuy-su made his second visit to Peking as chief of a royal mission and returned home with many books on Western ideas and ways again. He opened a class for young promising boys of *yangban* (aristocratic class) families at his home and taught them Western ideas and ways, while encouraging them to read the new books he brought from Peking and the *Sirhak* books.

Pak Yong-hyo, one of the leading figures of the coup of 1884, later recalled how he learned the enlightenment thought from Pak Kyu-su:

> The new thought came from the home of Pak Kyu-su, one of my relatives. I learned this thought with Kim Ok-kyun, Hong Yong-sik, So Kwang-bom and my eldest brother (Pak Yong-gyo).
>
> I learned the thought of equality from *Yonam-jip* (Collection of Yonman's Writings) as it contains essays attacking the aristocrats.

Shin Ch'ae-ho wrote thus on how Kim Ok-kyun learned the enlightenment thought from Pak Kyu-su:

> When Kim OK-kyunvisited Prime Minister Pak Kyu-su at his home, Pak brought a globe from a wall closet and showed it to him. Pak told him that the globe had been brought from Peking by his grandfather Pak Chi-won, whose pen name was Yonam. Turning the globe once, Pak told Kim with a smile, "Where is the Middle Kingdom today? When you turn the globe that way the United States will be the Middle Kingdom, and when you turn it this way Korea can be the Middle Kingdom. Thus any country can be the Middle Kingdom, depending on which way you turn this globe. There is no absolute Middle Kingdom. Right?

Kim Ok-kyun thus began to argue for trade relations with other countries on the basis of his study of the new books that Pak brought from Peking. Kim woke up from the traditional thought of hundreds of years that China was the Middle Kingdom of the world and the nations surrounding it were barbarians. Kim came to know that so long as this thought of looking up to China as the Middle Kingdom of the world prevailed, Korea could not become independent of China. Later Kim Ok-Kyun led the coup of 1884.

O Kyong-sok, a Chinese translator-interpreter of the *chungin* (middle people) class, visited Peking in 1853-1854 and also returned home with many books on the Western world. Naturally he studied these books and began to embrace the enlightenment thought. In 1872, he again visited China as an interpreter for Pak Kyu-su who was chief of a royal mission. Observing the developments in Peking, he felt that Korea was also in danger of heavy Western influence, and then he had his friend Yu Tae-ch'i (Yu Honggi), read the books he had brought from Peking. They discussed these books, worrying about the future of Korea. Later, O Se-ch'ang wrote about his father as follows:

> My father, O Kyong-sok, had frequently visited China as an interpreter for the annual Winter Solstice Emissary and other envoys of the Korean government sent to Peking. While in Peking, he witnessed the Chinese capital turning into an arena of power struggle among the Western countries and worried about the possibility that Korea might become such an arena. Later he studied the histories of Western powers, especially their rise and fall, and was aware that Korea was far behind these Western countries. He also deplored the corruption that prevailed in the government and warned that Korea would face a big tragedy should the corrupt, conservative government continue to remain in power....My father had a friend named Yu Hong-gi, alias Taech'i. Taech'i was a man of both letters and character. My father gave him the "new books" he had brought from Peking and encouraged him to study them. Later their friendship was solidified as they came to hold the same opinion that the only way to save the country from the brink of a fall to the Western power was to launch a great reform movement. One day Yu Tae-ch'i asked my father how the reform movement should be launched, and my father said that they should first make friends with young people of the *yangban* families in Pukch'on (North Village) of Seoul and then infuse them with the reformist thought.[4]

Yu Hong-gi was born of an interpreter's family of the *chungin* class, but he studied herbal medicine and practiced it near Kwanggyo

4. Kim Ok-kyun cited in Shin Yong-Ha (1989). *Formation and Development of Modern Korean Nationalism*. Seoul: Dae Kwang Munwhasa. p.52.

in Seoul. After reading the books that O Kyong-sok had brought from China, he came to embrace the enlightenment thought. A devoted Buddhist, he tried to fuse the enlightenment thought into Buddhism.

The enlightenment thought was thus developed by the above-mentioned three pioneers during 1853-1860s at the latest. The gist of the enlightenment thought developed by these three reformists can be summarised as follows.

First, a crisis is brewing up in Asia because of the Western powers' encroachments, and Korea is also faced with such a crisis.

Second, in order to overcome this crisis, Korea must be transformed from a pre-modern society to a modern society in a great reform movement.

Third, Ch'ing China has already succumbed to the Western powers, and Korea cannot be saved from such a crisis by relying on China.

Fourth, there is no absolute Middle Kingdom, and any country can be Middle Kingdom; so Korea should strengthen its independence from China and decide its national fate on its own, while striving to build a rich and powerful country of high civilisation.

Fifth, Western science and technology are farther advanced than oriental science and technology, and Korea should import and apply Western science and technology to build a rich and powerful country.

Sixth, Korea should initiate commercial and trade relations with Western countries on an equal and reciprocal basis, and accept Western ideas and ways on a selective basis in building a rich and powerful country.

Seventh, the *yangban* status system must be abolished because the ruling class privileges based on this system have caused the most serious injury to the nation, and an egalitarian social structure must be established for all in order to recruit competent and talented people for government positions.

Eighth, the government must be reformed and reorganised, because corrupt and inefficient government officials are incapable of saving the country from the encroachment of Western powers.

Ninth, the Western powers have powerful forces of artillery and warships and Korea should establish a modern army equipped with new weapons so as to strengthen the defence system.

Tenth, a new political force should be established without much delay by providing modern education to promising young people of the ruling class and exposing them to new thought and new knowledge based on Western ideas and ways.

It was in 1870, when Kim Ok-Kyun was around 20, that Kim, who was to become the leader of the coup of 1884, first learned the enlightenment thought from Yu Tae-Ch'i. O Se-ch'ang wrote about their meeting as follows:

> Kim Ok-kyun made the acquaintance of Yu Tae-ch'i when Kim was 20 years old. Kim learned the new thought from Yu and made friends with the young men who had interest in this thought. Kim passed *kwago* (the civil service examination) to serve in the government, where he devoted himself to gathering the young enlightened people.[5]

The enlightenment thought was developed in the latter half of the 1860s, and from 1870, when Kim Ok-kyun was 20, young people of the ruling class began to study this thought seriously. O Se-ch'ang said that Kim Ok-kyun learned the enlightenment thought around 1870 and gathered young enlightened people when he passed the civil service examination to serve in the government. It was in 1872 when he was 22 that Kim passed the examination and two years later, he was appointed a member of *Hongmun-gwan* (Office of Special Advisors). According to O Se-ch'ang, it was, therefore, in 1874 that Kim Ok-kyun started to gather young enlightened people of the ruling class.

At the same time, Kim Ok-kyun said that it was in 1874 that the *Kaehwadang* (Progressive Party) was formed. This is in agreement with the above-mentioned records of O Se-ch'ang. In his *Kapshinillok* (Journal of 1884), Kim wrote as follows:

> There is a court lady (Yi U-sok?) who is 42 years old. She is so strong that she is a match for five or six ordinary men in strength. So we

5. Kim Ok-kyun cited in Shin Yong-Ha (1989). *Formation and Development of Modern Korean Nationalism*. Seoul: Dae Kwang Munwhasa. p.53.

call her *Kodaesu* (an amazon) and she, in addition to being strong, is one of the favourites of the queen. She has worked for our party as a court agent for 10 years.[6]

In 1884, Kim wrote that there had been a secret court informer of the party from 10 years before, and this, together with O Se-ch'ang's records, leads to the conclusion that the Progressive Party was organised in 1874.

In sum, the enlightenment thought was developed by Pak Kyu-su, O Kyong-sok and Yu Tae-ch'i, and it was developed into the Progressive Party as a political force by Kim Ok-kyun and his friends. Under the guidance of Pak Kyu-su, O Kyong-sok and Yu Tae-ch'i, Kim Ok-kyun infused his friends with the new thought. Kim sought and gathered friends widely from among the military *yangban* class, the *chungin* class, merchants, and even commoners. He also won court ladies and eunuchs over to his side.

But when Korea opened its doors to Japan under the Treaty of Kanghwa-do concluded in 1876, the power of the Progressive Party was so weak that it could do almost nothing. Under the treaty, Pusan was opened in 1876, Wonsan in 1880, and Inch'on in 1883, and this necessitated that the Choson dynasty government employ young people who had knowledge of the outside world. As a result, many Progressives found their way into important government positions to propagate the enlightenment thought among government officials, thereby contributing to the wider dissemination of enlightenment thought. But in 1881, the conservative Confucian literati, who called for defending orthodoxy and rejecting heterodoxy, sent a letter to the king attacking the enlightenment policy based on foreign ideas. This letter was occasioned by Huang Tsun-hsien's *ChaohsienTs'e-lueh* (A Strategy for Choson) which Kim Hong-jip had brought from Japan in 1880. In reaction to the letter, young Progressives also sent letters to the king, explaining the need for an enlightenment policy. For instance, in September 1882, Ko Yong-mun wrote a letter to the king, spelling out the following set of recommendations:

6. Ibid.: 54.

1. Introduction of Western Technology: A mission should be sent to Western countries to observe their culture and institutions and establish friendly relations with them. Western engineers should be invited to the country for technical training of young people.
2. Establishment of a Public Council: A public council should be formed as a non-government organisation, and this council should draw on those who are well versed in specific problems in formulating its policy recommendations to the government.
3. Development of the Mining Industry and the Monetary System: A law should be enacted to promote the mining industry, and precious metal money should be issued for permanent circulation so as to make nobody live in idleness.
4. Establishment of a Police System: A police district should be established for every 50 households, and each district should have four policemen, in addition to the district chief, for control of theft, fire, flood and overdrinking in the district.
5. Establishment of National Bank and Chamber of Commerce: A national bank and a chamber of commerce should be set up in Seoul for the development of commerce and industry.
6. Establishment of a Navy: A navy should be established, with its base in lnch'on, for defence of the sea routes and the capital from any sea invasions.
7. Tax Reform: Unnecessary posts in the government should be abolished and a modern tax system should be established for a reasonable tax burden on the people. Under this system, public servants will get subsistent wages and the opportunity for competent people to enter public service will be broadened.

The Progressives, who found their way into important government positions after opening of the country to Japan and Western countries, had such influence on the king that their enlightenment policy was pursued. Between 1880 and 1884 when the *Kapshin Chongbyon* broke out, the Progressives implemented the following enlightenment programmes, among other things:

1. Establishment of a modern government office called *Tongni kimu amun* (Office for State Affairs) in 1880.
2. Despatch of *Yongson-sa* (Mission of Ordnance and Technology) to foreign countries in 1881.
3. Despatch of an observation mission in Japan in 1881.
4. Establishment of a modern army, called *Pyolgigun*, in 1881.
5. Establishment of *Kimu-ch'o* (Deliberative Council of Important State Affairs) in 1882.
6. Establishment of *Kamsaeng-ch'ong* (Office of Budget Austerity) in 1882.
7. Execution of balance of power policy to foreign countries in 1882.
8. Announcement of sea defence policy in 1882.
9. Establishment of *Hae-gwan* (Customs Office) in 1882.
10. Establishment of a modern school, *Wonsan Haksa*, in 1883.
11. Establishment of an English School, *Tongmunhak*, in 1883.
12. Publication of a modern newspaper. *Hansong Sunbo* in 1883.
13. Establishment of modern post system in 1883.
14. Establishment of *Ch'ido guk* (Office of Road Improvement and widening of streets in Seoul in 1883.)
15. Establishment of modern police system in Seoul in 1883.
16. Reform of custom system (introduction of Western customs) in 1883.
17. Despatch of students to foreign countries in 1881-1884.
18. Establishment of agricultural and livestock-farming experiment stations in 1884.
19. Establishment of 26 modern commercial and industrial companies in 1881-1884.

These modernisation programmes of the Progressives were designed to build a modern nation state in Korea. Had the progressive been able in continue their modernisation programmes without facing any hindrance, Choson dynasty would have become a modern nation strong enough to maintain its independence. But the situation began to deteriorate with the Military Mutiny of 1882 serving as a turning point.

The military mutiny forced the Conservative Party led by Queen Min out of power and the Taewon'gun took over the reins of government. The Conservatives asked for Ch'ing China's help, and Li Hung-chang. China's North Sea Minister, decided to sent troops to Korea to consolidate China's suzerainty over Korea. As a result, a force of 3,000 troops was sent to Seoul and Taewon'gun, the king's father, was invited to a Chinese warship off Inch'on and taken to China abroad the ship. He was put under detention at Paotingfu in China.

China put the Conservative again in power on the strength of its troops stationed in Seoul and claimed its suzerainty over Korea with positive interference in Korea's domestic and foreign affairs, thus greatly infringing upon Korea's sovereignty. Wu Ch'ang-ch'ing and Yuan Shih-k'ai, commanders of Chinese troops in Korea took the reins of Korea's military affairs and Chen Shu-t'ung, financial advisor to the Korean government, had financial control in hand. Paul Georg von Molendorff, whom Li Hung-chang sent to Seoul as the customs advisor, intervened not only in customs affairs but also in foreign affairs broadly.

Moreover, China, considering the Progressive Party's enlightenment movement under Kim Ok-kyun's leadership as having the aim of Korea's independence from Chinese suzerainty, employed all means to oppress the Progressives and hinder their movement. The modernisation programmes after the Military Mutiny of 1882 were carried out under Chinese oppression and persecution, and they were thus not satisfactory to the Progressives.

The Conservative Party led by Queen Min was subservient to China's suzerain policy in return for Chinese assistance in their rise again to power, which they had lost after the Military Mutiny of 1882. The Conservatives were bent on pursuing theirself-interest, paying no heed to the infringement upon Korean sovereignty and the hindrance to modernisation programmes due to Chinese suzerainty. Furthermore, they, in collaboration with China, oppressed the Progressives to eliminate them from the political world.

In 1884 when the Sino-French relation became tense over Annam (Vietnam), China moved 1,500 troops of its 3,000 man force in Seoul to Annam in May, leaving only 1,500 troops in Korea. In August of that year, war broke out between China and France in Annam. Taking advantage of the situation, the Progressive Party launched a coup d'état on 4 December 1884, employing 1,000 Korean troops and 150 Japanese troops stationed in the Japanese legation in Seoul.

In the coup, the Progressives executed Conservative ministers on the first day and established a new government on the following day. On the third day of the coup, they even announced a reform platform. But on the evening of the day, their government collapsed under the attack of Chinese troops. The Progressive Party's social thoughts underlying the coup of 1884 are reflected in the reform platform they announced in the coup, and in the following section I will introduce this platform of the Progressive Party as it is known today in an attempt to shed light on the nature of the coup.

Platform of the Progressive Party

Some thoughts of the Progressive Party which launched the coup of 1884 are directly reflected in the party's reform platform. Of course, the platform does not represent the whole of the party's social thoughts because it contains only those which could be put into practice immediately after the coup. But it still presents well the basic reform direction into which the Progressive Party wanted to lead the country during those days.

On the evening of 4 December 1884, the Progressive Party launched the coup, making opportune use of a banquet hosted by Hong Yong-shik, director of the Postal Administration, to celebrate the opening of the new building of this agency. The following day, the Progressives took over the reins of government and immediately started formulating a reform programme. On the evening of 5 December, they met in Ch'angdok-gung palace to discuss the platform, without eating supper. Participating in the meeting were Hong Yong-sik, Pak Yong-hyo, Kim Ok-kyun, So Kwang-bom, Pak Yong-gyo, Yi Chae-won. Yi Chae-wan and Sin Ki-son. They had an all-night meeting to finish the platform. Kim Ok-kyun presided over the meeting.

Around nine on the morning of 6 December, they announced this programme of political reform in the form of a royal circular and pasted up it on the walls at major places of the capital, even before the king approved it. The Progressive government occasionally announced major policy measures immediately after a cabinet meeting and sought the king's approval later in view of the urgent need of the situation. The fact that the Progressive government announced the reform platform to the public, prior to the king's approval, shows that these Progressives did not adhere to an absolute monarchy.

Two points deserve attention here. One is that the programme of political reform was formulated as a collective thought after long hours of discussion at a meeting. The other is that government policy was announced to the public beforehand in the form of a political platform, which had never before occurred in Korean history. All the previous governments, including the one ruled by the Conservative party led by Queen Min, had never announced their policy to the people. According to Confucian political morality, people as the ruled need not and should not know the intricacies of government policy making. Thus the Progressive government's policy announcement to the public was an unprecedented and epoch-making event at the time.

On 6 December, Right Prime Minister Hong Yong-sik of the State Council submitted the reform platform to King Kojong for his approval, and at three in the afternoon the king issued an edict proclaiming that the country would be run on the basis of the reform platform.

Today, the Progressive Party's entire programme of political reform is not known because Queen Min's Conservative Party, which took over power again after the collapse of the Progressive Party, collected documents containing the platform and destroyed them. A Japanese who was in Seoul during the Progressive Party's coup said that the platform contained 80 planks, but this is not reliable because he failed to put down those planks. The authentic record of the platform remaining today is found in Kim Ok-kyun's *Kapshinillok* (Journal of 1884) which he later wrote in exile. This journal contains

14 planks, and these are only part of the platform because Kim said, "the platform can be summarised as follows." The 14 planks Kim Ok-kyun put in his journal are:

1. Seek the immediate return of the Taewon'gun and an end to the empty formalities of tributary relationship with China.
2. Abolish ruling cases privileges and establish equal rights for all; stop making appointments on the basis of finding suitable office for the privileged seekers of position and instead seek out men whose talents suit them for official appointment.
3. Revise the land tax laws for every region of the country and root out extortionate practices of the petty officials who administer them thus alleviating the distress of people and at the same time ensuring receipt of sufficient revenue to meet government expenditure.
4. Abolish the Office of Eunuch Attendants (*Naesi-bu*), but employ those eunuchs who are men of superior talent.
5. Punish the most notorious officials whose evil and venal acts past and present have brought the nation to its present state of infirmity.
6. Cancel all outstanding grain loan debts owed to the government.
7. Abolish *Kyujang-gak* (Palace Library and Archives.)
8. Quickly establish police patrols to prevent thievery.
9. Abolish the Office for the Benefit of Peddler-Trade (*Hyesang kongguk.*)
10. Review the cases of those who have been banished or barred from office and as warranted, revoke their sentences.
11. Merge the Four Barracks Commands into a single unit, then select able soldiers among them and immediately form a Royal Guards Division under the command of the Crown Prince.
12. Put all internal fiscal administration under the jurisdiction of the Ministry of Finance, abolishing all other fiscal agencies.
13. Convene regular meetings of the ministers and councillors at the State Council chamber in the palace to discuss policy,

submit proposals to the king, make his decisions known, and then transmit them for implementation.

14. Abolish all superfluous government agencies with the ministers and councillors to study the matter and submit proposals to the throne.

Inoue Kakugoro, a Japanese translator of the *Hansongsunbo*, a thrice-monthly gazette published by the Office of Culture and Information (Pangmunguk) in the Office for Extraordinary State Affairs, recalled the reform actions of the Progressive party as follows (he witnessed the coup in Seoul):

1. Abolish the tributary relationship with China; immediately send an envoy to China to declare Korea's complete independence from China and seek the Taewon'gun's return.
2. Elevate the status of the king to that of emperor so as to be equal to the Chinese emperor, and address him as *P'yeha* (Your Imperial Majesty) and call his orders edicts. The emperor should address himself *Chim* (first-person term, used by the Chinese Emperor) so as to establish the proper etiquette as an independent nation's sovereign.
3. Control arbitrariness of the *yangban* class and promote civil rights of the commoner.
4. Abolish the eunuch system, but employ those eunuchs who are talented.
5. Severely punish all corrupt officials.
6. Establish the Ministry of Imperial Household Affairs so as to separate court affairs from state affairs.
7. Reform the government system and establish a cabinet consisting of eight ministers.
8. Abolish the civil service examination (*kwago*) system.
9. Select young men of talent and send them abroad for study.
10. Issue public bonds to raise funds for the promotion of industry, transportation, education and defence.

The historical characteristics of the coup of 1884 are well represented in the Progressive Party's reform platform, and the platform as it is known today is so briefly summarised that it requires annotations and explanations. In the following pages, I will review and explain the Progressive Party's reform platform on the basis of the 14 planks found in Kim Ok-kyun's *Journal of 1884* and other historical documents.

Analysis of Reform Platform

A. Declaration of Complete Independence

The first plank, to press for the immediate return of the Taewongun from China and an end to the tributary relationship with China, was a declaration that Korea and the new Progressive government was completely independent from China.

With the Military Mutiny of 1882 serving as a turning-point, Ch'ing China intensified its suzerainty over Korea in its policy to put the country under its control, thereby greatly damaging the sovereignty of Choson. The reform platform of the Progressive government was a flat rejection of the suzerain policy of China toward Korea and a declaration of Korea's complete independence from Chinese control. Before the coup of 1884, Kim Ok-kyun wrote his idea of national independence as follows:

> It is shameful that China has traditionally considered Korea its subject state, and it is partly because of this tributary relationship with China that we have no hope for development as an independent nation. So the first task facing us is to eradicate all vestiges of Chinese political influence and establish a completely independent nation. To be an independent nation, we should build up our political and diplomatic power.[7]

So Chae-pillater recalled Kim's independence thought as follows:

> He (Kim Ok-kyun) was highly resentful of the humiliating China-centred history of Korea, and was ceaselessly engaged in the thought of relieving the people of this humiliation by making Korea a free country and elevate its status as equal to other countries of the world.[8]

7. Kim Ok-kyun cited in Shin Yong-Ha (1989). *Formation and Development of Modern Korean Nationalism*. Seoul: Dae Kwang Munwhasa. p.76.

8. Sŏ Chae-p'il cited in Shin Yong-Ha Ha (1989). *Formation and Development of Modern Korean Nationalism*. Seoul: Dae Kwang Munwhasa. p.77.

> The ideal and goal Kim Ok-kyun sought at the time was to eliminate Chinese influence and take steps so an independent government could be established.
>
> Kim Ok-kyun was indignant about China's abduction of theTaewon'gun because he considered it an unbearable shame to Korea. So he started organising a force to eliminate the pro-Chinese aristocrats.[9]

So the reform platform of the Progressive Party rejected in its first plank the suzerain policy that China began to intensify in Korea after 1882, and abolished the empty formalities of tributary relationship with China which had existed before 1882. It was thus a declaration of Korea's complete independence from China. In other words, it was a declaration that Korea, being an independent nation, could now take an equal rank with other nations of the world.

The reform platform of the Progressive Party marked a very important milestone in modern Korean history, in that it not only flatly rejected China's suzerain policy in Korea after the Military Munity of 1882, but also pressed for bringing to an end the empty formalities of the tributary relationship with China for the first time in nearly 500 years since founding of the Choson dynasty, thus declaring before the world that Korea was a completely independent nation.

B. Abolition of the Yangban System and Nepotism and Emphasis on Appointments of Talented People.

The second plank of the reform platform called for the abolition of ruling class privileges and the establishment of equal rights for all so that men of talent could be appointed to official positions, instead of making appointments on the basis of finding suitable offices for the privileged seekers of positions. This was the pronouncement of equal rights for all by eliminating social status differences and rejecting nepotism and by guaranteeing appointments on the basis of men's talent.

---

9. Kim Do-t'ae (ed.) cited in Shin Yong-Ha Ha (1989). *Formation and Development of Modern Korean Nationalism*. Seoul: Dae Kwang Munwhasa. p.77.

At the time, the most evil system that checked development of the country was the *yangban* system. Kim Ok-kyun wrote in a letter to the throne about evils of the *yangban* system as follows:

> Your Majesty must still remember what I have told about the need to chop down the yangban system on the basis of my study for a long time. In ancient times when the nation was prosperous, Korea was better than the two oriental countries (China and Japan) in technology and industry, but today such prosperity has all gone with no trace remaining. This is because of the arbitrariness of the yangban.
>
> When people manufacture articles, the yangban officials take them, and when people make a fortune with hard work, the yangban officials snatch them illegally. People complain that when they support themselves by hard work, the yangban officials not only usurp the result of such hard work but even threaten to kill those who refuse to give up their property. As a result, many people have given up agriculture, commerce and industry, and the number of idle and wandering people is on the increase; this has only brought the nation to its present state of infirmity.

Kim Ok-kyun wrote this letter calling for elimination of the *yangban* system in 1876, and evidently he had already championed the cause of elimination of the *yangban*-based status system before he staged the coup of 1884. He used the phrase "to chop down" in requesting the elimination of the *yangban* system, and by this he must have meant that the *yangban* system should be chopped down as we chop down weeds with a sickle. So the phrase had a stronger meaning than the words abolition and elimination. In other words, Kim Ok-kyun demanded that the *yangban* system be done away with once and for all.

Other major agenda of reform, formulated by Kim Ok-kyun were economic reforms, reform of the defence system, abolition of *Kyujanggak* (Palace Library and Archives), the symbol of Confucian knowledge, and the establishment of modern police and judicial systems. Economic reforms included such clauses as cancellation of the outstanding debts owed by farmers, development of modern industries and creation of the Ministry of Finance which could assume overall authority of the fiscal administration. Establishment of modern police and judicial reform represented a modernist vision of the Progressives. Kim Ok-kyun wrote:

> A close look at the present judicial system reveals that the country's criminal law is outdated, and officials abuse and flout the law with impunity. People have been exiled to remote places just because they happened to use offensive words against officials.[10]

Kim Ok-kyun emphasised social justice, and in his view a modern police constituted the bedrock of internal peace and stability. His reform agenda, therefore, called for the establishment of a new system of constables on patrol (cop) as well as a new judicial system so as to ensure the release of those people who were unjustly imprisoned or banished under the harsh, feudalistic judicial system. This agenda demonstrated the progressive government's generosity, and indeed, it was intended to win the hearts of people, and at the same time to abolish the feudalistic judicial system.

C. Punishment of Officials Harmful to the Nation

In the fifth clause of its reform agenda, the Progressive Party demanded that the crimes of those most notorious officials whose evil and venal acts brought the nation to the present state of infirmity be punished. This was aimed at a purge of the corrupt officials who had amassed a fortune in the Conservative government—the punishment of such officials depending on the degree of harm they did to the national interest.

The purge of the corrupt officials who did great harm to the national interest under the old regime can be considered a natural course of action to be taken by the Progressive Party after it took over power in the coup of 1884.

As discussed above, the reform platform of the coup of 1884 was inspired by the modernist vision of the Progressive Party, and it was aimed at reforming the whole spectrum of state affairs.

---

10. Kim Ok-kyun cited in Shin Yong-Ha (1989). *Formation and Development of Modern Korean Nationalism*. Seoul: Dae Kwang Munwhasa. pp.92-93.

Historical Characteristics of the Reform Platform

The reformation thought of the coup of 1884, as expressed in the reform platform, was the pursuit of measures for construction of a modern nation-state. So Chae-p'il who took part in the coup, recalled Kim Ok-kyun's ideal as the construction of a "strong modern nation".

> Although he did not receive modern education, Kim Ok-Kyun had a keen insight into the historical trends of the time and devoted himself to building a strong modern nation in Korea. He strongly felt the need to reform the government and society by introducing new knowledge and new technology into the country.[11]

In training members of the Progressive Party as its leader, Kim Ok-kyun said, "Japan is endeavouring to be the England of the Orient, and we must make Korea the France of the Orient." So Chae-p'il also recalled him saying as follows:

> Kim Ok-kyun treated us as his brothers and told us everything in his mind. He was frank and honest with us. He told about our mission and responsibility in the reform programme and expected and believed that we would make a great contribution to the development of Korea. He often told us that while Japan was endeavouring to be the England of the Orient, we must make Korea the France of Asia. This was his dream and ambition. We believed him and made up our mind to fulfil our responsibility no matter what might happen to us.[12]

The strong modern nation Kim Ok-kyun and his Progressive Party members wanted to build was the France of Asia. Seeing that Japan was becoming a strong nation and trying to encroach upon other countries, as England was doing, they thought that by making Korea the France of Asia, it could become a strong modern nation to check the aggressive policy of Japan and other countries. In other words, the Progressive Party pursued the construction of a self-reliant, powerful nation in Korea.

In order to implement their political agenda without any delay, they launched the coup of 1884 which was a means to seize power

11. Sŏ Chae-p'il cited in Shin Yong-Ha (1989). *Formation and Development of Modern Korean Nationalism*. Seoul: Dae Kwang Munwhasa. p.99.

12. Sŏ Chae-p'il cited in Shin Yong-Ha (1989). *Formation and Development of Modern Korean Nationalism*. Seoul: Dae Kwang Munwhasa. pp.99-100.

first and then carry out their reform programme from above. To them the coup was necessary because the Conservative government led by Queen Min hindered such reforms in collaboration with Ch'ing China. Japan, which had once planned to invade Korea, was rapidly developing as a modern nation strong enough to encroach on Korea. Under the circumstances, the Progressives could no longer put off their programme to construct a modern, self-reliant, strong nation because without this programme Korea would soon be in the danger of colonisation by Japan. They planned to outset the Conservatives from power by force and form a new government capable of carrying out their reform programme. The first guidelines of this reform programme were the planks of the reform they announced after the coup of 1884.

The reform programme of the Progressive Party covered the whole spectrum of state affairs, because it was designed to transform the country from a pre-modern society into a modern one.

In the political and diplomatic area, it rejected China's suzerainty over Korea and declared Korea's complete independence from China. It aimed at transforming the feudalistic absolute monarchy into a modern constitutional monarchy and reforming the government organisation on the basis of a cabinet system, thereby making Korea powerful enough to be equal to other countries of the world and free from any interference by any foreign power.

In the social system, the reform platform pressed for an end of social caste distinctions and nepotism perpetrated by the ruling clique, and establishment of equal rights for all the people. In other words, it proposed a transformation of society from the *yangban*-ruled pre-modern society into a modern free one, in which all members of society are equal. The Progressive Party wanted to recruit men of talent from all walks of social life for employment in the building of a modern nation.

In the economic and financial area, the platform called for a drastic tax reform to bring to an end to all corruption and irregularities involving the old feudalist tax system and it also provided for a modern capitalistic economic reform to abolish the medieval commercial privileges of packmen. Free enterprise of modern capitalism was encouraged in manufacturing, mining, commerce, agriculture, transportation and communication. The Progressives wanted to put all internal fiscal administration under jurisdiction of the Ministry of Finance in order to control the treasury for carrying out of their reform programme.

In the cultural area, it pressed for an end to the *yangban*-oriented aristocratic cultural system for the establishment of modern culture based on popular education. To this end, it demanded the building of 'new' schools across the country for education of people in 'new' knowledge.

In the defence system, the platform included measures to transform the medieval military system into a modern defence system and to establish a military academy to train leaders of a modern army. Warships were imported to build a modern navy and a Royal Guards Division was activated. These measures were designed to establish a strong, self-reliant defence posture.

In the administration of justice, it sought to bring to an end the pre-modern police and judicial system and establish new laws to pave the way for modern police and judicial systems.

In sum, the reform of the new government born of the coup of 1884 can be considered a declaration of the measures for transforming Korea from a pre-modern society intomodern one. It was the first modern government's public announcement of a reform programme to establish a modern society in Korean history, and this may be said to be the historical characteristic of the platform.

Conclusion

It is obvious that *Sirhak* represented the first glimmers of nationalism in Korea because by decentring China and placing Korea at the centre of Korean consciousness, it facilitated the growth of a Korea-centred worldview. The *Sirhak* scholars' emphasis on Korean history, culture, geography and language as the source of pride for the nation contributed immensely towards the erosion of Sinocentrism in Korea and to the attendant nation-building process. The Progressive Party (Enlightenment Faction) inherited the spirit of *Sirhak* and sought to create a modern and independent Korea.

The coup of 1884, staged by the Progressive or Enlightenment faction, represented an effort to build a strong, self-reliant nation, that was able to cope with the national crisis which hit the country in latter half of the 19th century. This idea failed to materialise because of the failure of the coup. As a result, the Korean people lost the opportunity of building a self-reliant, strong nation to join the ranks of world powers through a great reform programme at an opportune time in world history. Although the coup of 1884 failed, the Progressive Party's reform thought remained, stimulating modernisation movements in later days. *Kabokyongjang* (Reforms of 1894) was a programme that realised the Progressive Party's reform thought related to the coup of 1884 under different circumstances. And the Independence Club and the Manminkongdonghoe (People's Assembly) movements in the 1986-1998 period and the patriotic enlightenment movement in the 1904-1910 period also stemmed from the reform thought behind the coup of 1884.

Furthermore, the reform ideas of the coup of 1884 were the spiritual source of all independence movements against foreign aggression and oppression in the early 20th century. In this connection, the reform thought of the coup of 1884 can be considered the origin of modern Korea's nationalism. It may be thus said that the reform platform of the coup d'état of 1884 marked an epoch-making milestone in the modern history of Korea.

11

ADITYA MUKHERJEE

Colonialism and India's Development Experience[1]

Introduction

There is an argument which calls itself 'revisionist', though it actually is a rehash of a nearly 150-year-old argument, which seeks to portray colonialism in a positive light. This view has now once again become fashionable. This is particularly true for countries which in recent years have been doing very well, countries in East, South-East and South Asia such as China, South Korea, Indonesia and India. Surprisingly, the view that is now being aired is that the current success of this region is closely connected with the colonial experience. It is suggested that it is the colonial opening up which created conditions for the economic take-off in these countries.

"White Man's Burden" in the Era of Globalisation

A peculiar argument has emerged and it tries to claim the credit for the current success of this region to their colonial past. By a virtual sleight of hand, the two processes of globalisation—one under colonialism between the 16th and the 19th centuries, and the other after the Second World War adopted by independent nation states—are conflated. The fact that in the colonial period there was an enormous movement of labour and capital, and an enormous

1. This paper draws from my Presidential Address to the Indian History Congress (Modern India) entitled "The Return of The Colonial in Indian Economic History: The Last Phase of Colonialism in India" in December 2007 (Reprinted in *Social Scientist* 36(3-4), March-April 2008 and in *Social Science Probings*, June 2008) and Mukherjee, Aditya (2010). "Empire: How Colonial India Made Modern Britain", *Economic and Political Weekly* (hereafter EPW) XLV(50), 11 December.

expansion of trade is being conflated with a similar expansion, in fact in some ways even a larger expansion, of trade and a movement of capital witnessed in the 20th century, especially since the 1960s. No mention, of course, is made of the fact that in the latter phase, labour did not move as easily as it used to move in the early colonial phase or of the fact that the earlier process occurred under colonial hegemony for colonial purposes, leading to the "great divergence" between Europe and Asia, while the latter process was essentially mediated through independent nation states in a vastly changed global capitalist system, which was gradually bridging the gap that had been created in the colonial period.[2]

In this colonial understanding, the bad phase in post-colonial countries like India was the nationalist, protectionist phase, which attempted to un-structure colonialism and promote national development. That is, in the Indian case, the fly in the ointment was the Nehruvian phase. The good phases were the colonial period, when the colonial economies were opened up to the world, and again the open economy after the so-called neo-liberal economic reforms in the second half of the 20th century.

This kind of position is found not only in the writing of Niall Ferguson, the very title of whose book *Empire: How Britain Made the Modern World* sums up his basic conclusion that Britain made the modern world through the empire.[3] One finds such positions taken in the writing of Tirthankar Roy, whose neo-colonial work as the *Economic History of India* would in my opinion embarrass even the conservative British Viceroy Lord Curzon because of the blatant manner in which it argues the colonial paradigm.[4] Similar positions are taken currently by economists like Lord Meghnad Desai, a former Marxist, who has moved considerably to the Right. The basic position

2. For a brilliant analysis of the globalisation occurring post World War II with world capitalism having reached a new phase, see Hobsbawm, Eric (1994). *Age of Extremes: The Short Twentieth Century*. Harmondsworth.

3. See Ferguson, Niall (2003). *Empire: How Britain Made the Modern World*. London: Penguin, for an unabashed defence of colonialism.

4. Roy, Tirthankar (2000). *The Economic History of India: 1857-1947*. New Delhi: Oxford University Press. Second edition, 2006.

argued by these neo-colonialists is that colonialism had a positive impact on the colonies and that particularly expansion of trade, creation of transport and communication infrastructure, etc. under colonialism was very beneficial for the colony and created positive initial conditions in the post-colonial situation. The endnote below summarises the position taken by Tirthankar Roy.[5]

It is also argued that the early post-colonial phase, which was relatively protectionist, was what was wrong in the development of these societies. As Desai put it, "the first 40 years of India's Independence (including the Nehruvian years) were wasted." He also argued that colonialism developed India and at Independence left

5. Here are just a few samples of Roy's position selected from various parts of the book which he himself calls "no more than an updated and shorter version of the *Cambridge Economic History of India,* Vol. II." He argues: (i) "...Colonial India experienced *positive economic growth....* In the nineteenth century ...it was driven by India's integration in a rapidly growing world market .... Other key factors encouraging economic growth ...were a strong state and modern transport and communication." "Real income in industry and services grew *rapidly throughout* the colonial rule." (ii) "The notion that commercialization was forced upon the peasants by taxes or debt, and not driven by profit motive, is seriously disputable" (iii) The proverbial "indebtedness" of the peasantry could be "a sign of *prosperity* and not poverty of the peasants" (iv) "Drain of resources from India can neither be precisely defined nor correctly measured". In any case "economic gains from colonies were neither as large as was imagined nor as crucial to the origins of industrialization." (v) The 'de-industrialization' thesis is unsatisfactory and needs to be replaced by an "alternative story" that of "commercialization" (vi) "The most important legacy of British rule was modern infrastructure and public goods that it created.... assets India *could not* believably have acquired in such extent and quality had it not developed close political links with Britain," i.e., British rule was *necessary* for India's transition to modernity. (vii) The modernity, if not benevolence, of the colonial state was also seen from the fact that "it spent less on luxuries and more on the *genuine* duties of the state such as *defence*, welfare, infrastructure and institutions." (viii) "Any explanation of slow growth rates must *focus on* the role of *local characteristics* and peculiarities..." Rather than hold colonialism responsible for stagnation one had to look at "conditions within India" such as: (a) "scarcity of water" despite investments made by the British which "go to the credit of this (British) regime"; (b) "scarcity of capital was always present and always acute"; (c) accelerated population growth rates; (d) social institutions like "caste...introduced market imperfections"; (e) the Indians' "hunger for gold and silver" and inclination "to spend the extra income on sumptuous marriage feasts and jewelry rather than on irrigation or road building"; (f) "agriculture...was subject to high climatic risks"; (g) " poorly developed institutions... such as banks and insurance ," etc. Roy, *op. cit.* no.4: vi,14-18,91,130,217,240-43,257, 273, 310-11, emphasis mine.

India among the top 10 industrial countries of the world![6] I have in detail critiqued these colonial views elsewhere.[7]

These revisionist arguments do not link with the more than a century-long tradition of critiquing colonialism, but does so with the liberal imperialist ideology of the early 19th century, of the "white man's burden" and the goal of imperialism being to "modernise" and develop the colonial "child people" and even train them towards self-government. For example, B.R. Tomlinson argues that "British rule in India...successfully achieved by 1947" was the 19th century objective of Elphinstone: "We must not dream of perpetual possession but apply ourselves to bring the natives to a state that will admit of their governing themselves..."[8] With such "progressive", "paternalistic" colonialism, there was no need for a national movement and indeed, as the Cambridge school argues, there was no national movement, it was only an "annual Tamasha" put up by the Indian elite to grab the loaves and fishes offered by the colonial state.[9]

---

6. Address at Bhoothalingam Centenary celebration, Nehru Memorial Museum and Library (NMML), New Delhi, 21 February 2009, organised by the National Council of Applied Economic Research. See also his *Rediscovery of India*, Bloomsbury, 2011.
7. Mukherjee, Aditya, Presidential Address to the Indian History Congress (Modern India) entitled "The Return of the Colonial in Indian Economic History: The Last Phase of Colonialism in India" in December 2007 (Reprinted in *Social Scientist* 36(3-4), March-April 2008 and in *Social Science Probings*, June 2008) and Mukherjee, Aditya (2010). "Empire: How Colonial India Made Modern Britain", *EPW* XLV(50), 11 December. The title of the paper is a play on the title of Niall Ferguson's book cited above (f.n.3). This is a revised version of a paper written as part of a global book project initiated by Sven Beckert (Harvard), Dominic Sachenmaier (Duke) and Julia Seibert (Trier), called *The Global Origins of the Old World* where an attempt was made to arrive at a non-Eurocentric explanation for Europe's rise and examine the important ways in which other parts of the world contributed to Europe's rise. The paper was read at a conference at Freiberg, Germany, 27-29 May 2010. The following section draws heavily from the first work cited above in this footnote.
8. Tomlinson, B.R. (1979). *Political Economy of the Raj 1914-47: The Economics of Decolonisation in India*. London; Macmillan. p.152.
9. For a critique of such positions, see my Presidential address cited above (f.n.7). For an important and detailed critique of the treatment of nationalism and popular resistance to colonialism by the 'subaltern studies' and associated scholarship, see Mukherjee, Mridula (2004). *Peasants in India's Non-violent Revolution, Practice and Theory*. New Delhi: Sage, especially Book II in this work titled "Interrogating Peasant Historiography: Peasant Perspectives, Marxist Practice and Subaltern Theory". Also see Mukherjee, Mridula (1988). "Peasant Resistance and Peasant Consciousness in Colonial India: 'Subalterns' and Beyond", in *EPW*, 8 and 15 October. The 'subalterns', to my knowledge, have not responded to this critique.

It appears that now we are going one step further than repeating liberal imperialist positions as breakthroughs. We have Maria Misra[10] of Oxford University, (out-competing her Cambridge school colleagues, who buy into the liberal imperialist point of view) arguing that the "conservative modernisers" or the conservative imperialists like Lord Curzon, who relied on a strategy of colonialism that tried to create a support base among the princes, *taluqdars* and the feudal "Indian Aristocracy", too had their contribution. The current economic success of Karnataka, Gujarat, Kerala, etc. is linked to the existence of princely states in this region in the colonial period and then by a strange sleight of hand to the conservative imperialists. Misra argues: "It is precisely these princely states that have become the industrial and technological powerhouses of modern independent India. Lord Curzon would have been proud." As we shall see below, the recent development of these regions had nothing to do with any form of imperialism, liberal or conservative. It had a lot to do with the breaks from imperialism after Independence. It may have also had something to do with the enlightened rulers in some of these princely states, like Mysore and Travancore-Cochin, and their relative autonomy from imperialism rather than their subservience to it.

In recent historiography emerging from the first world, such as the Subaltern school, there is a tendency to undermine the legitimacy of the national movement in India and a growing tendency to argue on continuity between the colonial state and the post-colonial state.

In this paper, I shall first, in brief, argue that the colonial legacy did not create positive 'initial conditions' and that the path to development necessitated the 'un-structuring' of colonialism. Second, I shall show how the post-colonial state marked a definite break with colonialism and under the leadership of Jawaharlal Nehru tried to un-structure the inherited colonial structure. I shall outline some of the elements of the Nehruvian strategy for 'un-structuring' colonialism in the economic sphere.

10. See Misra, Maria. "Aristrocracies and Modernities: India After the Great Rebellion", paper read at this symposium.

Colonial Legacy

A typical colonial economy often acquired features which, though they appeared to be 'modern' or capitalist, performed completely different and distinctly colonial roles as they occurred within the colonial framework. For example, a colonial situation could witness, as it did in India, a high degree of commercialisation (or generalised commodity production), rapid growth in transport and communications, close integration with the world market and a high degree of "potential investible surplus" raised from within the economy—all features associated with capitalist development. Yet in the colonial context, all these developments led to not only capitalist development in the metropolis but further colonial structuring in the colony. It ended up, to use the early Indian nationalist Bal Gangadhar Tilak's expressive phrase, "decorating another's wife" while disfiguring one's own.

In the Indian colonial economy which was forcibly internally disarticulated and extroverted, the above changes did not stimulate internal inter-sectoral exchanges between Indian agriculture and industry, or between the Indian consumer goods industry and capital goods industry.[11] The circuit of commodity circulation was completed via the metropolis, where colonial agriculture was linked to the metropolitan industry, or the colonial consumer goods industry (if and when it was allowed to develop) with the metropolitan capital goods industry; the multiplier effects of these exchanges were thus transmitted abroad. Similarly, the surplus generated in the colonial economy did not lead to extended reproduction through investment (the key feature which distinguishes capitalism from pre-capitalist modes of production), thus raising the organic composition of capital and productivity to a higher level on a significant scale within the indigenous economy, but facilitated this process in the metropolis.[12]

11. The question of exchange between the sector producing capital goods for the capital goods industry and the capital goods industry did not arise.

12. See Mukherjee, Aditya (2010). "Empire How Colonial India made Modern Britain" *EPW*, December, for a detailed discussion on how the colonial process contributed to the capitalist development of the colonising countries. Also see Hamza, Alavi (1981). "Structure of Colonial Formations," *EPW* 16(10/12); Amin, Samir (1974). *Accumulation on a World Scale.* New York; and Amin, Samir (1974). "Accumulation and Development: A Theoretical Model", *Review of African Political Economy*, for a brilliant enumeration of what constitutes a colonial/peripheral structure as opposed to a metropolitan/central one.

The traditional artisanal industry was destroyed,[13] (i.e., a process of de-industrialisation occurred in a country that was the world's largest exporter of textiles in the pre-colonial era) and not replaced with the modern capital-intensive industry on any significant scale.

Capitalism did not grow in agriculture either. Commodity production in agriculture was in response to a forced commercialisation to primarily meet the colonial state's revenue demands and not with a capitalist rationality, i.e., to earn profit for investment. Typically, agriculture witnessed a high degree of differentiation but it did not lead to capitalist farming through extended reproduction. The petty mode of production was perpetuated in agriculture with the large estates being let out to tenants with small holdings who continued to cultivate at more or less the same traditional levels of technology.[14] Moreover, agricultural output and exports, even when they grew,[15] remained articulated with metropolitan industrial and other needs.

Colonialism has to be viewed and evaluated as an overall structure. Growth in one or the other sector of the colonial economy or society cannot be evaluated as partial development (to be offset against the lack of such growth in another sector) if that sectoral growth was instrumental in creating the colonial structuring, which led to overall stagnation and even decline. The development

13. In some cases even existing modern industry was destroyed, which witnessed the destruction of the textile, shipbuilding and armament industry, started by Mohd. Ali in Egypt in the 1830s, through colonial intervention. See for example Lutsky, V. (1969). *Modern History of the Arab Countries.* Moscow: Progress Publishers.

14. This tendency has been shown to be true even in areas like Punjab in India, which it has been wrongly claimed was moving in the direction of capitalist agriculture, by Mukherjee, Mridula (2006). *Colonialising Agriculture: The Myth of Punjab Exceptionalism.* New Delhi; Sage. See also Mukherjee, Aditya (1979). "Agrarian Conditions in Assam 1880- 1890: A Case Study of Five Districts of the Brahmaputra Valley", *The Indian Economic and Social History Review* XVI(2); 207-32, April-June, for a discussion on how colonial structuring of Indian agriculture occurs in a vastly different situation (from Punjab).

15. In some instances, such as the sugar plantations of Indonesia in the late 19th century, they were operated by foreign capital at high levels of investment and technology, yet they remained totally articulated to colonial needs and had no positive effect towards growth of capitalist agriculture in Indonesia. See for example Geertz, Clifford (1963). *Agricultural Involution: The Process of Ecological Change in Indonesia.* Berkeley and Furnivall, J.S. (1944). *Netherlands India.* New York; and Furnivall, J.S. (1956). *Colonial Policy and Practice.* New York.

of railways, foreign trade, telegraph, agrarian transformation, a colonial civil service, etc. occurred in a manner that they became critical instruments in converting the pre-capitalist and sometimes emerging capitalist societies[16] into a stillborn colonial structure. The very instruments of the subversion of modern capitalist development in favour of colonial structuring cannot be treated as the residual or partial benefits of colonialism—a fallacy which unfortunately creeps into the thought of otherwise staunch liberal nationalists at the highest level and even some Marxists.

The structural distortions created by colonialism made the transition to self-sustained growth much more difficult. It required the overthrow of colonialism, and the un-structuring of the colonial structure for India to start its attempt to build independent capitalism, after colonialism for nearly 200 years ravaged its economy and society and deprived it of the opportunity of participating in the process of modern industrial transformation occurring in other parts of the world. Despite certain positive developments in the Indian economy in certain areas,[17] since World War I until 1947, India remained essentially backward and structurally colonial. The Indian economy at Independence was still basically dependent on stagnating, low productivity, semi-feudal agriculture with modern industry (in 1950) contributing a mere 6-8 per cent of national income and (in 1951) employing 2.3 per cent of the labour force (in 1946).[18]

What India inherited after 200 years of colonial "benevolence", which allegedly gave India the "advantages of commercialization", "exposure to the world market", "transport and communication", "a strong state", "western scientific skills", etc.—the benefits that

16. For example, Mohammad Ali's Egypt in the 1830s.

17. I have shown elsewhere how even these positive developments were not the result of colonialism but were wrenched from it and occurred in spite of and in opposition to colonialism. See for example, Mukherjee, Aditya (2002). *Imperialism Nationalism and the Making of the Indian Capitalist Class*. Sage. Chapter 1.

18. Goldsmith, Raymond W. (1983). *The Financial Development of India: 1860-1977*. New Haven: Yale University Press. p.68 and Chandra, Bipan (1992). "Colonial Legacy", in Bimal Jalan (ed.), *The Indian Economy: Problems and Prospects*. New Delhi. pp.8-9.

Tirthankar Roy could hardly stop listing—was a very sorry state of affairs indeed.

India's Own Heritage

As Angus Maddison's monumental work shows, India was the largest economy of the world for entire thousand years of the first millennium, accounting for close to 30 per cent of the world's GDP. Even as late as the beginning of the 18th century, India's was still the largest economy with about 25 per cent of the world's GDP, more than eight times that of the United Kingdom. The decline started soon after and at the end of nearly 200 years of colonial rule (during which Tirthankar Roy claims "colonial India experienced positive economic growth"),[19] India's share had been reduced to a mere 4.2 per cent in 1950. A few decades were needed after Independence before India could sufficiently shrug off the colonial legacy and begin to gradually claw her way back into improving her share of the global pie.[20] This aspect we will deal with shortly.

The impact of colonialism in human terms was traumatic and all too visible. At Independence, the average life expectancy was barely 30 years. The poor obviously died much younger. India was faced with acute food shortages, creating near-famine conditions repeatedly in different areas. The Bengal famine of 1943, just four years before the British left, claimed more than three million lives.[21] (A great tragedy, which Tirthankar Roy predictably underplays, putting the famine deaths only at "some half a million", a figure much lower than even the official famine Inquiry Commission and other government estimates.) Between 1946 and 1953 about 14 million tonnes of food

---

19. Roy *op. cit.* no. 4: 14.

20. Maddison, Angus (2006). *The World Economy: Vol. I A Millennial Perspective and Vol.II Historical Statistics*. OECD. Indian Edition (2007), New Delhi: Academic Foundation. Table 8b, p.641

21. See Sen, Amartya (1982). *Poverty and Famines: An Essay on Entitlements and Deprivation*. Delhi; OUP, Appendix D, pp.195-216 for a comprehensive exercise in estimation of famine deaths during the Bengal famine. While the Famine Inquiry Commission put it at 1.5 million, Sen convincingly argues why the figure is closer to around 3 million. See also, Greenough, Paul (1982). *Prosperity and Misery in Modern Bengal: The Famine of 1943-44*. New York, where he argues a higher figure, and Batabyal, Rakesh (2005). *Communalism in Bengal: From Famine to Noakhali, 1943-47*. New Delhi: Sage.

grains worth ₹1,000 crore had to be imported, seriously affecting India's planned development. In 1951, 84 per cent of the people (92% women) were illiterate.

India after Colonial Exploitation

It was from such abysmal initial conditions that Independent India under Nehru had to commence its journey towards modernisation. An important element at the beginning of this journey was setting up the process of un-structuring the colonial structure so that the Indian economy and society were ready for take-off. We will outline below the contours of the strategy followed to un-structure colonialism.

That there was some positive economic growth in India between 1914 and 1947 has often been cited either as the result of colonialism and its policies[22] or as the proof of decolonisation by which the colonial state was gradually pulling out, handing over to Indian interests.[23] However, it can be easily shown that the positive non-colonial type of developments seen in the inter-war period was not the result of any process of decolonisation because, as I have argued elsewhere,[24] there was no such process occurring. Neither were these developments the result of colonialism itself. They were the product of space wrenched from it. As I have argued earlier,[25] it is easily demonstrable that all the developments listed above occurred (to list some of the causes) either (a) as a result of the struggle, political and economic, against imperialism, whether through the national

22. Roy *op. cit.* no. 4: Chapters 4 and 5.

23. See, Dewey, Clive (1978). "The End of Imperialism of Free Trade: The Eclipse of the Lancashire Lobby and the Commission of Fiscal Autonomy to India", in Clive Dewey and A.G. Hopkins (eds.), *Imperial Impact: Studies in the Economic History of Africa and India*. London, and Dewey, Clive (1979). "The Government of India's New Industrial Policy 1900-1925", in Clive Dewey and K.N. Chaudhuri (eds.), *Economy and Society: Essays in Indian Economic and Social History*. Delhi; and A.D.D. Gordon *op. cit.* and Drummond, I.M. (1972). *British Economic Policy and the Empire, 1919-1939*. London.

24. See my Presidential Address, *op. cit.* no. 7.

25. In this section I have drawn heavily from Mukherjee, Aditya (1982). "The Indian Capitalist Class: Aspects of its Economic, Political and Ideological Development in the Colonial Period, 1927-47", Paper read at Indian History Congress. Kurukshetra and reprinted in Bhattacharya, S. and Romila Thapar (eds.) (1986). *Situating Indian History*. Delhi: OUP and Mukherjee *op. cit.* no. 17.

movement, legislative assemblies, business chambers or directly by entrepreneurs, as most demonstrably in the case of shipping,[26] or (b) when the grip of imperialism weakened or loosened due to world factors autonomous of the logic of colonial system in the colony, such as the World Wars and the Great Depression,[27] or (c) when the principal metropolis, Britain, lost out in competition to other metropolitan centres and preferred to permit indigenous enterprise in the colony to grow rather than allow other foreign powers to capture the colonial market, e.g., protection to cotton, iron and steel, matches and sugar was related, respectively, to competition from Japan, Belgium and Germany, Sweden and Java, a Dutch colony,[28] or (d) due to the inner contradictions of colonialism itself, e.g., the increasing need for revenue from the colony to meet imperial financial interests could no more be met from by now stagnating or even declining agriculture but through tariffs on imports, which provided indigenous manufacture a certain amount of protection against imperial industrial interests.[29] In other words, the specific non-colonial type of developments in the 20th century occurred not as a result of colonialism but in spite of or in opposition to it.

The very limited growth of the positive, non-colonial developments was occurring in an embryonic form in the hostile womb of colonialism, whose continuation was making the birth of capitalism in India more and more difficult.

---

26. There was a direct correlation between surges in the Indian national movement and economic concessions conceded by the colonial state. I have in great detail documented the efforts collectively as well as individually of Indian business to resist the 'collective monopoly' of British capital and wreak concessions from the colonial state in my Imperialism, Nationalism... *op. cit.* no. 17. See also Bagchi, *Private Investment...op. cit.*, Ch.6.

27. Bipan Chandra has documented how the spurts of growth experienced by Indian industry in this period was a result of the "loosening of the link" with colonialism during the two wars and the Great depression in *Colonialism and Modernisation*.

28. See the classic study by Adarkar, B.P. (1941). *The Indian Fiscal Policy*. Allahabad. pp.468-73 and my *Imperialism, Nationalism...op. cit.* no. 17, ch.6.

29. As discussed in section V above. Also see Ibid.

The legacy of colonialism, which Tirthankar Roy misjudged so completely,[30] was anticipated by Rabindranath Tagore, shortly before his death in 1941 in his inimitable way:[31]

> The wheels of fate will some day compel the English to give up their Indian Empire. What kind of India will they leave behind, what stark misery? When the stream of their centuries' administration runs dry at last, what a waste of mud and filth will they leave behind them.

How India Developed in the Post-Colonial Era

The growth that India witnessed after Independence was not all about carrying on the good work started during colonialism. It was a product of a structural break painstakingly crafted through a multi-pronged planned effort—a unique effort of trying to industrialise and build capitalism with democracy and civil liberties. Jawaharlal Nehru and other leaders were deeply aware that India was experimenting with a hitherto uncharted path as none of the industrialised countries of the world had democracy and civil liberties during the initial period of transition to capitalism and industrialisation. I have evaluated elsewhere the nature of this stupendous effort since Independence.[32] I will only outline here a brief comparison of some of the features of the colonial period, especially the period of so-called decolonisation and positive growth since World War I with those of the period after Independence. This may help underline the enormity of the break required, and to a considerable extent achieved.

The growth of per capita income in India in the colonial period was either zero or very low, remaining way below that of the independent countries of Europe, the US, and Japan between 1820 and 1913 (see Table 11.1). In the last decades of colonial rule after

30. See f.n. 35.

31. Quoted in Chandra, Bipan, Mridula Mukherjee and Aditya Mukherjee (1999). *India After Independence*, New Delhi: Penguin. p.19.

32. Ibid., Mukherjee, Aditya and Mridula Mukherjee (1988). "Imperialism and the Growth of Indian Capitalism in the Twentieth Century", *EPW* XXIII(II), 12 March. Also reprinted in Shah, Ghanshyam (ed.) (1990). *Capitalist Development: Critical Essays.* Bombay and Chandra, Bipan, Mridula Mukherjee and Aditya Mukherjee (2008). *India Since Independence.* Delhi: Penguin. chs. 25-33. See also Chandra, Bipan (1989). "Aspects of the Transformation Period of the Modern and Contemporary World", *Hitotsubashi Journal of Social Studies* XXI(1), August.

Table 11.1

Rate of Growth of Per Capita GDP (Annual Average Compound Growth Rates)

	1820-1870	*1870-1913*	*1913-1950*	*1950-1973*	*1973-2001*	*2001-2007*
	(1)	(2)	(3)	(4)	(5)	(6)
France	1.01	1.45	1.12	4.04	1.71	
UK	1.26	1.01	0.93	2.42	1.86	
USA	1.34	1.82	1.61	2.45	1.86	
Japan	0.19	1.48	0.88	8.06	2.14	
India	0.00	0.54	0.22	1.40	3.01	5.65*

Note: *per capita net national product.

Source: Columns 1 to 5 from Angus Maddison, *op. cit.*, Table 8b, p. 643. Column 6 is based on *Economic Survey, 2006-07,* Government of India, New Delhi 2007, and Mukherjee, Aditya (2008). "Indian Economy in the New Millennium," in Bipan Chandra, Mridula Mukherjee and Aditya Mukherjee (eds.), *India Since Independence.* Delhi: Penguin.

colonialism had its full impact, per capita income in India actually declined at an average annual rate of 0.22 per cent between 1913 and 1950.[33] After Independence, on the other hand, it grew on average at 1.4 per cent a year in the first couple of decades (about three times faster than the best phase, 1870-1913, under colonialism) and much faster at the annual average of 3.01 per cent in the next 30 years, 1973-2001 (a rate considerably higher than that achieved by West Europe,[34] the US, or Japan) and at an astounding average of 7.0 per cent (it was over 8 per cent in 2006-07) from 2003-04 to 2006-07, comparable to the explosive rates achieved by Japan (though in very special circumstances) between 1950 and 1973.[35]

33. The figures are all from Table 11.2 which is based on Maddison *op. cit.* no. 20: 643 except where indicated. Sivasubramonian and Heston's estimates show an annual growth rate of per capita income between 1914 to 1946 which is somewhat higher at 0.26 and 0.13 respectively but nevertheless prove our point reflecting the sharp contrast between before and after independence. M. Mukherjee's estimates of income growth are much lower than even Maddison's. See Goldsmith *op. cit.* no. 18*:* Table 1.2, p.4.

34. West Europe as a whole grew at 1.88 per cent between 1973-2001. Maddison *op. cit.* no. 18: 643.

35. Figures for 2001-2007 are based on *Economic Survey, 2006-07,* Government of India, New Delhi 2007, Table 1.2, S-4, and Aditya Mukherjee (2008). "Indian Economy in the New Millennium," in Bipan Chandra, Mridula Mukherjee and Aditya Mukherjee (eds.), *India Since Independence.* Delhi: Penguin. I have taken the per capita income growth rate for 2006-07 at a

contd...

Similarly, the colonial period saw a process of de-industrialisation by which traditional industry was largely destroyed and modern industry grew very slowly. Despite the growth of modern industry since World War I at an average of about 3.8 per cent per annum, it contributed a mere 6-8 per cent of the national product in 1950, having started from an extremely low level of 4 per cent in 1913.[36] Moreover, modern industry was yet dominated by consumer goods with a near total and debilitating dependence on the advanced countries for capital goods and technology. Contrast this with the period after Independence. Industrial growth during the first three plans (1951-1965) averaged 7.1 per cent per annum. More important, "the *three-fold* increase in (the) aggregate index of industrial production between 1951 and 1969 was the result of a 70 per cent increase in (the) consumer good industries, a *quadrupling* of the intermediate goods production and a *ten-fold* increase in the output of capital goods".[37] This pattern of industrial development led to a structural transformation of the colonial legacy. From a situation where to make any capital investment, virtually the entire equipment had to be imported (in 1950, India imported nearly 90 per cent of even the machine tools it required), the share of the imported component in fixed investment in equipment in India had come down to 43 per cent in 1960 and a mere 9 per cent in 1974, whereas the value of the fixed investment in India increased by about two and a half times over this period (1960-1974).[38] This was

---

...contd...

conservative 8 per cent. S. Sivasubramonian's comprehensive and detailed study confirms the sharp break in aggregate growth rates as well as in different sectors of the economy between 1900-1947 and 1947-2000. See, e.g., Sivasubramonian, S. (2000). *The National Income of India in the Twentieth Century*. New Delhi: OUP. Table 9.35, Figure 9.5. pp.622-28.

36. Goldsmith *op. cit.* no. 18: 68 and Chandra *op. cit.* no. 18: 8-9.

37. Vaidyanathan, A. (1983). "The Indian Economy Since Independence (1947-70), in Dharma Kumar (ed.), *The Cambridge Economic History of India*. Vol. II. Delhi. p.961, emphasis mine.

38. See Mukherjee, Aditya (2000). "Planned Development in India 1947-65: The Nehruvian Legacy" in Shigeru Akita (ed.), *South Asia in the 20th Century International Relations*. Tokyo; also in Chandra, Bipan, Mridula Mukherjee and Aditya Mukherjee, *India Since Independence op. cit.* no. 32: ch.25. These figures are from an extremely persuasive piece by Kelkar, Vijay (1980). "India and the World Economy: A Search for Self Reliance", Paper read at Seminar on *Jawaharlal Nehru and Planned Development*. New Delhi.

a major achievement, and it considerably increased India's autonomy from the advanced countries in determining her own rate of capital accumulation or growth.

Agriculture, the largest sector of the Indian economy, was in a state of ruin under colonialism. Per capita agricultural output fell, on average, at 0.72 per cent per year during 1911-1941. The average rate of fall in per capita food grains output was even sharper at 1.14 per cent per year, a 29.0 per cent fall over the period.[39] All crop yields per acre declined on average by 0.01 per cent per year between 1891 and 1946 and again food grain yields averaged a more rapid decline at 0.18 per cent, and even more sharply by 0.44 per cent per year between 1921 and 1946.[40] No wonder the food shortages and famine conditions mentioned above. After Independence, a combination of institutional changes (land reforms) and massive state-sponsored technological change transformed this situation.[41] During the first three plans (leaving out 1965-66, a drought year), Indian agriculture grew annually at over 3.0 per cent on average, a growth rate more than eight times the 0.37 per cent achieved during the half a century (1891-1946) of the last phase of colonialism in India.[42] The Green Revolution in the late 1960s maintained a rate of growth ranging from about 2.5 to 3.5 per cent (primarily through increases in yield). Till the mid-1990s,[43] the Green Revolution areas like Punjab and Haryana did not have any continuities with trends in the colonial

39. Blyn, George (1966). *Agricultural Trends in India, 1891-1947: Output, Availability, and Productivity*. Philadelphia. pp.102 and 123. See also Goldsmith *op. cit.* no. 18: 68.

40. See Blyn (1966): Table 7.1, p.151, Table 5a, p.327 and pp.83-85 for an explanation of how he uses 10 'reference decades' for his analysis. See also Sivasubramonian *op. cit.* no. 35.

41. See my chapters on Land Reforms and the Green Revolution in Chandra, Bipan, Mridula Mukherjee and Aditya Mukherjee, *India Since Independence, op. cit.* no. 32.

42. See Blyn *op. cit.* no. 39: Table 5.8, p.119; and Raj, K.N. (1965). *Indian Economic Growth: Performance and Prospects*. New Delhi, for the pre and post independence figures respectively. See also my chapter on "The Indian Economy, 1947-65: The Nehruvian Legacy" in *India Since Independence op. cit.* no. 32.

43. See my chapter "Agricultural Growth and the Green Revolution" in Chandra, Bipan, Mridula Mukherjee and Aditya Mukherjee, *India Since Independence op. cit.* no. 32.

period as Tirthankar Roy, for example, argues.[44] Haryana was largely an extremely backward area in colonial times and even Punjab showed meagre average growth in terms of all-crop yields per acre of 0.36 per cent per annum between 1901 and 1941 by one estimate and of only 0.06 per cent between 1906-07 and 1941-42 by another. The highest increases in yield seen in Punjab were in non-food crops of an average of 1 per cent per annum between 1891 and 1951.[45] In contrast the value productivity of 11 major crops in Punjab increased between 1950-51 and 1969-70 by 255 per cent, i.e., an average annual increase of more than 12.5 per cent.[46] The huge productivity difference certainly signifies a structural break.

The rate of capital formation, the key to economic development, occurred at a very slow pace during the colonial period. India was in fact losing to Britain as drain or tribute an equal proportion, if not more, of what was invested in India. The drain has been variously calculated to be between 5 and 10 per cent of her national income.[47] The average annual rate of capital formation between 1901 and 1913 was 6.92 per cent of GDP, falling to 6.75 per cent between 1914 and 1946 (see Table 11.2). Public expenditure, an important engine of capital formation in backward countries, declined sharply from an average of ₹75.4 crore annually during 1925-1930 to ₹41.7 crore during the Depression years (1930-1938), when the opposite needed to be done. The massive cut in government expenditure, along with other deflationary fiscal and monetary policies, greatly exacerbated negative effects of the Depression on the Indian economy.

---

44. Roy *op. cit.* no. 4: ch.3, p.51.
45. See Mukherjee, Mridula (2006). *Colonialising Agriculture: The Myth of Punjab Exceptionalism.* New Delhi: Sage. pp.157-61; the first estimate is computed from Blyn and the second is of John Lindauer and Sarjit Singh.
46. See Mukherjee Ibid.: 162.
47. See for example Habib, Irfan, "Colonization of the Indian Economy 1757-1900", in *Essays in Indian History op. cit.*: 304-05 and Bipan Chandra chapter on "The Colonial Legacy" in Bipin Chandra, Mridula Mukherjee and Aditya Mukherjee, *India After Independence op. cit.* no. 31: 10. See also f.n. 19 above for other estimates of the drain.

Table 11.2

Gross Domestic Capital Formation (GDCF) as Percentage of GDP, Public Expenditure at Current Prices and Public Expenditure as Percentage of GDP 1901-2006 (All Figures are Annual Averages)

	GDCF as % of GDP	*Public Expenditure ₹ Crore (current prices)*	*Share of Public Expenditure in GDCF as % of GDP*
1901-1913	6.92*	75.4 (1925-1930)#	
1914-1946	6.75*	41.7 (1930-1938)#	
1950-1955	9.04	331.8	3.14
1955-1960	13.3	769.6	5.62
1960-1970	14.66	1912.1	6.96
1970-1980	17.63	8003.4	8.19
1980-1990	21.23	26416.9	9.98
2004-2006	32.65		

Source: Computed from *Economic Survey 2006-07*, Government of India, New Delhi, 2007, Tables 1.4 and 1.5, S-6 to S-9.

* : Goldsmith *op. cit.* no. 18: Table 1-10, p.20 and Table 2-9, p.80.

#: Computed from Ray, Rajat K. (1979). *Industrialisation in India*. Delhi: OUP. Table 40, p.257.

The contrast between the colonial and the post-Independence scenario is evident. While public expenditure was low and declining during the last decades of colonial rule,[48] the initial 40 years of Independence (1950-1990) saw it rise by more than three times (see Table 11.2, column 2 and 3). Similarly, while the last 50 years or so of colonial rule (1901-1946) saw gross capital formation in the economy hover around 6-7 per cent of GDP annually, the first 50 years after Independence saw the rate of capital formation rise consistently and sharply, ending up at a rate of 33.8 per cent in 2005-06, about five times the colonial rate.[49]

There was also a rapid per capita increase in the availability of some infrastructural and social benefits as they grew several times faster than the population immediately after independence. In 1965-

48. Increase in expenditure during the Second World War was due to British War needs and not capital expenditure promoting development in India.

49. See Table 3, column 1 and *Economic Survey 2006-07 op. cit.*, I Table 1.5, S-9.

66, as compared to 1950-51, the installed capacity of electricity was 4.5 times higher, the number of towns and villages electrified was 14 times higher, hospital beds 2.5 times higher, enrolment in schools was a little less than 3 times higher and, very importantly, admission capacity in technical education (engineering and technology) at the degree and diploma levels was higher by 6 and 8.5 times, respectively. This, when the population increased only by 37.3 per cent over the period.[50]

Also, Jawaharlal Nehru and the early Indian planners were acutely aware of India's backwardness in science and technology (an area left consciously barren in the colonial period) and therefore made massive efforts to overcome this shortcoming. An unprecedented increase occurred in the educational opportunities in science and technology in the universities and institutes. National expenditure on scientific research and development kept growing rapidly with each plan. For example, it increased from ₹ 1 crore in 1949 to ₹ 450 crore in 1977. Over roughly the same period, the stock of India's scientific and technical manpower increased more than 12 times from 190,000 to 2.32 million. Spectacular growth by any standards, a type of growth whose benefits India reaps today as the world moves towards a "knowledge" society.[51]

The quantum jump in investment, growth rates, improvement in health, education, etc., listed above did not occur because of any dramatic change in India's "climatic risks," "resource endowments," "hunger for gold," or the tendency to "have sumptuous marriage feasts", some of the causes listed by Tirthankar Roy for the Indian economy stagnating in the colonial period.[52] They occurred because of the concerted effort to break away from disabilities created by the colonial structure.

---

50. Calculated from Bhagwati, Jagdish and Padma Desai (1970). *India Planning for Industrialisation.* London. p.74.
51. See Mukherjee, Aditya (2008). "Indian Economy, 1947-65: The Nehruvian Legacy", in Bipan Chandra, Mridula Mukherjee and Aditya Mukherjee (eds.), *India Since Independence. op. cit.* no. 32. p.349.
52. Ibid.

Conclusion

However, despite the paradigmatic change since Independence, India is still faced with intolerable levels of poverty and backwardness.[53] Undoing the ravages of nearly 200 years of colonialism was never going to be an easy task. What is certain, however, is that answers to the future challenges would not lie in building on the continuities with colonialism, but on the breaks.

53. See Mukherjee, Aditya (2008). "Indian Economy in the New Millennium", in Bipan Chandra, Mridula Mukherjee and Aditya Mukherjee (eds.), *India Since Independence. op. cit.* no. 32, New Delhi; Penguin, where I have highlighted the spectacular growth along with the immense human development challenges.

12

VYJAYANTI RAGHAVAN

Donghak and its Role in the Modernisation of Korea[1]

Introduction

Donghak, meaning 'Eastern Learning', started as a religion in Korea in the latter half of the 19th century and turned into a political movement within two decades. The armed Donghak Movement, which lasted from 1893-1895, gave rise to two consecutive broad based uprisings or two phases of the uprising—one which started in January and lasted till March 1894, and the other which lasted less than 20 days in October-November of the same year. The significance of the Donghak uprising of 1894, initially at Kobu in North Jeolla province and later in Gongju in South Chuncheong province of present-day South Korea, lies as much in its being one of the first large-scale, mass movements in Korea as in being rated by some scholars as the country's first war of independence. The independence that was being fought for was not only from the influence of foreign powers in Korean society and administration, but also from the existing system of domestic corruption and exploitation that was increasing in the latter period of Joseon Dynasty. It was thus an anti-establishment movement too.

However, it needs to be added here that there is a widespread feeling amongst scholars in Korea that the Donghak uprising was also the reason why Korea ended up losing its independence. In order to

1. The paper is in accord with the mainstream Korean historical assessment of the Tonghak movement. A variant assessment, provided by eminent historian Lew Young Ick can be found in his article, "The Conservative Character of the 1894 Tonghak Peasant Uprising", in *The Journal of Korean Studies* 7: 149-80, 1990.

suppress this uprising, the ruling Dowager Queen Min solicited the help of the Chinese army. Japan, which too had its eyes on Korea and had been involved in the factional strife within the ruling class, could not dispassionately watch the Chinese influence increasing within Korea and therefore, sent its army too. This led to the First Sino-Japanese War on the Korean soil in 1894-95, which led to Japan's first major victory in the modern era against an outside power. Having lost the war, China also lost control over Korea and Taiwan. Later, after its second such victory, this time against Russia in the Russo-Japanese War of 1904-05, Japan achieved dominance over Korea and colonised it in 1910. The Japanese army that had come ostensibly to suppress the Donghak revolt stayed on till 1945.

The Donghak uprising has also caught the attention of historians who have placed it amongst the various nationalist movements in which the resistance was rooted in new conceptions of a nation and in simultaneous visions of social reform. At the time the Donghak movement was conceived, the modern concept of nationhood might not have been fully formed but it certainly did arouse reactive and, at the same time, revolutionary forms of nationalism. It was reactive because the movement called for expulsion of the foreigners making inroads into Korea, and revolutionary because it simultaneously demanded some social reforms like breaking down the age-old stratification of society and doing away with old customs which were based on social class discrimination. Even to the limited extent that the Donghak movement resulted in traditional institutions being questioned and in efforts being made towards a restructuring of the social conditions, it can be viewed as a movement playing a role in the modernisation of Korea, in a period when the country was more broadly transitioning from a traditionalist society to modernity.

The pre-colonial history of a number of colonised countries is dotted with people's struggles including peasant uprisings which have arisen out of contradictions existing within those societies. The Pabna Uprising of the peasants of eastern Bengal (present-day Bangladesh), the Sepoy Mutiny of 1857 in other parts of India, and the Java Uprising in Indonesia are some cases in point. Vietnamese history is also full of similar events (starting as early as the 1st century CE) as is the history of some of the African countries like Tanzania, Zimbabwe etc. Therefore, before studying the Donghak movement, which was also largely, but not solely, peasant-based, it is necessary to begin with an analysis of the contradictions in economy, and social and political structure of the late Joseon dynasty.

Late Joseon Dynasty

Society and Internal Politics

Joseon Dynasty lasted from 1392 until 1910 when the Japanese took over the country as their colony. The late Joseon dynasty, roughly from mid-17th century onwards, largely remained an agrarian society with social, economic and political structures based on it. However, its main peculiarity was that the most valuable land belonged, or was distributed only, to the bureaucratic office bearers who had passed the highly competitive civil or military examinations called *gwageo*, and could theoretically be held by them only during their tenure. It was, again in theory not inheritable, but in reality there were varied practices. Landholding and office-holding were heavily linked. Therefore, the main concern of bureaucrats was to keep the peasants, whether small-plot owners or tenants, happy so that they could get them to till their land, while simultaneously exploiting them.

The society in Joseon or Yi Dynasty, as it was also called, was highly stratified, consisting of a top layer of *yangban* class (literally meaning two wings or branches—civil and military). This elite class which was numerically very small, by virtue of having monopolised the competitive *gwageo* exams conducted by the government, held top ranks of the civil and military administration. Separated from this ruling class was the rest of the population, which was further divided into three major layers—the *chungin* or literally the middle-men, the *sangmin* or commoners that consisted of the occupational group, and finally the *chónmin*, consisting of slaves and other "low-born" groups.[2] None of these participated in the political affairs because of their general exclusion from the power-oriented education system. Of these, the *sangmin* or commoners was naturally the largest group and consisted largely of farmers who constituted about 85 per cent of the entire population.[3]

The Joseon period, since the very beginning, was also afflicted with various internal power struggles. On one hand was the strife between the in-laws and other relatives of the royal family,[4] and on the other was the struggle between two *yangban* factions representing different brands of conservatism—the entrenched *hungu* power elites and the *sarim*, (literally meaning 'forest of scholars') scholars of the Neo-Confucian school (the Neo-Confucian literati) who were also collectively called *seonbi* and considered to be upstarts. Very early in the period, between 1498 and 1545, there had taken place a number of bloody purges, called the 'literati purges' (*sahwa* in Korean)[5] to get rid of many *sarim* scholars. Over the years, especially from the 17th century, many *yangban*, mentioned earlier as the elite class,

2. The *chungin* or the middle class consisted of the technical posts of medical officers, technicians, translators, interpreters, accountants, government artists etc., as also the lower level civil functionaries and military cadre members. The *sangmin* class or 'the freeborn commoners' consisted largely of the peasants who were mainly tenant farmers. Besides farmers, the class included merchants, artisans, fishermen etc., who were marginal in numbers. In the lowest commoner stratum were the "low-born" *chónmin,* who were largely the musical and acrobatic entertainers, the female entertainers or *kisaengs*, the butchers, tanners, jail keepers and, interestingly, even Buddhist monks. The lowest social class as a whole were the slaves or *nobi* which included household slaves or 'live-in' *nobi* as well as "out-resident" *nobi* who tilled their owner's land. There were systems in place to ensure that the peasants could not move and would cultivate, in perpetuity, the land assigned to them. But over a period of time, many "low-born" moved up to commoner status. For details refer, Lee, 1984: 182-88.

3. Kim, C.I Eugene and Han-Kyo Kim (1967). *Korea and the Politics of Imperialism 1876-1910.* Berkeley and Los Angeles: University of California Press. p.7.

4. The 'in-laws' politics started over the question of successors to kings who either had no legitimate son or were too young to rule. It began when King Seonjo was enthroned at the age of eleven, following the death of his father King Jeongjo in 1800. Queen Dowager Jeongsun who was the step great-grandmother of Seonjo became his guardian and ruled as regent from 1800 to 1805. After her regency, Queen Suwon of King Seonjo, who belonged to the Andong Kim clan, got involved in the politics because Seonjo's grandson, Heonjong was only eight when he was enthroned. The Andong Kim clan threw the state into complete disorder and they remained in control for most of the 19th century.

5. Wagner, Edward (1974). *The Literati Purges: Political Conflict in Early Yi Korea.* Harvard University Press.

started to lose their power and influence both because of the internal politics afflicting their leadership as well as being on the losing side of the larger national politics. As a result of these purges, many got excluded from the government post and retreated to the country side and fell to the status of local gentry[6] and many also became small-scale farmers.

However, towards the latter half of the Joseon dynasty with a large number of purged and displaced *yangban* going to the countryside, there was significant social mobility happening. There was some downward mobility because of the *yangban* becoming farmers and therefore *sangmin*, but a lot more upward mobility because of sale of the *yangban* titles to aspiring and resourceful commoners. The sale of the title and the forging and purchasing of genealogies became prevalent when the deficit-ridden Joseon government found this as a new source of revenue.[7] In effect, the strict Neo-Confucian orthodoxy was breaking down. The status of local *yangban* could also be acquired by marriage. On the other hand, with more families from the *yangban* class getting involved in farming, the techniques of farm production and management also started undergoing change gradually and becoming more sophisticated. Many privately run handicraft factories also gave rise to some wealthy merchants. Thus, there was a more influential mercantile class that was beginning to emerge, consisting of local manufacturers, local brokers who mediated between the merchants and the elite or between any two parties—the middlemen who had the capital and their clients—and other such people.

Alongside, the number of *yangban* was also increasing as the title was inheritable and therefore being extended to every descendant in each lineage. Consequently, the number of *yangbans* passing the civil and military exams was also increasing while the number of official posts that they could occupy remained fixed. This squeeze in numbers led to increased nepotism, corruption, sale of titles etc., on one hand, and confrontation, factional conflict and strife, on the other.

6. Lee, Ki-Baik (1984). *A New History of Korea*. Seoul: Ilchokak. p.250.

7. See "Korean History: Late Choson Period", available at *http://www.asianinfo.org/asianinfo/korea/history/late_choson_period.htm*. Accessed on 28 August 2012.

Over the course of time, there had also arisen a factional divide—Easterners (*tongin*) and Westerners (*seoin*)—amongst the dominant political families over the issue of holding government offices that had authority over personnel recruitment. There were further subdivisions of the Eastern faction into Northern faction (*bukin*) and Southern faction (*namin*) and the Western faction into Old Learning (*noron*) and New Learning (*soron*). The subdivisions extended to differences in the philosophical schools of thought, and they were accentuated by differences between members of the new commercial groups and proponents of the old class system. The differences also reflected regional feuds depending on which regions the leaders of philosophical factions hailed from. The provinces of Chúngchóng (central province) and Gyeongsang (southern provice) also stood to gain because of the increase in the number of candidates successful in higher civil service examinations from these particular regions.[8]

The factional affiliation came to be inherited and carried on for decades and the conflict between them was apparent not only in the capital but throughout the country, including the neo-Confucian literati at large. With factions developing sub-factions, there appeared more and more challenges to power. Corruption too started when grants of land began to be made to members or supporters of the royal family. Right of inheritance began to be granted. Some members of the gentry continued to belong to the gentry even if they failed the exams. Thus the rise of a disgruntled group of gentry who could not get official posts became inevitable. There was also an increase in the number of offspring from either interclass marriages or relationships, which was mostly between *yangban* men and non-*yangban* women. This also started posing serious social problems because the sons from these relationships or marriages were considered outcasts and were banned from government jobs. The ruling stratum of *yangban*, including those commoners who had acquired that status and entry into officialdom either by marriage or

8. Lee *op. cit.* no. 6: p.251.

by buying the title, comprised only 3 per cent of the total population at the end of the Joseon dynasty.[9]

The Economic Problems

As mentioned before, the *sangmin* or commoner class was the largest and consisted largely of farmers who constituted about 85 per cent of the entire population.[10] Only 25 per cent of these farmers were land owners and the rest were either tenants or held only part of the land they tilled.[11] The burden of tax was also very heavy on the *nobi* or slave class even though their numbers had become greatly reduced following the government banning inheritance of the *nobi* status in 1886.

The main source of income for the government was land revenue. But with large tracts of land being gifted to those who had been loyal to the founder of the dynasty, the elites possessing agricultural estates in perpetuity kept increasing. This brought about a reduction in the government revenue from land-tax receipts. Therefore, the burden of making good this loss was placed on the helpless farmers, who had to pay a land tax that fetched between 65 and 70 per cent of total government revenue.[12] This proved a heavy burden on petty landowners and landless peasants. This hardship was aggravated further by the levy of a tribute tax on the special items produced locally by them during the non-cultivable winter months. The corrupt officials left no method of exploitation out. Unable to meet their tax obligations, many peasants started abandoning their land. Moreover, the grain loan system and the usurious interest rates charged either by the state officials or by the private moneylenders, all added to their woes.

9. Kim and Kim *op. cit.* no. 3: 4.

10. Ibid.: 7.

11. Ibid.

12. Ibid.: 11

As Bruce Cumings notes:

> At this time Korea's taxation system was an ornery of infuriating exactions, most of them attached in one way or another to agrarian production. Because it was fundamentally weak in relation to the aristocracy, the state tried to raise money every which way and grabbed everything it could put its hands on, giving next to nothing in the way of service. There were government taxes, land taxes (not one but a variety, plus surcharges and handling fees), taxes on fallow fields, military taxes (one bolt of cloth for every able-bodied male, often more ruinous than the land taxes), taxes to the local officials, taxes to the local estates, all this not counting taxes on salt, fish, boats, and many other commodities. Every living thing that could be taxed was taxed, including tiny babies and the elderly, relatives and neighbours of people who had fled the tax collector, not to mention dead people. When the tax man got you, you could pay him off by getting a loan at usurious interest—from state officials through the infamous grain loan system, or from local moneylenders, who had been a thorn in everyone's flesh from time immemorial.[13]

In addition, during the entire 19th century, the rice fields and farms of Korea were struck by drought and floods alternately causing large scale famines. Moreover, to add to their misery, the burden of financing the fresh expenses that the government had to meet subsequent to the opening of the Korean ports to Japan in 1876, was also placed on the shoulders of helpless peasants. The extortions had reached such a point that it only needed a spark to ignite a peasant revolt.

After signing of the Chemulpo Treaty in 1882 under Japanese exaction, Korea had to pay as much as 500,000 won as reparation for damages caused by rioters launching a military attack (known as the Imo Incident) on Japanese legation. The Korean government also had to permit the stationing of Japanese troops in the capital. It also had to conclude a number of agreements for commercial activities of Japanese residents in Korea which were very disadvantageous to Koreans, especially the tax rates. In addition, Japan began to look

13. Cumings, Bruce (1997). *Korea's Place in the Sun: A Modern History.* New York: W.W. Norton & Co. p.115.

to Korean agricultural production of rice and soyabeans to meet its growing demands for them. Korean peasants were made dependent on Japanese capital and were forced to produce more and more of the high-quality rice coveted by the Japanese. The outflow of grain was so much that it devastated and impoverished the Korean peasants. The exploitation had reached a point where even during crop failures in some regions in certain years, the peasants had to pay exorbitant indemnities for losses suffered by the Japanese merchants.Under such circumstances, the only recourse left for the peasants was to revolt. Their indignation at this point was directed against the ruling class who they felt were responsible for their plight.[14]

The Donghak Doctrine and Movement

The basic economic contradiction in the late Joseon dynasty society thus revolved around land and agricultural production, and this therefore, led to the maximum number of widespread conflicts between the peasants and the bureaucracy. The critical point was reached when the land tax imposed gained an intolerable magnitude after the construction of a reservoir in Jeolla-do province.

An outlet seems to have been provided by Choe Je-u and his teachings called Donghak (meaning Eastern Learning), as a reaction to Seohak (or Western Learning, referring to Catholicism) making inroads into the country. Catholicism, or Christianity in general, was introduced into Korea by Yi Seung-hun who was baptised by a Catholic priest in Beijing, in the late 18th century. It found appeal amongst the common people of middle and lower classes. But the practitioners suffered persecution by the government because Catholicism disapproved of, among other practices, the tradition of ancestor-worship which was a basic tenet of Confucianism, as a form of idol-worship. The government thus perceived the Catholic faith as a threat to the existing social fabric.

In such a situation of domestic crisis and external threat, Choe Je-u started this new religion called Donghak. Choe was

14. See *http://www.asianinfo.org/asianinfo/korea/history/challenges_of_modernisation.htm,* Accessed on 23 October 2012.

a disenfranchised *yangban* who had failed the civil service exam and had reached a point of despair and desperation at the state of things, and was looking for a solution. He combined the teachings of Confucianism, Buddhism, Taoism and even some elements of Catholicism and started the Donghak doctrine. He promised the people a way out of their misery. His teachings appealed to the populace because it combined native Korean spiritual beliefs with the contemporary need of driving out the Japanese and the Westerners. His doctrine proclaimed unity of humankind with God and, more importantly, equality of all human beings here on earth, thereby transcending class or status distinctions. This greatly appealed to the peasants and, therefore, Choe Je-u was able to gather a large number of followers who were mostly the exploited peasants. While the initial Tonghak movement was suppressed with Choe's execution as a subversive by the state in 1864, it remained resilient underground and reemerged in the early 1890s as a more forceful campaign under other leaders. While one Choe Si-hyeong assumed mostly a spiritual-social leadership, a political activist named Jeon Bong-jun now unfurled a new banner of revolt because the economic situation had worsened beyond any recovery. Starting in the Cholla region, the violent uprising rapidly spread to other areas.

It was the first time that peasants were involved in political affairs on an organised, mass basis, with numbers going upwards of 20,000, combined with elements of a modern, sharpened consciousness of social justice; it included better treatment of women in demand for the dismantling of all systems of discrimination and expolitation. The peasants along with other disgruntled groups expressed their resentment through many linked uprisings, the frequency of which had started increasing at a rapid rate from 1892 on. Driven by the slogan "*poguk anmin*" ("protect the country, secure the people"), the rebels attacked government facilities, freed prisoners and slaves, humiliated the *yangban* and destroyed their houses, and plundered grain from government storehouses.[15] (More on their specific demands will be said later.)

---

15. Lee, Chong-Sik (1963). *The Politics of Korean Nationalism.* University of California Press. p.30.

The more the rebel groups protested, the more the government tried to restrain and check the movement by arresting leaders and seizing their properties. However, these uprisings could not be easily quelled, thereby exposing the weakness that had also set into the military, many members of which had also been exploited and felt disgruntled. So much so that this rebellion of 1894 could be suppressed only with the help of the Chinese forces called in by the Korean throne. This was something that proved to be a grave mistake in the long run. Korea seeking outside help to settle matters within the country, as in this instance and a few other times, is what in latter years generated the feeling among the foreign powers that Korea was incapable of taking care of its affairs without outside help.[16]

It is necessary also to add a word or two about the larger ideological milieu as well. The existing ruling philosophy i.e., Neo-Confucianism, did not offer any viable solution for social or economic progress. It was also an era of religious vacuum. Buddhism, which had been a state religion during the earlier Koryo dynasty, had been suppressed in the Choson period and the Neo-Confucian ideology had taken over as the official orthodoxy. However, this was a philosophical and ethical system affirming the hierarchical status quo than either a spiritual or a progressive outlook. The existing value system had clearly failed to solve the problems that existed. Therefore, the time was ripe for a new promising doctrine. Donghak's concise but effective slogan "drive out the Japanese dwarfs and the Western barbarians, and praise righteousness" provided the much–needed impetus for the movement in its last phases.[17] The leaders of the movement also realised the power they wielded in the economy, which is apparent from their petition with Mencius-like words:"The people are the root of the nation. If the root withers the nation will

16. Towards the end of World War II when the matter of stripping Japan of the territories it had seized and restoring independence to Korea was discussed at the Cairo Conference in 1943, the U.S., Britain and China resolved to place postwar Korea under trusteeship, preparatory to independence "in due course". This idea was reinforced at the Moscow Conference in 1945 and Korea was placed under the joint American-Soviet Union trusteeship, thereby losing the only chance of establishing a unified government.

17. Cumings *op. cit.* no. 13: 115.

be enfeebled."[18] This self-belief gave them the inner strength to carry on their drive. However, athough the movement gathered enough momentum, the leaders could not see it to its logical end—firstly because the envisioned end was a desire and not a well-planned outcome and secondly, and as we have seen, their strategy was no match for the forces that came from outside the country.

The External Political Scenario

A linked dimension of the Donghak movement was its focus on stemming the foreign encroachments on Korea. The Meiji government of Japan had made several attempts earlier to establish official relations with Korea but unsuccessfully. However, in 1876, a military expedition was sent with the objective of concluding a treaty of friendship and commerce with Korea. The interplay of three factors at this time resulted in signing of the treaty called the Kanghwa Treaty, named after the port city where it was signed. The three factors were: the strong Japanese determination to open Korea which until then had been strongly resisted by the Korean regent Taewongun, who was a traditionalist; China's acquiescence to this though it ensured that it did not totally relinquish its suzerainty over Korea; and a change in the Korean government with the Taewongun having yielded power to the Min family which was pro-China.[19] After signing of this treaty, there was a sharp increase in the Japanese presence in Korea, and by the end of 1880, a permanent Japanese diplomatic mission was established in Seoul.

Internally, there was a conflict between the traditionalists who were pro-China and the reformists who were pro-Japan, over the issue of opening Korea and widening its contact with the outside world. The factional struggles led to political turbulence in the form of conspiracies, intrigues, arrests and executions. The more radical among the reformists who wanted to modernise Korea on the lines of Japan conspired to take over the government and carried out a coup d'état in 1884 called *Gapshin Jeongbyeon*. It led to the first encounter

18. Ibid.: 117.

19. Kim and Kim *op. cit.* no. 3: 17.

of the Chinese army with the Japanese army at *Hanseong* (old name for Seoul) in which the former won. However, after the crisis, the Joseon government in its attempt to move away from both China and Japan reached out to Russia. Russia took the opportunity that fell in its lap to extract concessions for itself to facilitate its trade with Korea. This precipitated the British occupation of *Gomun* Island (Port Hamilton) to check the potential Russian influence. The increasing presence of foreign traders severely affected the share of Korean small-scale merchants and peasants in the market and as a result people living in rural areas started facing starvation.[20] The situation made it easy for the Donghak to gather momentum and spread easily.

Taewongun, the regent who had been ruling in the name of King Kojong but had gone into semi-retirement, became a symbol and a source of inspiration, like Bahadur Shah in the Indian context, for the anti-foreign outbursts. The ruling Min faction solicited Chinese help in suppressing the domestic opposition. This is significant because outside help was sought to solve domestic partisan problems. But one needs to note that this was not something new in Korean history.

With the opening of the Korean ports to Japan, the inevitable happened and Korea soon had to sign similar treaties with other countries too—America, Britain, France, and Germany. Thus began not only the multiple foreign influences within Korea, but also a conflict of foreign interests and an international power struggle. It was not as though Korea was new to foreign influences either. For centuries, Korea had adopted the principle of *sadae* or "serving the great" regarding its relations with China, and that of *kyorin* or "friendly relations with the neighbour" regarding its relations with Japan.[21] Even so, the exchange was largely in the form of visits by emissaries which was ceremonial and followed strict protocol, and there was very limited and guarded exchange between these countries in trade and culture. Korea turned into a hermit nation only because of aggressive policies of the western powers and missionaries towards China, Japan, and Korea followed by aggressive moves by Japan

---

20. Young-Woo, Han (2009). *The History of Korea.* National Institute of Korean History. pp.191-97.
21. Ibid.: 12.

itself. However, this isolationism of Korea is viewed by some as more a result of a calculated policy based on rational assessment of its self-interest rather than a reflexive policy.[22] Be that as it may, the increased influence of foreign powers ended in the Sino-Japanese War of 1894-95, and with the victory of Japan the Chinese influence on the peninsula ceased, and with the defeat of Russia in the Russo-Japanese War of 1904-05, the Russian influence also came to an end.

According to many scholars, the earliest decisions of Japan to expand its role in Korea were out of concern about its own weak strategic position in the region and therefore with the goal of denying control to any other power, rather than with any clear-cut objective of expanding into overseas territory for economic or political reasons.[23] This at the outset may seem as a major difference in the motives of British imperialism and the Japanese one. On the other hand, it has also been said that in the post-Meiji period when the issue of protecting Japanese political, security and economic interests were being discussed, Korea figured prominently in the Tokyo's discussions.[24] What is certain is that economic reasons did figure in the Japanese calculations even if only in the latter years. Korea and Taiwan (then Formosa) by virtue of being contiguous pieces of land adjoining Japan, became easy targets of Japanese economic interests. At the same time, these two lands also became perceived as easy stepping stones for the more advanced western powers to gain access into Japan; Korea was particularly viewed as "a dagger thrust at the heart of Japan".[25] There had been very few invasions in Korean history and it had led a comparatively calm existence especially during the previous 200-plus years. The main invasions were by the Japanese in 1592-1598 and by the Manchus in 1627

22. Buzo, Adrian (2007). *The Making of Modern Korea.* London: Routledge. p.3.

23. Duus, Peter (1987). "Economic Dimensions of Meiji Imperialism: The Case of Korea, 1895-1910", in Ramon H. Myers and Mark R. Peattie (eds.), *The Japanese Colonial Empire, 1895-1945.* Princeton: Princeton University Press. pp.128-29.

24. Schmid, Andre (2002). *Korea Between Empires 1895-1919.* New York; Columbia University Press. p.26.

25. Peattie, Mark R. (1987). "Introduction", in Ramon H. Myers and Mark R. Peattie (eds.), *The Japanese Colonial Empire, 1895-1945.* Princeton: Princeton University Press. p.15.

and 1636. The new foreign intrusions in the period under discussion were from multiple sources: western powers such as France, America, and Russia; a more aggressive China; and an even more threatening Japan. They now waged or caused tension and bloody conflicts on the Korean soil. Therefore, the decades immediately before and after the opening of Korea in 1876 and before its later annexation by Japan in 1910 were very crucial years for Korea. It turned the country from an isolationist nation to a critical area for big nations like China, Russia and Japan in their struggle for power.

The Role of Donghak in the Modernisation of Korea

The basic tenet of Donghak was, as we have seen, "the equality of all human beings" and could be called "Marxist" in nature, though it was by no means Marxism-inspired. The Donghak Movement also came to be known as Donghak Revolution as it was anti-feudal, anti-government and anti-foreign in nature. Yet it was not as though all the rebels were driven by all these motives. The movement brought together the traditionalists who were against foreign influences and the reformists who wanted to reform and modernise. The movement provided a common platform and a meeting point. The drive for modernisation in Korea began after a fashion with the Kabo Reforms of 1894-95 which were initiated as an outcome of the Donghak uprising. But they were not effective enough to be able to safeguard Korea's sovereignty because modernisation on the social and political front was still very early and superficial. It was still too early for the people of Korea to have developed the ability to unite and operate effectively and set up all the viable political, economic, social, educational institutions needed. Japan, on the other hand, was able to perceive the threat from the West early and was able to modernise at a much faster speed to strengthen itself, which helped it win two major wars. Korea soon ended up becoming a colony of Japan as we know.

A major reason why Donghak failed was that it did not get the widespread support that a movement needs despite its reformist and nationalistic goals. The reforms demanded by the rebels were staunchly opposed by the upper classes, and the masses were largely ignorant. According to Chong-Sik Lee, only a modern education system would have brought about the change in outlook that was needed, and that could not happen immediately. Yet Lee also adds that the Donghak movement provided political education on a gigantic scale. The Korean masses became aware of their own potentialities and therefore, started having hopes for the future.[26] It can be said that the seeds of a new national identity had been sown. The changing situations in the vicinity and the very presence of Japanese on the Korean soil contributed to an awareness of change. It also constantly stoked feelings of nationalism.

That the feeling of nationalism itself does not arise merely by the presence of something that is "foreign" and merely as a reaction to it, has been well acknowledged.[27] That it is difficult for the concept of nationalism to evolve in isolation within the boundaries of a nation and in the absence of a feeling of "the other," is also a well-known fact. The situation within and around Korea, since 1876, had led to a lot of exchanges of culture, ideas and philosophies. The Donghak philosophy was a product of both—a realisation of what was wrong internally brought about through increased interactions with the western countries and with a reformed Japan, and a reaction to what was being imposed on the country from outside. This amalgamation gave rise to initial forms of nationalist sentiments and these nascent nationalist sentiments and doctrines played a role in emergence of the Donghak movement. In other words, Donghak was a nationalist movement that erupted due not necessarily to any fully developed nationalist ideas but certainly traces of this nationalism were beginning to emerge. The kind of nationalism it aroused preceded the sense of a more developed and articulate popular national identity, which is a modern concept. This does not mean, however, that Korea did not exist as a nation with clear boundaries and a ethnic and racial identity before that.[28] It only means that as yet a more modern idiom

---

26. Lee *op. cit.* no. 15: 33.
27. See Chatterjee, Partha (1986). *Nationalist Thought and the Colonial World: A Derivative Discourse.* London: Zed.
28. Cumings *op. cit.* no. 13: 141.

had not taken hold across the country. The concept of a nation-state in its modern garb was yet to take birth. The Donghak uprising itself was a result of progressive thinking, but it is unfortunate that the leaders did not have the far-sightedness of anticipating the direction it would take, and Korea ended up being colonised. However, this in turn led later to instilling an anti-colonial nationalism amongst the Koreans, one that gave rise to a more modern sense of nationhood.

The point also needs to be made that while Donghak may have been an important landmark in the evolution of modernity in Korean thought and philosophy, still it is not as though Korea had left behind its Neo-Confucian norms completely. In fact, because the Neo-Confucian social value systems are so deeply ingrained in people's psyche, even today these values can be perceived in the Korean people's day to day life and their social relations. That, however, does not take anything away from the fact that the Donghak movement was adopting more and more modern concepts in its drive.

The kind of nationalism that Donghak teachings and the movement gave rise to was reinforced due to the presence of foreigners on the Korean soil. The Donghak leaders wanted Korea to be rid of Japanese and other foreign encroachments. This was the other side of the kind of nationalism in Japan of the 1870s that called for an invasion of Korea, or *seikan ron* (*jeong han non,* in Korean); in other words, advocating a punitive expedition into Korea for the insulting and humiliating treatment meted out to the Japanese who wanted to open trade links with Korea.[29] These two kinds of nationalism are two sides of the same coin. Donghak was more a reactive nationalism than one that had a well thought-out ideological basis. It was an emotional nationalism fuelled by instinctual responses to protect the interests of those affected by socio-political changes and degradation that was taking place, and to the presence of foreigners. However, it would not be right to say that the Donghak rebels had a clear imagery of the end result of what they wanted. It was the intervention of the strong external military forces

29. Norman, E.H. (2001). *Japan's Emergence as a Modern State.* Delhi: Khosla Publishing House. pp.85-86.

that disrupted and destroyed their effective operation and prevented them from proceeding on the path that might have helped them retain their momentum and power.

The doctrine of Donghak provided the ground for creating certain ethos of belonging amongst the people—a sense of shared identity. Donghak in effect had made the people conscious of an incipient national identity *vis-à-vis* the foreigners. In other words, it had set in motion a kind of conscious and articulate identification of the people of Korea as a separate entity that is said to be possible only in the case of those who have an authentic identity, which in turn is said to be not possible without modernity.[30]

Even if Donghak started off as being merely reactive, it did play a major role in Korea's modernisation because of the attention it drew to the need for societal change. The major demands of the rebels are quite revealing of the kind of reforms they visualised and desired. They asked for:

1. Removal of *yangban* oppression.
2. The burning of slave registers.
3. An end to strict social hierarchy.
4. Redistribution of land.
5. Removal of compulsion on the outcastes to wear their distinctive hat.[31]

Thus, there was a degree of consciousness of human rights that was beginning to set in, which is indicative of the beginning of modernisation. The reforms demanded by the rebels became the basis for reforms proposed by the Korean government with Japanese support immediately after the uprisings. However, these sudden drastic changes were opposed by various strata of society, especially some officials, the conservative literati, and the more diehard traditional *yangban*, and therefore had to be abandoned in 1895. But again, while traditional institutions were being questioned by the rebels, no clear-cut new institutions were proposed or even conceived

30. Verma, Roop Rekha (1994). "On the Interpretation of Traditional Cultures", in Eliot Deutsch (ed.), *Culture and Modernity*. Delhi: Motilal Banarsidass Publishers. pp. 533-34.

31. Cumings *op. cit.* no. 13: 118.

by them; therefore, the period could be looked upon only as a time when Korea was groping for a transition from traditionalism to modernity.

However, as noted before, prior to the annexation, Japan got into the process of suppressing the rebels by force and violence. This, on one hand, exterminated or otherwise neutralised the rebels, some of whom then started functioning from outside the country; and, on the other, it also drove many Korean commoners into the rebel camp, turning the rebel movement into a mass movement.[32]

Its concepts were modern not because they were a rejection of the past or tradition, but because they initiated a review and modification of institutions and value system. If we are to accept the basic tenet of all modernisation theories that "societies develop through a series of evolutionary stages," then Donghak had certainly set Korea on to the next evolutionary stage by giving rise to many nationalists who when suppressed by the colonial power went on to function even outside the country. Many of them went on to establish provisional seats of power outside Korea and came back later to play a role in their struggle against the colonial power. These protests flowered into a militant nationalism in latter years, which found expression in various kinds of anti-Japanese protests including the famous March First Movement of 1919.

In sum, Donghak played a major role in widely sowing the seeds of nationalism both as an ideology and a movement with two referral points, one internal and the other external. The external reference here is to the other nations and cultures that were beginning to influence Korea's domestic culture. The movement initiated a feeling amongst the masses to liberate Korea's own independence and culture from the deleterious influences and interferences of external forces and cultures. The internal dimension was more of a modern notion of seeking a new politico-civil society of equal rights by breaking down the hierarchical structure of relations, rules, rights, duties, and privileges in polity and society; thus a movement for breaking away

32. Kim and Kim *op. cit.* no. 3: 223.

from the past ensued.[33] To be sure, most of these seeds were not new as the broad survey by Shin Yong-ha in this volume demonstrates. The difference between the prior attempts covered by Shin and the Toghak movement was that while those attempts were top-down ones and were confined to small groups of people, the Tonghak movement was a genuinely rural and grass-roots phenomenon with a truly mass base. Only the Independence Club was close to bridging the elite-masses gap, but it too remained largely an urban body. Thus, the Tonghak uprising was part of larger and wider, though far less articulate, stirrings for reform and independence.

The socio-economic-political conditions during the latter period of the Joseon dynasty were such that they made the disgruntled peasants and dispossessed social leaders to group together to overcome internal constraints from below. The Donghak doctrine provided them the platform for this thrust. This grouping gave them an identity when it was targeted against the external constraints unitedly. This identity gave them later what in the modern concept is known as national identity, that is, the mature, full-fledged sentiment of belonging to a specific nation which is an important ingredient of the nation-state—a modern political institution. (For another take on top-down reformist efforts, refer to Vipan Chandra's contribution to this volume.)

Bibliography

Lee, Ki-Baik (1984). *A New History of Korea*. Seoul: Ilchokak. pp.182-88.

---

33. For a more detailed discussion of fusion between power and culture and their role in nationalism refer to, Aloysius, G. (1997). *Nationalism Without a Nation in India*. New Delhi: Oxford University Press. pp.15-19.

13

MRIDULA MUKHERJEE

Anti-Colonial Movements in India

A Study of the Relationship Between the National Movement and the Peasants

Conquering India had not been easy for the British East India Company. It took them a full 100 years to bring most of India under their control. Beginning with the victory in the Battle of Plassey in 1757, which secured for them the crucial province of Bengal, and ending with the brutal suppression of the great national revolt of 1857, the process was marked by numerous wars, revolts and rebellions. To name only some, the battle of Buxar against the Mughal emperor and his allies, the two Mysore Wars, the three Maratha Wars, the two Anglo-Sikh Wars, numerous expeditions against the tribes of the North-east, the Sanyasi rebellion in Bengal, the Polygars revolt in South India, revolts of the Kols and Santhals, and the uprising of 1857. Kathleen Gough, an American scholar, had documented many years ago that in the first 100 years of British rule, there was a rebellion or war of resistance every year in one part of India or another. Contrary to the famous colonial notion that the British had acquired the Indian empire in "a fit of absent mindedness", it had taken a great deal of concentration, resources, and the support of the monarchy and parliament for the Company to become the ruler of what was to become "the jewel in the crown".

However, this phase of resistance is characterised as anti-British, but not yet anti-colonial, since it was not based on an understanding of the colonial nature of British rule. Understanding of colonialism as a system came only with the writings of Dadabhai Naoroji beginning in the 1860s, and other early nationalists in India. This understanding formed the basis on which the national movement and its main forum, the Indian National Congress, was founded in 1885. There were other organisations and movements as well. The Indian National Congress was the mainstream but not the only stream: there were, over time, many other streams flowing into the swelling river of India's freedom struggle. Apart from the pre-Congress peasant and tribal movements, there were the Revolutionary Terrorists, the Ghadar and Home Rule Movements, the Akali and Temple Reform movements of the 1920s, the struggle in the legislatures and in the Press, the peasant and working class struggles, the movements of the Left inside and outside the Congress, the state people's movements, the politics of the capitalist class, the Indian National Army, the RIN Revolt, etc. These political movements formally happened outside the Congress. But we do not treat these 'non-Congress' movements as 'parallel' streams, as some have maintained. Though they were outside the Congress, most of them were not really separate from it. They cannot be artificially counter-posed to the movement led by the Congress, which, with all its positive and negative features, was the actual anti-imperialist movement of the Indian people, incorporating their historical energies and genius, as in the case with any genuine mass movement. In fact, nearly all these movements established a complex relationship with the Congress mainstream and at no stage became alternatives to the Congress. They became an integral part of the struggle against imperialism. The only ones that may be said to have formed part of an alternative stream of politics were the communal and casteist movements, which were not nationalist or anti-imperialist but in fact betrayed loyalist pro-colonial tendencies.

In this paper, we take up the question of the relationship between the national or anti-imperialist movement and the peasant movement, which increasingly became anti-colonial in the 20th century.

In the early 1920s, peasant protest emerged as part of the Non-cooperation Movement in United Province (UP) and Kerala, and in many other parts of the country as well. In 1928, a landmark peasant movement was led by Sardar Patel, the senior Congress leader from Gujarat, with Gandhi's blessings in Bardoli in Gujarat, which brought the government to its knees and galvanised the whole country. In the Civil Disobedience Movement 1930-1932, peasant participation was very high in most parts of the country, and no-tax and no-rent campaigns were very prominent. The growth of the Left forces from 1934 onwards, in the form of the Congress Socialist Party and the Communist Party, further consolidated the process of peasant mobilisation and in 1936 the All India Kisan Sabha was set up, holding its first meeting along with the Congress session at Faizpur. The formation of Congress ministries in many provinces in 1937 enabled a series of legislative measures that provided debt relief, security of tenure for tenants, restoration of lost lands, and other relief to peasants. The enhanced civil liberties also created a climate conducive to greater political participation and expression of peasants and peasant organisations. *Kisan sabhas*, *ryotu sanghams*, *karshaka sanghams*, as the name may be in different parts, mushroomed everywhere. Peasants were very much in evidence in all national campaigns, including the Individual Civil Disobedience movement in 1940-41. The Quit India Movement in 1942 was sustained by peasants for months despite severe repression after the first few days of urban protest. The post-war phase from 1945-1947 saw another wave of peasant protest and some Congress ministries in provinces even initiated the legislative process for *zamindari* abolition.[1]

Clearly, the national movement and the peasants and the peasant movements had developed a very close relationship over this period. Peasant protest in 20th-century colonial India increasingly became an integral and inseparable part of the anti-imperialist movement, especially in terms of its ideology, but also by way of its impact and often even in terms of leadership and organisation. One question

1. For an overview of peasant protest and peasant participation in the national movement, see my chapters 15, 16, 22, and 27 in Chandra, Bipan, Mridula Mukherjee, Aditya Mukherjee, K.N. Panikkar and Sucheta Mahajan (1988). *India's Struggle for Independence*. Penguin. This paper is based on a large number of interviews conducted with peasant leaders and activists in Punjab and some other parts of the country by me and my colleagues as part of my research on Punjab and also as part of a project on the history of the Indian national movement, headed by Prof Bipan Chandra. It is also partly based on material presented in Mukherjee, Mridula (2004). *Peasants in India's Non-violent Revolution: Practice and Theory*. New Delhi: Sage.

that can then be asked is: did the peasantry's involvement with the Indian national movement further or retard the peasantry's struggle for a better life? Did the involvement lead to a heightening of their political and class consciousness, did it enhance their ability to struggle against exploitation or did it obstruct the process of political awakening and social struggle?

It is my contention that the answer to the question posed has to be in the affirmative for many reasons. The national movement familiarised the peasants with modern forms of politics and organisation, with the modern ideology of anti-imperialism as well as viable strategies and techniques of resistance; it generated leaders and the cadre who spent their lives among the peasants. In addition, by enhancing the peasants' awareness of their exploitation by imperialism, the national movement increased their capacity to perceive other types of exploitation as well, such as that carried on by landlords and moneylenders. And by increasing their capacity to struggle against a particular form of oppression, that is, imperialist oppression, it simultaneously increased their capacity to fight other types of oppression. This is because the enhancement of political awareness of a specific situation or the capacity to understand a specific structure of exploitation simultaneously creates the capacity and the potential for understanding other structures of exploitation, just as the capability and experience of struggling against a particular type of oppression generates and enhances the capacity to fight other types of oppression.

Further, the peasantry's association with the national movement helped its struggle against indigenous exploiters in a more direct way as well. Since imperialism was the main guarantor and at times even creator of the indigenous exploiting classes of princes, landlords and moneylenders, any advance of the struggle against imperialism had an immediate and automatic effect on the fortunes of these classes as well. Any weakening of imperialism, any blow struck at the heart of the colonial structure of exploitation, led simultaneously to the enfeebling of those who derived surety of their existence from that very structure. The relative ease with which the process of integration of the princely states into the Indian Union and the abolition of *zamindari* was accomplished after Independence, that is, without generating any major social upheaval, is proof both of the extent to which these elements were dependent on the colonial state and the colonial structure as well as of the extent to which they had been weakened or neutralised.

The struggle against imperialism helped in another way as well. Often under the pressure of the anti-imperialist movement and of the peasant struggles that constituted an important part of it, the colonial state itself was forced to sacrifice the interests of its traditional social base—it accepted the need for protective tenancy legislation for regulating interest rates and usurious practices, etc. How far these measures helped the majority of peasants is indeed debatable, but the fact remains that they did hit at the interests of those that constituted the traditional social base of the colonial state. Thus, it could be said that the struggle against the primary contradiction helped in no small way to tackle the secondary contradictions of Indian society.

And further, the integration of the peasant movements with the national movement and the enmeshing of the peasant struggles with that for national liberation meant that peasant struggles were no longer only sectional economic struggles against particular instances of exploitation and oppression, but were increasingly becoming political struggles in the highest sense of the term so as to bring about a transformation of society from a colonial, backward one to an independent, developing one. Participation in the national struggle also helped to remove the fear of authority of the mighty British government, under which peasants lived. The mass defiance of laws, courting of arrest and non-payment of taxes, all helped to give the peasants a new self-confidence in their ability to successfully defy the government and resist oppression. This psychological change was crucial, for without it there could be no peasant organisation and peasant struggle. The association of the peasants and of peasant movements with the national movement also acted as a shield against repression. Once nationalist leaders and the cadre were associated with any particular peasant struggle, the government was wary of using strong methods against it for fear of the nationalists making a hue and cry in the cities and in the Press, and turning public opinion against the government.

The national movement also secured economic concessions for and provided economic relief to the peasants. In Bardoli, for example, the fact that prominent nationalist leaders like Patel assumed leadership of the movement, and succeeded in making it an all-India issue was certainly important in securing tax reduction for the peasants.[2] In Punjab, nationalists of all hues, Central Sikh League, Akalis, Naujawan Bharat Sabha, Kirtis, Gandhians and others together built up the movement, which secured major remissions in taxes in the early 1930s.[3] In the UP, in 1930–31, the no-rent no-revenue campaign led by the Congress secured important remissions in revenue and rent. The Congress ministries that assumed office in 1937 were responsible for rent and revenue reductions, tenancy legislation, debt relief legislation and for abolishing feudal levies like *salami*.[4]

The struggle for greater civil liberties, which was an important and continuous part of the national movement, also considerably enhanced the freedom of the peasantry to organise and express itself.

---

2. See Mehta, Shirin (1984). *The Peasantry and Nationalism: A Study of the Bardoli Satyagraha*. New Delhi; and Mukherjee, Mridula (1988). "Peasant Movements and Nationalism in the 1920s", chapter 16 in Chandra *et al. op. cit.* no. 1, *India's Struggle for Independence.*
3. Mukherjee *op. cit.* no. 1. Chapters 2, 3 and 4.
4. Even the record of the Bihar ministry, which was supposed to be the most "right-wing" of all, was not so bad. B.B. Chaudhuri lists the following measures taken by the Bihar Congress ministry during 1937–1939 which in his view "undoubtedly helped the peasantry": "1) Rent was reduced by 25 per cent, on an average. The Ministry persuaded the *zamindars* to agree not only to a reduction of the cash rent, but also of the share of the crop. 2) Peasant holdings were made transferable without the prior consent of *zamindars*, and the *salami* that was payable to them at the time of such transfers was greatly reduced. 3) Sales by *zamindars* of the entire holdings of peasants on grounds of non-payment of due rent were made illegal. *Zamindars* were to sell only a part of the holdings, which was enough for the realisation of the arrears of rent". Chaudhuri, B.B. (1971). "Agrarian Movements in Bengal and Bihar, 1919-1939", in B.R. Nanda (ed.), *Socialism in India*. p.364.

   Also see Chandra, Bipan (1988). "Twenty-Eight Months of Congress Rule", chapter 26 in Chandra *et al. op. cit.* no. 1, *India's Struggle for Independence.*

Again, the Congress ministries by increasing civil liberties of the people, provided the *Kisan sabhas* with greater freedom to carry on their work and therefore 1937–1939 were years of a great spurt in the peasant movement all over India.[5] A sharp contrast is provided in Punjab by the Unionist ministry, which came to power in 1937 and kept up relentless pressure on peasant activists through arrests, externments from the province, internments in the village, and bans on newspapers and journals.

The idea of national unity, of Indians being one people, which permeated the consciousness of the peasantry as a result of the efforts[6] of the national movement, created the basis for all-India unity of the peasants as well. Without the idea of an Indian nation, there could be no all-India peasant movement or All India Kisan Sabha. For peasants to understand that they had interests that were common with those in other parts of the country, they had to first grasp the idea that there was an Indian nation, and in this the national movement played a crucial role. It was only then that peasant struggles could, however gradually, overcome their localised character and assume an all-India character and significance. That this was well understood by the leaders of the peasants is beyond doubt:[7]

> No longer are our peasants' satyagraha campaigns isolated struggles unobserved by the peasants of other parts, as Lenin found Russians to be. Wherever there was a struggle, the peasants of the whole of India came to be interested in it, collected funds, observed sympathetic all-India Days and helped the sufferers in every possible manner...True, the All-India Peasants Congress had come to knit all the peasants together under the aegis of a National Peasant unity. But it was Mahatma Gandhi and the Congress that laid the foundations for the growth of the new consciousness and familiarised the peasants with the potent idea of their national unity.

---

5. Ibid.
6. Mukherjee *op. cit.* no. 1. Chapter 5.
7. Ranga, N.G. (1949). *Revolutionary Peasants.* New Delhi: Amrit Books. p.58.

Historiographical Approaches

Of the three basic approaches that have emerged in the writing of modern Indian history—the imperialist or neo-imperialist, the nationalist and the Marxist—it is to the broad Marxist approach or tradition that the vast majority of writings on peasant resistance have tended to belong. The imperialist and neo-imperialist school is virtually silent on this aspect and the nationalist contribution has been quite meagre.

More recently, however, a new trend of historiography has emerged, popularly identified as the "subaltern" school,"[8] which dismisses all previous historical writing as élite historiography which has little to offer by way of an understanding of the history of the people. It seeks to replace this "old", "blinkered", "élite" historiography with what it claims is a new "subaltern" or people's historiography.

Unlike the subalterns, the traditional Marxist writers[9] do recognise many, though not all, of the features of the relationship that we have discussed here. They clearly accept that the national movement after 1918 and especially Gandhi played a crucial role in mobilising and organising the peasantry in anti-imperialist mass struggles that expressed the peasantry's primary contradiction with imperialism. They also acknowledge that this process made available to the peasantry a modern nationalist ideology that was an advance over the peasantry's own existing level of understanding or

---

8. The volumes edited by Ranajit Guha under the title of *Subaltern Studies* are an obvious part of what goes by the name of the "subaltern school", but the other writings of the scholars who form part of the "subaltern" group are also treated as part of the writing of this school. On this basis, I have included Gyanendra Pandey's *The Ascendancy of the Congress in Uttar Pradesh*, Sumit Sarkar's *Modern India and Popular Movements and Middle Class Leadership*, Partha Chatterjee's *Bengal 1920–1947: The Land Question*, Stephen Henningham's *Peasant Movements in Colonial India* and of course Ranajit Guha's *Elementary Aspects of Peasant Insurgency in Colonial India* as part of the writing of this school. I have, however, omitted David Hardiman's article in Subaltern Studies I as well as his Peasant Nationalists of Gujarat from consideration as part of the subaltern school, because I believe that neither of these two studies reflect the "subaltern" approach.

9. R.P. Dutt, *India Today*, and A.R. Desai, *Social Background of Indian Nationalism* and *Introduction to Peasant Struggles in India*, would be good examples of this approach, as would many others.

consciousness and the traditional ideologies available to them.[10] They are able to perceive this because they do not share the "subalternists'" romantic image of an inherently rebellious and even revolutionary peasantry.

However, they simultaneously believe that the national movement and especially Gandhi had a negative impact on the peasantry and its struggles because of: (a) the tendency to withdraw or curb movements just when peasant militancy was about to break the bounds set by the bourgeois or upper-class character of the movement,[11] (b) its insistence on non-violence in order to protect the interests of the propertied sections, (c) the lack of incorporation of the "class" demands of the peasantry, that is, anti-landlord and anti-moneylender demands, into the programme of the national movement (which was confined to anti-colonial demands such as reduction in land revenue, water rates, salt tax and taxation in general, or to demands for irrigation, industrialisation and the like), and lack of encouragement to struggles based on these demands and (d) its unwillingness to promote and encourage class organisations of the peasantry.

The explanation for these negative features is found in the traditional Marxist assumption that the national movement was led by a weak and compromising bourgeoisie that tended to vacillate

10. A.R. Desai, for example, accepts that "even the limited calls given by Gandhi and the Indian National Congress unleashed gigantic political ferment among the peasantry, deepened the anti-imperialist consciousness in various strata of rural India and linked the rural masses with the larger nationalist anti-British movement ... By pointing out that the grievances of the masses could be removed only if British political control was eliminated, the Indian National Congress succeeded in linking up the immediate demands to political demands and enabled various exploited strata to lift their consciousness from immediate grievances to politico-structural causes, which subsequently helped them to see their problems in the context of larger issues of Socialism and Capitalism.... The Gandhian strategy included many programmes which took up the issues of securing relief to the poor peasantry, the tenants, share croppers and the exploited tribals as well as specially aggrieved strata like the untouchables and the artisans of lower classes.... The role of Gandhi and the nationalist movement in involving the peasantry in political struggles and thereby politicizing them and awakening them cannot be denied." A.R. Desai, "Introduction" to Part IV, in A.R. Desai (1979), *Peasant Struggles in India*, pp. 280–81.

11. The withdrawal of the Non-Cooperation Movement in February 1922 after the violence at Chauri Chaura, the signing of the Gandhi–Irwin Pact and the negotiated transfer of power in 1947 are cited as proof of this tendency of the Congress by almost all Marxist writers.

in its struggle against imperialism and that this vacillation often led to compromise and negotiated settlements with imperialism in which the interests of masses were betrayed; in the assumption that bourgeois or propertied class (and not national) interests were the first concern of the nationalist leadership and this led to their ignoring or sacrificing the peasants' class demands and class struggles and to a discouragement of their class organisation; as well as in the assumption that non-violence and needs of common struggle were merely ready tools which helped to obfuscate the reality and cloak the real class reasons for this behaviour.[12]

The traditional Marxist position, however, despite the apparent similarity of some of its conclusions with those of the "subalternists", is still quite fundamentally different from the "subaltern" one because it flows from a different set of assumptions—its reasons and methodology for arriving at even some similar conclusions are different. The duality of their position and their characterisation of the relationship as both positive and negative, springs from the duality or contradictions in their own understanding of the nature of contradictions in Indian society and the character of the national movement. While they believe that the central contradiction in the colonial epoch is to be located in the conflict of interests between colonialism and the Indian people, they do not accept the logic and full implications of this theoretical position when they get down to concrete analysis of specific historical situations and conjunctures. Similarly, while on the whole they accept the anti-imperialist credentials of the national movement and its leadership, they also believe that this anti-imperialism, based as it was on the bourgeoisie's vacillating position *vis-à-vis* imperialism and on the fear of mass militancy, was not sturdy and uncompromising but prone to surrender and betrayal. The "subalternists", while rejecting positive aspects of the Marxists' evaluation of the national movement, have

12. See, for example, Desai *op. cit.* no. 10, *Peasant Struggles in India,* especially p.756; and Dutt, R.P. (1949). *India Today*. Bombay. p.353 (especially).

no hesitation in accepting the negative ones, despite their belief that Marxist historiography is also "élite".[13]

The "subaltern" brand of historiography places the national movement led by the Congress and the politics of the peasants in two separate and autonomous domains of politics—one "élite" and the other "subaltern". It sees their relationship, such as it was, as being characterised by a "structural dichotomy"; in other words, it was basically antagonistic. This dichotomy was so pronounced that any effort at "braiding together of the two strands of élite and subaltern politics led invariably to explosive situations indicating that the masses mobilised by the élite to fight for their own objectives managed to break away from their control and put the characteristic imprint of popular politics on campaigns initiated by the upper classes". The national movement, being an "élite" movement, could have nothing positive to contribute to a peasantry that already had, before its association with the national movement, a political consciousness of which "resistance to élite domination" was an "invariant" part. Its greater association with "élite" nationalism could only lead to efforts at its domination and hegemonisation, though these efforts could not really succeed and would only lead to "explosive situations".[14] The subalternists, thus, either deny the fact of the close relationship between the peasantry and the national movement or, when it is too obvious to be successfully denied, assert that it was marked by efforts on part of the élite Congress leadership to "control and, if necessary, suppress the stream of popular politics".[15]

---

13. For example, Sumit Sarkar refers to the "dependent bourgeoisie of colonial India" which was inhibited by "its relations of dependence and collaboration with foreign rule and British capital, close connections with pre-capitalist forms of exploitation of the small producer through rent, usury and trade..., fear of an already fairly militant working class as well as the lack of cultural hegemony in so far as there was little permeation of modern bourgeois values throughout society." Sarkar (1983). *Popular Movements and Middle Class Leadership in Late Colonial India: Perspective and Problems*, p.72.

14. Guha, Ranajit (1982). "On Some Aspects of the Historiography of Colonial India", in Ranajit Guha (ed.), *Subaltern Studies I: Writings on South Asian History and Society*. Delhi. pp. 4–6.

15. Gyanendra Pandey (1978). *The Ascendancy of the Congress in Uttar Pradesh, 1926–34: A Study in Imperfect Mobilisation*. Delhi. p.217.

The subalternists also question the conventional wisdom about the growing participation, over time, of the peasantry as a whole in the national movement and in the major mass struggles launched by it—a wisdom that had not hitherto been questioned by any strand of historiography, including the traditional Marxists who otherwise have their own critique of the interaction between the peasants and the national movement. The subalternists believe that "on the contrary ... as the organization and strength of the Congress increased and the scale of its campaigns widened, the social depth of the movement actually diminished."[16] This assertion is based on the notion that the extension of Congress organisation, which enhanced the ability of the "élite" national movement to impose its own "élite" forms of mobilisation and struggle on the people, led to a decline in the participation of many "subalterns" whose autonomous forms of struggle, which tended to be more violent, and whose mobilisation, which was horizontal, could not fit into the pattern of vertical mobilisation and constitutional and non-violent forms of struggle that characterised the "élite" national movement.[17]

Peasant Movements and the National Movement

Unfortunately, the real flesh and blood peasants that form the subject of my story refuse to fit into the mould cast for them by the subalternists. At no stage do we find them expressing the kind of reservations about the national movement that are expected of them. They appear to have been quite willing to be vertically mobilised by nationalists of all hues, the Akalis, Gandhians or Leftists; they seem to have adopted, without any explosive situations, "élite" forms of struggle based on non-violence; and those of them that bravely defied the British in the Civil Disobedience Movement of 1930–1932 would surely have objected to the implied trivialisation of their protest by it being described as the reaction of "hard-pressed apolitical men and women" to the "economic conditions" brought about by the

16. Ibid.: 207–08. This is also echoed in Sarkar, Sumit (1983). *Modern India: 1885–1947*. Delhi. p.183.

17. Guha *op. cit.* no. 14: 2, 4.

Depression[18]—as they did show their resentment, even to their own well-loved Communist leaders, in 1942, when they tried to keep them away from the powerful nationalist current that was surging through the country.

Indian peasants also refused to furnish any evidence for the proposition that greater distance or autonomy from the élite anti-imperialist stream was a recipe for greater militancy or resistance to élite domination. By this logic, militant peasant struggles should have emerged, and with greater vehemence, in areas and among peasants who were outside the influence of élite anti-imperialist politics and the élite ideology of nationalism. But again, real life failed to copy theoretical mythology. On the contrary, a particularly striking feature of the political landscape was the considerable congruence of lines that defined the boundaries of influence of the peasant movement and the national movement. Peasant struggles in the 20th century, and especially after 1918, tended to emerge either along with or as part of the national struggle or in areas and among sections that had at one time or another felt the impact of anti-imperialist struggles. Significantly, peasant movements were also usually unable to break through the same limits of space, religion, or class and caste that defined boundaries of the anti-imperialist struggle. (This neither means that the peasant movements occupied all of the political space created by the national movement, nor that they could on occasion step outside that space—the generalisation made here, like all generalisations in the social and human sciences, is meant to indicate the dominant trend.) This congruence between the areas shaded on the political map of 20th century colonial India by the peasant and national movements was linked to the fact that in most parts of the country, it was the anti-imperialist movement that created the initial political space in which peasant movements emerged. By mobilising the peasantry into anti-imperialist political action, it created a new political awareness and awakening among them which made them receptive to the more radical or "class"-oriented ideas of peasant

18. Pandey *op. cit.* no. 15: 155–57.

organisations and peasant struggles. This is so widely accepted by participants, contemporaries and later commentators that any substantiation is really redundant. To give just two examples:

> Indian peasants...became politicised in the wake of the nationalist movement. The general spirit of defiance of authority generated by the nationalist movement from 1920 onwards and Gandhi's charisma surely promoted the growth of peasant movement almost throughout the country.[19]

> The various national evolutionary struggles led by Mahatma Gandhi and the national Congress in 1921, 1930–34 and 1940–43 have roused the Indian masses, particularly peasants as nothing else in recent centuries had done...Naturally when we began to organise peasants, we found them already with their feet well planted on the modern plane of national consciousness and determination to beard the British Imperialism in its den through the new weapon of Satyagraha with confidence in their ability to win freedom. Our task was thus very much facilitated.[20]

The national movement also provided another crucial pre-requisite for organising the peasantry into their own organisations and leading their struggles: the political cadre and workers activated by the national movement were to form the cadre of peasant movements as well. The Non-Cooperation Movement at the all-India level and in Punjab the Akali Movement as well (which was enmeshed with the Non-Cooperation Movement) created a new generation of young political workers who fanned out to villages and many continued even after their withdrawal to work among the peasants as constructive workers and often became the agents for organising peasant struggles (as in Bardoli or Midnapore). Others

---

19. Sen, Sunil (1982). *Peasant Movements in India.* Calcutta. p.28. Sunil Sen was a participant leader of the Tebhaga Movement and is a recognised analyst of peasant protest.

20. Ranga *op. cit.* no. 7: 54. N.G. Ranga, one of the most colourful personalities of Indian politics, returned from an Oxford education to work among the agricultural labourers and later the peasants in his native coastal Andhra in the early 1920s. He was a major inspiration in the founding of the All-India Kisan Sabha, apart from being deeply involved in nationalist politics from the early 1920s. He was also a recognised scholar and has written extensively on Indian peasants and their problems.

gravitated towards more radical politics and joined the Workers' and Peasants' Parties, the Nau Jawan Bharat Sabha (NJBS) and the like and went to the peasantry with their own new ideas. Similarly, the Civil Disobedience Movement drew a whole new generation of youth to itself and it was chiefly from among these that the new cadre of the Kisan Sabha Movement in the 1930s emerged. Quit India played a similar role, as did movements such as those of the Ghadar Party, the Akali Movement and the like.[21] In those areas and among those groups that remained outside the ambit of the anti-imperialist struggle, and where therefore there was both a lower level of political consciousness as well as a shortage of political cadre, the peasant movement also generally remained weak.

This is more than borne out by the example of Punjab. A marked feature of the political landscape, which is bound to hit any student of Punjab politics before Independence in the eye, was the continued concentration of the peasant movement in the pre-Independence era in central Punjab, its virtual absence in western Punjab and its negligible presence in south-eastern Punjab or present-day Haryana. This was obviously not because the peasants of central Punjab were more depressed in their conditions of existence than those elsewhere. On the contrary, peasants in western Punjab, a region dominated by big Muslim landlords, were mostly tenants-at-will who were certainly worse off than the self-cultivating peasants of central Punjab and as oppressed and exploited as any in the country, while much of the south-eastern region was almost chronically a victim of drought, famine and the like and its peasantry led an extremely precarious and insecure existence. One is also immediately struck by the fact that it was not only the peasant movement that was concentrated primarily in central Punjab, the rural base of the broad anti-imperialist movement also conformed to this regional pattern: it was the

21. To list just a few of the well-known names of radical leaders who emerged via these movements: Bhagat Singh and most of his comrades, P. Sundarayya, A.K. Gopalan, Keralyeean, Ravi Narayan Reddy, Sahajanand Saraswati, Karyanand Sharma, Biswanath Mukherjee, Kamalashankar Pandey, N.G. Gore, Nana Patil, Bhagwan Singh Longowalia, Jagir Singh Joga, Sohan Singh Josh and Sohan Singh Bhakna.

strongest in central Punjab, non-existent in western Punjab and weak in south-eastern Punjab.[22]

That this was not a mere coincidence and that there was a deeper connection between these two phenomena was fully visible to contemporaries, as shown by the responses of some of the Communist leaders whom we questioned on this aspect—on the subject of inability of the Communists to organise the peasantry in areas other than central Punjab. The Communist leaders repeatedly pointed to the importance of the anti-imperialist movement and especially the Akali Movement in mobilising the primarily Sikh peasantry of central Punjab, in breaking its political apathy and producing a general political awakening.[23]

These movements also threw up an array of political workers or cadre and it was these already politicised elements who were later attracted towards the Left and peasant movements and became its cadre. In the initial stages in the late 1920s, and even in the 1930s, a disproportionately large share of the leadership of the peasant movement was provided by Ghadar Party veterans—known affectionately as Ghadri Babas—as well as by the Ghadar/Kirti Party activists, whose nationalism was so strong that their socialism remained suspect in the eyes of their CPI comrades for many years.[24] Similarly, the Civil Disobedience Movement of 1930–1932 also threw up a new generation of political workers, as did the NJBS, led by

22. Peasant leaders were very conscious of this. Interviews with many, including H.S. Surjeet, Sri Ram Sharma, Jagir Singh Joga, Dalip Singh Tapiala, Chhajju Mal Vaid, Jagjit Singh Anand, Narain Singh Shahbazpuri. As Jagjit Singh Lyallpuri pointed out: "Communist influence was in the peasant movement in Central Punjab and in parts of the colonies and mainly among the Sikh peasantry. Unionist party's influence was weak among the Sikh peasantry and in the towns and strongest among the Muslim peasantry, quite strong in Haryana, though here the Congress influence was also there" (interview).

23. Interviews with Baba Bachhitar Singh, Jagir Singh Joga, G.S. Randhawa, Jagjit Singh Lyallpuri, H.S. Surjeet, Jagjit Singh Anand and many others. Baba Bachhitar Singh and Jagir Singh Joga had themselves joined politics during the Akali Movement, along with most other Patiala leaders. Jagjit Singh Lyallpuri also pointed out that his family had been very active in the Akali Movement and this was an important political influence on him, though he came straight to left politics (in the late 1930s).

24. Bhagat Singh Bilga, who came from the Ghadar/Kirti stream, said: "There was a view against us that our communism was 'different'. It was not of a different kind, but it was also anti-British" (interview).

Bhagat Singh. This is not to suggest that the Left movement or Kisan movement did not attract any new cadre, but that the initial base and hard core of leadership as well as cadre were all provided by those who had entered politics via the anti-imperialist movement.

The Communist leaders also pointed out that their main problem in reaching out to the Muslim peasantry of west Punjab was that of shortage of a local Muslim cadre and lack of any political links or contacts in the villages, without which it was impossible to approach the peasants. This, in turn, was a result of the fact that these areas had been untouched by any political movement, the peasant masses had never been part of the anti-imperialist movement and, therefore, there were no political workers or cadre who could be attracted towards the Communist movement and provide it with an initial foothold among the peasantry.

In fact, the degree of unanimity on this question among all our witnesses is unmatched by any other issue. I cite next a few examples from responses during interviews to this question. Harkishen Singh Surjeet agreed that it was the lack of influence of the national movement on Muslims that led to shortage of the Muslim cadre and this in turn acted as a major constraint on mobilisation of the Muslim tenants in western Punjab and the canal colonies. He pointed out that when the peasant movement was sought to be extended into the canal colony areas of Nili Bar/Montgomery in 1938, though 50 per cent of the tenants were Muslim, the movement was based primarily on the non-Muslim tenants who belonged to the Rai Sikh and Kamboh castes.

This was because Hindus and Sikhs were already affected by the national movement and there were cadre available from among them, including at the local level.[25] Jagjit Singh Anand too commented on the fact that the influence of the peasant movement did not extend to the Muslim belt in west Punjab. "That can be explained—actually the national movement itself was confined mostly to the central districts of Punjab," he said. He went on to elaborate at length on how the general consciousness among the masses was brought about by the

25. Interview.

national movement, in which he included the Akalis, the Ghadar/Kirti Movement, etc.[26] But the best and most succinct formulation on this was made by Jagir Singh Joga, the legendary leader of Patiala who began his political career as a young school student on a visit to Amritsar during the Non-Cooperation Movement and then went all the way through the Akali, Praja Mandal, and Muzara movements, as well as through the Lal Communist Party and later returned to the CPI to continue till the end of his life to lead the Kisan Sabha in Punjab. To quote:

> The cadre emerges from a political movement...and among the Muslims, there had been no movement at all. The national movement was also very weak among them. And where there has been no national movement, the question of Communists, of a Communist movement does not arise at all. [This is because] the people were backward, not aware, not politically conscious, Communists on their own cannot break this. Only nationalism could bring awareness, break this barrier. Communists could not do this on their own, without nationalism.[27]

If this was the reality, that the Communists on their own with all the theoretical understanding of class struggle and class structure and all their commitment to the cause of the peasantry, were unable to break through the limits defined by the spread of the anti-imperialist movement, does it not raise important questions of theory, of the possibly organic relationship between the peasant movements and the national movement and even the Left and national movements, of the possibility that, in the absence of a

26. Interview.

27. To continue in Jagir Singh Joga's words: "The cadre emerges from a political movement, of which some goes to Congress, some to us, and some which comes to us goes back. We did not have much cadre and the movement could only progress slowly". To the question: "Did you have discussions in the Kisan Sabha about spreading the movement to west Punjab?", he replied "Yes, we did. We tried to attract as much Muslim cadre as possible, but without success. The movement in the Nili Bar Colony was also confined to the non-Muslim tenants, who were either Rai Sikhs or Kambohs" (Interview). Jagjit Singh Lyallpuri also confirmed that the tenants in the movement in the Nili Bar Colony were non-Muslims—Rai Sikhs, Kambohs and Ods and that this area was closer to Lahore and there were already political contacts in the area with Congressmen and this made the task easier (interview). Also interviews were done with Chhajju Mal Vaid, Narain Singh Shahbazpuri, Dalip Singh Tapiala, and Master Hari Singh.

general political consciousness or political awakening, even the most radical economic programme could not mobilise the masses, in fact it could not even be reached to them?

Nationalism as Ideology

For colonial people, nationalism becomes a powerful, almost elemental urge—its appeal is akin to, and can perhaps be matched only by, religion and not by ideologies of class struggle, no matter how well formulated and coherent they may appear. Certainly, the ideology of class or economic struggle had no chance of success if it ranged itself against nationalism. Each age, each epoch in the history of people has its own dominant thrust—or, in Marxist terminology, its own central or primary contradiction. Only an ideology and movement that expresses that dominant thrust or primary contradiction is capable of moving people into political action on a mass scale for social transformation. Nationalism, because it expresses this dominant thrust of a colonial society, and because it alone expresses the deeply-felt experiences of cultural humiliation and marginalisation, economic exploitation and political subordination that are an inevitable part of the colonial interaction, is the only ideology that acquires this privileged position in the colonial epoch. It is, in Bipan Chandra's evocative phrase, "a prime mover of history".[28] Colonialism can be seen, in the words of one of the foremost nationalist Marxist revolutionaries of our time, Amilcar Cabral, as:

> "a denial of ... [the] historical process" of a people, then nationalism—its opposite, its "other"—becomes the vehicle for "the regaining of the historical personality of that people...their return to history through the destruction of the imperial domination to which they were subjected". Cabral, in fact, goes so far as to say that in colonial conditions, class struggle itself takes the form of the national liberation struggle that is fought by the "nation class".[29]

---

28. Chandra, Bipan (1988). *Indian National Movement: The Long Term Dynamics.* New Delhi. p.9, reprinted in *Writings of Bipan Chandra: The Making of Modern India from Marx to Gandhi,* Orient Blackswan, New Delhi 2012.

29. Cabral, Amilcar (1980). *Unity and Struggle.* London. pp. 130, 133.

I have stated earlier that religion was the only possible competitor to nationalism. It is arguable, however, that in a colonial society even religion—which is a centuries-old ideological formation that has provided to the mass of people one of the major ways of making sense of the world in which they live—may not have been sufficient. Even when Jinnah gave the call that religion was in danger, as in 1946–47, if it had not been articulated by the Muslim League into a political discourse of which nationalism was also a major constituent, it may not have succeeded. It can be argued that even communalism, to become a mass force, especially among the peasants, needed the crutch of nationalism. After all, the Muslim League, when it actually succeeded in reaching out in the 1940s into the countryside in many parts of the country, had to recruit nationalism as its aide by demanding Pakistan—an independent Muslim state—and could not just continue demanding protection for Muslims in a colonial India ruled by Great Britain as it had demanded earlier. Similarly, the Hindu Mahasabha failed to become a mass force during the national movement when it pitted itself against the Indian National Congress, the leading party of the national movement.[30] On the other hand, the recent runaway growth of the Hindu communal forces has much to do with the projection of their religion-based communal politics as symbolic of the assertion of Hindu nationalism.

I might also advance the hypothesis that it appears that for people to engage in a struggle that requires immense sacrifice and for them to be able to sustain this struggle over a prolonged period of time (as distinct from engaging in short-lived bursts of revolt or acts of desperation), what is required is a movement with an ideology that has a large vision, a big ideal—this is, after all, one reason why revolts are inspired by millenarian ideologies. Only such a vision can

---

30. For a full-length study of communalism in colonial India as well as for the relationship between communalism and nationalism, see Chandra, Bipan (1984). *Communalism in Modern India*. New Delhi. Also see his three essays (Chapters 31, 32, 33) on communalism in Chandra, Bipan, Mridula Mukherjee, Aditya Mukherjee, K.N. Panikkar, Sucheta Mahajan (1988). *India's Struggle for Independence*. Penguin. New Delhi.

inspire people and sustain them in their determination.[31] And the Indian national movement did offer such a vision and an inspiring ideology.

Communists could not hope to substitute this with calls for class or economic struggles, which is what they tried to do, though most often only in theory and mercifully less often in practice. They at least needed to encapsulate these calls within a larger vision of an egalitarian system, of socialism representing a new kind of society. In India, however, Communists often reduced the socialist ideal in their practice to the doctrine of struggle for economic demands—perhaps one reason for this was that they were weaned on what Bipan Chandra has called Stalin-Marxism, a particularly reductionist and mechanistic variety of Marxism. However, it is not as if had they successfully projected the socialist ideal, it could have replaced the nationalist vision as the prime mobilising force in colonial India—it could have only allied with nationalism and left its stamp on it in the hope of a better tomorrow—after Independence. That Communists registered the successes they did was because in practice—for long periods of time, as during 1927–1929, 1935–1939, and even to an extent during 1940–41—they functioned as good nationalists and fully identified with the ideology of nationalism to establish their presence among the people in general and peasants in particular.

For Punjab, for example, the oral testimony of many of the left-wing leaders bears this out in ample measure. After all, these activists had talked, like other nationalists, about the drain of wealth from India to Britain, of the need to throw out the British; they were, like others, members of the Congress and like others, and often even more than others, office bearers of the Congress in their areas of influence. The following examples from some of the interviews conducted for this study will corroborate this. Harkishen Singh Surjeet, the late general secretary of the Communist Party of India (Marxist), who was a major grass-roots level organiser of the peasant

31. To quote Bipan Chandra: "Ideology and ideological preparation are important in any form of popular, mass-based struggle ... [because] active opposition involving immense sacrifice cannot be offered only on the basis of exploitation or a sense or knowledge of exploitation. It requires strong, very strong ideological commitment." Chandra *op. cit.* no. 28: 8–9.

movement from about 1935, while discussing the ideology of the peasant movement, said:

> The question is [that] everything was done for the struggle against imperialism. So that is why all the propaganda, even the mass organization, [the] issues which were being posed, everything was linked with imperialism...Government [was] also a foreign government. That is why political propaganda was inherent. The conferences [were] not the type of trade union conferences which [are] being held today, mainly on the basis of economic demands. Everywhere it [was] connected with the political view.

Ujagar Singh Bilga, who was a grass-roots peasant organiser since the late 1920s and had worked in many parts of the province, also said that their refrain was that "our problems cannot be solved till we throw out the British."

Bhagat Singh Bilga, one of the prominent Ghadar/Kirti leaders, echoed the same: "The planned kisan movement thus brought a national awakening among the kisans."

Wadhawa Ram, the son of a poor tenant-at-will who sacrificed his job as a *patwari* to become one of the major organisers of the tenants in the colony areas of Nili Bar/Montgomery/Multan, said:

> In the villages we, [that is, the Communist peasant activists] were the Congress. Even if we didn't claim it, the people thought we were Congressmen. Nobody knew the name of Communists, but the Congress was a big party. Even where our influence was strong, we were known as Kisan workers, but not as Communists.

Jagjit Singh Lyallpuri, another important Communist leader, also emphasised the close identity between nationalism, the national movement and the peasant movement:

> Till 1942, there was no demarcation between us and the Congress. At the village level, we were known as Congressmen. In fact, we made more sacrifices for the Congress cause than the traditional Congressmen. The Congress flag we considered our flag—the flag of anti-imperialism. We defended the flag more avidly than them. The main current of politics was anti-imperialism and Congress was the main symbol of this and all anti-imperialist currents had to work within it.

Narain Singh Shahbazpuri, a peasant organiser of Amritsar District, recounted at length how he would, in his speeches before peasant audiences, reproduce the standard nationalist critique of British rule, dwell on the drain of wealth from India to England, describe India as the golden bird (*sone ki chirya*) that was fleeced and say that if only we could retain this wealth here, we could have more development and become prosperous.[32]

The Communist leaders of the peasants appeared before their audience in their nationalist or Congress incarnation also because the ideology and programme of anti-imperialist nationalism provided a basis, a focus, a rallying point around which different sections and strata of a fairly differentiated peasantry could be united. It may not be too rash to advance the hypothesis that, given the fact of deep economic and social divisions within the peasantry,[33] this was perhaps the only ideology and programme that could, in the given context, form the basis of common action and common organisation of different sections of peasants.[34]

The only other possibility, and one that was explored by the Unionist party in Punjab especially by Chhotu Ram and to some extent by the Krishak Praja Party in Bengal, was of mobilising the peasants around an ideology of anti-urbanism, or ruralism, which may even sometimes, given the necessary popular pressure, acquire peasantist overtones. But such ideologies were, at least in

32. Many others made the same point in different ways. For example, see interviews with Chain Singh Chain, Ram Singh Majitha, and Dalip Singh Tapiala. See also Mukherjee *op. cit.* no. 1: Chapters 3 and 4.

33. Many scholars have noted the difficulties caused by sharp class divisions within the peasantry for the task of organising a common struggle. See, for example, Chaudhuri, B.B. (1971). "Agrarian Movements in Bengal and Bihar, 1919-1939", in B.R. Nanda (ed.), *Socialism in India* and Gough, Kathleen (1979). "Peasant Resistance and Revolt in South India", in A.R. Desai (ed.). *Peasant Struggles in India.* New Delhi. especially pp. 369 and 723.

34. This difficulty in uniting different classes, especially sections of the landowning peasantry with agricultural labourers, in a common struggle has been experienced more sharply since Independence, once anti-imperialist nationalism could no longer fulfil the same function and also once agricultural labourers' organisations emerged as an important constituent—which they were not in the pre-Independence days. It is possible to argue that just as these conflicting class demands could not be subsumed in a single movement in the pre-Independence days without a wider ideological orientation in the direction of anti-imperialism, similarly they cannot be incorporated today without a longer-term vision of national societal development.

the given historical context and perhaps are at all times, in spite of their apparent pro-peasant bias, ultimately reactionary. In the specific context of colonial India, they were successfully incorporated into the imperialist ideological discourse because their anti-urban emphasis helped, as in the case of the Unionists in Punjab, to blunt the anti-landlord (landlords being rural and not urban elements) and pro-nationalist (nationalists being identified as urban and the national movement as an urban-dominated movement) edge of the emerging peasant movement. In the case of the Krishak Praja Party, which retained its anti-*zamindari* edge, the pro-nationalist potential of the peasant movement was blunted. Of course, both in the case of the Unionists in Punjab and the Krishak Praja Party in Bengal, these ideologies were also happily married with communal and semi-communal and casteist ideologies which made it even easier for them to become part of the imperialist discourse.[35]

It would then seem that anti-imperialism was the only historically appropriate progressive ideology that could form the basis of unity and common struggle of the different strata of a peasantry, which was otherwise divided not only on the basis of caste, religion, and language, but also increasingly differentiated at the economic or class plane as well. It is not surprising that, in practice, even the left-led peasant organisations, the All-India Kisan Sabha and its numerous provincial wings, including the Punjab Kisan Committee, functioned on the basis of this understanding—anti-imperialism was a crucial component of the ideology which was transmitted by the massive propaganda and organisational efforts of Kisan Sabha activists in Punjab and other parts of the country in the 1930s and 1940s. And, as in the case of the Indian national movement which could not be conciliated even in its mild, moderate phase,[36] this clear-cut anti-imperialist ideology made it difficult for the colonial authorities to either conciliate or co-opt the peasant movement from the 1920s.

35. For the Unionists in Punjab, see Mukherjee *op. cit.* no. 1: Chapter 1; for the Krishak Praja Party in Bengal, Sen *op. cit.* no. 19: 53–54 and Chandra *op. cit.* no. 30: 84, 87.

36. Chandra *op. cit.* no. 28: 8.

Conciliation had been possible in the case of the 19th century peasant movements such as the Indigo Revolt, the Pabna Uprising and the Deccan Riots by conceding much of their demands.[37] Further, it was this anti-imperialist ideology that made it possible for the peasant movement in Punjab to demarcate itself from the Unionists, especially when Chhotu Ram was in a militant mood and raised demands and talked a language which sounded very similar to that of the Kisan Sabha activists. The one way in which the Kisan cadre could prevent their movement from being usurped by him was by constantly reminding the peasants of his pro-British politics—and their own anti-imperialism.[38]

I may clarify that the argument does not hinge on whether this modern nationalist political consciousness reached the peasantry through the organisational network of the Congress or through numerous substitutes such as the Akali Movement in British Punjab and the Punjab princely states during its anti-imperialist phase from 1920–1925, the Andhra Mahasabha in Hyderabad State, the numerous Praja Mandals in the Indian states, N.G. Ranga in coastal Andhra from the 1920s, Swami Sahajanand in Bihar till the late 1930s and Communist, Congress Socialist and other leaders and cadre of the Kisan Sabha Movement in various parts of the country, including Punjab. After all, in China it was primarily the Communist Party that took this consciousness to the peasantry. I am referring to modern nationalist ideology and politics in general and not to the specific organisational form through which it was disseminated at various local levels. However, insofar as the Indian National Congress was the main organisational form—on a national, all-India plane—of the Indian national movement, a primary role was played in this process by it and the movements it launched, as well as by its leaders, especially Gandhi.

37. Ibid.: 8, footnote 3.

38. Harkishen Singh Surjeet says this was the big difference in perceptions of Unionists between peasants of central Punjab and other areas: the peasants of central Punjab saw them as pro-British, elsewhere they were seen as pro-peasant (interview). Jagjit Singh Lyallpuri also asserts that the Sikh peasants of central Punjab were conscious that Unionists were pro-imperialist in the larger context, even though they may pass some pro-peasant legislation (Interview).

14

VIPAN CHANDRA

Were So Chaep'il and Yun Ch'iho Oriental Orientalists?

New Reflections on the Korean Enlightenment

Were So Chaep'il and Yun Ch'iho, two eminent Korean champions of reform in late 19th century Korea, oriental orientalists, or as some takers on Edward Said would have put it, self-orientalising orientalists? This is the main question I want to examine in this paper.

In the countries that I taught about until 2012—India, China, Japan, and Korea—there were quite a few eminent intellectuals and political activists who adopted intense and wide-ranging critiques of their societies and cultures, along with espousing an enthusiastic adoption of western civilisation in the pursuit of both personal development and national progress and strength. Here my focus is entirely on reexamining the main ideas of the munmyong kaehwa (enlightenment and civilisation) movement in a summary fashion as championed by So and Yun through pages of The Independent, the newspaper they ran, and in the case of Yun, additionally through his private diary in the last decade of the 19th century. On occasion I may refer to some statements of Yun from the early 20th century, only because they put some of his late 19th century ideas in sharper relief for us.

My choice of So and Yun is not because they were the only notable figures in the Korean version of this movement. There were also others—Kim Okkyun, Yu Kilchun, Pak Yonghyo, Yi Sangjae, and the like. It is simply because So and Yun had had the longest direct exposure to the civilisation and societies of the west; they had studied in a rapidly westernising Japan, with Yun also having travelled in Russia and western Europe, Shanghai and the British colony of Hong

Kong; they received their degrees from American higher educational institutions; they were early converts to Christianity; and they wrote far more knowledgably, extensively, and articulately than others on the need for Korea to adopt the western model of progress and strength—both the direct one and the indirect one they saw unfolding in Japan. Western political, educational, technological, medical, social, commercial, military and religious ideas and practices had as a package enthralled their minds. This package stood for light and the rest mostly signified darkness.

I will first give a summary description of the So-Yun reformist thought in the form of representative statements, directly or in paraphrase, from their own writings. I will then offer a somewhat updated critique of the Christian-Western prism that shaped their intellectual and moral views on Korea, something through which So and Yun viewed virtually everything. On the margins, they also incorporated parts of their own history and culture. They clearly did have a good grasp of that history and culture, but they chose not to make a public stand in support of it, except where it seemed to serve their westernising agenda.

Let me say as a starting point that there were very few in the late 19th century missionary groups with whom So and Yun were closely involved, who showed any willingness to embrace any part of Korea's intellectual and moral heritage, in the sense that while giving others what one has, one also receives from them what is admirable in matters that should carry some weight in all inquiring minds—i.e., in the philosophical concepts and moral visions that undergird and inform every rich civilisation. Even J.S. Gale and Homer Hulbert, perhaps the most scholarly of all missionaries in Korea, did not develop the kind of, shall we say, catholicism and inclusiveness of mind that one associates with Matteo Ricci or James Legge in China or with Hermann Hesse and Sir Edwin Arnold in India (there were many more such Western figures in India). For the most part, Korean culture was, even when the missionaries were polite about it, a spiritual "adversary"for their conversion-focused, evangelical enterprise. Korean converts like So and Yun therefore developed a more rejectionist attitude toward their own culture, and it conditioned their modernisation project.

My second preliminary point is that on most though not all ideas, So and Yun, in the period discussed here, can be seen almost as identical intellectual twins, even when Yun at times expressed exasperation with So's allegedly arrogant personality in his private diary. On most public issues they were close enough to be able, I think, to finish each other's sentences. They collaborated, after all, on the Independence Club and on the *Tongnip sinmun* and its English-language twin, *The Independent*. Hence, even when using the words of one or the other, I believe one can justifiably refer to them as representing the thoughts of both.

Let me cite here a short critique of Confucianism that Yun wrote in the 1895 issue of the Korean Repository, a missionary magazine well known to most Koreanists. It is rather self-explanatory, and coming from the horse's mouth, so to speak, warrants a full reproduction. In his prefatory remarks, Yun asserted that he was expressing his views "not from the standpoint of a philosopher—which I do not pretend to be—but as a Korean who has paid some attention to its practical results." "What has Confucianism done for Korea?" Yun asked, and then provided the following answer:

> With diffidence yet conviction I dare say that it has done very little, if anything for Korea. What Korea may have been without Confucian teachings, nobody can tell. But what Korea is with them we too well know. Behold Korea, with her oppressed masses, her general poverty, her treacherous and cruel officers, her dirt and filth, her degraded women, her blighted families—behold all this and judge for yourselves what Confucianism has done for Korea.

Yun then proceeded to give a list of some of Confucianism's "glaring faults, any one of which," he argued, "may injure a people who build their political or social fabric on it." First, according to Yun, was that Confucianism "enfeebles and gradually destroys the faculty of faith. It is an agnostic system. He who is imbued with its teachings finds it hard to believe in any truth beyond this material world of bread and butter."

Second, "Confucianism nourishes pride. It tells you that your heart is as naturally inclined to be good as ... water is to seek the level. In the name of wonders, where did the first evil come from, then? Further, it overlooks the distinction between things moral and mental. It holds that if you are moral—that is, if you love your father and mother—you will know everything under the blue sky. It places no bounds to the human understanding and thus makes every pedant who can repeat the classics a boundless fool, serene in the flattering contemplation that he is verily omniscient!"

Third, "Confucianism, knowing no higher ideal than man, is unable to produce a godly or god-like person. Its followers may be moral, but never spiritual.... On the other hand, a Christian, having God to look unto as the author and finisher of his faith, is a man all the way up, however small he may be in himself. In other words, a Confucianist begins in and ends in man. A Christian begins in man but ends in God...."

Fourth, "Confucianism is selfish or rather encourages selfishness. It never says go and teach, but come and learn. In trying to make men to keep the doctrine of the mean, it makes them mean, narrow, calculating, revengeful, ever ready with specious excuses and never given to generous adventures."

Fifth, "While Confucianism exalts filial piety to the position of the highest virtue, and while a Confucianist makes this very common principle to hide a multitude of uncommon sins, the whole system saps the foundation of morality and prosperity by classifying women with menials and slaves...."

Sixth, "Confucianism aims to make people good through legislation.... It is amazing how short-sighted Confucianists seem to be not to have seen the folly of committing the moral welfare of a nation into the hands of absolute monarchs whose surroundings and temptations were and have been notoriously unfavorable to the growth of virtues. The idea of reforming society through the reformation of each individual of the mass seems to have never crossed their mind[s]."

Seventh, Yun assailed "the hunger and thirst after office for which Confucius himself set a conspicuous example. Most readily do I admit that he was actuated by the purest motives to seek after office. Yet as a drunkard throws over his weakness a kind of religious sanction by quoting Paul's injunction to drink a little wine for the stomach's sake, every Confucianist who runs after office for nothing but the squeezing there is in it, sanctimoniously tells you that he is following the steps of Confucius."

Yun concluded by advising Koreans to part with this "system of ethics"—"the sooner the better."

There were numerous reiterations of this theme in Yun's diary and So Chaep'il's editorials in The Independent. Some of these reiterations use the broader words Western or Occidental rather than just Christian. Let's cite just a few brief but telling statements on the subject.

In one editorial in *The Independent*, So wrote:

> Wherever Western civilisation has made its appearance, the place was transformed into a new country altogether.... We hope the time will come when Western civilisation will penetrate every corner of the continent of Asia and make use of the Creator's beautiful soil for the good of His [the H is in upper case here] people the world over.

Yun echoed this theme later:

> What we want is the rich,nay, revolutionising ideas of the West introduced and naturalized, as it were, in Korea.....[We need] the epoch-making and world moving thoughts of the Occidental races.

The Anglo-Saxon missionaries, So asserted in another editorial, had with energy and devotion, brought both "truth" and a range of beneficent activities to the East. The Gospel of Christ evidently was, as So put it, "the bedrock of Anglo-Saxon civilisation."

Let's now pursue this with reference to an individual-focused episode.

Sin Ki-son, who had been associated with the failed progressive coup of 1884 (discussed extensively by Shin Yong-Ha in this volume), had transformed himself into an egregiously pro-Chinese leader once he became education minister in early 1896. In a memorial to the throne, he bitterly attacked the new western-style hair of some Korean men, the wearing of western uniforms by soldiers, policemen and students, the increasing use of Han'gul, then called Onmun, and the adoption of the Western calendar as expressions of ungratefulness to China. He called the use of Han'gul a "beastly" practice. These innovations to him were ominous signs of the impending destruction not only of the venerable Chinese classics, but also of government itself. In another document, called Yuhak kyongwi (The Warp and Woof of Confucianism), he vented his anti-westerrn and anti-Christian vitriol even more vehemently. He referred to Europeans as birds and beasts and their languages as the chirping of fowls. He called Christianity vulgar, shallow and erroneous, and a type of barbarian vileness. He praised China as a grand and glorious center of civilisation and the largest and richest empire in the world.

Answering this diatribe against the west, So asked Sin to look at China and see how it was tottering to its fall and how its boasted classics were plunging her deeper and deeper into the mire.

So then exposed the hypocrisy of Sin and of men like him in the following sarcasm-laden counter-assault:

> Mr Sin has a fine contempt for Europe and Europeans, but let us see how it would work practically. He wears cotton pants which were woven in Manchester. The watch he wears was perhaps made in Switzerland. He lights his pipe with matches from Vienna unless he prefers the cheaper Japanese product. He reads by the light of American kerosene oil. He probably wears a piece of amber from the Baltic in his top-knot. If it were not for European glass he would not be able to look out of his windows in winter.... And [referring to King Kojong's refuge in the Russian legation] his sovereign is the guest of one of these "low-down, bird-chirping" Europeans.

The image of official obscurantism as exemplified by Sin was just one illustration. In Yun's diary, one additionally finds numerous denunciations of abuses of power, and beyond that, a whole lot of other unacceptable social and cultural habits of Korea—all of which he attributed to Chinese ideological and political influences on Korea. Many of these statements, since they are terse words recorded on different occasions in a private diary, sound like angry outbursts in which all problematic issues of Chinese and Korean culture or behavior are randomly thrown into a trash basket called China and Chinese influences, as it were; conversely, the admirable traits of nearby Japan, an able follower of things Western, are displayed in a flower vase at the center of the family dining table. Herewith are a few of Yun's choice tirades. [I have put down a composite sketch from various entries in Yun's diary.]

Chinese influences in Korea, for example, were described as "infernalness" and the Korean government itself as "infernal" and "evil-saturated." For Yun, it followed from this blanket characterisation that all the problems that he saw in both Korean society and government were directly or indirectly connected to a pervasive Chinese virus in the body politic. The cowardice, the lying, the tendency toward theft, the effeminate male character, the deceit, the trickery and fraud, the instances of embezzlement, the vanity, the wickedness and hellish exactions by government officials, the bighting effects of patronage, and the stagnancy of Korea were all attributed to the Chinese connection.

Some of this was duly echoed in So's editorials as well, though in less strident words. To Yun, in addition, the Chinese were dirty people and an abomination—"the filthiest people in the world except (possibly) the Coreans." Although Yun did not directly extend this baleful tie to fellow Koreans' treatment of their natural landscape, one sometimes wonders if he didn't think so.

> The unsightly, slovenly mud villages and treeless hills of Korea drew his attention not in contrast to any greener, more eye-pleasing and respectful treatment of nature in China but in Japan. Everything, he said, was ugly in Korea. The Koreans had disfigured and disgraced nature; the Japanese with exquisite taste had preserved, improved and glorified the charms of nature.

Japan, he rhapsodised, was "a blessed paradise," a "Garden of the world."

Not even the Chinese writing system escaped Yun's contempt. He asserted that it had an excellent faculty for "clothing Lilliputian thoughts in Brobdingnagian expressions."

When enumerating the presumed superior traits of Japan and the Japanese, in addition to their stewardship of nature, he lauded their manly and martial spirit; their courage and bravery; their forward looking mentality; their self-reliance; their high degree of discipline; their loyalty and patriotism; their watchfulness on behalf of the nation, in part due to their devotion to the exalted throne connected to the Sun Goddess "cultivated, nursed and perfected" in feudal times; their super-abundant energy; their respect for public order; their intelligence; their polite and peaceful manners; and the like.

During the Sino-Japanese War of 1894-95, Yun knew exactly where his sympathies should be. The war was a conflict between what he called "the regenerating civilisation of the West [as seen in Japan] and the degrading barbarism of the East [as seen in China]. The success of Japan would mean the salvation of Corea and the reformation of China." The reverse "would plunge Corea into a bottomless pit of Chinese corruption."

To both So and Yun, the most shocking political contrast between Japan and Korea was the independent spirit of Japanese and the alleged China-worshiping servility of Koreans. In numerous newspaper editorials, they castigated the debilitating psychological effects of Korea's long history of living under Chinese overlordship. That deep-rooted habit, according to them, had drained their national pride and made them timid and dependent on China. This attitude had become so ingrained in the Korean character that a Korean, Yun wrote in one diary entry, "takes to foreign vassalage as naturally as a duck takes to water."

The democratic political and legal systems of the West; the respect for individual rights; the, by comparison, better treatment of women; the less rigid class boundaries; the trends toward general social egalitarianism; the industrial, technological and economic advancement; and other praiseworthy qualities of western societies were products of their Christian religious base. Nowadays, some in the West add the word Judeo before Christian, but one does not come across that prefix in the words of So and Yun. Nor does one see any acknowledgement of the role of Catholicism in the progress and strength of the West. Christianity to them meant Anglo-Saxon Protestantism, pure and simple. And the connection between that brand of Christianity [hereafter just Christianity, for brevity's sake] and advanced western civilisation was given on a take it or leave it basis. There was no attempt to plumb deeply how this nexus came about or whether one might, on the contrary, seek a better explanation of western advancement in the alternative ideas of the Enlightenment and other purely secular forces. Although both So and Yun were well versed in them and made good use in their discourse of eminent figures produced by those forces, they always did so with an insistence on their connection to an inseparable Christian umbilical chord. Since the only westerners they interacted with were men and women of the Christian faith, this Christianity-equals-human-progress proposition was self-evident to them.

While I have seen no direct comments from So or Yun on the contradiction of their Christian credo in the non-Christian foundations of Japan's Meiji Restoration and its rapid march toward modernity, Yun seemed to imply that the unifying effects of Japan's imperial mythology and its *bushido* (samurai code)-derived values were wedded to Christian–shaped western institutions and practices. That combination had what made that nation an enviable model; it had enthusiastically embraced the secular products of the Christian west, hence it was indirectly Christian-influenced anyway in its fervent commitment to the cause of progress. The path toward Korea's modernity had to be more directly Christian because in Yun's reckoning Korea had nothing akin to Japan's *bushido*. And while the Japanese had largely thrown away the *joi* part of the *sonno joi* ("revere the emperor, expel the foreigners") slogan and moved with spectacular speed toward western-style advancement, a vast majority of Koreans had remained unreconstructed rejectionists, in the *wijong ch'oksa* ("defend [Confucian] orthodoxy, reject heresy ") mould, in their attitude toward Western civilisation.

At the political level, So and Yun waxed eloquent on the benefits of introducing into Korea the western concepts of debate, respect for dissent, a free press, elected local officials, modern political parties seeking to win public support for their platforms through public canvassing, and limited monarchy of the western kind via a partly-elected national assembly at the outset. And they sought to buttress them all by a public enlightenment campaign that would gradually domesticate the notions of natural rights, popular sovereignty, rule of law, and the like. As many Korean scholars and I have pointed out before, most of these ideas were clearly derived from the philosophy of social contract as embodied in the writings of John Locke, Rousseau, Thomas Jefferson, and the American Declaration of Independence.

Both So and Yun did realise that both at home and abroad, western nations had committed and continued to commit grave injustices—racism, annexation and exploitation of overseas colonies, etc.—but their democratic systems of government and law, a free press and the presence of many God-fearing and high-minded men in those nations made the exposure and rectification of errors and abuses an ongoing process, leading to the ever-expanding betterment of all. Yun, particularly, had a high opinion of the British; using Lord Macaulay as his source and prefiguring the later Curzonian, Kiplingesque, and Churchillian rhetoric, he held up the British government of India as a model of enlightened foreign rule of people who had proven themselves to be unfit for self-government. The occasional atrocities, follies as he called them, committed by some Englishmen in India were an unavoidable cost borne by a few for the benefit of many. Indians should not "whine" about those costs, he advised. (In later times, he was to add for good measure that while Gandhi was undoubtedly a great man, it was the British who "let him become great"!) Since Korea had also not proven its fitness for enlightened self-government, privately Yun on occasion wished that if the country were to fall under foreign rule, it should ideally be British rule, with Japanese rule as the second best alternative.

Korea's existing political and social systems, even with the legal reforms enacted since the "opening" of the country in 1876, had shown no real improvement in people's lives because the political system was still embedded in an intellectual and moral ideology and a social structure that remained dominantly Confucian, authoritarian and undemocratic.

Let me now turn to the big question I raised at the outset about whether the So-Yun ideas could be called examples of Oriental Orientalism. Without going into an extended exposition of this theme, let me rely on Sinologist Arif Dirlik who has examined the issue in the context of China to help us get a handle on it in the Korean context. Evidently, So and Yun, especially the latter, echo many of the Orientalist themes although it is clear that Yun was making an exception for Japan. China and Korea, and remote India, all were seen in need of western or western-style tutelage to overcome their perceived stagnancy, their perverse resistance to reform, and their general unworthiness to be members of the civilised world. Similar in approach to many Orientalists, So and Yun reduced Korea to what may appear as an essentialised portrait of unmitigated negativity. Yun's outbursts are of course particularly extreme in this portrayal.

Yet one needs to be cautious about several facets of this issue. In his discussion of Orientalism in China, Arif Dirlik, borrows Mary Louise Pratt's concept of "contact zones" to offer a more nuanced understanding of China's own version of Orientalism. Briefly stated, he argues against Orientalism as a product solely made in the west and brought to China or Asia and forced upon the natives, but presents it as a collaborative enterprise between easterners and westerners. Put simply, the areas or circles where westerners and easterners came into close contact and continued sustained interaction with one another, provided all kinds of stimuli from which western as well as Asian critics of Asia emerged. Chinese intellectuals who became critics of Chinese culture or civilisation were thus not just paid or unpaid mouthpieces of critical westerners or their theories, but were autonomous agents who used, by their own choice, standards borrowed from the west to analyse and reform their societies in the western image that they came to admire as the model of human progress. I find this proposition substantially persuasive because my own study of China, India and Korea has long convinced me of what is clearly its commonsensical foundation. Propaganda, schooling, wealth and other means of conversion were no doubt powerful tools in the hands of the imperial west, but they never uniformly led to pliant success. In fact, as is well known, in India the recipients of western influence as often as not turned their new education against the west itself even when they appreciated many of its virtues. Numerous intellectuals and political activists thus developed their autonomous responses.

At first blush, one may see the ideas of So and Yun as nothing but brain-washed refrains of the deeply prejudicial, often ignorant, and self-serving denigrations of Asian societies and cultures propagated by western advocates of imperial expansion in Asia and Africa. Unruly children; savages in beliefs and practices; lecherously hedonistic; dishonest and impervious to the meaning of truth; impractical and otherworldly dreamers; superstitious; bound by fatalism and gender and caste–based concepts of immobility; servile to narrow group interest and devoid of goodwill toward human beings beyond that pale; mired in putrefying stagnancies of mind and soul and resistant to enlightenment; effeminate; dependency-oriented; craven and obsequious in manner and treacherous in conduct—these and other damning descriptions of non-white peoples were common fare in western societies. They provided good justification to many for western imperial expansion all over the world—loftily in the name of divinely sanctioned civilising missions, whatever the real, economic and political goals might have been. Edward Said systematically and, before him Albert Memmi in more subdued and general ways in his study of the effects of colonial ruling psychology on the colonised, have pointed out the demeaning impact on many among the subject countries' hapless elites of being bombarded by various combinations of this sort of pernicious propaganda coming from western quarters. It is scarcely surprising that some among the native elites sought to join the foreign ruling or dominant circles or at any rate those of power and prosperity by mindlessly parroting the received propaganda no matter how degrading to their countries and cultures. Some even helped the cause of western imperial penetration of their lands (or later in East Asia specifically, of similar expansionist designs by Japan).

Such social climbers under alien dispensations of power thus did exist and may rightly be called a variety of Oriental Orientalists. I am not convinced, however, that So and Yun merit such a mocking label categorically in the period under discussion (and in the case of So, also not in the rest of his public life which he continued to dedicate to Korean national causes). As for Yun, though he incurred the wrath of nationalist Koreans for later ardently supporting the Japanese rule of Korea, Koen De Ceuster's 700-plus-page study of Yun shows that it was not because he had sold his soul to Japan for selfish ends but because this was the only way he could salvage some benefit for his people under a most trying set of circumstances beyond his control.

The reason I say they were not categorical Oriental Orientalists is this: If by reason of comparing one's own society and culture with others, one draws harshly unfavorable conclusions about one's own, it does not *ipso facto* follow that one is some sort of a cavalier and self-seeking follower of the admired model. If that was the case, we might as well dismiss some of the most admired Indian leaders of our age as belonging to such a category of men. The critiques that M.G. Ranade, G.K. Gokhale, Mahatma Gandhi, and J.L. Nehru drew of their own societies often echoed those of western critics of Indian culture, but whereas the western critics often spoke with unmixed malice, derision and self-righteousness, they spoke with the clear aim of reforming India toward something better. It is worth recalling that when Katherine Mayo's scurrilous portrait of India, called Mother India, appeared in the 1920s, Gandhi India aptly called it the drain-pipe view of India; it was suggested by others that while westerners should not rely on it, Indians should read it. Their point was that Mayo was just representing a vicious kind of collective self-satisfaction in the west (in the way Arthur Smith did on China by his book titled *Chinese Characteristics*) based on a random compilation of all that was wrong with India and none that was right, Indians in contrast might usefully become concentrated on how they should improve what needed to be improved in their society.

In China likewise, Liang Qichao, Qiu Jin, Chen Duxiu, Sun Yatsen, Hu Shih, Lu Xun, Lin Yutang, and Mao, for example, wrote trenchantly and unsparingly about what was wrong with China, ideologically, institutionally and in terms of alleged national traits. Yet no one has called them crassly hostile to China because they sought to bring to China what they found better in Japan or in the west or in the early Soviet model. They have all had their critics, but not on grounds of being mindless or self-centered imitators of any western model. Meiji-era Japanese reformists, from the intellectual mentors, such as Ueki Emori and Nakae Chomin, of the *jiyu minken undo* (people's rights movement), to Fukuzawa Yukichi and Ito Hirobumi; and Japanese documents, from the Charter Oath of 1868 to newspaper editorials in the 1870s and 1880s, likewise freely used harsh words to describe many Japanese customs and practices. All reform endeavors sought their abolition and their replacement by the "civilized"and "enlightened" models of the west. The Charter Oath in one translation even spoke of abolishing the "evil" customs of the past.

The motives of the Chinese and Japanese reformists, like those of Indian ones, in criticising their societies and cultures may indeed be called patriotic—a kind of "tough love" version of patriotism. It would be unfortunate to label such men and Yun and So as Oriental Orientalists, for then we would denigrate their own independent agency and suggest that though mature and educated, they could only parrot foreign propaganda against their nations and were incapable of making autonomous investigations into what afflicted their societies. It can be said without any reservations whatever that such a simple depiction of their lives and careers would be grossly inaccurate and unjust.

It needs to be reiterated that both So and Yun, especially the latter, also spoke out against the blatant and stinging racism of some westerners against Asians including against Yun himself when he was studying in the US. He also noted with condemnation the equally objectionable behaviour of many individual Japanese in Korea. He had once experienced rejection from an inn in Georgia when traveling and had had to spend an entire night in a railroad station. This had caused him to have what sounds from his diary as a clinical-level depression under which he had temporarily come to question the very worth of his life. Yet he had overcome that, presumably with the help of more enlightened Christian missionary educators. It is not surprising that while often attacking western imperial behavior and racism, he on one occasion seemed to shout in his diary, God bless the missionaries! On the other side of the Pacific, while admiring the Japanese in general, he was unsparing at the shortsighted and self-defeating aggressiveness of the Japanese government as well as individual carpetbaggers in Korea as they went about hunting for railway, mining, timber and other concessions in cahoots with corrupt Korean officials. In great anger, Yun used the J-word expletive against those Japanese in one diary entry.

In fact, both So and Yun in their public statements wanted Korea to become an independent state if at all possible by learning from the western and Japanese examples. The three-year campaign of the Independence Club (1896-1898) was sharply focused on that issue, though, as we know, it failed to achieve its goal. Yun in particular wanted to see Korea become the Switzerland of the East as Japan was fast becoming its Great Britain. Later, after Japan had taken over Korea and become settled in the colony, Yun still thought Korea might someday become this Asian United Kingdom's Scotland, conceptually an equal partner with Japan as England, just as some other pro-Japanese Koreans before World War I had naively hoped to see Korea's 1910 annexation by Japan as a step toward an Asian Austro-Hungarian empire. Like other collaborators of Japan, even hoping against hope, Yun wished Japan to mend its ways in Korea and use friendlier and respectful methods of winning Koreans over. When in the late 1930s, the policy of banning any public discourse in the Korean language followed by the forcible conversion of Korean names into Japanese names began, Yun pleaded, though unsuccessfully, as Koen De Ceuster points out, with the Japanese authorities that they should abandon their ill-conceived moves, and argued cogently that different cultural identities can and should be allowed to coexist within the empire for the benefit of all its members.

Yet, clearly, Yun's uninformed praise for the British rule of India and his dismissive attitude toward Indian nationalism later, based as his views were on mostly British sources on India, were a form of Oriental Orientalism as well as, perhaps, a reflexive, distant and vicarious cover for his collaboration with Japanese rule. There is a simple but important difference here between attacking one's own society from knowledge and experience in order to improve it and unwittingly helping perpetuate, without real knowledge or direct experience, the negative images of another society held by its western imperial rulers. I should also mention that the severest attacks of Yun on the personal-character type failings of his own countrymen were recorded overwhelmingly in his private diary and not exposed for public mockery in the pages of the *Tongnip sinmun* or *The Independent*. So, likewise, never used any generalised public assaults on some race-based Korean national character as such, only on the country's outdated, warped and unprogressive institutions, beliefs and habits. In that distinction, I see another vital difference between the general Orientalism of westerners and the So-Yun critique of their own society.

A further nuance to add here is that as far as I can trace this matter, western missionaries themselves were often more circumspect and indirect in their salvos against Korean culture. The writings of Henry Appenzeller, Horace Underwood, Homer Hulbert and contributors to the missionary organ, The Korean Repository, were relatively benign and showed mostly friendly curiosity rather than any kind of venom against Korean culture. They hoped, it seems, that through their positive church sermons, door-to-door proselytism led by Korean converts, connections with the court, educational and medical work, and broad sympathy for emerging Korean nationalism, they would be able to make better headway in their enterprise than by aggressive and open, fire and brimstone-type rhetoric. They were either more genial personalities or simply played smart on this front because they knew well that strident assaults on Korean faiths and practices would invite only violent and deadly counterattacks from those in the *wijiong ch'oksa* school. It was So, Yun and other Koreans for the most part who engaged in heated debates more directly with their Confucian opponents. This again lends credence to Pratt's "contact zones" as a matrix where pro-western ideas were produced as much by Asian reformist minds through their own intellectual and moral agency as by westerners directly.

I would suggest that if one can find weaknesses in So and Yun's advocacy of the western-Christian model of progress for Korea, they might be of two kinds.

First, one is struck by the unbalanced vehemence of their pro-western stances. Back in the early summer of 1990, my colleague Lew

Yong Ick drove me to Chunch'on on a scenic route. Over a winding road we passed some low but lush hills, meadows, ponds, streams and a river and some of those charming rural hamlets that dot the Korean countryside. It was quite an idyllic, picture postcard view that I was savoring with much delight until we suddenly came across a set of rusting ship containers next to a ramshackle and eerily silent factory that had the look of having been locked up for good. At one time it had either manufactured those steel containers meant to carry Korean goods all over the world or was merely a place to turn discarded containers into scrap metal. I remarked that seeing that ugly sight was like suddenly encountering an awfully jarring note in a visual symphony, and wondered if the wijong ch'oksa stalwarts of yore did not fear, among other things, this kind of desecration of Korea's pristine landscape (despite what Yun said about its utterly unappealing nature) when they thundered their opposition to all things western. One knows, of course, that they were extremists in many other ways, but then were So and Yun also not extremists on the other side of the equation?

Second, there was little in So and Yun, other than an expedient collaboration with some *Sirhak*-type contemporaries in the Independence Club's popular campaign, to suggest that they were eager to create a synthesis between the best of the west and that of the Sinic and Korean traditions. It was all a relentless condemnation of Korean heritage other than the celebration of Han'gul, King Sejong, and some remote military heroes before Confucian values allegedly emasculated the country. A good bit in their writings sounds so much like an exaggerated caricature of Korea that it begins to make even the more credible parts of their critiques rather tiresome.

In them, one looks in vain for an intellectual and moral engagement with Wonhyo, Chinul, Yi T'oegye, Yi Yulgok, Yu Hyongwon, Chong Yagyong, Pak Chega and the like, or with the wisdom of, shall we say, Zhuangzi. There was nothing but a dismissive stance toward them. And while Confucianism was at least recognised as a force to be reckoned with, Buddhism and Daoism were generally treated as if they didn't even exist in Korea. Likewise, there was no interest on their part to forge ties with leaders of the unhappy peasantry whose political, social and economic grievances and reform ideas as seen in the failed Tonghak Rebellion had substantial parts in common with the So-Yun platform (as Vyjayanti Raghavan's paper in this volume demonstrates); the Tonghak rebels were both anti-Christian and anti-Japanese and were beneath any consideration as potential allies in a western-type movement for change. One also sees in this contempt for the Tonghak, a subtle transference of Orientalist elitism over those whom Antonio Gramsci might have called the Korean subalterns. Elite leadership might conceivably do things for them or speak for their interests, or as Yun did once, even speak with mild praise for them from a distance, but it need not stoop to invite them to share co-decisive roles. Reform had to proceed in a top-down fashion, just as the "higher" civilisation of the west could only give things to the "lower" societies of the east, not show any willingness to receive anything from them.

J.L. Nehru once suggested that both for individuals and nations, it was healthy to blend multiple points of view as long as the blend was not random but based on some core concepts lending equilibrium. Open societies in his view could also be like a palimpsest allowing successive waves of cultures from inside and outside to leave their marks on its history without obliterating any preceding ones, for no culture as such to him was a categorical evil. He was a synthesiser of east and west par excellence, a Fabian socialist and a champion of multi-party parliamentary democracy and a free press, and a secularist who felt perfectly at home in the spiritual and ethical though agnostic message of the ancient Upanishads. Likewise, Gandhi could thoughtfully blend Sufi Islam, Hindu and Jain spiritual thought with the Christian Sermon on the Mount.

I was looking for a quest somewhere in the writings of So and Yun for a similar synthesis but found none. What that synthesis could or should have been is not for me to say, but the fact that the attempt was absent shows a very narrow, theocratic intolerance potentially in conflict with their otherwise democratic ideology. The western-Christian groups in Korea of which So and Yun were members, were mostly engaged in an evangelical enterprise and in that enterprise all truth was embodied in the gospel of Christ. Accommodation to non-

Christian ideas was simply out of question. With that approach, what, one wonders, would eventually remain of the Korean-ness of historic Korea. Would the pre-Christian intellectual and moral traditions eventually become nothing but the dregs of Korean history, part of a primitive and unenlightened cultural landscape to be studied only as an embarrassing foil to the only true faith, in the manner of the Christian Greece and Rome against their pagan precedents?

It would be tempting, as a closure, to try to put this narrative under some overarching, unifying theory of personality, thought and action. I have decided not to go there. I don't know if such a neat theory exists. In history, especially in the history of public figures' lives and careers, one sees many zigzag turns over time and many wise and foolish, principled and arbitrary, thoughtful and impulsive, generous and selfish, courageous and timid, words and actions in different contexts. Public figures both shape events and are shaped by them. All those twists and turns and contradictions simply do not allow for any grand, trans-temporal explanation. All I see in these two lives is, thus, a mixed package of much that was admirable and some parts that reflect, to paraphrase Sir Isaiah Berlin from another context, the crooked timber of humanity. At least some of their early ideas could also be attributed to the impatient idealism of their youth. The truth of history, to me, therefore, is not in the middle of things but in the muddle of things. I would be quite satisfied if I have provided some fresh food for thought to affirm the validity of that proposition.

A Note on Sources:

I have presented this short paper as a reflective essay rather than as a conventional piece of research, even though it is, of course, research-based. Thus, instead of listing all sources or footnoting every quoted statement, I have listed below the major sources from which my raw data and some ideas were drawn. They are acknowledged here in order of their importance in my paper, not alphabetically.

First I want to express my deep indebtedness to Koen De Ceuster, a fellow Koreanist, whose 1994 PhD dissertation, "Modernisation to Collaboration, the Dilemma of Korean Cultural Nationalism: The Case of Yun Ch'iho (1865-1945)," submitted to K.U., Leuven, Belgium, is the largest comprehensive study of this modern Korean intellectual-activist. While he and I have both used some common sources, especially Yun's multi-volume diary, he has mined all sources more extensively than I did back in the 1970s. In my composite portrait of So and Yun, I have relied much more on Dr De Ceuster's findings than on my own as far as Yun is concerned. This is especially true of Yun's statements on the alleged traits of Chinese and Koreans, his views of India under British rule, and his later collaboration with Japan. My two references to Dr De Ceuster in this paper do not adequately cover my debt to him. I want to state my gratitude to him here more fully.

Also of much value is Dr De Ceuster's article, "Through the Master's Eye: Colonized Mind and Historical Consciousness in the Case of Yun Ch'iho (1865-1945)" in Bochumer Jahrbuch zur Ostansienforschung, Band 27, 2003. I am very thankful to him for sharing this article with me after I completed my own. It resonates well with my own point of view. Of course, I alone remain responsible for any errors of interpretation.

Next in importance is my own 1988 monograph titled "Imperialism, Resistance, and Reform in Late 19th-Century Korea: Enlightenment and the Independence Club," published by the Institute of East Asian Studies, University of California, Berkeley. It discusses the ideas and activities of not only So and Yun, but also of many of their colleagues and followers. Yun's essay on Confucianism is drawn from the missionary magazine, *The Korean Repository* (Seoul, 1895) as mentioned in the text.

In this paper, I have taken a more critical—and I hope more rounded—view of So and Yun than in that monograph; it was more laudatory than my recent thinking can continue to justify.

Edward Said's much cited book *Orientalism* (Vintage Series, 1979) gave me some key ideas to test as is evident throughout. Likewise, Arif Dirlik's essay, "Chinese History and the Question of Orientalism," in *History and Theory* 35(4) (December 1996), was extremely useful for framing my interpretations.

On references to Indian events and historical figures, I found the following works very useful:

Two chapters drawn from the writings of J.L. Nehru in Martin Lewis (ed.), *The British in India: Imperialism or Trusteeship?* (D.C. Heath, 1962); and *Sources of Indian Tradition*, Vol.2 (Columbia University Press, 1988). On Chinese and Japanese events and ideas referenced in the paper, I drew heavily on a similar series from Columbia on each of the two countries. All Columbia volumes are anthologies of primary sources.

15

RAKESH BATABYAL

Gandhi's Critique of Colonialism

Introduction

Mahatma Gandhi, on his return from South Africa, entered the national movement for freedom in India. In the first four years of his engagement with various issues and movement, from intervening in the strike at the Ahmedabad textile mill to Champaran Satygraha and finally his leadership in the Khilafat movement indicated a line of thought which has been very crucial in understanding the larger phenomenon of the Indian national movement. In recent times, his small tract that he wrote in 1907, namely *Swaraj*, has been the treated as the complete exposition of his politics and critique of British rule. However, a deeper and more critical understanding would indicate that Gandhi's critique of colonialism was far more broad-based and deep in terms of its intellectual and political linkages than is generally assumed.

Gandhi: A Visionary Critic of Colonialism

His critique was in many ways an evolution over the earlier critique of colonialism by the late 19th and early 20th century intellectuals who had presented a strong economic critique and placed colonialism on a systemic pedestal with the help of logic and data. Gandhi, while premising his critique on the same sophisticated economic critique, provided it with a new political strategy, i.e., strategy to link this critique to people's lives and bring them to the movement, and create a future vision out of the same. The vision of freedom was what Gandhi made and thereby he unshackled the political critique of colonialism intimately linked to the movement of the people to bring a new order. The vision of freedom was now based not on a Westminster model but on a theory of struggle, where the ideal of freedom can aspire to become a continuously evolving model. The adoption of the Non-Cooperation resolution by the Congress in 1920 helped to change the shape of the Indian national movement.[1,2] It brought new sections of the population into the movement, created new leaders and threw up new issues to be tackled by the leadership. It also created a situation where many old slogans were seen in a new light. At the special meeting of the Indian National Congress at Calcutta in September 1920, Gandhi promised "*Swaraj* in a year". This was a slogan heard during the Swadeshi movement in 1905-1907, first in Bengal and then in many parts of India.[3] In the heat of the 1920s, however, the word began to take new meanings. Its career saw new twists and turns.

'*Swaraj*' became the Mantra for Freedom Struggle

"*Swaraj* means a state", Gandhi declared, "that we can maintain our separate existence without the presence of the English."[4] However, the existence without the presence of the British was not an end in itself. *Swaraj* was intimately connected to the conception of "natural life" and that of a perfect life. *Swaraj* did not define them. "For me the only training ground in *Swaraj* we need is the ability to defend ourselves against the whole world and live our natural life in perfect freedom even though it may be full of defects. Good government is no substitute for self government."[5]

"*Swaraj*" was a slogan given in a political movement and it was therefore incumbent on Gandhi to connect his ideas to the political

---

1. See, for a wonderful account of the way the movement changes the lives of many women who got involved with the movement and even went to jail, Menon, Visalakshi (2004). *Women and Nationalism: The UP Story.* Delhi: HarAnand Publications. For an overall account of the movement, see Chandra, Bipan, Mridula Mukherjee and Aditya Mukherjee (1989). *India's Struggle for Independence.* Penguin.

2.

3. For a brief history of the Swadeshi movement, see Mukherjee, Uma and Haridas Mukherjee (1958). *India's Fight for Freedom or The Swadeshi Movement 1905-1906.* Calcutta.

4. Government of India, (1980). *Swaraj in One Year, Collected Works of Mahatma Gandhi* (hereafter CWMG). Delhi: Publication Division Delhi. Vol.19. p.11.

5. Ibid.: 12.

movement. This he did by arguing that the "movement of non-cooperation is nothing but an attempt to isolate the brute force of the British from all the trappings under which it is hidden and to show that brute force by itself cannot for one single moment hold India."[6] And the moment this process of isolation is achieved, *Swaraj* too is achieved. Here he is using the idea of disillusionment to refer to this isolation.[7] The notion of disillusionment can be explained only when one has explained the idea of illusion. And the instruments of this illusion Gandhi found in schools, law courts and legislative assemblies because they, he thought, were tools which constituted the legitimising instruments. However, at the same time, he linked the disillusionment to something beyond. Disillusionment itself does not guarantee self-realisation or disengagement. And here the notion that Gandhi uses as the next stage to that of the disillusioned self is to achieve a state of perfect freedom, which also cohabits with a natural life.

Gandhi, who had promised *Swaraj*, was also giving meanings to the term. "*Swaraj* is not a gift,"[8] he argued, and that it was to give India external freedom that "India should be able to regulate her life without the outside rulers."[9] At the same time, there is a hint of metaphysical transportation when *Swaraj* was linked with the "state of being." "*Swaraj* is a state of being of individuals and nations. Just as only a person who eats will have his hunger satisfied, so alone can he be free who throws off subjection."[10] *Swaraj* was invoked for "self-sufficiency,"[11] while winning *Swaraj*[12] was important for "being able to defend ourselves."[13] But in a significant way it was soon linked with a different idea of democracy, "*Swaraj* means government by the

6. Ibid.: 15.
7. Ibid.: 25.
8. Ibid.: 23-4.
9. Ibid.: 58.
10. 15.5.1921, CWMG, Publication Division Government of India, Delhi, 1980, Vol.20, p.99.
11. Ibid.: 154.
12. Ibid.: 274.
13. Ibid.: 422.

many." "Where the many are immoral or selfish, their Government can spell anarchy and nothing else. I am in this movement only as I believe that many are good and true at the bottom, but being cowardly and careless, are ignorant of their inherent qualities, and that when once they have realised the power of goodness, they will begin to practice it and succeed in the attempt."[14]

This new acceptance of democracy by Gandhi was in contrast to his trenchant criticism of parliamentary democracy of the Westminster type in his *Hind Swaraj*. One witnesses Gandhi's rumination over the idea of *Swaraj* during the course of the Non-Cooperation movement. The idea of *Swaraj* acquired a new shape barely a year and a half after he made the promise of *Swaraj* in a year. One of the significant changes in 1920 was the near absence of the notion of civilisation, which constituted the core of the idea of *Swaraj* in his *Hind Swaraj* in 1908-09. In 1920-1922, one hardly finds civilisation as a defining criterion of *Swaraj*. As we have seen, in the beginning of the movement, while articulating his moves, he had talked about two conditions defining the nature of *Swaraj*.

Throughout the Non-Cooperation movement, the attempt was to advocate a kind of disillusionment that the people should go through *vis-à-vis* the apparatus of the colonial system, i.e., education, economy and governance. From the mid-1970s, historians, particularly those of Marxist persuasion, began to use the Gramscian notion of hegemony to explore this process of disillusionment, which was effected by the Indian intelligentsia.[15] *Swaraj*, in Gandhi's thought, seemed to be on the other side of this disillusionment: "The moment we are disillusioned, we have *Swaraj*," he declared in 1920. *Hind Swaraj* was also a strong statement on disillusionment. The difference is that by 1920, one could glean that he was trying to come to grips with the kind of society that he envisaged. It is in this process that he begins to accept some of the elements that he had rejected in his *Hind Swaraj*, such as parliamentary democracy which he had condemned as

---

14. Ibid.: 423. See '*Swaraj* is lack of the fear of death'. Ibid.: 503-05.

15. Chandra, Bipan (2008). *Indian National Movement Long Term Dynamics*. Delhi: HarAnand Publications (first published in Vikas, Delhi, 1978); Chandra *et al., op. cit.* no. 1.

a "sterile woman" and "prostitute". There are two further changes that one sees gradually unfolding:

a) First, a clearer object was identified, and it is the colonial state and not western civilisation that becomes the object of direct attack. It placed him face-to-face with the challenge of countering two major planks now. While he had placed a critique of the machine civilisation at the core of his vision in the *Hind Swaraj*, the colonial state becomes the core now.
b) Second, a position against the colonial state would bring him into the intellectual and political stream which had defined India's nationalist core.[16] Locating himself in this stream, Gandhi had to envision a society premised on concrete social contexts.

One notices two other significant dimensions in Gandhi's thinking at this time and they were indicative of these changes that began to colour his perception. First, unlike most of the leaders of the national movement, he showed no inclination to explore Indian history in detail, and second his idea of *Swaraj* had to denote a life of self-reliance. Now implications for these will soon be clear.

Gandhian 'Liberty'

The two understandings of freedom that we most often talk about are the absence of restraint (negative liberty) and a kind of self-realisation as freedom (positive liberty).[17] In Gandhi's notion of freedom, given the colonial situation in which he lived and worked, one finds both the notions operating. However, it would be a disservice to Gandhi's thought to bind him to these theoretically explicated notions. A self-realisation account of freedom meant

16. This included an economic definition of nationalism, a powerful thrust on equity, social transformation and a strong democratic current. For an overall understanding of India's nationalism in the words of its founding fathers, see, Batabyal, Rakesh (2007). *Penguin Book of Modern Indian Speeches*. Penguin.
17. For a thorough discussion on the issue from the point of view of the western philosophical tradition, see Berlin, Isaiah (1969). *Four Essays on Liberty*. Oxford: OUP; Rawls, John (1999). *A Theory of Justice*. Cambridge (Mass.): Harvard University Press.

that he must have had some notion of human nature.[18] At this juncture, the human nature that he postulates was based on universal premises. The 'Indian', therefore, was self-deceived by apparatuses of the modern West, which had awakened the brute in her. By positing a Universalist position on human nature, Gandhi sought to critique a particular western and modern phenomenon, colonialism, which in turn created problems for him.[19] His answer was to broaden the definition of freedom in his notion. By claiming a universalistic nature of humanity, the attempts would be to realise freedom within the existing universe, for a person to lead a natural life.

But once in the movement, Gandhi was addressing a national situation under colonial conditions.[20] The freedom that he wanted here was also the absence of restraint. However, his definition of Indian society was not a historical one. He was talking about Hindu and Muslim in a manner which, if not ahistorical, was a kind of given.[21] This may have been the reason which prevented him from committing himself to any strong notion of community, except in the sense of what was a given community as such.

When he was condemning the western or modern civilisation in *Hind Swaraj,* he was not premising himself on such a historical

18. One of the finest expositions on Gandhi's philosophy can be seen in Mrinal, Miri (1997). "Gandhi and Empowerment", in Ananta Kumar Giri, *The Modern Prince and the Modern Sage: Transforming Power and Freedom.* Sage Publications. Though Prof Miri never expanded on this in his other writings, one gets a deep sense of Gandhi's notion of freedom in this article.

19. Those who try and engage with this issue often avoid speaking of colonialism. The category of 'colonial modernity' is a convenient term but it has more to do with modernity and its critique than to colonialism and its critique—how colonialism defines the distorted modernity.

20. It seemed akin to the Marxist dilemma over arguing for universal solidarity of labour and the existence of nationalism—a dilemma that became very acute in Marx's lifetime itself, which further deepened after the First World War. For a significant introduction to the issues involved in this dilemma, see, Avineri, Shlomo (1991). "Marxism and Nationalism", *Journal of Contemporary History* 26(3&4); 637-52.

21. This is a central theme in the running battle between Indian historians and those who wish to define India in essentialist terms. Here even Karl Marx who otherwise has studied India carefully gives the same idea of India—self-sustaining village society. Those who now try to situate the notion of community at the centre of the discourse critiquing nationalism and modernity, interestingly fall into the same trap as their idea of community too is very warped, and exists quite often in some text.

phenomenon. The idea of human nature and the western civilisation were still the reigning ideas that made him look for a global solution. *Hind Swaraj* was written as a response to a very specific case. It was a critique and attack on the advocacy of violence as a means for liberation.[22] Now, Gandhi was thinking about *Swaraj* not just an antidote to violence, but something much broader—a social vision for a specific historically located society. It has become quite common now to view *Hind Swaraj* as a historicist document by those who saw in it a vindication of their own anti-modern and localist agenda.[23] Intrinsic in these positions is the critique of any universalistic paradigm. But in the year Gandhi was immersed in his anti-colonial movement, he was rather going back to universalist roots, and took certain stands on universalist grounds. And it is here that I come back to the notion of self-realisation.

When Gandhi spoke of disillusionment, he was referring to disillusionment with the colonial items of illusion. Colonialism had made the Indian a liar, coward, etc., hence they needed to come out of this to lead a natural life.[24] This means that by now he had come to accept that a particular process, i.e. colonialism, had been instrumental in obfuscating certain universalist merits of Indians. The way out of this was to realise one's true nature. Gandhi's self-realisation account of freedom was, therefore, deeply ensconced with a critique of colonialism.[25]

---

22. Note to the second edition, *Hind Swaraj*.

23. Chaterjee, Partha (1986). *Nationalist Thought and the Colonial Discourse: A Derivative Discourse*. London: Zed Books.

24. An interesting text written and published in Calcutta on the eve of the Non-Cooperation movement lists these three as the major issues that had depraved the society and that Gandhi has arrived particularly to solve this situation.

25. In fact, his idea of decolonisation in this sense seems to be a much broader concern than the decolonisation of mind project, which has been the mainstay of many intellectual and academic projects. See, for some pioneering work in this area, Thiong, Ngugiwa (1981). *Decolonising the Mind: The Politics of Language in African Literature*. Nairobi: East Africa Educational Publishers Limited.

Swaraj as Freedom for Individual

Gandhi accepts the universalistic paradigm and conjoins the self with society's quest for freedom. Interestingly, he does not take problematic of the self to a metaphysical level. This, it seems, enables him to engage with the world retaining at the same time the problematic of self. This is very significant from the contemporary vantage point when the intellectual as well as spiritual attempts to engage with the question of self have led to a disengagement with society and politics. The idea of self-reliance that Gandhi makes inseparable from the idea of *Swaraj* embraced that of the self. In his *Hind Swaraj*, he was very clear that society and the self has an interestingly intimate relationship. "Civilization is that mode of conduct which points out to man the path of duty. Performance of duty and observance of morality are convertible terms. To observe morality is to attain mastery over our minds and our passion. So doing, we know ourselves. The Gujarati equivalent for civilization means 'good conduct'."[26]

Gandhi's attempts to retain both the self and the community in his problematic bring him close to the post-Socratic Greek thinkers.[27] For them, the most significant problem was to have an account of autonomy while retaining the notion of community. Gandhi had in his earlier reading of Indian society found that the "tendency of Indian civilization" was "to elevate the moral being", while that of "the western civilization is to propagate immorality. The latter is godless, the former is based on a belief in god."[28] One can argue that in the *Hind Swaraj* account, he found the European civilisation bereft of a strong moral universe. This moral universe he also connected with God. Later on, Gandhi was to argue about his conception of God, an issue we would not be concerning ourselves with here.

But in 1920, his criticism of the colonial order apparently lacked this moral critique. It was a positive self-realisation account in which

26. *Hind Swaraj*, p. 64.

27. Lutz, Mark (1997). "Civic Virtue and Socratic Virtue", *Polity* 29(4): 565-92, Summer; Lucca, John de (1965) "Three Interpretation of Pre-Socratic Philosophers", *The Classical Journal* 60(4) 158-63, January.

28. Ibid.: 67.

self-reliance comes to occupy central place. At the same time, however, the negation of the colonial order had to precede such a realisation. One can sense that Gandhi's arguments began to locate themselves around a universalist notion of human nature which allowed him to argue for the morally powerful individual action, i.e. *ahimsa*, to attain the perfect freedom that *Swaraj* could usher in. And it is here that Gandhi's idea on well-being, though not self consciously anti-nation or cosmopolitan, presented itself as full of possibilities for individual freedom while at the same time not rejecting community and nation.

For Gandhi, it can be discerned, *Swaraj* did not merely mean freedom replacing unfree status. Rather, *Swaraj* meant the state of being of every individual in the community. The sense of being of the community of such individuals was an expression of the natural life. Artificial life, in contrast to the natural life, prevented self-actualisation by the individual. Colonial rule presented impediments to self-actualisation of a natural life in many ways and therefore could not be termed as facilitating natural life. Gandhi's advocacy of self-government, therefore, was also an attempt to create conditions for natural life of self-actualisation.

On the one hand, machine civilisation influenced the natural life of self-actualisation. On the other, colonial rule too prevented such natural life. The two are clubbed together because, in India, colonial rule also brought in the machine and the consequent socio-cultural elements. However, even if colonial rule was over, for Gandhi the quest for *Swaraj* was not, as mere political decolonisation was no guarantee for the realisation of *Swaraj*. The freedom of *Swaraj* is ultimately an inner freedom, and a form of self-actualisation. Hence, the concept is universalist and the agenda is also universalist.

Is *Swaraj* a notion, the meaning of which is derived from the meaning of an India (or Indian nation), ultimately dug up from the history of India? Partly, and only partly, it may be so. The *swa* or self, which is to qualify the *raj* or government, may have its root in the traditional Hindu philosophical notion of *atman*. Inner freedom of the right kind is attributed to this traditional notion. But beyond this point, *Swaraj* does not carry an India-centric local meaning. The inner freedom that characterises the true self is also talked about in all traditional cultures and the idea of self-realisation in a natural state—an authentic state—is part of the moral history of the West as well, especially ancient Greece.[29] An independent Indian nation may instantiate *Swaraj*, but *Swaraj* cannot be said to have only one understanding, namely an independent India. The most significant problem, therefore, for us is then how Gandhi's *Swaraj* is to be seen. We propose that it is here that Gandhi has to be located in the stream of political and intellectual consciousness that his predecessors had brought to the nationalist agitation in India, where they too had tried to define *Swaraj* and made it a signifier for the popular imagination.

Genesis of *Swaraj*

Not long before Gandhi began penning his *Hind Swaraj*, Bal Gangadhar Tilak, speaking at Belgaum in 1907, tried to delineate the idea of *Swaraj*. He was very clear that the idea of *Swarajya* should be separated from the idea of good governance—an interesting dimension which Gandhi continued to maintain. Tilak argued that the "question whether this rule of English Government is good or bad is one thing. The question of 'one's own and alien's rule is quite another'". Exhorting us not to confuse the two, he further suggests that when "you say bad then what are the improvements that must be made in it? This question is different".[30] He even goes further and points to a deeper debate as to the goodness or badness of many of the *Swarajyas*—what to choose from. He argues that one should make a clear distinction between the questions of *Swarajya* and goodness or the otherwise of the government. "If you say good", he argues,

> It must be seen what good there is under it which was not under the former rule. These are different points of view ... formerly there were many kingdoms in our India—in some places there was Mohammadan rule, in some places there was Rajput rule... Were

29. The idea of Hindu nation is not to be confused with the idea of *Swaraj*, for the former concept is given a historical base by its proponents, the latter is not, not at least in relation to any specific or exclusive historical tradition. If we fail to appreciate the non-local significance of *Swaraj*, or interpret it as inextricably bound up with the historical notion of the independent Indian nation, whose character is defined by the key concepts of the Hindu civilisation, we might end up doing injustice to the imaginative originality of Gandhi.

30. Bal Gangadhar Tilak, *Tilak Samgra*. Pune: Kesari. p.99.

these swarajya good or bad? I again remind you that this is a question different from our theme."[31]

Tilak, thereafter, discusses the nuances of what he called the invisible sentiment and visible form of government. In a significant manner, he brings the issue to a very sophisticated head by explaining in detail:

> Some able men who have been educated in England and have received college education there come to India and the State administration of India is carried through them. Emperor is a word. When you give a visible form to the sentiment which arises in your mind at the mention of the word raja, i.e., King, there is the present Emperor. This sentiment itself is visible. When a visible form is given this invisible something there is the king—emperor. But the emperor does not carry the administration. The question of Swarajya is not about the Emperor, not about this invisible sentiment. This must be remembered at the outset.[32]

> Swarajya relates to visible government and means the demand that the management of our affairs should be in our hands is the demand for swarajya.[33]

In the demand for *Swarajya*, therefore, there has been an intense attempt to distinguish it from the mere demand for freedom leading to good governance. Tilak put the two on two different pedestals. It was, however, left to Bipin Chandra Pal to give the issue a detailed treatment, particularly in his *Swaraj* addresses in Madras in 1907, again much before Gandhi wrote his *Hind Swaraj*. Pal was the most articulate spokesperson of the new wave of nationalist leaders and he presented *Swaraj* with all its intellectual underpinnings.

His point of departure was the proclamation by Gopal Krishna Gokhale of the Congress goal of self-rule, which was translated as *Swaraj*. Gokhale's comment was that *Swaraj* as an ideal was all right but was not practical, as it was not achievable in the near future. Pal contended that what was not practical cannot be an ideal and that

31. Ibid.

32. Ibid.: 99-100.

33. Ibid.: 115.

Swaraj was an ideal precisely because it was practicable.[34] He criticised another dominant theme that *Swaraj* or self-rule could be gained by being in the Empire, a critique of the goal of dominion status.[35]

Interestingly, speaking of the true nature of *Swaraj*, he pointed out three significant possibilities which he called his confessions. First, the true character of *Swaraj* was not known except that it would be a real people's *Swaraj*; second, the form of *Swaraj* was also not known and that the only guess that he had was that it would be a united states of India. Third, he was convinced that the methods of getting that *Swaraj* would be peaceful and non-violent. This he attributed to "peaceful ways of the Indian culture". On the form of *Swaraj*, he argued that though *Swaraj* assured development, this "development along European lines would be wrong as the material and spiritual cost of such development was very high". He championed a sense of national determination, *nishtha*, for making people not use certain goods for consumption and it is here he joined this *Swaraj* with his argument for boycott of foreign goods.

The key to his critique was disillusionment—a point on which Gandhi's understanding too was centred. In some sense articulating an incipient understanding of the later-day nation of hegemony, Pal suggested that through the method of boycott and national determination the prestige of the British government would be killed, and this would kill the *maya* or illusion about the latter, which people thought was their government.[36]

During 1909-10, Gandhi was presenting a critique of civilisation in his *Hind Swaraj*. Though described as the fundamental text to study Gandhian thought, Gandhi was not expounding any attack on the colonial government, nor was he expositing any major tactical moves through this text. At this same time, Pal was attacking one of the basic ideas that Gandhi would premise his own methods of struggle on, i.e., the space for human perfection.

34. Pal, Bipin Chandra (1954). *Sawraj and Swadeshi*. Calcutta. p.38.

35. Ibid.

36. Chandra *op. cit.* no. 15.

Gandhi believed, following Tolstoy, in the idea of efficacy and possibility of individual perfection. An individual can achieve spiritual and moral perfection in this world. Pal had, however, attacked this idea of Tolstoy. He believed that as long as society was based on tyrannical rulers and uncivil individuals, there was very little space for individual perfection. Therefore, the change in society must precede any thought of individual perfection. He had argued that the latter was going back to the medieval times and to philosophical currents which abstracted the ideal from the real and made the individual look ethically and spiritually independent of the social and civic institutions of his country. He argued that it was in the modern times that it has become possible for the individual to attain freedom through civic institutions. Gandhi, a couple of years later, would try and propose quite forcefully that the possibility of attaining individual moral perfection can go hand in hand in the struggle against tyranny or oppression. In fact, the quest for moral perfection was to be embedded in the process of struggle itself. In the struggle for attaining *Swaraj*, this point would come out more forcefully. Pal, for instance, believed in peaceful methods to get freedom, but this peaceful method to him comes naturally from the social ethos of Indian society. For Gandhi, on the other hand, peaceful methods for attaining *Swaraj* itself were part of the struggle. As he would argue, *Swaraj* resides in the methods of attaining it. One can see, therefore, that the idea of *Swaraj* connects Gandhi to a very powerful intellectual current in the national movement.

Deconstrcution of *Swaraj* by Nazrul Islam

In Bengal, one hears at this time the voice of Kazi Nazrul Islam, a poet who after having a stint in the British army began to emerge as a very radical voice in the literary circles of Bengal. His powerful vocabulary, use of locally rooted cultural metaphors, and trenchant critique of the colonial powers made his writing singularly effective. His was the voice of the post Non-Cooperation movement youth who had been politicised in a new kind of politics. The government proscribed collections of his poems, particularly *Sarbahara* and

Visher Banshi, and he was sentenced to a year's imprisonment.[37] What distinguished his rebellious poetry was its rhetorical stance, which can be seen in his contestation of the meaning of *Swaraj*. The rhetorical element of his poetry was soon reflected in his prose, and editorials that began to appear in his *Dhumketu*, which he began to edit from 1922, were replete with examples. In the issue of 22 August 1922, *Dhumketu* presented a very passionate account of the perception of *Swaraj*. Nazrul began by posing a question: "What does *Swaraj* mean?" The answer for him was: *Swaraj* meant "that a man is his own king, or that all are kings—that I am subjected to none, that we are not seated either on the throne or under the flag of any one". "But this king has to be rebel who could utter this cry in an unrestrained voice, without being frightened by any terror and with an inflated chest". Now *Swaraj* could only be won if this kind of cry could be shouted out by anyone.

But the "real question" he further deliberates is who is the rebel who has the courage to utter this cry, "I am my own king". The reason for the paucity of such kings was due to the fact that, as he saw it, India "is a country of men devoid of faith in their own selves." Therefore, he invokes people to be the king, be free, and asked them to:

> Arise awake, know yourself, do not obey anybody. The liar, who stands in your path—crush him as you go—you will see the world rolling its head at the foot of your flag. Cut off the bondage of dependence with your ideal and, sitting in a row under the shade of the broad, open sky, cry 'I am the best of men. I am always invincible'. Cry: 'victory to truth'. Come o king of men; O rebel: in the highest pleasure of yoga, declare the message: 'I am all over the universe'. That is Swaraj, cry: 'O waking God! O waking God'.[38]

Soon however, the rhetorical stand was taken over by an overtly political one in which the content of *Swaraj* was spelt out in terms of freedom from foreign domination. It had to be a freedom of complete nature. He wrote:

37. Mitra, Priti K. (1993). "The Rebel Poet and Mahatma: Kazi Najrul Islam's Critique of Gandhi's Politics in the 1902s", *South Asia Research:* 46-55, May.

38. Ibid.: 21.

> We do not understand Swaraj or the like ... not a single iota of India shall remain subject to the foreigner ... The whole responsibility for India, the entire charge of defense, administration everything should rest in the hands of Indians. No foreigners should have the slightest right ... You should do what your minds want you to do. Do not obey religion, society, the king, God, anybody.[39]

Interestingly enough, the earlier invocation was referring to God, here even God was not made any allowance. This was a concept of freedom of reason, that of the mind. But how to root it in society remained the problem. While Nazrul was trying to define his meaning of *Swaraj*, there were indications that the political programme within the concept of *Swaraj* was now examined more closely and, in fact, there were alternative versions of "*Swaraj*" beginning to be articulated.

While contours of the movement began to attract criticism, one could see that *Swaraj* began to acquire a contested meaning. Add the challenge that came from sections of workers and the peasantry. In a self-reflexive mood, a newspaper catering to the middle class declared: "[T]he peasants were not enchanted by our ideal of *Swaraj*."[40] What was the ideal of *Swaraj*, which it said was theirs? Thus, one finds that there was a class character being imposed on the ideal of *Swaraj*. "Namshudra peasants would not have the same ideal of *Swaraj* because it was preached by the Bhadralok." This would be problematic in the long run as we would see.

Those who had just returned from the villages were asking why there is no enthusiasm, no hope—why the *charkha* was lying idle. The oppression of the police may be one cause of it, but not the sole cause. "The peasants have not been enchanted by our ideal of *Swaraj*."[41]

Nayek, a radical peasant newspaper, wrote that in fact the class dimension or socio-economic readings of society was now coming to be attached with the tussle over the meanings of *Swaraj*. The

39. Ibid.: 22.

40. Ibid.

41. Ibid.

newspaper, a representative of the peasant cause, deepened its arguments:

> One of our friends lectured on Swaraj to an old Namashudra for half an hour. At the end, the old man asked what people like him would gain by Swaraj. Their troubles are about rents, taxes, naibs and darogas. The zamindars and darogas belong to the bhadralok class and the members of which are preaching Swaraj, and so these men cannot be expected to treat the lower classes better than now when Swaraj will come. These words deserve careful consideration.[42]

The programmatic depiction of an alternative version of *Swaraj* interestingly also involves a critique of the organisation of the Congress. One can see the beginnings of an interesting correlation that began to take shape where composition of the political party was linked directly to its political programme. Here the absence of peasants from the Congress was being depicted as the party being one of the middle classes and therefore the *Swaraj* that was articulated from the Congress platform was a *Swaraj* of that class.

So long, the question of the poor had no place in the Congress. The Congress was in the hands of the middle classes and they hoped that power would come into their hands when the British left. The members of the Congress were mostly lawyers and merchants, who wanted to gain something by taxing foreign goods when *Swaraj* would come and the lawyers thought they would then get high posts. So the ordinary public did not care much for the Congress.[43]

The reading of the idea of *Swaraj* along these lines provides the idea with a life of its own and it linked Gandhi to the political contestation that ensued within the movement. More often than not, this fact is ignored. The communists and the Marxists attacked Gandhi and the Congress for not being pro-poor and being bourgeois, and their line of criticism can be gleaned from the incipient critique of *Swaraj* that was written in *Nayek* in 1922.

The solution was seen in a procedural change in the Congress. *Nayek* also pronounced "our spiritual *Swaraj* must be brought down

42. *Nayek*, Calcutta, 26 July, 1922.

43. Ibid.

to the level of the earth" because "no more experiments on spiritual *Swaraj* should be made with the poor coolies and day labourers". Thus, Gandhi's ideal of *Swaraj* was first pronounced as the ideal of the middle class and then as different from that of the peasantry and coolies and then declared a spiritual *Swaraj*. This then was shown to be the cause why there was no enthusiasm among those sections. There were attempts to evaluate Gandhi through the programme devised by others and here he has been compared with other thinkers in that historical context.

Retrieving a person from the sediments of imagination may be a case for the psychoanalyst, or as has been argued recently the work of a different trope of the historical imagination. Through rhetoric and critique an idea or a person can be evaluated in a deeper sense, but one is still not sure whether they sufficiently lead us to recover the popular psyche of the time in which the idea or the person in question is entrenched. The notion that a person, the subject of retrieval, has to be located within the historical process, and not just in a context, is a powerful argument in favour of rhetoric being subjected to scrutiny. But how does one yoke rhetoric to scrutiny? And it is here that comparison is suggested as a way to put realism in practice, which could give the historians points of reference outside the rhetorical realm.

Critics of Gandhian *Swaraj*

While Gandhi was still trying to come to terms with the promise of *Swaraj* in a year, sections of people had begun to question the promise itself. One such line of criticism was that Gandhi's politics was impractical. The very idea of non-violence was discarded as an ascetic activity not suited for politics. From this stemmed an entire range of criticism. One of the significant lines of criticism was employing a comparison, particularly with Aurobindo's line of politics. B.C. Chatterjee, one of the early leaders of the Hindu Sabha in Bengal, for instance, writing just after the movement, contrasted Gandhi's call for *Swaraj* with that of Aurobindo's Swadeshi and found that Gandhi had done disservice to the cause of freedom. An analysis of his attack on Gandhi brings out a very interesting aspect. In the ultimate analysis, the premise of this attack was a constitutional developmental position, or rather the strong belief that the British would have given some new reforms had Gandhi not joined the movement and given it an orientation. Writing 65 years later, Ashutosh Lahiry, long-standing general secretary of the Hindu Mahasabha, blamed Gandhi for delaying freedom. His critique was again the same as that expressed by Chatterjee: Gandhi should not have blocked the path of constitutional development.[44] Interestingly, many of those who were close to the Hindu Mahasabha criticised Gandhi's idea of the movement in the light of the Swadeshi movement and found the earlier one more effective. Most of these writings, however, are bereft of any analysis of the idea of *Swaraj* or Gandhi's social and political world-view entailed in the idea.

Gandhi was received through his notions of *Swaraj* and the *Charkha*, which were critiqued in the public domain. The perceptions regarding Gandhi no longer involved just an individual and his relationship with Gandhian ideas, but also how these ideas as well as the personality of Gandhi travelled to the public domain. Thus, after the Non-Cooperation movement, Gandhi and his notions influenced the shaping of the domain where these ideas were publicly perceived and debated, and at the same time the public domain itself helped in shaping those ideas that would ultimately constitute the perceptions of Gandhi. One of the tools that the domain provided was that of analogy. For an individual, history quite often provides the pool from which the memory, with the help of the recently shaped public domain, selects and creates analogies to understand another individual or phenomenon. The Swadeshi movement provided people with such an analogy to examine the Non-Cooperation movement and the notions of *Swaraj*, while on the other hand individuals of the post-Swadeshi movement phase of Bengal politics provided the pool to examine Gandhi's individual position.[45] Thus, history constituted a very significant source for the public domain.

---

44. Lahiry, Asutosh (1976). *Gandhism in Indian Politics*. Delhi.

45. Ibid.: 26.

Historians on Gandhi's Critique of Colonialism

Historians have arrived relatively late on the scene with regard to employing Gandhi and his ideas in their understanding of modern Indian history. When they did do so in the 1970s, the task was to understand and critique his mobilisation processes during the national movement for freedom. There were two dominant approaches to study the national movement at this juncture. The imperialist and neo-colonialist approach had a long pedigree, following in the wake of the colonial official writing. The history of such history writing is closely related to the understanding of society and politics in India and the role of the British in this. Therefore, the understanding of Gandhi, Gandhian ideas and their place in the national movement had a sociological pre-history. He was either a *baniya*, or a part of the upper class, solidifying the interests of this section against all those whose protector the British were supposed to be, or he was a Hindu leader blackmailing the British through his tricks to leave the country. All these categorisations defined initially a cruder and later a sophisticated historiographical approach, quite often defined by its detailed work of the local and regional dimensions of movements that began to colour the political, social and cultural landscape of India in the 20th century. There is interestingly a common telos of most of these works, that the movement which nationalist historians and others saw as a movement for national liberation was nothing but mobilisation of few of the native sections, namely the upper-caste English-educated groups in different domains, motivated by their enlightened self-interest. Gandhi and the phase of the movement led by him were placed in this milieu. It was shown how limited and fragmentary his mobilisation or influence was—it did not reach as many people as the national movement might have projected. There is a retrospective justification of the colonial policy of invalidating the claims of Gandhi and the Congress that they represented all sections of the Indian people. Then in the official records and now in the works of Cambridge historians, Gandhi represented only the upper-caste Hindus. The subaltern studies, which emerged in the 1980s, very interestingly began with a serious note on colonial sociology. It tried to critique sociological studies as Orientalist sociology. But more significantly, in its enthusiasm to anchor a politics of fragments, it began by positing a fragmentary politics—society was shown to be permanently divided into two sets, the subalterns and elites. Thus, while the colonial historiography tried to anchor history on to sociology, subalterns tried to anchor sociology on to history. Here, it was useful for the national movement to be shown as an upper-caste, elite phenomenon. However, Gandhi proved to be a difficult proposition. The masses were with him. Two kinds of efforts were made—to show that the masses did not come to Gandhi influenced by his message but they had their own, uninfluenced message, and/or they acted independently of Gandhi's message. In another way, Gandhian ideas were significant enough for the intellectual predicament to be appropriated and shown to be at variance with the nationalist movement, which was an elite phenomenon. Thus, Gandhi was deprived in many such writings of his location and made to preside over a critique of modernity with his decontextualised ideas, and interestingly, his idea of *Swaraj* becomes the key to such an appropriation.

Marxist historiography has seen vicissitudes in the characterising of Gandhi in its overall evaluation of the social and political processes. Beginning with Rajani Palme Dutt's characterisation of Gandhi as the leader of the bourgeoisie nationalist revolution to the recent sympathetic understanding of him being the leader of one of the largest mass movements in human history, this change in perspective occurred with the change in the understanding of the national movement led by Gandhi. Except for the works of A.R. Desai, one is not sure whether even today the Marxian characterisation of the movement followed from a proper sociological study or the sociology followed the strategic. Gandhi proved to be extremely crucial in their debate over social composition of the movement. However, there has been not much work on the ideological orientation of Gandhi's movement except that there was an automatic imposition of class character upon the movement. The late 1970s saw a change. Bipan Chandra argued in 1977 for a rigorous theorisation of the national movement in terms of its long-term dynamics.[46] He, for the first time, showed Gandhi to be having a programmatic coherence. This was in many senses the first theoretical exercise, with regard to the national movement and Gandhi, on their own terms and not on the basis of a colonial sociology or imperative, and the diktat of international communism. In all such historiographical exercises, the modes, methods and metaphors that Gandhi used in his mobilisation drives were seriously studied. Satyagraha, nonviolence, etc. have been the key ideas that were explored. A fetish of violence has made many Marxist scholars shy away from working on the serious aspects of the programmatic ideas of Gandhi.

This was taken up by non-Marxist political scientists who employed Gandhi's idea of *Swaraj* to critique the post-independence Indian state and the leadership. This was also because of the premises of the Marxist historiography, which was closely linked to their understanding of the current political landscape where their contest was with the hegemonic nationalist ideology.

Conclusion

Gandhi's idea of *Swaraj* also engaged political scientists, who began to read and employ Gandhian ideas in their study of contemporary politics in India. One viewpoint, decidedly anti-Marxist, was rooted in the tradition of American political science, which began to argue since the late 1960s that the post-independence Indian state is avowedly working against democracy. Thus, this academy promoted work that encouraged fragmentary politics so that the state's extension could be curbed. The state was to be attacked on two grounds, namely that it was anti-democratic, and that it was part of modern impositions which needed to be overcome. Significantly, Gandhi and some of his ideas were found to be handy to show that they were completely at variance with ideas of the post-Independence Indian state and therefore could be used in attacks against the Indian state.

46. Chandra *op. cit.* no. 15.

16

HULAS SINGH

Rationalism and Nationalism in 19th Century Maharashtra

Introduction

The rise of Indian nationalism in the 19th century is often viewed as a political phenomenon, linking its inception primarily with the emerging political consciousness to the virtual exclusion of its cultural dimension. Cultural consciousness, which preceded political agitation, is generally seen as a separate sphere of activity or at best epiphenomenal to the emerging political process. Historically speaking, however, it was in the realm of culture that nationalism in India found its initial incubation in the 19th century. The intellectual awakening that came to the fore during the period saw the shaping of nationalist consciousness, particularly among the emerging intelligentsia. When nation, as distinct from region or province, became the fundamental frame of reference, identity and aspirations among certain sections of society, in particular the educated middle class, intellectual nationalism was decidedly born. Indian nationalism, as would be seen, found its first intellectual expression in rationalism of the 19th century much before the political form of nationalist consciousness germinated in the country. The notion of India as a nation found articulation in literature and orature for the first time in the 19th century ideas of reform, apart from the ongoing process of India's objective knit-togetherness. Although the first intellectual soundings were heard in Bengal, Maharashtra emerged as a prominent theatre of nationalist manifestation at the time-point. Perhaps no other contemporaneous intellectual tradition in the country seemed to be as passionate in propagating the nationalist agenda as in Maharashtra during the period. In this exercise, an attempt has been made to study intellectual ideas for hastening the process of cultural revitalisation and national invigoration in the context of Maharashtra in the 19th century.

The movement in Maharashtra was essentially an intellectual initiative at a socio-cultural renewal of the country in the context of colonial rule. Rationalism was a prominent strand of thought at this time-point. It was characterised by faith in reason as the ultimate arbiter of assessment, as the supreme touchstone of truth. Its epistemological orientation was, however, marked more by concern for the country than by quest for knowledge for its own sake. Social regeneration for overall national reconstruction constituted its core content. Almost all the intellectuals concerned themselves with the social side of nation building. Society and nation were seen holistically for the purpose of reform and not as separate spheres of activity or as dichotomous entities. Rationalism and nationalism were closely connected almost as a means-and-end continuum.

The main Maharashtrian thinkers of the time were, to mention the prominent figures, Bal Shastri Jambhekar, Dadoba Pandurang Tarkhadkar, Bhaskar Pandurang Tarkhadkar, Gopal Hari Deshmukh, better known as 'Lokahitwadi', Vishnu Bhikaji Gokhale, popularly known as Vishnubawa Brahmachari, Jyotirao Phule, R.G. Bhandarkar, N.M. Parmanand, M.G. Ranade, Vishnushastri Chiplunkar, K.T. Telang, B.M. Malabari, N.G. Chandavarkar, G.G. Agarkar and Pandita Ramabai. They condemned the prevalent customs and practices such as caste, the condition of women, child marriage, polygamy, enforced widowhood and disfigurement of widows, idolatry, polytheism, priesthood, ritualism and other superstitions as culturally corrupt, nationally debilitating, humanly heinous and rationally repugnant. For social renewal, they advocated the elimination of caste distinctions, uplifting the position of women, marriage only on maturity, monogamy, widow marriage, monotheism, end of ritualism, eliminating religious intermediation and emphasis on spiritual worship. This was part of the nationalist agenda, and not an exercise in isolation. National invigoration remained the main aim of rational reform. The nationalist orientation of the intellectual movement in

Maharashtra may be broadly studied under the following six sub-heads:

Idea of India as a Nation

Indian nationalism, particularly at the level of subjective consciousness of the people, found its initial expression in the realisation and propagation of the idea of India as a nation by intellectuals in the 19th century. Almost all of them came to view India as a national collectivity, as distinct from diverse regional identities. This was a novel realisation. The medieval mystics, either of the Bhakti or Sufi tradition, had no notion of India as a national entity. Nationalism in the 19th century was, however, not a linear movement; its path was quite complex and tangled. It grew gradually, wave by wave, with provincial pride at times coming to the fore in the process. Provincialism seemed to be quite palpable in certain expressions, particularly of Ranade, Chiplunkar and Tilak. Ranade painted pre-British Maharashtrian political and religious upheavals in a much superior light compared to those in the rest of the country. Shivaji and his successors were viewed to have been far far-sighted and formidable native potentates engaged in the process of nation-making, in contrast to their counterparts in other parts of the country. He wrote:

> Unlike the Subhedarships of Bengal, Karnatik, Oudh and Hyderabad, the rise of the Maratha power was due to the first beginnings of what one may well call the process of nation-making... It was a national movement or upheaval in which all classes cooperated...The histories of Hyder and Tipu, and of the Mahomedan rulers of Hyderabad, Karnatik, Bengal and Oudh, present nothing parallel to it.

He even drew a parallel between the Reformation in Europe and the struggle waged by the saints and prophets, particularly of Maharashtra in medieval times. He also at times tended to conflate or even equate the Maratha region, kingdom or territory with country or nation as if India consisted of different countries or nations—countries within country, nations within nation, so to say. At the Indian National Social Conference held in Lahore in 1893, he termed the Conference "the great gathering of the Indian Nations."

Prachi Deshpande in her work *Creative Pasts* has highlighted this tendency in terms of the "creation of a Marathi regional consciousness that clearly demarcated itself from the larger Indian nation". She further finds "slippages between region and nation" quite "frequent" in 19th century consciousness. Chiplunkar's following passage from his *Nibandhamala* has been quoted as an example to question the nationalistic intent in his writings and to highlight his tilt towards Maharashtrianism:

> It is not even a hundred years since our country witnessed great warriors. We can still remember how even at the very end we dazzled all of Hindustan with our royal brilliance, even as the whole world watched, bewitched by our glory!

Tilak's invocation of the Ganapati and Shivaji festivals—started in 1893 and 1895, respectively—highlighted the efficacy of the Maratha legacy for an anti-colonial agitation, while being viewed as divisive in terms of region and religion.

Such dimensions of thought in the context of 19th century Maharashtra, however, need not be blown out of proportion without situating its actual say in the overall structure of ideas. No doubt, provincial pride did assert itself at times. The understanding of India as a larger national reality was, however, never in question. At no stage was Maharashtrianism counterposed to pan-Indianism as the objective of intellectual pursuit. The notion of India as a nation, a larger entity and a bigger frame of identity subsuming within itself different regions and aspirations to a common collective purpose remained unsullied throughout in their thoughts and deeds during the period. The provincial pride derived its validity, if at all, as a frame of reference only in relation to other similar regions within the country; it was not in contradiction to pan-Indianism as the overarching consciousness of identity. The founding of the Indian National Social Conference in 1887 under the leadership of Ranade and the holding of its meetings at different locations ranging from Madras to Allahabad, to Bombay, to Calcutta, to Lucknow and to Lahore exemplified, apart from others, the efforts on the part of social reformers to socially weave the entire country into an integrated national pulsation, thus laying the social foundations of

Indian nationalism. Expressing satisfaction at the participation of reformers from Bengal, the Northwestern Provinces, Punjab, Madras and Bombay at the second Indian National Social Conference held at Allahabad in 1888, Ranade remarked:

> We are in a sense as strictly national socially, as we are politically. Though the differences are great for purposes of immediate and practical reform, yet there is a background for common traditions, common religion, common laws and institutions and customs, and perversions of such customs, which make it possible for us to deliberate together in spite of our differences.

Ranade further termed the social reform movement a "national awakening" during his speech at the fourth Indian National Social Conference held in 1890 in Calcutta.

National Self-Strengthening

The question of national regeneration remained a dominant theme in writings and speeches of the intellectuals in Maharashtra. In his convocation address delivered as vice-chancellor at the University of Bombay in 1894, Bhandarkar voiced his national concern. He said:

> If the people do not see the good that is there in foreigners, they are incapable of learning; if they do not see their own faults and defects and the evil that there is in their manners, customs and institutions, there can be no improvement, no progress; and the nation must lag behind while others are going on, and must suffer

In his presidential address at the Indian National Social Conference held in Allahabad in 1902 he said, "Social Reform, a National Movement—This has been my creed since the year 1853." Social reform was thus conceived in the context of the nation; it had no separate or sectoral agenda or purpose. In his another address given in 1915, Bhandarkar further emphasised the national perspective to the reform initiatives. He said:

> We have been thinking of the evils from which our nation is suffering. And endeavouring to remove them by the introduction of reforms, political, social, moral and religious. These constitute the national question and the elevation of the nation is what we have been seeking.

Mahatma Phule's notion of nation, however, went beyond the conception of nationality viewed primarily through the educated middle-class perspective. In his concept of nation, unity and equality, education and the emotional integration of the masses, particularly the depressed and downtrodden sections of society, constituted the defining moment. He argued:

> If the mass of the people are so riven and divided among themselves, they form a veritable hotch-potch. How can such a hotch-potch ever form a 'Nation'? (be ever called a 'Nation'?) There cannot be a 'Nation' worth the name until and unless all the people (nationals, inhabitants) of the land of King Bali—such as the Shudras and Ati-Shudras, Bhils (tribals) and fishers, etc. become fully educated, are able to think independently for themselves and are uniformly unified and emotionally integrated. If (a tiny section of the population like) the upstart Aryan Brahmins alone were to found the National Congress who will take notice of it.

Admiration or Collaboration

Most of the intellectuals in Maharashtra were ardent admirers of British rule and had a firm faith in its regenerative role. They even viewed it as a divine dispensation, destined to civilise and modernise India on modern European lines. Jambhekar, who heralded the beginning of intellectual awakening in Western India, was highly impressed by efforts of the British government towards the country's amelioration.

The establishment of law and order and the introduction of modern education were prized by him as golden British gifts to India. Lokahitwadi also, particularly in the beginning, held British rule to be a divine dispensation. In one of his letters, he argued that the British had been sent to India by God to awaken the Hindus to the evils of terrible customs such as *sati* and infanticide.

Mahatma Phule surpassed all bounds in his admiration for the British. He saw in their advent the real prospect of Shudra emancipation. To quote:

> The All-merciful Providence took pity on the Shudras and brought about the British Raj to India by its divine dispensation which

> emancipated the Shudras from the physical (bodily) thraldom (slavery). We shall never forget their kindness to us. It was the British rulers that freed us from the centuries-old oppression of the Bhat and assured a hopeful future for our children. Had the British not come on the scene (in India) (as our rulers) the Bhats would surely have crushed us in no time (long ago).

He recalled with a sense of relief the defeat of the Indian Revolt of 1857. "It was through Providential dispensation that the revolt engineered by Bhat Nana (Peshwa and his henchmen) was put down by the brave English rulers." Besides, each member of the Satyashodhak Samaj ('Society of Seekers of Truth'), founded by Phule in 1873, had to take a pledge of loyalty to the British Empire. His sense of indebtedness to British rule was also at a personal level. He listed in 1883, three major formative influences on the evolution of his own consciousness: childhood interaction with Muslim friends and neighbours, the Scottish Mission in Poona and their work on the spread of education on human rights, and finally the British rule encouraging the freedom of expression.

In a booklet *A Warning*, written in 1885, Phule was again effusive in his praise for colonial rule. He wrote,

> By divine dispensation, the English rule (or supremacy or raj) came to be established here, a rule which was at once just and merciful, wholesome, beneficial, righteous and merciful—for the comfort and benefit of the long-suffering masses in India. May this regime last long! After the advent of the English raj here, the common people were freed, at long last, from the inhuman oppression and tyranny.

Admiration or even eulogising British rule, at least in the early years, constituted a conspicuous feature of the mainstream intellectual strand represented largely by Jambhekar, Lokahitwadi, Bhandarkar, Ranade, Telang, Malabari and Chandavarkar, though the degrees differed. This, however, does not mean that they were collaborationists, and not nationalists as some of the others who later argued eloquently against the rationale of the Raj in the country. Notably, the mainstream intellectuals stood for India and not England as the fundamental frame of reference, identity and aspirations. They wished and worked for developing their own motherland and were not the agents of colonial rule. If England figured in reference, it was only in terms of its being an aid or means to the ultimate aim of national rejuvenation and reconstruction. England, after all, represented the might of European modernity and its potentiality in steering modernisation on similar lines in India seemed to be well within the realm of possibility. Historians have, however, quite copiously dealt with the context of intellectuals' admiration of colonial rule, which need not be repeated. The persistent pursuit of a nationalist agenda by these intellectuals need also not be dismissed either by dubbing them as collaborationists. It may be noted that their belief in British beneficence was, moreover, not blind; it was on occasions quite critical and qualified. As years rolled on and the seamy side of the colonial rule became more and more visible, these very believers of divine dispensation grew sceptical of British rule. Eulogism turned into criticism whenever they found it faulting or wanting.

Open Condemnation of Colonial Rule

Nineteenth-century Maharashtra constituted a unique stage of rational resurgence and even nationalist militancy simultaneously. The dominant doctrine of divine dispensation faced its severest challenge and criticism during the course of the 19th century itself in Maharashtra, significantly in early years of the century.

Dadabhai Naoroji delineated the subject of drain in detail subsequently and his theory of drain came to form the kernel of the Moderates' economic critique of colonialism. It was, however, Bhaskar Pandurang who first highlighted the idea of India's drain through trade as the real face of British rule, despite a certain degree of naivety and emotion noticeable in his expressions. Naoroji's theory of drain, on the other hand, exemplified masterly erudition and analysis and stood strongly substantiated by meticulous facts and figures. It was highly authoritative and rigorous in research in comparison to Pandurang's views, which relied more on the sharpness of his observation and incisiveness. It is, however, the historicity of Pandurang's formulation that denotes its signification and value in modern Indian history. He could visualise that the drain was instrumental in India's poverty and pauperisation, thus falsifying the doctrine of divine dispensation at a time-point when belief in British beneficence was a predominant perception in the country.

Drain was a matter of concern also with other intellectuals in the 19th century. Malabari, in particular, criticised the colonial connection for the annual drain of India's wealth. He wrote:

> It is this exhausting drain—carrying off the life-blood of the nation in the shape of pay, pension, annuity, purchase money, profits of enormous business, and interest on still more gigantic loans—that has naturally riveted the attention of far-seeing critics. Is it not a grievous economic fallacy that India, the poorest country in the civilized world, should be administered on a scale of remuneration, too high even for the richest country...

Pandurang tried to expose the hollowness inherent in the British claim that they brought about prosperity, law and order, and peace and security in India. He argued,

> To say that a country taken possession of by a horde of foreign usurpers whose sole aim is to enrich themselves at the expense of its real masters, is prospering under them, is as absurd as to conclude that a town left at the tender mercies of a gang of robbers is enjoying all the advantages of peace and security in spite of their depredations and oppressions.

He also took the British to task for their racial arrogance and discrimination, and criticised the British system of law and justice for being biased and inequitable.

Economic Critique

The anti-colonial current of the rationalists extended even to the economic field, although concern for culture predominated over that of the economy in the overall rationalist thinking during the period. It would not be hyperbolic to say that it was the rationalists who first provided the economic critique of British rule in India. Jambhekar, despite being impressed by the scientific and technological superiority of the West, was perhaps the first reformer in Western India to highlight the discriminatory taxation policy of the British to be responsible for India's industrial and agricultural stultification. He observed:

> European goods are exempted and pass free, while native products, and thereby native industry, which ought to be protected and encouraged, are heavily taxed. The very grain the cultivator raises on land that pays a high rate of assessment, is burthened with land customs at various stages on the way to market. The articles manufactured by native artisans cannot be conveyed from one place to another for use or sale, without payment of everlasting transit customs. What, in our opinion, would contribute to the prosperity of the country is the abolition of all inland duties, the amount or collection of which obstructs the internal traffic.

He called upon the British government to provide encouragement to the commerce of the country and not to stultify its economic growth. We have already seen that Bhaskar Pandurang defined Drain as the most potent instrument of British exploitation in India. Lokahitwadi, a great believer in the doctrine of divine dispensation, also highlighted the adverse economic impact of British rule on India. In one of his letters of the *Shatapatre* published in Prabhakar, during 1848-1850, he linked the phenomenon of growing poverty in India to the "ruin of industry and commerce of the country" under foreign rule. The export of raw materials from India and import of manufactured goods played, according to him, an instrumental role in India's impoverishment. He, therefore, strongly advocated the reversal of this negative trend.

Lokahitwadi, one of the most incisive intellectuals of 19th century India, emphasised that industrialisation was crucial to India's uplift. It was he who first conceived the idea of *swadeshi* and boycott, much before it was made into a major plank of the nationalist agitation in the country. He emphasised that Indians should not only manufacture their own products but also use them, even if of poorer quality than the foreign items, and that they should boycott the imports. It was, however, Ganesh Vasudeo Joshi, popularly known as Sarvajanik Kaka, who founded the Poona Sarvajanik Sabha on 2 April 1870, to represent the wants and wishes of the Indian people, who first took the vow of *swadeshi* to propagate its use. He had been practising it since 1869.

As already indicated, even Mahatma Phule was highly critical of the exploitation of the Indian people under British rule. He closely observed and criticised instances of the increasing taxation of peasants, flooding of Indian markets with foreign manufactured goods, de-industrialisation and pauperisation of the artisans. It was, however, Ranade from among the 19th century intellectuals in India, apart from Naoroji, who most forcefully articulated the economic critique of colonial rule in India. In his inaugural lecture at the first Industrial Conference, held in Poona in May 1890, he highlighted the grim fact of India's acute poverty, malnutrition and even starvation. Again, in his lecture on the "Indian Political Economy" at the Deccan College, Poona, in 1892 he stated, "Stagnation and dependence, depression and poverty—these are written in broad characters on the face of the land and its people. To these must be added the economic drain of wealth." He, however, did not believe that India's poverty emanated largely from the drain of wealth as Naoroji did. He made this quite clear in his address in Poona in 1890 itself. He said:

> We should husband our little resources to the best of our power, and not exhaust them by vain complaints against the drain of the Indian Tribute or by giving battle with Free Trade ... State help is after all a subordinate factor in the problem. Our own exertion and our own resolutions must conquer the difficulties, which are chiefly of our own creation.

He did not single out British rule for all of India's woes and apportioned a sizeable blame for poverty to the indigenous weaknesses such as idleness and lack of enterprise. On the other hand, he exhorted Indians to learn and not spurn the advantages of the East-West contact through colonialism. The poverty of India "is a very old inheritance and not the result solely of foreign conquest and competition", he observed. He held, however, that colonial rule had led to the complete collapse of Indian pre-eminence in commerce and manufacturing. He stated:

> Political ascendancy is not the only particular vantage ground which we have lost. Commercial and manufacturing predominance naturally

> transfers political ascendancy, and in this our collapse has been even far more complete.

He was deeply disturbed at the deteriorating share of Indian enterprise in commercial activities of the country and the concentration of commercial and manufacturing hold in foreign hands. In his own words,

> The increased trade and commerce of the country represents a steadily diminishing proportion of Native enterprise and skill engaged in it, and the monopoly of political power is made more invidious by monopoly of commercial wealth and manufacturing activity.

Culture and Civilisation

Nationalism in 19th-century Maharashtra found further expression in the subtle but conscious distinction made between culture and civilisation, as far as their approach to the West was concerned. This was a distinctive feature of Maharashtrian thought, there being a blurring between the two in the case of Bengal. The intellectuals in Maharashtra admired the material aspects of Western society, i.e., its advancement in science and technology, education and industrialisation. They opted for adapting Western civilisation for India's development on modern lines. Right from Jambhekar onwards, nearly all stood for Westernisation in its civilisational sense. The "Prospectus" of *Sudharak*, a weekly authored by Agarkar, exemplified this general refrain.

In his first editorial in *Sudharak*, Agarkar stated: "If we accept in a proper way the new Western education and the new ideas which come along with it, do not cast away our basic heritage i.e. our Indian Aryan culture, then only we will progress happily." Similarly, Chandavarkar stated that education must be related to our past national culture.

Conclusion

The reform movement in 19th-century Maharashtra was an integral part of the emerging nationalist consciousness in the country. The rationalist phase constituted the embryonic stage in the history of evolution of nationalist consciousness in the country.

It formed the phase of social self-correction and strengthening and was perceived to be a prelude to political reform. Society and nation were seen almost synonymously. "A nation socially low cannot be politically great" was the general intellectual refrain. "There can be no advancement politically without social and moral advancement." "There is no hope of political elevation for as long as we live and apparently love to live, in such social degradation."

The rationalist resurgence in Maharashtra symbolised the incubation of a nationalist consciousness and provided the ideational infrastructure for the Moderates and even the later nationalist leadership to further build upon. The Indian national movement, which evolved subsequently, incorporated many of the lessons and legacies of the rationalist phase. The idea of India as a nation, drain and de-industrialisation, poverty and pauperisation, exploitation of the rural peasantry, stultification of Indian industries, racial discrimination, exclusion of Indians from positions of power and authority and subordination of the entire Indian economy to the needs of colonial economy formed some of the significant areas of rationalist concern, which the later nationalists took up and elaborated further. Emphasis on modern education, end of caste discrimination, abolition of untouchability, improvement in the position of women and their education, stress on industrialisation and scientific development, moralism, secularism, individualism and constitutionalism were other important nationalist legacies of 19th-century rationalism. The phase of rational reform was actually an intellectual adumbration of India as a nation in the making, an inchoate manifestation of a nationalist awakening in the shaping, and thus it constituted the initial stage of India's struggle for independence. The 19th-century rationalists could well thus be termed the early nationalists in modern Indian history.

17

SUCHETA MAHAJAN

Strategies of Imperial Retreat
Independence and Partition of India

Introduction

In this paper, I intend to retrieve the story of the end of empire from the context of decolonisation and locate it within that of the struggle of the nationalist forces to wrest independence from the colonial power. I will also show that partition was an imperial strategy not specific to India. The discussion of the complex reality of 1947 is framed against the colonial past and the post-imperial scene. There is a wide divergence in historical interpretations of two of the momentous events, indeed processes, independence and partition.

Indian independence: Retreat or deal?

In the imperialist view, independence is the culmination of the process of devolution of power or self-government initiated by the colonial regime. The partition of the country, in this view, was the result of the age-old divide between the Hindus and Muslims. In the nationalist interpretation, independence was the culmination of the freedom movement; whereas partition was the consequence of the divide and rule policy of the British.

Independence was not real independence in the view of some left historians; it was only a transfer of power. A certain section of the left even described it as a deal between the imperialist and national bourgeoisie. It was even termed a sell-out, for which the nation paid the price of partition. I believe that independence and partition were but two sides of the same coin. Independence was wrested by the nation in the making, a process in which communities and classes were welded in one nation. By 1947, there were enough people constituting the nation, and demanding independence.[1]

However, partition took place because the nation-building process was incomplete in 1947, and particularly an important community, the Muslims, were not well represented. Let's take a look at what independence was not—independence was not a voluntary withdrawal by the imperial power, for whom empire had become a millstone around their neck, as has been argued with differing emphasis by Gallagher, Seal, Drummond and Dewey.[2] By the time of the Second World War, the colonial rulers would have it that they were paying for the defence of the empire. This claim was belied by India's forced contribution to the war effort, which amounted to sterling balances to the tune of over 1,200 million pounds sterling. Britain was to pay this back to India after independence, but tied it to British capital goods and divided the payment into instalments, rendering it almost worthless.[3]

Independence was not decolonisation, which suggests an unravelling of empire; the opposite of acquiring it.[4] Decolonisation has become a popular term today in historical writing as it lacks ideological imperative of the terms "national liberation revolution" or even "independence". It obviates the need for using terms like "anti-colonial", let alone "national".

1. Mahajan, Sucheta (2000). *Independence and Partition: Erosion of Colonial Power in India. Sage Series in Modern Indian History.* New Delhi. pp.391-92.

2. Gallagher, John (1982). *The Decline, Revival and Fall of the British Empire.* Edited by Anil Seal. Cambridge; Gallagher, John and Anil Seal (1981). "Britain and India between the Wars", *MAS* 15(3); 387-414; Drummond, I.M. (1972). *British Economic Policy and the Empire, 1919-1939.* London; Dewey, Clive(1978). "The End of Imperialism of Free Trade: The Eclipse of the Lancashire Lobby and the Concession of Fiscal Autonomy to India", in Dewey and Hopkins (eds.), *Imperial Impact: Studies in the Economic History of Africa and India.* London.

3. Mukherjee, Aditya (1986)."The Indian Capitalist Class: Aspects of its Economic, Political and Ideological Development in the Colonial Period, 1930-47", in S. Bhattacharya and Romila Thapar, *Situating Indian History.* New Delhi. pp.239-82.

4. Mahajan, Sucheta (2014). "Towards Freedom: The Making of a History", in Thierry de Costanzo/Guillaume Ducoeur (eds.), *Decolonisation and the Struggle for National Liberation in India, 1909-1971, Historical, Political, Economic, Religious and Architectural Aspects.* Anglo American Studies No. 48. Frankfurt.

Independence was not a gift, it was wrested by the anti-colonial movement. Why was this achieved in 1947? By then imperial hegemony had been eroded substantially to make the continuation of the enterprise of empire in India untenable.[5]

The erosion of hegemony was a process, not an event. Over time, the pillars of the colonial state, the bureaucracy and the army were whittled down. The ideological apparatuses such as the rule of law, Pax Britannica and the district officer, the *mai-bap* of the people, were also under challenge. The colonial state was a semi-hegemonic state that preferred to rule through acquiescence rather than repression in the first instance. For functioning of the administration, they relied on loyalists, who were nominated to the Councils and worked in the government. Colonial policy was one of keeping loyalists on board and trying to be one step ahead of the anti-colonial movement. Concessions of a substantial nature were to be made. For instance, the reform initiatives culminating in the Government of India Act 1935, were to perpetuate colonial rule, not to move to self-government as claimed by the government.[6]

Chronology of the Retreat

The strategy of the national movement was not only one of eroding hegemony.[7] It was also one of building up counter-hegemony. Here the task was to mobilise different social sections, communities and regions and wean away loyalists and liberals by exposing the authoritarian underpinnings of the colonial state. The intention was to reduce colonial policy to a mess of contradictions. This process had taken off by the 1930s. There were resignations of officials during the Civil Disobedience struggle and even earlier in the Non-Cooperation movement. Then the period of provincial autonomy and formation of popular ministries saw officials scurrying after ministers, wearing *khadi* shirts, and rendered helpless in the face of politicians

5. Mahajan *op. cit.* no. 4: Chapter 5.

6. Ibid.

7. Chandra, Bipan (1984). "Long Term Dynamics of Indian National Movement", Vikas. Reprinted) in Mukherjee, Aditya (ed.) (2013). *Selected Writings of Bipan Chandra.* Orient Blackswan.

undercutting the authority of the government, by people coming to them for redressing grievances; that is, the functioning of a virtual parallel government.[8] During the Quit India movement, there were instances of officials helping nationalists escape arrest when underground, giving sympathetic judgements, as pointed out by Partha Sarathi Gupta in *Towards Freedom 1943-1944*.[9] The repression-conciliation dyad placed the colonial official in a dilemma. How was one to handle a political agitator who was likely to be a minister in a few years? This was the case regarding senior Congress leaders like Govind Ballabh Pant in the United Provinces.

By 1945, hegemony of the colonial state was heavily undermined. The influence of nationalist forces was greater than that of the colonial state. Some loyalists and liberals had moved to the side of the nationalist forces. For some, like Tej Bahadur Sapru, the attitude of the colonial government towards Gandhiji when he went on a 21-day fast in 1943 was the last straw. The importance of non-violence is evident here. The three members of the Executive Council who resigned in 1943 did not consider resigning in protest against the repression of the 1942 Quit India movement, perhaps because it was violent.

By 1945, the importance of a settlement was recognised by the colonial rulers. This would ensure British prestige and transform the empire into a Commonwealth. Else it was feared we would be reduced to the position of commercial bag men in the East, in the words of the Viceroy.

By 1946, His Majesty's Government was clear it would leave soon and a time period of 2-3 years was even referred to. Prime Minister Clement Attlee in 1946 ruled out the option of staying on for 10-15 years when Viceroy Lord Wavell suggested it.[10] He pointed to the paucity of troops and other commitments such as Greece and

8. Mahajan *op. cit.* no. 1: Chapter 5.

9. Gupta, Parthasarathi (ed.) (1997). *Towards Freedom, Documents on the Movement for Independence in India, 1943-44*. New Delhi: Indian Council for Historical Research and Oxford University Press.

10. Note by Attlee, c.13 November 1946, Mansergh, N. (1980). *Constitutional Relations between Great Britain and India: Transfer of Power, 1942-47*. Vol. IX. p.68.

Palestine. Also, public opinion in Britain and indeed the world would not be in its favour. So it was deemed best to exit while in control. This date, to begin with fixed as June 1948, was later revised to August 1947.[11]

Conclusion

If one aspect of imperial retreat was the negotiated nature of the settlement, the partition of the colony along religious lines was a strategy of imperial retreat in India, as it had been in Ireland and was to be in Palestine.[12]

Later, in Africa in the 1950s and 1960s, it was often a case of dividing countries along the lines of tribal groupings, as in Nigeria. So there was no single pattern. Also partition was not the definitive conscious strategy. Partition could be the only option left as earlier politics meant running out of better options. Unity in the case of India was eventually precluded as the colonial rulers could not break with their past of fomenting divisions. So all that remained was lip service to unity—"we tried hard but we couldn't leave behind a united India" (Prime Minister Attlee).[13]

The British could not turn the clock back; divide and rule had created and crystallised communal identities and politics, which could survive without being propped up by the colonial state. They had acquired an autonomy of their own, like the Muslim League, which had loyalist roots and moorings but increasingly spoke in their own voice. So strategic defence considerations inclined the colonial rulers to try for united India, which would have depth in defence.

But politics, that is, the relationship with Muslim League, suggested partition and politics held sway over strategy. Eventually the colonial rulers could not break with their past. They had been too anti-Congress for long. British officials resented the Congress for

11. Mahajan, Sucheta (ed.) (2013). *Towards Freedom: Documents on the Movement for Independence in India, 1947*. New Delhi. p.29.

12. Fraser, T.E. (1985). *Partition in Ireland, India and Palestine*. London.

13. Williams, Franco (1961). *A Prime Minister Remembers: The War and Post War Memoirs of the Rt. Hon Earl Attlee*. London. pp.211-12.

subverting war efforts when Britain was fighting with her back to the wall.

Also the situation on the ground dictated the policy eventually, and here there was virtual civil war by 1946-47. This hastened the slide towards partition. Whether it was partition or united India, the emphasis by His Majesty's Government was on an agreed solution, on a settlement. The Cabinet Mission plan was all about coming up with a scheme that accommodated the central concern of the Muslim League, namely Pakistan, and the Congress' insistence on unity, put it together to the two parties, and get agreement somehow, even if this were to collapse soon once the inherent contradictions came to the fore. The primary concern was to demonstrate to the world that the policy was not the responsibility of the British, it was that of the Indians (represented by their parties Indian National Congress and Muslim League). The British could then exit gracefully while Indians remained embroiled in the worst kind of communal violence, which could be traced back to the colonialist-initiated divisive politics of separate electorates. Mountbatten's game plan was one of quick exit after getting agreement—on whatever the option, unity or partition.

Yet the post-imperial scene was important. Imperial interests had to be safeguarded. One must not confuse this with neo-imperialism, as is done by sections of the left. In 1946, the departing colonial rulers were looking for a formal defence treaty, which was a precondition to a political settlement. When this seemed increasingly unlikely, given the stress on political sovereignty by the Indian leaders, a Commonwealth solution to the post-imperial scenario emerged. Under this, the dominion(s) would be encouraged to join the Commonwealth and in time its informal ties would work to affect the desired result of defence cooperation. One might say as an aside that the Commonwealth did not really work as intended, and remained a club rather than a successor to empire. Hostilities between the dominions as early as 1947 over Kashmir precluded cooperation. Also, given Britain's declining power by the mid-1950s, Nehru had a bigger stature in the world than the British Prime Minister, Anthony Eden.

Finally a look at the mechanism through which independence was effected—this was not a seizure of power or violent overthrow of a regime. From the side of the Congress too, negotiations were generally tried out before going in for a confrontation. When independence seemed to be on the cards, Congressmen were willing to wait to see the substance of the offers being made—as Gandhiji said, a great nation has declared its intention to quit, what would be lost by waiting?[14] The Congress kept up preparedness for a mass movement, however, in the eventuality that agreement was elusive.

Such examples of negotiated settlement prior to independence are many, including in countries where communist movements were at the helm, such as Mozambique, Guinea-Bissau and Vietnam. The negotiated manner of the settlement does not make these transitions any less revolutionary. Neither should the substance of India's independence be considered any less—as the slogan of the communists of the day, "*yeh azadi jhooti hai*" (this freedom is false), indicated—because of the form of the transition. By focusing on the form of the transition, on the temporary constitutional continuity and continuation of the form of institutions like the civil services and the armed forces, as is done by some Cambridge scholars, one ignores and underestimates the content of the transformation. The revolutionary nature of the transformation lies in the break from colonialism, in snapping the fetters, in emerging out of the circle of colonial underdevelopment.[15]

---

14. *Hindustan Times*, 24 February 1946.

15. See chapters titled "Introduction" and "The Colonial Legacy in Bipan Chandra", in Mridula Mukherjee and Aditya Mukherjee (2008). *India Since Independence*. New Delhi.

VYJAYANTI RAGHAVAN

Conclusion

With the advent of industrialisation and technological developments in navigation, it had become a norm for the powerful states to access distant lands and subjugate the weaker ones. India and Korea both became victims of such quests of the imperial powers. British motivations at colonisation centred on finding raw material and markets for its products post industrialisation, while Japan's goals were to find land and expand its power throughout Asia after the Meiji Restoration and its defeat of China and Russia in wars with them.

The Japanese considered the Koreans to be "uncivilised and illiterate people", thereby rationalising their activities as probably a "civilising mission" just as western imperial powers did elsewhere. This, despite the fact that the literacy level of Koreans at that time was considered to be higher than that of the Japanese.[1] Britain, of course, entered India for trade in the 17th century along the coasts and gradually made inroads into hinterland and expanded its hold. The Indian economy was very well developed by the 18th century and had a lot to offer to the British by way of raw material and artisanal skill. Britain made India its focus to expand its own economy, much in the same way as Japan did in Korea. The British attempt at colonising was far more successful than the Japanese one because, having had a long head start and experience, they used more judicious policies than the Japanese did.

Debates, both in India and Korea, on the nature of the colonial period and the colonial society, have two clear points of views—one which looks at the capitalist growth in the colonies that took

1. Joe, Wanne J. (2000). *A Cultural History of Modern Korea*. Seoul: Hollym. p.268.

place during that period and believe that it gave the momentum for growth and development, and the other which emphasises mainly the collapse of the colonial economy as a result of colonial rule and its exploitative nature. There is also enough scholarship in India and Korea that argue on both points of view. That the colonisers undertook the development of roads, railways and other such infrastructure in the two colonies not as a philanthropic gesture, but to better network the entire economy of the colony is an accepted fact. That the growth and development that took place were fallout of it is also not denied. Therefore, what is emphasised by the two schools of thought might be different, but the basic point remains that motivations of the colonisers for colonising were exploitative in nature.

It must however be granted to both the imperial powers that they contributed greatly to scholarly work and to the production of knowledge and data on various aspects of the colonies. It is on this scholarship and in particular the data gathered by them that scholars rely heavily even now. And it is only since a few decades ago, as part of the post colonial theoretical study, that scholars have engaged in deconstructing and analysing the colonial interpretations of native colonies.

The colonial patterns of Imperial Britain and Imperial Japan reveal certain similarities which are discussed later, but there were also stark differences emanating from the fact that the former colonised a race which, to their mind, was an inferior one, while the latter colonised people of the same race who in some ways felt superior to the colonisers and therefore found it much more difficult to come to terms with it even to this day. The Koreans have always treated Japan's colonisation of Korea as an ethnic betrayal and have never forgiven them for it. For, until the Meiji Restoration, Japan and Korea both had had tributary relationships with China. In fact, Japan was the last link in the chain of exchange of goods and culture between these countries. Being colonised by Japan was something that had not been in the realm of possibilities for Korea and it was therefore taken completely by surprise.

While Britain ravaged India and its resources for merely mercantile goals, Japan also ravaged the minds of the natives totally through their *naisen ittai* policy of assimilation, and in the process charted a course of cultural disruption and destruction which made their rule far more exploitative. They then extended it to human resource subjugation too. While both sets of colonisers benefitted greatly by establishing profitable enterprises and infrastructure, the British reaped the profits over a longer period than the Japanese. Japan's first Governor-General might have hoped for the righteousness and justice of the Sun Goddess Amaterasu to shine on Korea, but it is not as though these were merely noble wishes for welfare of the natives.

Recent post-colonial studies have also included studies to see whether former colonies, after independence, have been able to achieve the same level of economic development as the country that had colonised it. It has been found that amongst countries that gained independence after World War II, it is only Korea and Taiwan whose per capita GDP has managed to catch up with that of Japan which had colonised them in the first half of the 20th century.[2] This has been largely dependent on how quickly the colonies have been able to either shed or capitalise on the colonial heritage, as the case may be, and set their economies on the track of development suited for their economies.

It has also been found that the colonial powers had invariably left the colonies in a state of unbalanced development resulting from catering only to the needs of the colonial power. For instance, while Britain's investment was in the industrial sector, Japan focused on the agricultural production. India came to possess modern textile and steel industries, a network of railways and roadways and a banking system, but the agricultural sector remained neglected. For a country whose population growth rate increased exponentially, this had far-reaching implications in the long run. On the other hand, whatever improvements and investments Japan made was

2. Hsiao, Frank S.T. and Mei-Chu W. Hsiao (2005). "Colonialism, Learning and Convergence: A Comparison of India and Taiwan, *Journal of Asia Pacific Economy* 10(2): 146-77.

in agricultural production to help it reach a level of self-sufficiency. For this purpose, it invested in an extensive network of irrigation, transport and communication systems while the industrial sector remained neglected. Despite these odds, South Korea has been able to make tremendous progress in a very short time and achieve the 'Miracle on the Han River' kind of economic growth. India has yet to fully realise the institutional reforms required for such growth.

Returning to the points of similarity in the two colonial powers, it can be said that both depended on their colonies for the supply of personnel for their expansive military ventures. The training of the army under the colonial powers in both colonies was not only to make them professional soldiers to act cohesively on the battlefield outside the country, but also to quell internal disturbances. The Japanese army stationed in Korea was called the Joseon Army and it served two purposes. They were, firstly, to regulate and protect their own boundaries and serve as a frontline military base for attacking mainland China, and secondly, to offset elements within Korea that might disrupt the power of the Government–General therein. Sri Krishan has in his paper revealed how the British extended linguistic and caste divisions within the Indian society to the army and created separate regiments, making sure that their vision did not extend beyond their own regiment and was quite segregated from the civil society. This division ensured total allegiance to the colonial power. However, following the Mutiny of 1857, in order to avoid unity amongst the native soldiers, an Indian Army was created which was composed of soldiers of different castes, regions and even nationalities. They also followed the martial race theory, looking for races that exhibited more warrior-like qualities thereby ensuring that they remained loyal and did not turn against the colonisers again. They thus used ethnicity to promote their own imperial interests. Japan, through its policy of forceful conscription, enslaved the Koreans to work on their farms and fight their wars. But, by the time the second Sino-Japanese War was on its way in the late 1930s, the Japanese colonial administration was all set to transform the Korean peninsula as a war supply base. Japan had occupied Manchuria and had started needing forces for its Kwantung Army there and had therefore started enlisting Korean soldiers on a large scale. Many were also engaged to work in the military industrial sector. It is said that the number of conscripted Koreans reached its peak just before the War in 1944, at 200,000 men. The Japanese trained them such that many of the Koreans became far more brutal than the Japanese soldiers. Many were convicted of Class B and C war crimes. But the more long-lasting damage to Korea was the fact that Japan created a division amongst the people by creating a set of soldiers loyal to the Japanese Army and another lot that became loyal to the Chinese Red Army. They were the people who had escaped to mainland China from Korea. Many joined the Chinese Red Army and fought against the Japanese Imperial Army in the Sino-Japanese War. Other means of promoting their interests involved co-opting the elite in the two countries to run their administration, but at the same time ensuring that they were kept only at the second rung. Similarly, they recruited the poorer natives in the police and created a network of informants.

In the field of education too, the role of the British during the initial years was only to provide grants to the locals for setting up schools. But with the coming of the missionaries towards second decade of the 19th century, their motive for setting up educational institutions was to evangelise the Indian mind. The British administrators like Viceroy William Bentinck and Thomas Macaulay wanted to use education as a means to ensure that the native Indians would not rise against the British if their minds were naturalised with European knowledge. They created a parallel educational system which mimicked the curricula in England. The fact that we continued with this curricula so many years after independence reflects that it bore some positive elements. According to Venkataramanujam (chapter 5), the British used the façade of justice and fair play in the form of promoting education and camouflaged their true intention of controlling the Indian mind.

Neerja Singh has discussed how the Indian intellectuals had come to realise that any kind of social reform or transformation, including the emancipation of women, could be achieved only through education. This kind of self-introspection could be said to have been triggered by the exposure to western ideas that had come in during the colonial period. However, neither did the exposure extend to equality in education for men and women, nor for the independent growth of women. The idea of educating women was largely to narrow the asymmetry in gender relations within India. That it did not get implemented effectively and has had adverse effect on the policies of health and family welfare in the country is a matter for another debate. Nevertheless, calculations of the British backfired because education opened the minds of some of the Indians into seeing the British rule in all its starkness.

Japan, on the other hand, played an active role in the public education system of Korea right from the start with the intention of assimilating the Koreans into the Japanese culture and thereby making them "imperial citizens". This is even more true of the period post the March 1st Movement in Korea, following which their interference in the Korean education system became total. The Japanese policy following this resistance movement became one of obliterating Korean culture completely. They did this under the slogan of *Naeson Ilche*, meaning 'Japan and Korea are one entity'. They wanted the Koreans to view themselves as Japanese and espouse Japanese values. All this was to mentally prepare them to perform the duties as Japanese citizens.[3] However, they lacked the rights as Japanese citizens. As part of this policy, they banned the teaching of the Korean language and Korean history and instead insisted on the school curricula including Japanese language and history. They insisted on the Koreans adopting Japanese names too. Some scholars have explained the reason for harshness of the Japanese colonial rule by the fact that Japan was still a novice at the game of colonialism as compared to the west. It had its own insecurities resulting from the expansionist mode of the western powers that it was surrounded by at the end of the 19th century.

It is not as though that prior to Japan colonising Korea there were no efforts at modernising the prevailing education system. In

3. Jeon, Sang-sook (2011). "The Characteristics of Japanese Colonial Rule in Korea", *The Journal of Northeast Asian History* 8(1): 67-68, Summer.

fact, after Japan forcefully got Korea to open three of its ports—Busan, Wonsan and Incheon—for trade following the signing of the Kanghwa Island Treaty in 1876, the local people of Wonsan felt the need for leaders who were educated under the new modernised system of education of the west to give direction to the resistance to this onslaught. Therefore, the first western-style school called the Wonsan school was established in 1883.[4] The curriculum, for the first time, included subjects like astronomy, geography, arithmetic, algebra, etc. Until then, the local village schools called *seodang* taught only Chinese classics. Following the Kabo Reform movement of 1894 and the education rescript of 1895, many innovative laws pertaining to school education and curriculum were developed. The reforms proposed drastic changes right from elementary school to the university level education. However, these could not be implemented as Korea soon became first a protectorate and then a colony of Japan. Then the Japanese followed a discriminatory educational policy under their colonial rule.

Ito Hirobumi, the first Resident General of Korea changed the education system as soon as he took charge in 1905. He brought all schools under government management, reduced their numbers, reduced the period of education, brought about changes in the content of the curricula and even lowered their level. The elementary schools came to be known as 'Common Schools' and were reduced to 4 years of education from 5 to 6 years earlier. They also followed a discriminatory education system where the Japanese students attended 6 year elementary school while Korean students attended only a 4-year Common School. Also, there wasn't much of a difference in the content of the basic and advanced level. As a result of reduction in the number of schools, only about 25 per cent of school-aged students were enrolled in the schools.[5] It is believed

4. Lee, Sang-Gu, Jihwa Noh and Sung-Yell Song (n.d.). "Educational Policy and Curriculums of Korean School Mathematics in the late 19th and early 20th Century", available at *http://matrix.skku.ac.kr/Series-E/2009/2009-SE-10-LeeNohSong.pdf*. Accessed on 15 April 2013.

5. Uchida, Jun (2011). *Brokers of Empire. Japanese Settler Colonialism in Korea, 1876-1945*. Cambridge: Harvard University Press. p. 340.

that this kind of restricted education was the main reason for the stunted growth of an indigenous entrepreneurial class in Korea.

However, while Japan's forceful educational policies might have been tolerated in the initial years, they certainly met with a lot of resistance later on. In the initial years, there was an emergence of a viewpoint that saw the Japanese-style modern education as the best route to rising in the new society that they saw being shaped around them.[6] A large section of the commoners in the Korean society under Japanese rule looked forward to undermining of the status and power of the *yangbans* who had been exploiting them. But when Japan started following a discriminatory policy of education, their feelings turned from one of ambivalence to that of disillusionment.

In Korea, there also rose a new group of enlightened middle-class Korean women who had been empowered through interactions with Japanese women settlers in the process of Japan's assimilation policy. These new women started mounting a double-barrelled attack on the Korean patriarchal system and the Japanese assimilation policy and at the same time took an active interest in social reform programmes.[7] Thus, while the Japanese government tried to assimilate the Koreans, though only at the lower levels through discriminatory educational and other policies, they also ended up giving rise to a class of people, including women, who had become more aware of their rights and intellectually more empowered.

As far as the approach of the Imperial powers to religion is concerned, unlike the Spanish kings who dispatched missionaries with clear instructions to convert the local people, the British left the native religion alone and made no effort at converting the natives. Venkataramanujam (chapter 5) has discussed how the British under the East India Company maintained religious neutrality and gave precedence to trade over religion. They, in fact, viewed the religious institutions as sources of revenue and brought

6. Toshihiko, Matsuda (n.d.). "The Korean People in the "Military Rule" Period" in *Governance and Policing of Colonial Korea 1904-1919*. Kyoto: International Research Centre for Japanese Studies. pp. 138-39.

7. Uchida *op. cit.* no. 5: 338-40.

them under the purview of the Board of Revenue. They further strengthened their control over these through legislations. But with the growing influence of missionaries in England, the Company's lack of interference in some of the local social and religious practices like *sati*, *thugee* and 'hookswinging' was vehemently criticised in England. With an increase in missionary activities in India in the latter half of the 19th century, there was also an increase in communal clashes within India. It was eventually the British interference in socio-religious and political practices that led to the revolt of 1857, following which the colonial government distanced itself from the missionary activities.

Japan, during its phase of assimilation, did insist on the Koreans adopting the Japanese native Shinto religion, but there was no forceful conversion. Buddhism took on a new form with the management being more controlled in the Japanese style. The other new religions, prominent amongst which was 'Cheondoism' or the 'Heavenly Way', which had sprung up as a reaction to Catholicism that had started making inroads into Korea after the forceful opening of its ports in 1876, were all suppressed.

In Korea, Christianity, which had first come as Catholicism via China in the 17th century, was outlawed by the Joseon dynasty and its practitioners persecuted. But by the time Protestantism and Presbyterian missionaries came into Korea via America in the late 19th century, the Koreans, by and large, had become tolerant towards it. In the years under Japanese colonial rule, many Koreans started adopting Christianity both as a tool to promote nationalism and as a reaction to counter the Japanese efforts to promote Japanese language and Shintoism. But there was also a section of people within Korea with whom communist literature, which was stealthily finding its way into Korea, was finding popularity. The concept of class struggle was very appealing to the peasants and the lower class citizens of colonial Korea. They protested against all religious activities, particularly that of the missionaries. But the missionaries used education effectively to evangelise the minds of the people and, as years went by, Protestantism became the religion of the intellectuals and the middle class urbanites in Korea and became central to Korea's pursuit of modernity.

Nothing captures the Japanese colonial government's attitude towards the various religions prevalent in Korea at that time better than the words of Henrik H. Sorensen when he says:

> The Japanese colonial government in Korea, during the first ten years of the occupation, utilized a wide range of tactics in order to promote loyalty and cooperation from the religious groups. Whenever it was possible they sought to influence, and change the individual religions in a congenial manner, so that they were better suited for these purposes. However, when resistance was too strong, or, as in the case of the majority of the Christian groups and many of the new religious movements (like *donghak* or *cheondogyo*), they did not refrain from using false accusations, or even violence, in order to get their way.[8] (matter within brackets added.)

He adds that this kind of control over colonial subjects through religion was something that Japan had learnt from the great imperialist powers of the west.

The manifestations of the resistance of the colonies to colonial rule in the two countries took various forms, some violent and some non-violent, like the March 1st Movement in Korea and the Quit India Movement in India. One of the first rebellions to the presence of the Japanese took the form of the Donghak Revolt (in its second phase) and that to the British took the form of the 1857 Revolt. Both these revolts were suppressed by the might of superior technology and organisation of the foreign powers. During the harsh Japanese colonial rule, the independence movement of the Koreans could not be coordinated within Korea and had to be done by the provisional governments set up by the Korean national leaders in Manchuria and China. It therefore could not gather enough force to overthrow the colonial power. But in India, the series of non-violent civil disobedience movements called for by the national leaders in

---

8. Sorensen, Henrik H. (n.d.) "The Attitude of Japanese Colonial Government Towards Religion in Korea", Available at *http://cjas.dk/index.php/cjas/article/viewFile/1822/1842*, Accessed on 10 July 2014.

the 1920s and 1930s became the driving force that eventually forced Britain to give up its colony.

Eventually, the imperial powers retreated from their colonies, but the manner in which this happened in India and Korea was very different. The divide and rule policies of Britain had created communal identities and politics that had acquired an autonomy of their own. As a result, while Britain exited following the demand for political sovereignty, the Indians got embroiled in the worst kind of communal violence which ended up partitioning the country. In Korea, Japan did not retreat; in fact, in the course of World War II, it was forced to surrender. Its harsh and aggressive policies within Korea had not allowed any single representative organ to rise that could take over the reins of power from Japan. The Committee for the Preparation of Korean Independence organised by leaders of the Korean Provisional Government could not get the support of the left-wing forces within the country. The latter group had hastily put together an administrative mechanism called the Korean People's Republic. Due to a lack of consensus amongst them, the US and Soviet armies appeared on the scene to take over from, Japan when it surrendered.

Korea, which was to become free and independent "in due course" as per the Cairo Declaration of 1 December 1943, came under the Trusteeship plan of the great powers and ended up being divided along the 38th Parallel—the line along which the US and Soviet Union forces drew their zones of occupation. It has remained divided since then.